Urban Health in Africa

Urban Health in Africa

Edited by
Elaine O. Nsoesie and
Blessing Mberu

JOHNS HOPKINS UNIVERSITY PRESS   BALTIMORE

© 2025 Johns Hopkins University Press
All rights reserved. Published 2025
Printed in the United States of America on acid-free paper
9 8 7 6 5 4 3 2 1

Johns Hopkins University Press
2715 North Charles Street
Baltimore, Maryland 21218
www.press.jhu.edu

Library of Congress Cataloging-in-Publication Data

Names: Nsoesie, Elaine, 1985– editor. | Mberu, Blessing, editor.
Title: Urban health in Africa / Elaine Nsoesie, Blessing Mberu.
Description: Baltimore : Johns Hopkins University Press, 2024. | Includes
    bibliographical references and index. |
Identifiers: LCCN 2024025906 | ISBN 9781421451152 (paperback : alk. paper)
    | ISBN 9781421451169 (epub)
Subjects: MESH: Urban Health | Africa
Classification: LCC RA418 | NLM WA 380 | DDC
    362.1/042096—dc23/eng/20241122
LC record available at https://lccn.loc.gov/2024025906

A catalog record for this book is available from the British Library.

*Special discounts are available for bulk purchases of this book. For more information, please
contact Special Sales at specialsales@jh.edu.*

Pauline Bakibinga, MD, PhD
(April 25, 1978–July 30, 2022)
Photo courtesy of the family of Paulina Bakibinga

    This book is dedicated to Dr. Pauline Bakibinga, winner of the 2022 Turman Corrah Prize for Excellence, whose medical practice and research on urban health in sub-Saharan Africa spanned over a decade. We are deeply grateful for her important contribution to this book—"Case Study of Prospects of Digital Health for Africa in Nairobi, Kenya," which she completed before her sudden departure. Pauline's vision to strengthen Africa's health systems from below, and across the most vulnerable points in the last mile, particularly by using digital innovations, speaks loudly to the future that we must embrace in pursuit of universal health coverage that leaves no one behind. She was passionate about addressing the needs of the most vulnerable and marginalized among the urban poor, especially those in informal settlements in African cities. We are inspired by her work and share in her commitment to and vision for urban health in Africa. We hope that her last contribution and those of other chapter authors will inspire urban health researchers and practitioners both now and in the future.

Contents

Acknowledgments   xi
List of Contributors   xiii

1   Urban Health in Africa   1
Elaine O. Nsoesie and Blessing Mberu

Part One: History and Background

2   Looking to the Past to Understand Today's African Cities   15
Elaine O. Nsoesie

3   What Is an African City?   32
Elaine O. Nsoesie and Blessing Mberu

Part Two: Social Determinants of Health

4   The Challenges of Informal Settlements and Slums
in Urban Africa   49
Marylene Wamukoya and Kanyiva Muindi

5   Urban Food Insecurity in Eastern and Southern Africa during the
Era of Sustainable Development: Making a Case for Slums   66
Linda Beyer

6   Housing as a Determinant of Health in African Cities   96
Meggie Mwoka

7   Water, Sanitation, and Hygiene (WASH) in Urban Areas of Africa:
Situational Analysis and Opportunities for Improvement   113
Sheillah Simiyu and Phylis Busienei

8   Ambient and Household Air Pollution in African Cities   142
Kanyiva Muindi

9   Transportation and Urban Health Risks in Africa   159
Peter Elias and Femi Ola Aiyegbajeje

10 Road Access and Health Care Inequality in Urban Africa 183
Mansoureh Abbasi, Aissata Boubacar Moumouni,
Marie Christelle Mabeu, and Roland Pongou

11 Conflict in Urban Areas in Africa and Implications
for Urban Health 195
Eme T. Owoaje and Edward Asemadahun

Part Three: Demographic Impacts and Health Behaviors

12 Sexual and Reproductive Health of Young People
in Urban Africa 213
Donatien Beguy, Blessing Mberu, and Kevin Nyamai

13 Urban Environments and Healthy Behaviors: Preventing
the Epidemic of Chronic Diseases in African Cities 231
Meelan Thondoo, Feyisayo A. Wayas, and Tolu Oni

Part Four: Case Studies

14 Case Study of Participatory Data-Driven Approaches to Improve
Urban Air Quality in Kampala, Uganda 255
Deo Okure, Engineer Bainomugisha, Daniel Ogenrwot,
Richard Sserunjogi, Priscah Adrine, and Gabriel Okello

15 Case Study of Mental Health, Illness, and Resources
in Yaoundé, Cameroon 271
Michael Guy Toguem and Barnard Christian Bela Zomo

16 Case Study of Improving Education to Address Determinants
of Health in Arusha, Tanzania 282
Neema Mduma and Dina Machuve

17 Case Study of Integrated Planning as Pathway for Healthy Informal
Settlements in Nairobi, Kenya 292
Jane Weru and Patrick Njoroge

18 Case Study of Prospects of Digital Health for Africa
in Nairobi, Kenya 302
Pauline Bakibinga, Dennis J. Matanda, and Elizabeth Bakibinga

Part Five: Looking to the Future

19 Educating the Next Generation of Urban Health Scholars 325
Damilola Odekunle, Feyisayo A. Wayas, Lambed Tatah,
Meelan Thondoo, and Elaine O. Nsoesie

20 Urban Health: 2030 and Beyond 341
Blessing Mberu and Elaine O. Nsoesie

Index 349

Acknowledgments

We thank Robin Coleman for editorial guidance, writing advice, and consistent support for this book. We are indebted to Dr. Sandro Galea for encouraging us to take on this project and for his mentorship and enthusiasm throughout. We would also like to acknowledge Olubusola Oladeji for helping us research the book proposal. As always, we thank our families for their support, kindness, and unwavering interest in our work.

—*Elaine and Blessing*

Contributors

Mansoureh Abbasi
University of Ottawa, Ontario, Canada

Priscah Adrine
AirQo, Department of Computer Science, Makerere University, Kampala, Uganda

Femi Ola Aiyegbajeje
Department of Geography, University of Lagos, Nigeria

Edward Asemadahun
Department of Community Medicine, University College Hospital, Ibadan, Nigeria

Engineer Bainomugisha
AirQo, Department of Computer Science, Makerere University, Kampala, Uganda

Elizabeth Bakibinga
Commonwealth Secretariat, London, United Kingdom

Pauline Bakibinga
African Population and Health Research Center, Nairobi, Kenya

Donatien Beguy
World Bank and UNHCR Joint Data Center on Forced Displacement, Copenhagen, Capital Region, Denmark

Linda Beyer
Sustainable Urban Development, University of Oxford, England, and Primary Care and Chronic Disease, Health Prince Edward Island, Canada

Phylis Busienei
African Population and Health Research Center, Nairobi, Kenya

Peter Elias
Department of Geography, University of Lagos, Nigeria

Marie Christelle Mabeu
Stanford University, Stanford, California

Dina Machuve
Devdata Analytics Limited, Arusha, Tanzania
Dennis J. Matanda
Population Council, Nairobi, Kenya
Blessing Mberu
African Population and Health Research Center, Nairobi, Kenya, and Demography and Population Studies Programme, Schools of Public Health and Social Sciences, University of the Witwatersrand, Johannesburg, South Africa
Neema Mduma
School of Computational and Communication Sciences and Engineering, Nelson Mandela African Institution of Science and Technology, Arusha, Tanzania
Aissata Boubacar Moumouni
University of Ottawa, Ontario, Canada
Kanyiva Muindi
African Population and Health Research Center, Nairobi, Kenya
Meggie Mwoka
Fellow, Rockefeller Foundation and Boston University Commission on Health, Determinants, Data, and Decision Making (3D Commission), School of Public Health, Boston University, Boston, Massachusetts
Patrick Njoroge
Akiba Mashinani Trust, Nairobi, Kenya
Elaine O. Nsoesie
School of Public Health, Boston University, Boston, Massachusetts
Kevin Nyamai
Institute of Statistics, University of Neuchatel, Switzerland
Damilola Odekunle
Department of Urban and Regional Planning, University of Lagos, Nigeria
Daniel Ogenrwot
AirQo, Department of Computer Science, Makerere University, Kampala, Uganda, and Department of Computer Science, Gulu University, Gulu, Uganda
Gabriel Okello
AirQo, Department of Computer Science, Makerere University,

Kampala, Uganda; Cambridge Institute for Sustainability Leadership, University of Cambridge, United Kingdom; and African Centre for Clean Air, Kampala, Uganda

Deo Okure
AirQo, Department of Computer Science, Makerere University, Kampala, Uganda

Tolu Oni
Global Diet and Physical Activity Research Group, MRC Epidemiology Unit, University of Cambridge, United Kingdom; UrbanBetter Lab, Innovation Africa @UP, and Department of Architecture, University of Pretoria, Tshwane, South Africa

Eme T. Owoaje
Department of Community Medicine, University of Ibadan, Nigeria

Roland Pongou
University of Ottawa, Ontario, Canada

Sheillah Simiyu
African Population and Health Research Center, Nairobi, Kenya

Richard Sserunjogi
AirQo, Department of Computer Science, Makerere University, Kampala, Uganda

Lambed Tatah
MRC Epidemiology Unit, University of Cambridge, United Kingdom

Meelan Thondoo
Global Diet and Physical Activity Research Group, MRC Epidemiology Unit, University of Cambridge, United Kingdom

Michael Guy Toguem
Department of Psychiatry, Polyclinique IDIMED, Douala, Cameroon

Marylene Wamukoya
African Population and Health Research Center, Nairobi, Kenya

Feyisayo A. Wayas
Research Centre for Health through Physical Activity, Lifestyle and Sport, Division of Physiological Sciences, Department of Human Biology, and Division of Public Health Medicine, School of Public Health and Family Medicine, Faculty of Health Sciences, University of Cape Town, Cape Town, South Africa

Jane Weru
Akiba Mashinani Trust, Nairobi, Kenya
Barnard Christian Bela Zomo
Unit of Mental Health Promotion, Ministry of Public Health,
Cameroon

Urban Health in Africa

1

Urban Health in Africa

Elaine O. Nsoesie and Blessing Mberu

1. Introduction

Africa, with 43 percent of its 1.3 billion people living in urban areas, is currently the least urbanized region in the world, but it is also the continent with the fastest urbanization rate. Fifty-six percent of the population is projected to live in urban areas by 2050 (United Nations 2018). Cities in Africa offer similar advantages (e.g., employment and improved quality of life) and challenges (including inadequate housing and transportation) as cities in other parts of the world. Some challenges are unique to African cities, however, owing to historical, political, cultural, economic, and demographic factors.

African countries have gone through different periods of demographic growth, from stagnation during the precolonial era to exponential growth postindependence (Heinrigs 2020). Yet rapid urbanization across African countries has been associated with significant variations in wealth and resources within cities. Slums, which have increasingly become an important aspect of cities in many low- and middle-income countries, are an important feature in many African cities. Among the over 1 billion people living in slums or informal settlements, 238 million (24 percent) live in sub-Saharan Africa (United Nations 2021). Yet informal settlements remain generally unseen in some national data systems, official statistics, urban averages, and policy priorities, and scientific literature on slum health remains largely underdeveloped (Ezeh et al. 2016).

Governments have struggled to develop the infrastructure and provide the resources needed to keep up with urban growth. This means many urban areas struggle to address challenges such as housing, transportation, and health care. Also, the increase in urbanization and the unconfined movement of people, commodities, capital, and services have resulted in changes in lifestyle factors. While the depth of these challenges and opportunities differs from one urban area to another and from one country to another, these factors influence health in both positive and negative ways. For example, cities offer educational opportunities that can shape behavior and circumstances across multiple generations. Education can also lead to higher paying jobs. Higher income in turn is associated with higher obesity prevalence. Obesity is a risk factor for many chronic diseases. This complexity in the impact of urban health determinants is partly what makes the study of how African cities are influencing and shaping population health important.

In AbdouMaliq Simone's book *For the City Yet to Come*, he argues that the unique challenges faced by African cities do not imply that African cities do not work. Simone writes, "In city after city, one can witness an incessant throbbing produced by the intense proximity of hundreds of activities: cooking, reciting, selling, loading and unloading, fighting, praying, relaxing, pounding, and buying, all side by side on stages too cramped, too deteriorated, too clogged with waste, history, and disparate energy, and sweat to sustain all of them. And yet they persist" (Simone 2004, 1). Through four case studies, Simone examines informal economies and social collaborations to make a compelling argument that overlooking the successful aspects of African cities—including the creativity, innovation, and collaboration of residents involved in robust informal economies and associated political economies—we miss the opportunity to learn about a type of urban configuration whose realities can be applied to other cities in the world (Njeru, Prytherch, and Kenny 2006; Simone 2004). While Simone's argument is largely focused on informal economies, a similar argument can be made for African cities more broadly. Although many problems arise from factors that shape health, as this book demonstrates throughout, many complex, effective solutions and resources exist in African cities.

To fully understand health in African cities, we need to dig deeper into the different dimensions and interlinkages among Africa's rapid urbanization, demographic characteristics, and the growth of urban informal settlements, enabling an understanding of how urbanization is changing how people live—what they eat and drink, and how they think and interact with one another. This book combines these ideas with case studies that illustrate factors associated with the rapid growth of cities in Africa, capturing the current state of urban health knowledge; builds on growing African and Africanist scholarship on urban health in Africa; and offers a springboard for future research investments. The chapters also highlight innovations and successful implementation of policies aimed at improving the lives of urban residents. Urban health requires interdisciplinary study; therefore, the book includes contributions and perspectives from Africans and Africanists from multiple disciplines. Most of the chapters focus on specific social determinants of health while centering the challenges of the most vulnerable populations, which include individuals who reside in slums, women, and young people. Furthermore, case studies provide specific examples of how cities in Africa are addressing challenges such as air pollution, mental health, and school dropout rates.

The book starts with two chapters that provide the reader with a historical perspective of cities and health in Africa, as well as the similar and varying ways in which African countries define cities. The next three parts consist of a range of perspectives on the determinants of health; demographic impacts and health behaviors; and case studies. First, we present chapters about the social determinants of health, grouped to highlight or build on related ideas. The discussions in each chapter are based on published research, and when data or evidence is limited, the authors incorporate novel data and analysis. The chapters are ordered as follows: informal settlements and slums; food insecurity in slums; education; housing; water, sanitation, and hygiene (WASH); ambient and household air pollution; transportation; road access; and conflict. The chapter on road access presents a specific example of how transportation infrastructure serves as a pathway to health by presenting new data on the association between road access and perinatal health outcomes.

The next part focuses on demographic impacts (i.e., the sexual and reproductive health of young people), the built environment and health behaviors, and their association with chronic diseases. The third part presents case studies. We focus on select African cities and issues, namely, air quality in Kampala, mental health in Yaoundé, education in Arusha, informal settlements in Nairobi, and digital health in Nairobi. The high representation of cities in East Africa is coincidental and largely due to the availability of authors. Through these case studies, we hope readers can have a better orientation of how African cities are creating opportunities and addressing challenges related to social determinants of health.

We conclude with two chapters looking forward: one on training the next generation of urban scholars, who would keep pace with the rapid urbanization happening on the continent, and another on the future of urban health in Africa.

2. Opportunities, Challenges, and Policy Solutions

Compared to rural health, which has a well-established foundation across Africa, the field and study of urban health in Africa is nascent (Declaration of Alma-Ata 1978; WHO Regional Office for Africa 2008). With the rapid growth of urban populations in Africa, an increased emphasis on the impact of urbanicity on health and the translation of knowledge into policy and action to improve the health of urban residents is urgently needed. This requires an appreciation of the determinants and the broader cultural, historical, and economic contexts. The authors in this book digged deep into the different dimensions and interlinkages among Africa's rapid urbanization, its demographic characteristics, and the growth of urban informal settlements, enabling an understanding of how urbanization is changing how people live. The chapters also draw on interdisciplinary contributions and perspectives to challenge current limitations in policy, while broadening the knowledge base.

2.1. Learning from a History of Cities in Africa

In 1691, Portuguese ship captain Lourenço Pinto wrote of Benin City in West Africa, "Great Benin, where the king resides, is larger than Lisbon; all the streets run straight and as far as the eye can see . . . The houses are large, especially that of the king, which is richly decorated and has fine columns. The city is wealthy and industrious. It is so well governed that theft is unknown, and the people live in such security that they have no doors to their houses" (Koutonin 2016).

Scholars estimate that Africa's urbanization started in the fourth millennium BCE, with cities in Egypt emerging around 3300 to 3200 BCE. Abydos, one of the first settlements that could be considered a city, had about twenty thousand residents in 3200 BCE (Tarver and Miller 1993). Cities such as Edo City in Benin, Walata, and Timbuktu, situated on the border of the Sahara in the Sahel's Niger River basin; Koumbi-Saleh in Mali; Cairo in Egypt; and many others emerged later. Many of these cities have disappeared or evolved geographically, and only fragments of their history are captured or emphasized in global discussions of cities and their influence on major historical events, as with much of African history.

While cities in precolonial times were vastly different from cities today, are there lessons to be learned from these early cities? For example, what factors created security, wealth, and industry in Benin City? Are there lessons we can adopt today in Indigenous cultural processes and beliefs that shaped governance in precolonial cities? Are there lessons in poor governance that should not be repeated?

Much evidence shows that historical factors and policies influence present-day determinants of health (Galea 2017). While much of this research has been pursued outside Africa, there is no reason to assume that similar observations are not applicable. Many historical events and policies both within Africa and globally have shaped countries and cities, including slavery, colonialization, and specific political, conflict, social, cultural, and economic events. The consequences of many of these factors tend to intersect and may concentrate disadvantage on particular groups of individuals.

While the definition of a city, or an urban area, differs across the continent, certain characteristics associated with the urban advantage and "disadvantage" are similar across many cities. Some individuals who move to cities in search of better education, jobs, and other opportunities that contribute to health and well-being find what they seek, but others do not. Instead, many end up living in poverty and struggling with challenges such as food insecurity, water insecurity, pollution, and environmental disasters, among others.

Understanding how cities have emerged in Africa and what factors have shaped the culture, dynamics, and inequity in cities could be a first step toward addressing the challenges that affect urban residents. There is sometimes a dearth of knowledge on African experience, ingenuity, and successes. Compared to other regions of the world, African history is not well known beyond the influences of slavery and colonialization. There is a need to center the history of African cities in discourse about urban health, rather than propagating the narrative that Africa does not have a history, that the continent has not contributed to the shaping of the world (French 2021), or that no lessons from the past can be used to shape present-day policies. The history and definition of cities in Africa is discussed in chapters 2 and 3.

2.2. Determinants of Health in African Cities

Slums, youths, infrastructure, and data and technology are four major themes that emerge across many of the chapters in the book.

2.2.1. SLUMS

Across several chapters, authors emphasize the need to elevate the needs and voices of slum residents. More than 50 percent of urban residents are projected to live in slums by 2050 (UN-Habitat 2003, 2020; WHO 2000). In chapter 4, the authors discuss the many challenges experienced by slum dwellers, including marginalization, lack of formal employment opportunities, different forms of poverty (e.g., chronic versus transient poor), lack of convenient access to public transportation, absence of healthy housing, food insecurity, pollution, lack of access to safe drinking water and safely managed sanitation, and specific vulnerabilities experienced by children living in slums. Chapter 5 makes the case for creating specific policies for addressing food insecurity in slums. The author discusses how gender and employment intersect with slum residency to heighten food insecurity, and describes adaptive approaches slum dwellers implement to manage food insecurity. Chapter 6 delves deeper into the issue of housing insecurity, addressing issues of instability, affordability, quality, and safety. To address the lack of healthy housing in cities, policymakers require reliable data documenting what is available and what is lacking to tackle the needs of slum residents. Newer data sources, including satellite images, panorama street view images, and mobile phone data, can provide useful information on built environment indicators, as has been shown in many studies. These data, however, are not always available from companies, and often the quality of the available data is not timely and comprehensive enough to answer policy-related questions in urban Africa.

The intersection of the aforementioned social determinants of health reduces resistance to disease outbreaks and natural disasters. The authors stress the need for policymakers to prioritize policies that focus on increasing the resilience of slum residents through city planning and management. Slum health must also be separated from urban health planning broadly to develop specific and effective interventions that address the unique problems slum dwellers face.

Slum dwellers also have much to share and teach populations in cities in Africa and globally—such as how to develop resilience to shocks and a unique ability to organize that could be easily used to bring their opinions and influence to policy decisions. Through organizing sanitation campaigns to highlight issues of water insecurity and menstrual hygiene, as well as collaboration with county government, residents of the three largest slums in Nairobi (Mukuru Kwa Njenga, Kwa Reuben, and Viwandani) are creating change, as discussed in the case study in chapter 17. Chapter 7 discusses how cities have devised various ways of increasing access to sanitation facilities, including deploying new service delivery models and partnerships with all stakeholders. These efforts still need to be advanced through various approaches, including participatory co-design methods with the relevant disciplines and stakeholders, enhancing effective governance structures (including political will), increasing education and advocacy, and refining data collection systems for informed decision making. Improving the health of slum residents will also benefit nonslum urban dwellers; slum health is a key determinant of urban and national health indicators.

2.2.2. YOUTH

A conversation of urban health in Africa is incomplete without a discussion of the health challenges experienced by young people. About 40 percent of Africans are younger than 15 years, and almost 60 percent of the population are younger than 25 years (UN Department of Economic and Social Affairs 2022). The median age in Africa is 19 years, and more than two-thirds of city dwellers in the largest African cities (such as Lagos, Dakar, Accra, and Abidjan) are younger than 30 (OECD 2020). The discussion in the book focuses on the experiences of young people in slums with sexual and reproductive health and mental health challenges.

As noted in chapter 12, young people face similar challenges experienced by adults in slums (such as lack of access to quality education, inadequate housing, food insecurity, water insecurity, etc.) in addition to challenges that make them vulnerable (i.e., poor livelihood opportunities; high risk of gender-based violence; insufficient basic services, including poor schooling facilities; high levels of substance use). Many girls in slums have no privacy to change their pads during their menstrual periods and are at risk of sexual abuse. These youth are also more likely to engage in risky sexual behavior because of the lack of access to education on sexual and reproductive health, including information about and access to modern contraceptive methods.

This also increases their risk for adverse sexual and reproductive health outcomes, including sexually transmitted diseases and early pregnancies and motherhood.

Chapter 15 discusses mental health and challenges experienced by unhoused children. A recent systematic review found that 40.8 percent of adolescents in sub-Saharan Africa had emotional and behavioral challenges, followed by about 30 percent with depression and anxiety disorders (29.8 percent and 26.9 percent, respectively), and one-fifth with post-traumatic stress disorder (PTSD) and suicidal thoughts (21.5 percent and 20.8 percent, respectively; Mabrouk et al. 2022).

Policies that address the challenges experienced by young people in urban Africa in an ever-changing world are urgently needed. For example, in chapter 12, the authors highlight policies in countries such as Sierra Leone that focus on protecting girls, including declaring rape and sexual violence a national emergency in 2019, encouraging pregnant girls to stay in school, and providing free medical treatment for victims of rape and sexual violence. Addressing the challenges experienced by urban youth requires an intersectoral approach that focuses on ensuring a healthy and stable future for urban Africa.

2.2.3. INFRASTRUCTURE

The need for improved infrastructure, including housing, transportation, and water and sanitation systems, is significant in urban Africa.

A variety of door-to-door transport options are available in African cities, with many benefits including access to employment, schools, clinical centers, and leisure activities. These transport systems can be expensive, however, especially for the poor and are often unregulated, exacerbating other challenges such as financial insecurity and crime (Opondo and Kiprop 2018). These challenges are underlined in chapter 9, in addition to the absence of transport policy, the dominance of the informal sector, inadequately designed and poor transport infrastructure, low investment outlay, unregulated pricing systems, low adoption of digital platforms that aim to improve urban transportation, and lack of strong institutional capacity. As the population in urban Africa grows, tackling these needs with a focus on sustainability and health will help to address associated urban health burdens, including road traffic accidents, physical human inactivity, greenhouse gas emissions, and traffic-related environmental exposures, such as air pollution, noise, and local temperature rises.

To enhance urban transport systems and urban health, the authors suggest a focus on maintaining the function of public transport systems, enhancing modal diversity, reducing dependency on motorized transportation, increasing safe walking and cycling, among other ideas. The authors also make broader policy recommendations, including many already adopted in countries across Africa: smart land use and transport policy; allocation of adequate land for green spaces; improved multimodal transport systems; road hierarchy arrangement and management; effective transport governance supported by institutions, frameworks, and funding commitments; use of smartcard ticketing; among others.

The impact of transportation on health is further elaborated in chapter 10 with a focus on the importance of road access for maternal and prenatal care. Roads contribute to health outcomes in multiple ways, enhancing economic well-being by enabling access to markets, for example, and distributing health care services, such as ambulances, and medical care. Using novel data and analysis for twenty-eight countries in sub-Saharan Africa, the authors' findings suggest that roads do not equally benefit all individuals and population groups, with the strongest effects noted for mothers who are over 25 years, wealthy, educated, and employed. There is an overall positive correlation between road access and prenatal health care use, especially for child delivery services.

Similarly, the issues of inadequate, unsafe, and unaffordable housing are discussed in chapter 6. Individuals who live in slums and informal settlements experience forced evictions and harassment from housing authorities, which can affect physical and mental health, as well as livelihoods and social networks. While a single policy solution does not exist to address these issues, there is a need for a multisectoral partnership, involving health professionals, urban planners, city managers, and others, to ensure that houses are designed to address neighborhood needs and improve access to other needed resources, including safe water and healthy foods. Chapter 7 further assesses challenges and opportunities for improving water, sanitation, and hygiene (WASH) in urban Africa, also encouraging intersectoral collaboration. Solutions to a lack of sanitation facilities include shared community facilities, which have operation and management challenges but some successes (including improving WASH) in some countries. Further rigorous research that incorporates contexts and cultures in cities, improved data collection, development and implementation of WASH policies at multiple levels, community health education and awareness campaigns, and participatory co-design approaches that draw from multiple sectors and individuals affected are needed.

2.2.4. DATA, TECHNOLOGY, AND URBAN HEALTH

There are many opportunities to use technology and data to document and address urban health needs. Four of the case studies focus on innovations in urban health priority areas, including implementing digital health within health systems in Nairobi, Kenya; addressing mental health in Yaoundé, Cameroon; reducing school dropout rates for girls in primary schools in Arusha, Tanzania; and using technology to improve air pollution monitoring in Kampala, Uganda. Nairobi, Kenya's capital, is used to describe the potential of digital health technologies in reducing health care inequities in an African city with a fast-growing urban population. Technology and community participatory approaches are employed in Kampala, Uganda, to gather data on air pollution. This effort has expanded to several cities across Africa. Data science methods and community participatory design approaches are being employed to improve education outcomes especially for girls in Arusha, Tanzania. The authors discuss the implementation of a machine learning tool that considers the various factors associated with school dropout and alerts relevant individuals when a student's risk of dropping out of school increases.

Although many applications of technology address social determinants of health in African cities, they are not often known. Through the case studies, we attempt to highlight innovations in urban health and hope these lessons and examples can be adopted by other cities. We also hope that highlighting these examples encourages investments in their sustainability in regions where they have been implemented, as well as support for the progress and achievements of regional and global health agendas.

3. The Book's Approach

In this book, our aim is to provide a picture of the current state of urban health in the region, including perspectives on areas where data are urgently needed, case studies, and future prospects on how cities will shape health in African countries. We intend to present a careful examination of the current state of the science, illuminating what we know and where gaps exist in our knowledge to inform priorities for urban health research and training in Africa in the next decade. The book's sections aim to elucidate the factors shaping health, describe emerging challenges, and provide examples to improve our understanding of how African cities are addressing challenges. Despite the book's focus on Africa, the methods, ideas, and solutions presented are applicable to other regions of the world, especially countries facing similar opportunities and challenges. Most important, we consider this the perfect time for this book. Africa is rapidly urbanizing. To influence urban health in the next decade and beyond, we need to understand its current state.

REFERENCES

Declaration of Alma-Ata. 1978. "International Conference on Primary Health Care." *WHO Chronicle* 32 (11): 428–30.

French, Howard W. 2021. *Born in Blackness: Africa, Africans, and the Making of the Modern World, 1471 to the Second World War*. New York: Liveright.

Galea, Sandro. 2017. "History as a Determinant of Health." Boston University School of Public Health Dean's Note, March 12. https://www.bu.edu/sph/news/articles/2017/history-as-a-determinant-of-health/.

Heinrigs, Philipp. 2020. "Africapolis: Understanding the Dynamics of Urbanization in Africa." *Field Actions Science Reports: The Journal of Field Actions* 22:18–23.

Koutonin, Mawuna. 2016. "Story of Cities #5: Benin City, the Mighty Medieval Capital Now Lost without Trace." *Guardian*, March 18.

Mabrouk, Adam, Gideon Mbithi, Esther Chongwo, Ezra Too, Ahmed Sarki, Mary Namuguzi, Joseph Atukwatse, Derrick Ssewanyana, and Amina Abubakar. 2022. "Mental Health Interventions for Adolescents in Sub-Saharan Africa: A Scoping Review." *Frontiers in Psychiatry* 13:1696.

Njeru, Jeremia, David L. Prytherch, and Judith Kenny. 2006. *"For the City Yet to Come: Changing African Life in Four Cities*. AbdouMaliq Simone; *Metropolitan Phoenix: Place Making and Community Building in the Desert*. Patricia Gober; *Urban Informality: Transnational Perspectives from the Middle East, Latin America, and South Asia*. Ananya Roy and Nezar Al Sayyad, Eds." *Urban Geography* 27 (4): 388–92.

OECD. 2020. "How Is Life in Your City?" OECD, Sahel and West Africa Club. https://oecd-swac.shorthandstories.com/how-is-life-in-west-african-cities/.

Simone, AbdouMaliq. 2004. *For the City Yet to Come: Changing African Life in Four Cities*. Durham, NC: Duke University Press.

Tarver, James D., and M. Miller. 1993. "Urbanization in Pre-Colonial Africa." *Africa Insight* 23 (3): 176–78.

UN Department of Economic and Social Affairs, Population Division. 2022. *World Population Prospects 2022: Summary of Results*. New York: United Nations.

UN-Habitat. 2003. *The Challenge of Slums: Global Report on Human Settlement 2003 / United Nations Human Settlements Programme*. London: Earthscan.

UN-Habitat. 2020. *World Cities Report 2020: The Value of Sustainable Urbanization*. Nairobi, Kenya: UN-Habitat. https://unhabitat.org/sites/default/files/2020/10/wcr_2020 _report.pdf.

United Nations. 2018. *Revision of World Urbanization Prospects*. New York: United Nations.

United Nations. 2021. "Make Cities and Human Settlements Inclusive, Safe, Resilient and Sustainable." Sustainable Development Goal 11. UN Statistics Division. https:// unstats.un.org/sdgs/report/2021/goal-11/.

WHO (World Health Organization). 2000. *WHO Report on Global Surveillance of Epidemic-Prone Infectious Diseases*. Geneva: WHO.

WHO (World Health Organization) Regional Office for Africa. 2008. *Report on the Review of Primary Health Care in the African Region*. Brazzaville, Congo: WHO Regional Office for Africa.

I HISTORY AND BACKGROUND

Historical and contemporary factors have shaped urbanization in Africa. To fully appreciate the complexity of the problems, opportunities, and solutions in African cities, it is important to understand how forces such as colonialism shaped the built environment and sought to define urban citizenship to conform to European perspectives of what urbanization should look like. In part 1, we introduce the reader to a brief history of cities in Africa and how cities are defined across the continent. We discuss how different political and social contexts have influenced the growth of urban areas, from the precolonial period to the present era, and how these changes have shaped factors that affect health. We then describe the differences in how countries in Africa define cities, discuss how urbanization has varied substantially across the continent, and explain why there is a need to study cities in Africa without constantly comparing them to cities in other regions of the world. These chapters aim to frame the perspectives presented in the remainder of the book.

2

Looking to the Past to Understand Today's African Cities

Elaine O. Nsoesie

1. A Rich Urban History

Africa's urban history dates back centuries, exceeding two thousand years for some regions and cities (Chirikure 2020c; Coret, Zaugg, and Chouin 2020; Satterthwaite 2021a). While the information is incomplete, we gather from fragmented oral narratives, as well as archaeological, anthropological, literary, and historical data, that some of the current large African cities existed prior to the late nineteenth century, when colonial rule began to considerably expand (Coret, Zaugg, and Chouin 2020; Satterthwaite 2021a; Tarver and Miller 1993). Evidence suggests that urbanization was important in the precolonial era. Some urban centers were capitals of kingdoms, empires, and caliphates. Africa also had various shades of urban design, with a range of spatial expressions from the colossal to the satellite, and even to the nomadic; scattered homesteads formed networks with military cities and major urban centers (Chirikure 2020c). Regardless of how they are categorized, urban settlements were most importantly places for dwelling, working, practicing religion, and relaxing. Cities were first human settlements—places where people lived, services were exchanged, and authority was built and maintained (Chirikure 2020c).

There were local and regional similarities and differences in how these urban areas functioned. For example, the administrative, political, and ritual functions of peripatetic capitals were similar to those of the Luba and Kuba Kingdoms in Central Africa and the Zulus of South Africa. In contrast, ancient Egyptian and Nubian capitals practiced centralized control of resources, which was not the case in places like Great Zimbabwe, where households were free to participate in production and circulation of resources (Chirikure 2020b; Edwards 1994; Snape 2014).

Urban growth in Africa prior to the nineteenth century has been attributed to internal influences (such as Indigenous population growth, technological innovation, and internal trading networks) and trans-Saharan trading involving metallurgy and mixed agriculture (Segal 1988; Tarver and Miller 1993). For example, the cities of Walata and Timbuktu started as trading centers and then evolved to commercial centers, where goods from the north (e.g., salt, dates, silk, textiles, etc.) were traded for goods from Sudanese traders (including gold, ostrich feathers, ivory, grain, spices, kola nuts, woven cloth, and slaves; Tarver and Miller 1993). These "trading cities" were often on the edge of different ecological zones, sometimes characterized by different transport systems. Cities were also influenced by religious conflicts and wars, such as the Muslim conquest of northern Africa in the eighth century. They served as centers of schools, scholarship, administration, and magnificent mosques that attracted a flux of pilgrims (Coret, Zaugg, and Chouin 2020; Satterthwaite 2021a). The city of Alexandria, established in 332 BCE, was a center of commerce, culture, and intellectual activity. Home to prominent intellectuals such as Euclid and Ptolemy, it was also the capital of Egypt until 642 CE. The city of Cairo, founded in 641 CE, was a major center of East–West spice trade and Islamic study. The city has within its borders other ancient cities, including al-Fustat (the city of tents), al-Askar (the city of sections, or cantonments), and al-Qatta'i (the Quarters). It has remained one of Africa's largest cities for most of the previous fifteen centuries (Satterthwaite 2021a). It is estimated that close to 500,000 people lived in Cairo around 1340.

In West Africa, the Ghana Empire (ca. 300 to 1100) prospered from trans-Saharan trade in gold and salt, which influenced the emergence of large urban centers such as Bamako—an important market town and a center for Islamic scholars; it had two universities and several mosques in medieval times (Satterthwaite 2021a). The Oyo Empire, which was dominant during the mid-seventeenth to the late eighteenth century and marked the start of the documented history of the Yoruba people, was preceded by Ile-Ife, a city that began to emerge as an important artistic center between 700 and 900 CE. Other cities in the neighboring Benin Empire were also influenced by the Yoruba, including Benin City, Warri, Auchi, and Olene (Coret, Zaugg, and Chouin 2020; Tarver and Miller 1993).

In East Africa, evidence of urban centers has been noted along the Swahili coast, in Askum and Gondor in Ethiopia, and in Khartoum and Sennar in Sudan. Ancient cities like Kerma in Sudan, which was estimated to have about ten thousand inhabitants in 1700 BCE, thrived as the "first great urban center" in tropical Africa (Satterthwaite 2021a). By the eighteenth century, Swahili towns on the Benadir coast, such as Barawa, Marka, Mogadishu, Lamu, and Zanzibar, were trade centers. In southern Africa, Great Zimbabwe was a principal city between the eleventh and fifteenth centuries as well as a trade center. The Tswana agro-towns in present-day Botswana also remained for several centuries (Chirikure 2020c; Satterthwaite 2021a).

The largest cities in Africa in 1800 and in 2020 based on available data are listed in table 2.1; all cities with listed years existed before European colonial rule (Satterthwaite 2021b). Of the thirty-four cities, the largest were located in countries in northern and western Africa, including Morocco, Nigeria, and Egypt. Some of these cities became major transport, administrative, and military hubs during colonial rule. None of the cities listed is in southern Africa, but the population of Cape Town was estimated to be close to twenty thousand inhabitants in 1800. Only eight of the cities categorized as largest cities in 1800 were also considered on the list of one hundred largest cities in 2020, and a majority (i.e., five) are in northern Africa.

Like cities today, ancient cities in Africa had vast diversity. The shape and history of African cities have not been linear. Periods of urbanization have been followed by periods of deurbanization, when cities that once flourished lost their prominence. The shape, structure, and life span of various cities were affected by conquest, natural disasters (such as the bubonic plague), political crisis, demographic shifts, relocation, and political influences (Coret, Zaugg, and Chouin 2020). For example, Alexandria had transformed into an insignificant fishing town with about six thousand inhabitants by 1777, before becoming a large prominent city again. Archaeological evidence indicates that the modern city of Alexandria was built on top of the ancient one (Daniels 2022). Other ancient cities experienced different fates. Ile-Ife, for instance, experienced major demographic mishaps and then later reestablished in the same location; Djenné-Djenno appears to have been relocated to the current town of Djenné; and Savi was devasted after the Dahomey conquered Hueda in 1727 (Coret, Zaugg, and Chouin 2020).

The discussion in this chapter is in no way a comprehensive review of cities in Africa prior to the nineteenth century. Many papers, essays, and

Table 2.1. The largest cities in Africa in 1800

1800 rank (2020 rank)	City	Country	Founded	1800 population (thousands)	Region
1 (1)	Al-Qahirah (Cairo)	Egypt	641 CE	260	Northern Africa
2 (108)	Sokoto	Nigeria	1799 CE	120	Western Africa
3 (125)	Meknes	Morocco	940 CE	110	Northern Africa
4 (35)	Tunis	Tunisia	300 BCE	90	Northern Africa
5 (166)	Oyo	Nigeria	1300 CE	85	Western Africa
6 (28)	El Djazaïr (Algiers)	Algeria	1000 CE	73	Western Africa
7 (134)	Ife	Nigeria	1200 CE	72	Western Africa
8 (153)	Katsina	Nigeria	1320 CE	70	Western Africa
9 (51)	Fès	Morocco	786 CE	60	Northern Africa
10	Kazargamu	Nigeria	Unknown	50	Western Africa
11	Alkalawa	Nigeria	Unknown	50	Western Africa
12 (67)	Marrakech	Morocco	1070 CE	50	Northern Africa
13 (38)	Rabat	Morocco	1000 CE	43	Northern Africa
14	Obogun	Nigeria	Unknown	40	Western Africa
15 (20)	Kumasi	Ghana	1600 CE	40	Western Africa
16 (71)	llorin	Nigeria	1730 CE	40	Western Africa
17 (94)	Zaria	Nigeria	1536 CE	40	Western Africa
18 (127)	Ogbomosho	Nigeria	1650 CE	40	Western Africa
19	Segn	Mali	Unknown	30	Western Africa
20	Bonga	Ethiopia	Unknown	30	Eastern Africa
21 (13)	Kano	Nigeria	1100 CE	30	Western Africa
22 (197)	Kebbi	Nigeria	600 CE	30	Western Africa
23	Masenya	Chad	Unknown	30	Middle Africa
24	Yendi	Ghana	Unknown	30	Western Africa
25	Kiawa	Nigeria	Unknown	30	Western Africa
26	Constantine	Algeria	Unknown	25	Northern Africa
27 (156)	Asyut	Egypt	Unknown	25	Northern Africa
28	Mouzangaye	Madagascar	Unknown	25	Eastern Africa
29	Gbara	Mali	Unknown	24	Western Africa
30	Bulaq	Egypt	1500 CE	24	Northern Africa
31 (64)	Abomay	Benin	Unknown	24	Western Africa
32	Sangha	Mali	Unknown	24	Western Africa
33	Damietta	Egypt	500 CE	23	Northern Africa
34	Kairwan/ Kairouan	Tunisia	670 CE	20	Northern Africa

Sources: Data from Satterthwaite (2021b). Almost all city and urban population statistics from 1950 onward come from the UN Population Division's *2018 World Urbanization Prospects*. Almost all city population statistics prior to 1950 come from Tertius Chandler, *Four Thousand Years of Urban Growth: An Historical Census* (Lampeter: Edwin Mellen Press, 1987). This table also draws on Paul Bairoch, *Cities and Economic Development: From the Dawn of History to the Present* (London: Mansell, 1988); and Bill Freund, *The African City: A History* (Cambridge: Cambridge University Press, 2007).

Note: This list includes all African cities for which population estimates suggest they had 20,000 or more inhabitants around 1800. There are likely to be many more for which there are no estimates.

books have been written on the subject, with emerging and diverging opinions on the economic, social, and political factors that influenced and shaped these urban areas.

We have chosen to highlight in the next sections two cities lost to history: Great Zimbabwe in southern Africa and Benin City in western Africa.

1.1. Great Zimbabwe

Great Zimbabwe was a medieval city located in the southeastern part of today's Zimbabwe. The term *great* is used to differentiate it from the two hundred smaller ruins distributed across the Zimbabwe Highveld. The city is thought to have been an administrative and religious center during the Iron Age (Chirikure 2020b, 2020c). The ancestors of the Shona people, belonging to the Bantu group and native to southern Africa, started building the city in the ninth century and continued till the fifteenth century. At its peak, the city housed an estimated eighteen thousand people, but different surveys present varied population estimates, suggesting the need for additional studies (Chirikure et al. 2017; Garlake 1973; Huffman 2007; Kuklick 1991).

Monumental architecture, stone sculptures combining human and animal likenesses, external trade, leadership and ancestral power, and class distinction are hallmarks of Great Zimbabwe (Chirikure 2020c; Garlake 1973; Pikirayi 2002). In and around the urban area, remnants of crafts, such as weaving and metallurgy; subsistence activities, like food preparation; musical instruments; and entertainment and relaxation artifacts, including mangala board games, have been discovered (Chirikure 2020a). Stone walls built without the use of mortar, 11 meters high and 250 meters wide, are referred to as the Great Enclosure, the most prominent feature of Great Zimbabwe's edifice. In the eleventh century, construction began on the stone buildings and lasted for more than three hundred years. The ruins of Great Zimbabwe are among the largest constructions in southern Africa and are the second oldest after Mapungubwe in South Africa. The ruins form three distinctive architectural groups, which are thought to represent the work of successive kings. Other notable artifacts include eight Zimbabwe birds carved from a micaceous schist (soapstone) on top of monoliths the height of a person; soapstone figurines (one can be found in the British Museum); intricately worked ivory; pottery; iron hoes; iron gongs; copper ingots and crucibles; iron and copper wire; bronze spearheads; and gold objects, including pendants, bracelets, sheaths, and beats (Garlake 2002; Summers 1971). In addition to local agricultural trade, objects suggesting international trade and connections include glass beads and porcelain from China and Persia. Eight monolith birds, carved into soapstone, were found in a large stone ruin of the ancient city. They are said to represent the bateleur eagle, which in Shona culture is thought to be a good omen, protective spirit, and messenger of gods (Nelson 2015).

Great Zimbabwe was involved in local and long-distance trade and exchange, connecting it with other regions thousands of miles away, such as Central Africa (Pikirayi 2002). Moreover, it was a vital element of the Indian Ocean Rim–based circulation system supplying gold, ivory, food, and other resources. Recent research on the political economy of Great Zimbabwe shows that contrary to previous perceptions, rulers may not have monopolized all forms of trade. Instead, commodities were distributed by households located in different parts of the network, thus demonstrating the capillary approach of the political economy (Chirikure 2020b). In fact, the rulers made use of production without central control through ancestry and a communitarian ideology.

Great Zimbabwe had developed an oral literacy as well as a variety of engineering principles, which are carefully laid out in the massive walls and buildings that make up the city's dwellings. In general, urban development in Great Zimbabwe was scattered across the landscape, with nodes of congregation spread out to exploit agriculture, control public health, and enable collective action to organize labor in support of various activities, from public buildings to subsistence and crafts (Chirikure 2020c). Possible explanations postulated for the decline and abandonment of Great Zimbabwe include political instability, famine, water shortages due to climate change, depletion of gold mines, and decline in trade (Holmgren and Öberg 2006; Pwiti 1991). It is recognized as a UNESCO World Heritage Site and considered a national monument in Zimbabwe.

1.2. Benin City

Mawuna Koutonin (2016) writes, "with its mathematical layout and earthworks longer than the Great Wall of China, Benin City was one of the best planned cities in the world when London was a place of 'thievery and murder'. So why is nothing left?" Benin City was the capital of the Benin Empire, also known as the Edo Kingdom, in West Africa. The kingdom emerged around the eleventh century CE and was invaded by the British in 1897. Benin City was also looted and burned by British soldiers (Bradbury 2004; Cartwright 2019). The historical Benin City is largely forgotten, with no ruins or touristic attractions.

Benin City was surrounded by massive walls in the south and deep ditches in the north (Oliver 1977). Several other walls located beyond the city separated the surrounding area of the capital into about five hundred villages. The 1974 edition of the *Guinness Book of Records* describes the walls as "the largest earthworks in the world carried out prior to the mechanical era . . . In April, 1973, it was estimated that the total length of the earthworks was probably between 5,000 and 8,000 miles with a total of almost 600 million cubic yards of earth removed" (McWhirter and McWhirter 1974, 303). The planning and design of Benin City was carried out in accordance with the strict rules of symmetry, proportionality, and repetition, which are now known as fractal design (Eglash 1999). To create perfect fractals, the city and its surrounding villages were deliberately set up with similar shapes repeated in the rooms of each house, in the houses, and in the groups of houses in the village in mathematically predictable patterns (Koutonin 2016). The king's court was located at the center of the city, and thirty broad streets about 120 feet wide extended from it. Underground drainage in these main streets was constructed from sunken impluvium, with an outlet to drain storm water. Turf on which animals fed was located in the center of some streets. Bronze plaques depicting the victories and deeds of the former kings and nobles were affixed to the pillars of the palaces. The city was divided into eleven divisions, each a smaller replica of the king's court, comprising series of compounds, including living quarters, workshops, and public buildings, interconnected by doors and passageways, lavishly decorated with art.

Benin was actively involved in the trade of ivory, palm oil, pepper, and other resources with the Dutch and Portuguese from the fifteenth through the eighteenth century. Word of the beautiful African city quickly spread throughout Europe at the beginning of the sixteenth century, and new visitors from all parts of Europe came to see it, their admiration recorded in a number of voyage notes and illustrations. Benin City was described by early foreign explorers as a place free of crime and hunger, with large streets and clean houses, wealthy and industrious, a city filled with courteous and honest people and governed by a centralized and highly sophisticated bureaucracy (Elias and Akinjide 1988; Koutonin 2016).

A magnificent collection of artworks, sophisticated commercial networks, and the military tactics used by the warrior kings to defend and expand Benin are only a few examples of the historical artifacts that contributed to the empire's fascinating and imposing nature (Cartwright 2019). Benin possessed a sizable army of well-trained, disciplined troops, and the monarch acted as their divine ruler. The artists in Benin used various mediums, including iron, bronze, and ivory. They are known for their life-size head sculptures depicting the Obas and Iyobas, as well as bas-relief pieces, particularly plaques, typically depicting historical events. Ivory was carved into a wide variety of items, including masks, armlets, and combs (Cartwright 2019). Benin City was also one of the earliest cities to have a version of street lighting; huge metal lamps, several feet high, were placed around the city, particularly close to the king's palace (Koutonin 2016). These lamps were fueled by palm oil and lit at night to provide light for traffic to and from the palace.

Benin started to lose influence in the fifteenth century as a result of internal conflicts associated with slave trade at its borders and the growing European encroachment. The British invasion of Benin in 1897 was ultimately motivated by a desire for dominance over the trade and territory of West Africa (Igbafe 1970). After the destruction and looting of Benin City, the empire was occupied by the British and eventually became part of British colonial Nigeria (which became Nigeria after the country gained independence in 1960).

2. Cities and Colonialization

The colonization of Africa after 1884 was very different from that of ancient times; it encompassed almost the whole continent. Strained relations due to competition among European nations for African territory led to the convening of a conference in Berlin in 1884 to discuss what had become a "scramble for Africa" (Tarver and Chandler 1993). The resultant treaty defined "right to occupation" and led to the partitioning of Africa among European powers. Areas of Africa that were previously unoccupied by European powers were formally colonized. Liberia and Ethiopia are the only two present-day nations that were not colonized during this period. In the early nineteenth century, Liberia was founded to resettle freed enslaved people, and its independence was recognized in 1847. Italians invaded Ethiopia in 1935 and occupied the country for six years, but Ethiopia has always maintained an independent monarchy (Tarver and Chandler 1993).

Foreign powers have undoubtedly controlled Africa longer than any other major region of the world. Regions in Africa at different times have been colonized by many peoples and groups. including the Semitic groups from South Arabia and Merina, as well as Europeans, including Portuguese, British, and French. Some cities in Africa were occupied by foreign entities much earlier than the recognized colonial rule of Africa (Njoh 2007, 2009). Europeans set up outposts, mostly in the coastal regions before the beginning of the colonial era at the end of the nineteenth century, including outposts in Zanzibar (present-day Tanzania), Luanda (Angola), Badagri (Lagos, Nigeria), and Porto Novo (Benin). These outposts were used as holding points for enslaved people during the transatlantic slave trade (Njoh 2007). During the colonial era, the outposts acted as the nucleus around which colonial towns, such as administrative centers, were established. The location of these colonial cities is an important feature; these cities were usually located at the highest elevations, separated from the inhabited areas of the Indigenous population by a considerable distance (Njoh 2009). Examples include Hill Station (Freetown) in Sierra Leone; Buea Station, Bamenda Station, and Yaoundé, Cameroon; Bamako, Mali; Brazzaville, People's Republic of Congo; Abidjan, Côte d'Ivoire; and Niamey in Niger; among others.

The division of the continent among European powers introduced the phenomenon of political boundaries and established the pattern of colonial states in the 1890s, which largely remained as the basis for the political fragmentation of independent Africa. These forced borders restricted movement of tribes between territories and confined Africans to the "largely artificial states created by European imperialists" (Tarver and Chandler 1993, 253; Michalopoulos and Papaioannou 2016). Different types of restrictions on movements also existed within these states. For example, colonial cities in eastern and southern Africa were often considered "white man's country," and Africans were deprived of the freedom to permanently settle in these areas (O'Connor 1983). In South Africa, at the height of apartheid, Black-occupied townships located outside the "white" cities grew rapidly and cramped millions of Blacks into neighboring unserviced areas, which became slums (Obudho and Mhlanga 1988). Slums remain a major feature of cities in eastern and southern Africa today.

The economic and political changes wrought by colonial rule and postcolonial developments reshaped the placement of the largest cities and urban structures in Africa. City systems evolved to reflect government hierarchy—

in many instances passed down from colonial governance—including the prominence given to state and provincial capitals. Political authorities in cities strive to exert regulatory functions in relation to social interactions, commercial transactions, and religious and cultural life (Coret, Zaugg, and Chouin 2020). In material and symbolic terms, these authorities often play an important role in shaping these activities into a model of representation to demonstrate their legitimacy (Home 1983; Myers 2003; Njoh 2007). The rate of urbanization was comparatively low across Africa during the colonial era, and in 1950, only 15 percent of residents were living in areas that were classified urban, making Africa the least urbanized major region in the world.

2.1. Urban Planning, the Built Environment, and Segregation

Over a century ago, prior to colonization by European countries, alternative ways of living (such as hunting, gathering, and transhumant pastoralism) and their organizational logics existed together with varying magnitudes of urbanity and urbanism. For example, nomadic pastoralism was practiced in West Africa (Bassett 1986), Kenya and Tanzania (Robertshaw 1990), and southern Africa (Smith 1992). Like the Pygmies of Central Africa and the Hadza of Tanzania, the San people of southern Africa were devoted to mobile ways of living based on hunting and gathering (Chirikure 2020c; Mitchell 2002). Communities that clustered in place, lived sedentary lives, invested in architecture, and practiced mixed farming coexisted with populations that chose alternative livelihood options and their embedded organizational processes. Colonialism transformed these intricate approaches to existence by instating an urbanism that was connected to capitalist extractive economies. There were the previously mentioned colonial ports and administrative centers, and cities such as Johannesburg that were built because of the mining industry (Chirikure 2015, 2020c). Some scholars have questioned whether these variants of urbanism and urbanity during precolonial rule might be beneficial to today's urban Africa.

The land tenure system in Africa was based on communal ownership before the European colonialists arrived (Meek 1946, 1957; Chirikure 2020c). The worth of land was tied to its use and could not be translated to a financial or market value. Under this system, it was not permissible to sell or outright transfer land. People or families did not have to reside in the same area for thousands of years because property rights did not exist as they do in other regions (Chirikure 2020c).

At the same time as western Europe's scramble for territories in Africa, city planning emerged as a discipline. Thus, colonial Africa, like colonial Asia before it, offered European architects a unique opportunity to test the feasibility of newly acquired planning theories and concepts, which was not available to them in Europe, where they were severely constrained by limited space. Conversations about town-planning policies from the European colonial era in Africa tend to focus on their socioeconomic and political excellence or impact (Home 1983; Myers 2003; Njoh 2007). There is a dearth of knowledge on how planning policies were used as tools for domination, intimidation, and power in urban spaces (Njoh 2009). Manipulation of objects in the built environment was one approach to applying force. This was accomplished through, for example, the encampment of African workers, establishment of military bases, and installation of fences around the homes of Europeans (Njoh 2009). Colonial powers also constructed massive monuments and buildings of extravagant scale, such as government official and residential facilities, to display Europe's ingenuity and technological resources and to overwhelm and belittle the African with mere size. Surveillance is another way through which power and coercion existed in the built environment. By typically erecting offices and residential districts on elevated sites that overlooked the residential quarters of Indigenous people, the colonized were placed under the constant watch of the colonizer (Home 1983; Njoh 2016).

Urban planning laws adopted in colonies were merely duplicates of similar laws in Europe. French colonial agents enacted laws by the late 1950s that required urban master plans for major towns throughout France's colonized territories in Africa. The 1948 Town Planning Act, crafted by British colonial agents for Nyasaland (present-day Malawi), was based on an act of the same name already effective in the United Kingdom as of 1932, which also informed the 1946 official effort to control urban development in colonial Nigeria (Home 2013; Wekwete 1995).

Urban planning efforts during this period might be misconstrued as gestures encouraging the native population to relocate to these urban areas. In many territories, however, colonial authorities devised means to discourage African migration to towns. In some cases, only Africans with jobs were allowed in towns. In British colonies such as South Africa, so-called pass laws were implemented to restrict native populations' access to urban areas. In other colonies, such as Southern Rhodesia (current Zimbabwe), pieces of legislation limited urban access only to those working in the urban sector (Mamdani 1996). In 1926, a law in Brazzaville, which was a replica of a similar law effective across the Congo River in Leopoldville (now Kinshasa) in Belgian colonial Congo, set a 9 p.m. curfew on Africans of all ages (Martin 1995). Similarly, by housing employees in workers' camps, colonizers could more easily influence and control Africans' behaviors. For example, workers who worked in agro-plantations or mines were usually awoken in the early hours of the morning to be transported by trains or trucks. Further, housing employees provided the employers with a steady influx of extra income, which was usually deducted directly from the employee's pay. Thus, such policies requiring employer-provided housing reinforced the power of Europeans over the natives; Europeans did not participate in the colonial civil service.

Furthermore, colonial architects and urban designers were proficient at using their skills to complement efforts to realize broader colonial goals, including defending newly occupied territories from other European powers and appeasing resistance by natives within the territories (Wright 1991). Scholars state that their actions were not apolitical as some claimed. In pursuit of the former objective, colonial architects designed and built forts and castles in strategic locations within colonial centers that enabled a commanding view of the surrounding area. These forts or their ruins can be found along the coast of East and West Africa. The oldest and most prominent of these structures, St. George's Castle at Elmina in present-day Ghana, was built with dressed stones from Europe by the Portuguese in 1482 (Njoh 2009).

Additionally, access routes were carefully planned between regions to facilitate rapid movement of troops to defend the country's borders in wartime. For example, scholars note that the railway system in colonial Tanganyika (present-day Tanzania) linked agriculturally rich areas in the hinterland with the ports of Tanga and Dar es Salaam, but maybe most important, the rail enabled easy movement of troops to key defensive locations within twenty-four hours (Lugalla 1994). The Germans feared that British troops stationed in Kenya could attack Tanganyika anytime.

The architects of colonial Africa had unbridled power to influence spatial order and human behavior in the built environment. The distinction between coercion and expertise was often indistinct in colonial planning, especially in the case of zoning, which is an important component of controlling physical spaces (Njoh 2009). Zoning is authorized by the legal concept of police control, and police power denotes the right of entire communities to manage the use of private property with the purpose of protecting the interests of the general public (Njoh 2009). The institutional authority of planners to influence people and their environments is inspired by the police power of the state, whose interests are wide and can be misrepresented by many terms, including public welfare, public safety, and public health (Njoh 2009). The institutional authority vested in urban planners by colonial governments allowed them not simply to manage people and the environment for the public interest but, in many instances, to use the supposed grounds of promoting and protecting public health, welfare, and safety to develop spatial policies intended to buttress the power of the colonial state and to support efforts to effectuate social control on the colonized (Frenkel and Western 1988; Njoh 2009; Wright 1991).

For example, colonial planners used their institutional authority and technical expertise to develop land use policies enabling achievement of the "social" goal of maintaining racial segregation in the colonies under the guise of protecting public health (Njoh 2009). Routes to implementing such plans, however, were different depending on the colonizing nation. In the French colonies, there were attempts to disguise such plans, because the French population at home was not in favor of racial segregation policies in the colonies. For example, colonial planners in Madagascar insisted that a 1928 law requiring buildings in particular districts to be built using only European materials was not intended to attain the goal of racial segregation (Wright 1991).

While the British community were not strongly opposed to racial residential segregation policies, colonial planners still invented pseudo-scientific justifications for carrying out such racist policies in British colonial Africa. For example, in Sierra Leone, from 1899 to 1900, a team of scientists led by Ronald Ross identified the anopheles mosquito as the malaria-causing vector and recommended nighttime separation of the European population from the native as a way of protecting the former from malaria (Ebikeme 2019; Njoh 2009). The discovery that anopheles mosquitoes could not fly more than 430 yards was used as the basis of a spatial policy requiring the separation of European districts from Indigenous residential areas by at least 430 yards (Frenkel and Western 1988). Similar racial residential segregation policies had been implemented in India long before such public health activities provided a guise (Kenny 1985).

Racial segregation policies invariably provided Europeans access to larger and better located plots of land, while the Indigenous population was confined to the least desirable plots. Furthermore, by designing exclusively European districts, colonial authorities could neglect districts occupied by the native population, which created a stark distinction between areas occupied by natives, with few modern amenities, and European districts, with an excess of modern amenities. Scholars have suggested that racial and ethnic segregation uses "visibility as an effective means of oppression" (Njoh 2009).

3. Conclusion

The history of urbanism in Africa was contested by some scholars because it did not fit the Eurocentric definitions of urbanization. While the ruins of Great Zimbabwe were for a time contested to have been built by Africans, conversations about colonialism in Africa are even today often whitewashed to focus on what some claim were its important impacts on Africa's built environment and economy. Here we choose to focus on works that have challenged the singular narrative of European urban planning prowess in Africa by reflecting on evidence showing that colonial development in Africa was often not for the growth of the state but for the furtherance of broader colonial goals. The built environment continues to play a major role in the development of cities in Africa and is a major theme of discussion throughout this book.

REFERENCES

Bassett, Thomas J. 1986. "Fulani Herd Movements." *Geographical Review* 76:233–48.

Bradbury, R. E. 2004. "Continuities and Discontinuities in Pre-Colonial and Colonial Benin Politics." *History and Social Anthropology* 8:193.

Cartwright, Mark. 2019. "Kingdom of Benin." *World History Encyclopedia.* https://www.worldhistory.org/Kingdom_of_Benin/.

Chirikure, Shadreck. 2015. *Metals in Past Societies: A Global Perspective on Indigenous African Metallurgy.* Cham: Springer.

Chirikure, Shadreck. 2020a. *Great Zimbabwe: Reclaiming a "Confiscated" Past.* London: Routledge.

Chirikure, Shadreck. 2020b. "New Perspectives on the Political Economy of Great Zimbabwe." *Journal of Archaeological Research* 28:139–86.

Chirikure, Shadreck. 2020c. "Shades of Urbanism(s) and Urbanity in Pre-Colonial Africa: Towards Afro-Centred Interventions." *Journal of Urban Archaeology* 1:49–66.

Chirikure, Shadreck, Thomas Moultrie, Foreman Bandama, Collett Dandara, and Munyaradzi Manyanga. 2017. "What Was the Population of Great Zimbabwe (CE 1000–1800)?" *PLoS One* 12 (6): e0178335.

Coret, Clélia, Roberto Zaugg, and Gérard Chouin. 2020. "Cities in Africa before 1900: Historiography and Research Perspectives." *Afriques: Débats, Méthodes et Terrains d'histoire*, no. 11. https://journals.openedition.org/afriques/3088.

Daniels, Patricia S. 2022. "These Four Lost Cities Were Jewels of Ancient Africa: What Happened to Them?" *National Geographic History Magazine*, May 24. https://www.nationalgeographic.com/history/history-magazine/article/what-happened-to-these-four-lost-cities-of-ancient-africa.

Ebikeme, Charles. 2019. "The Future of Health in Africa Must Include Urban Health." *Cities and Health* 6 (1): 7–9.

Edwards, D. N. 1994. "Power and the State in the Middle Nile: Meroe in Context. An Example for the Study of State Development in Sudanic Africa." *Archaeological Review from Cambridge* 13 (1): 5–19.

Eglash, Ron. 1999. *African Fractals: Modern Computing and Indigenous Design*. New Brunswick, NJ: Rutgers University Press.

Elias, Taslim Olawale, and Richard Akinjide. 1988. *Africa and the Development of International Law*. Dordrecht: Martinus Nijhoff.

Frenkel, Stephen, and John Western. 1988. "Pretext or Prophylaxis? Racial Segregation and Malarial Mosquitos in a British Tropical Colony: Sierra Leone." *Annals of the Association of American Geographers* 78 (2): 211–28.

Garlake, Peter S. 1973. *Great Zimbabwe*. London: Thames and Hudson.

Garlake, Peter S. 2002. *Early Art and Architecture of Africa*. Oxford: Oxford University Press.

Holmgren, Karin, and Helena Öberg. 2006. "Climate Change in Southern and Eastern Africa during the Past Millennium and Its Implications for Societal Development." *Environment, Development and Sustainability* 8:185–95.

Home, Robert K. 1983. "Town Planning, Segregation and Indirect Rule in Colonial Nigeria." *Third World Planning Review* 5 (2): 165.

Home, Robert K. 2013. *Of Planting and Planning: The Making of British Colonial Cities*. New York: Routledge.

Huffman, Thomas N. 2007. *Handbook to the Iron Age: The Archaeology of Pre-Colonial Farming Societies in Southern Africa*. Scottsville, South Africa: University of KwaZulu-Natal Press.

Igbafe, Philip A. 1970. "The Fall of Benin: A Reassessment." *Journal of African History* 11 (3): 385–400.

Kenny, Judith T. 1985. "Climate, Race, and Imperial Authority: The Symbolic Landscape of the British Hill Station in India." *Annals of the Association of American Geographers* 85 (4): 694–714.

Koutonin, Mawuna. 2016. "Story of Cities #5: Benin City, the Mighty Medieval Capital Now Lost without Trace." *Guardian*, March 18.

Kuklick, Henrika. 1991. "Contested Monuments: The Politics of Archaeology in Southern Africa." In *Colonial Situations: Essays on the Contextualization of Ethnographic Knowledge*, edited by George W. Stocking, 135–69. Madison: University of Wisconsin Press.

Lugalla, Joe. 1994. *Crisis, Urbanization, and Urban Poverty in Tanzania: A Study of Urban Poverty and Survival Politics*. Vol. 4. Washington, DC: University Press of America.

Mamdani, Mahmood. 1996. *Citizen and Subject: Contemporary Africa and the Legacy of Late Colonialism*. Princeton, N.J.: Princeton University Press.

Martin, Phyllis M. 1995. *Leisure and Society in Colonial Brazzaville*. Cambridge: Cambridge University Press.

McWhirter, Norris, and Ross McWhirter, eds. 1974. *Guinness Book of World Records, 1975*. New York: Sterling.

Meek, Charles Kingsley. 1946. *Land Law and Custom in the Colonies*. London: Oxford University Press.

Meek, Charles Kingsley. 1957. *Land Tenure and Land Administration in Nigeria and the Cameroons*. London: HM Stationery Office.

Michalopoulos, Stelios, and Elias Papaioannou. 2016. "The Long-Run Effects of the Scramble for Africa." *American Economic Review* 106 (7): 1802–48.

Mitchell, Peter. 2002. *The Archaeology of Southern Africa*. Cambridge: Cambridge University Press.

Myers, Garth Andrew. 2003. "Designing Power: Forms and Purposes of Colonial Model Neighborhoods in British Africa." *Habitat International* 27 (2): 193–204.

Nelson, Jo. 2015. *Historium: Welcome to the Museum*. Somerville, MA: Big Picture Press.

Njoh, Ambe J. 2007. *Planning Power: Town Planning and Social Control in Colonial Africa*. Boca Raton, FL: CRC Press.

Njoh, Ambe J. 2009. "Urban Planning as a Tool of Power and Social Control in Colonial Africa." *Planning Perspectives* 24 (3): 301–17.

Njoh, Ambe J. 2016. *French Urbanism in Foreign Lands*. Cham: Springer.

Obudho, Robert A., and Constance C. Mhlanga. 1988. *Slum and Squatter Settlements in Sub-Saharan Africa: Toward a Planning Strategy*. New York: Praeger.

O'Connor, Anthony. 1983. *The African City*. New York: Africana.

Oliver, Roland. 1977. *The Cambridge History of Africa*. Vol. 3. Cambridge: Cambridge University Press.

Pikirayi, Innocent. 2002. *The Zimbabwe Culture: Origins and Decline of Southern Zambezian States*. Walnut Creek, CA: AltaMira.

Pwiti, Gilbert. 1991. "Trade and Economies in Southern Africa: The Archaeological Evidence." *Zambezia* 18 (2): 119–29.

Robertshaw, Peter. 1990. *Early Pastoralists of South-Western Kenya*. Memoir 11. Nairobi, Kenya: British Institute in Eastern Africa.

Satterthwaite, David. 2021a. "African Cities from 500 AD to 1900." *African Cities Research Consortium* (blog), May 10. https://www.african-cities.org/african-cities-from-500-ad -to-1900/.

Satterthwaite, David. 2021b. "What Are the Largest Cities in Africa—Today and in 1800?" *African Cities Research Consortium* (blog), April 26. https://www.african-cities.org /what-are-the-largest-cities-in-africa-today-and-in-1800/.

Segal, Aaron. 1988. "The Emergence of Cities and State Structures in Precolonial Africa." *Africa Today* 35 (3–4): 110.

Smith, Andrew B. 1992. *Pastoralism in Africa: Origins and Development Ecology*. London: Hurst.

Snape, Steven. 2014. *The Complete Cities of Ancient Egypt*. London: Thames and Hudson.

Summers, Roger. 1971. *Ancient Ruins and Vanished Civilisations of Southern Africa*. Cape Town: T. V. Bulpin.

Tarver, James D., and Tertius Chandler. 1993. "Urbanization in Colonial Africa." *Africa Insight* 23 (4): 250–54.

Tarver, James D., and M. Miller. 1993. "Urbanization in Pre-Colonial Africa." *Africa Insight* 23 (3): 176–78.

Wekwete, Kadmiel H. 1995. "Planning Law in Sub-Saharan Africa—A Focus on the Experiences in Southern and Eastern Africa." *Habitat International* 19 (1): 13–28.

Wright, Gwendolyn. 1991. *The Politics of Design in French Colonial Urbanism*. Chicago: University of Chicago Press.

3

What Is an African City?

Elaine O. Nsoesie and Blessing Mberu

1. Cities in Africa

What is an African city? What is an urban area in Africa? A quick search of "African cities" on the internet returns millions of results—from scholarly research to journalism, blogs to novels. Most of these writings reference current statistics on Africa's urbanization rates and projections of future growth. For example, the United Nations projects that the population of Africa will increase from approximately 1 billion in 2010 to 2 billion by 2050 (United Nations 2014). This population growth is expected to occur largely in urban areas, where more than 50 percent of the total population will dwell by 2035 (United Nations 2018). Africa has gone from having no megacities (i.e., regions with more than 10 million inhabitants) in 1950 to seven megacities, which currently include Lagos, Kinshasa, Accra, Cairo, Pretoria, Khartoum, and Johannesburg (Cobbinah 2015; Sumari et al. 2020; United Nations 2018). This number is expected to rise to fourteen by 2050 with cities such as Luanda, Addis Ababa, Dar es Salaam, and Nairobi joining the list (Sow 2015). This unprecedented growth in urban regions across the continent makes Africa, though currently the least urbanized, one of the fastest urbanizing regions in the world. Despite all these discussions of cities and urban areas in Africa, however, there is not a consensus definition of what constitutes an urban area. In fact, there is no globally accepted definition of *city* or *urban*. What then do we mean when we use the terms?

2. Urban Areas

The phrase *urban area* encompasses various urban morphologies, including cities, towns, metropolitan regions, and agglomerations. Most definitions of urban areas in Africa are administrative, functional, or morphological, implying that definitions tend to correspond with geographic boundaries determined by administrative responsibilities or rule, population size, or physical borders (Heinrigs 2020; Moriconi-Ebrard et al. 2008; Silimperi 1995). For example, Ethiopia defines urban areas as regions with a population of two thousand or more, while Botswana defines urban areas as agglomerations of five thousand or more residents, with most dependent on economic activities other than agriculture (OECD 2020). In contrast, Malawi's definition of urban includes "all townships, town planning areas and district centers," and Eswatini defines urban as "a geographical area constituting a city or town, characterized by higher population density and human construction in comparison to the areas surrounding it" (OECD 2020).

Similarly, definitions for cities are not consistent; different countries have their own criteria. A historical definition of the city that underpins the politico-administrative descriptions used in countries such as the United States, China, Germany, Egypt, and others is the notion that a city is a well-defined region with independent judicial structures and residents free from the control of landowners (OECD 2020). These differences in definitions make it challenging to compare urban statistics (such as urban population, population density, and even the number of particular urban areas) across countries. Varied definitions can also impede the comparison of health statistics across regions, especially when policymakers are deciding on the distribution of resources. To address these challenges, some scholars have proposed alternative and harmonized definitions of urban areas. An example is a project implemented by the Organization for Economic Cooperation and Development (OECD) called Africapolis, which focuses on using a spatial approach to capture urban dynamics in Africa (Heinrigs 2020). Africapolis claims that Africa is more urban than it is perceived, with hundreds of agglomerations still "unrecognized" (Heinrigs 2020). Nonetheless, while a more consistent definition of a city would be useful for statistical purposes, it is important to recognize the complex nature of each urban area, as well as the historical and geopolitical forces that have influenced the dynamics of these localities.

3. The African City

Cities in Africa are not all the same, and no single city can stand as a representation of all. Even the term *African city* suggests a generalization of a particular type or theme by which cities in Africa are identifiable. Each city is multifaceted, with a diverse range of contemporary experiences and history, governance reforms, informalization, and health challenges that make them different, but also with certain characteristics that are comparable to cities within the continent and around the globe (Myers 2011b; Obeng-Odoom 2010; Potts 2012). Ideas that are held as truisms across the entire continent are not always backed with data. For example, by comparing differences across regions and studying the characteristics of specific locations, scholars have challenged the notions of high rates of urbanization (Potts 2012), the idea that growth in cities is mainly driven by urban population growth (Sumari et al. 2020), and that Africa's urbanization rates are not associated with economic growth (Obeng-Odoom 2010; OECD 2020). Although significant differences exist in urban growth and development patterns across the continent, most writings on cities in Africa tend to focus on similarities, thereby overlooking or ignoring differences driven by politics, history, and other factors (Myers 2011b; Myers and Murray 2006).

Also, many cities in Africa look and function differently from cities in Europe and North America to which they are usually compared. Scholars argue that characterizing these cities as "marginal," "not yet," or "in the process of becoming" global are largely Eurocentric (Abdoul 2005). Others argue that if the patterns and processes exhibited by African cities are novel or unique from those in other parts of the world, then the knowledge gleaned from experiences, theories, and practices in African cities should be equally included in discussions about cities, even if these ideas are discordant from Western ideas of urbanism (Choplin 2012; Myers 2011a, 2011b). This notions are equally important when thinking about and discussing health in cities in Africa. It is challenging to apply some of the urban health theories established using cities in North America and Europe as models to the African contexts without dismissing the unique features possessed by cities in Africa.

Furthermore, there is a need to acknowledge the varied paths to urbanization (Fox 2012; Jedwab 2013). Even in progressive writings, a crisis narrative is typically used to collectively describe African cities. There is a major preoccupation in various forms of writing and art (including scholarly articles, documentaries, and novels) on the degraded aspects of cities in Africa. Many accounts and commentaries on African cities tend to present a simplistic view focused on disease, spatial incoherence, organized crime, civil disorder, poverty, inadequate social service provision, unruly behavior, ignorance, and the like (Abdoul 2005; Bouillon 2002; Cheru 2002; De Boeck and Plissart 2014; Mbembe 2001; Myers and Murray 2006; Simone 2004, 2005). This narrative furthers stereotypes about African cities and about the continent of Africa, promoting long-held ideas about Africa as a place of disorganization and ineffective governance. Several scholars have critiqued these limited and mechanistic accounts (e.g., Abdoul 2005; Ahonsi 2002; Gandy 2005; Gberie 2005; Myers and Murray 2006; Tostensen, Tvedten, and Vaa 2001), objecting to the focus on the seemingly endless chaos of daily life, arguing that this preoccupation stems from European and North American ideals of a "good city" (Swilling 1997). Instead, these scholars call for a more complete view of cities in Africa that acknowledges urbanization as a complicated, multifaceted, and inconsistent process with diverse trajectories without a single endpoint (Four African Cities 2002; Tostensen, Tvedten, and Vaa 2001). Additionally, a rounded viewpoint should consider the challenges, the uneven urbanization process, while acknowledging the contributions of urban residents in shaping and defining the city.

4. Factors Influencing Urbanization

Many scholars have presented population growth as a major driver of urbanization in Africa; the number of urban dwellers is projected to increase from 395 million people in 2010 to 1.3 billion in 2050 (Güneralp et al. 2017). For example, Kenya had more people living in urban areas in 2015 than the entire continent had in 1950. The urban population in Africa has grown by approximately 21 million each year since 2010 (Heinrigs 2020).

Others argue that urban-biased policies—government policies that channel resources from other regions to cities, thereby creating different levels of public good delivery between rural and urban areas—have led to urbanization (Ades and Glaeser 1995; Davies and Finch 2003). This idea is similar to another that links urbanization and rural poverty, the theory that population migration from rural to urban regions as people search for opportunities, including education and employment, has driven the urbanization rate (Barrios, Bertinelli, and Strobl 2006).

Other explanations include rural expansion; growth of inland urban Africa, which counters the dominant view of coastal cities and metropolitan regions; and spontaneous mega-agglomerations (OECD 2020). The in situ *urbanization* of rural areas occurs when areas classified as rural reach a population density that leads to reclassification as urban. Some scholars say that this calls for the study of rural areas in tandem with urbanization, partly because these reclassifications can occur quickly as urbanization rates increase, and because it also affects the activities in these areas, including a decline in agriculture. Another phenomenon is the merging of rural settlements into existing urban areas. For example, over time, Cairo has grown to include several rural towns and villages that were once classified separately from the city (Heinrigs 2020; OECD 2020).The dynamics of urbanization are also influenced by factors such as the economy, conflict, climate (including droughts), geography, and public policies (Aliyu and Amadu 2017; Henderson, Storeygard, and Deichmann 2014). These different influences on urban dynamics can also influence the health and well-being of city dwellers.

5. Urbanization and Economic Growth: Is There an African Exceptionalism?

The positive implications of urbanization for economic development have been historically documented for countries and cities in Europe and North America. The advantages of spatial concentration have become a major interest of mainstream economists, and a range of econometric studies in Europe and North America have found that large agglomerations contribute to higher productivity and stronger growth, albeit on a modest rather than a massive scale (Turok 2014). In other regions, particularly the African continent, the relationship between urbanization and economic growth has been the subject of quite a debate. Though sub-Saharan Africa is the least urbanized region of the world, its urbanization rate of 3.5 percent stands as the highest projected urban growth rate in the world up to 2050 ("African Development Report" 2007). People are attracted to cities because they generally offer more choices (such as good quality housing), opportunities (such as employment), and services (such as education and health care) to the residents (Muindi 2014). Cities also concentrate risks and hazards for health, however, and the impact of adverse events, such as contamination of the water supply, air or noise pollution, or natural disasters, is amplified in densely populated urban settings (WHO Centre for Health Development 2010).

Further, a mismatch between rapid population growth of cities and the ability of governments to provide infrastructure and livelihood opportunities heightens these risks and hazards. Instead of bringing inclusive growth and major developments to African cities, urbanization has resulted in the proliferation of informal settlements, or slums, widening income inequalities and increasing urban poverty. It is estimated that more than two-fifths (43 percent) of the urban population in sub-Saharan Africa live below the poverty line, and three-fifths (62 percent) live in overcrowded slums lacking basic services and vulnerable to extreme hardship, pernicious health conditions, and environmental crises (Artuso 2011; UN Department of Economic and Social Affairs 2014; UN Economic Commission for Africa 2008). Consequently, the commonly assumed urban advantage has been challenged in many low- and middle-income countries, raising intricate social policy challenges around resilience and viability of life in cities in many countries (Fotso et al. 2009; Muindi 2014), as well as fueling the debate on African exceptionalism in the face of urbanization without strong evidence of economic growth and development (Myers 2011b; White, Mberu, and Collinson 2012). This debate has been extensively documented in the last ten to fifteen years with strong evidence on a spectrum of positions. On one hand, a corpus of scholars has painted exceedingly pessimistic pictures, highlighting extreme conditions of squalor, degradation, decay, and pollution (Myers 2011b). On the other hand, others have presented a more optimistic image of Africa's urban poverty, pointing to the positive features of marginal communities, the energy and creative spirit of informality, and the coping strategies evident in invisible urban practices on the periphery (Myers 2011b). Accordingly, and echoing the position of many scholars, poor communities are characterized as not passive victims but active agents, with resilience and imagination to negotiate and survive the tough environments of African cities, making the most of the opportunities available through ingenuity and experimentation. Yet other experts point to how African economic potentials have taken a new upward trajectory in the last ten years, with African countries listed among the world's fastest-growing economies (World Bank, Africa Region 2011). The idea of Africa rising has been echoed across the continent, together with the optimism that major infrastructural investments and booming exports of primary commodities offer tangible signs of revival and a rising urban middle class capable of driving growth and spreading prosperity through a consumer boom (Myers 2011b).

The spectrum of positions and evidence provided indicates that the jury is still out on the relationships between urbanization and economic growth in Africa, calling for further investments in data collection and evidence generation on the interactions between contemporary economic and demographic changes across Africa vis-à-vis urbanization and economic growth in the region. Notwithstanding, while cities per se cannot be blamed for poverty, White, Mberu, and Collinson (2012) identified some aspects of exceptionalism that cannot be discarded altogether, insisting that cities in sub-Saharan Africa are not generating development at the same rate as other regions; meanwhile, the stark realities of growing poverty in the region's cities cannot be ignored. They conceded, however, that the roots of these problems are complex and cannot be attributed simply to changes in population distribution, and they identified four elements of exceptionalism that remain in Africa.

First is the history of urban settlements in the region with appreciably lower densities and the historical predominance of agro-pastoral economies. Second is the *scale* of current urban growth in the region, which is certainly greater than in previous transitions, with fertility decline being slower; hence rapid urban growth today is fed, in many countries, by high rates of natural increase in both rural and urban areas. Third is the tradition of circular migration and seasonal population movement, with implications for rural-urban linkages and the economic sustainability of urban destinations and rural origins. These links are important for resource flows, such as cash or nonmonetary remittances, information, and behavioral norms, and they expand the influence of urban living way beyond city and town boundaries (Chukwuezi 2001; Gugler 2002; Mberu 2015). This link is associated with a strong commitment to rural origin development, challenging the dichotomous model of urban versus rural areas and complicating simplistic renderings of the implications of rural-urban migration for development in urban destinations and rural origins (Smith 1999, 2004). While linkages are identified across the major regions of the world, they are exceptionally strong across the sub-Saharan African region (Mberu 2015). Fourth is the general recognition of the inability of cities to promote the level and kind of economic growth that would hasten the reduction of poverty in sub-Saharan Africa, together with economic and human development not at pace with the rest of the developing world. Implicated in the inability of national economies to deliver improvements in well-being are the weakness in the Human Development Index, high levels of national debts and consequent structural adjustment policies, exposure to broader pressures of global competition, limited outlets for external migration, weak governance structures, and lack of vision, foresight, and a participatory approach to planning (Kessides 2006; Lahariya 2008; White, Mberu, and Collinson 2012).

In sum, the overarching perspective is the view of migration as an intrinsic dimension of economic and social development, reflecting the rational decisions of millions of migrants to seek new opportunities away from local restrictive environments, and rural-urban migration is the major force in population redistribution to achieve that goal in the region (Chen, Valente, and Zlotnik 1998; Kessides 2006; Montgomery et al. 2013; White, Mberu, and Collinson 2012). A corpus of literature has demonstrated that rural-urban migration in sub-Saharan Africa is not only a household survival strategy, but also a partner in the economic and social development of migrant-sending communities. Yet the discrepancy between the urban promise and concrete economic growth realities remains unresolved. In the rest of this chapter and the book, African and Africanist scholars continue to interrogate available data, policy, and program inputs in the continued search for pathways to solutions for achieving sustainable, equitable, and inclusive urban health across the region.

6. Cities and Health

For some city dwellers, cities are places that carry memories of the past, where children are born, loved ones are buried, and life unfolds daily on the streets. Cities offer opportunities for these dwellers to launch and build businesses, find stable employment, obtain an education, and develop local and global networks, factors that can all lead to economic prosperity and health. For many others, cities are "points of departure or launching pads, facilitating movement to somewhere else" (Murray and Myers 2007, 27). For example, the neighborhoods in a city like Douala in Cameroon are always changing, as people move in and out for different purposes, thereby dismantling and reshaping physical, social, and interpersonal boundaries. Whether seen as transient or constant, physical, social, and interpersonal experiences can have significant influences on health.

Therefore, to fully understand features influencing health in cities, including how different cities are navigating factors such as governance regimes and postcolonialism, it is important to understand the history of these cities and the local and global economic factors contributing to their current state. It is also important to acknowledge that cities are complex environments—on one hand dealing with significant and sometimes global challenges, while on the other hand offering remarkable technological and cultural innovations. Furthermore, health in these contexts should be studied holistically—acknowledging that its residents are affected by both the good and the bad, and that they in turn influence and shape the city. The millions of ordinary people who dwell in cities in Africa are resourceful, innovative, and determined individuals who effectively navigate the troubles of everyday life. They are not merely victims of unavoidable structural processes but are active agents who are shaping their environments.

There are definitely challenges that influence the health and well-being of urban dwellers. These include urban inequality, poverty, unreliable urban service provision (housing, water, electricity), infectious diseases, and violence. Rapid urbanization across many African countries has been associated with significant variations in wealth and resources. Some governments have struggled to develop the infrastructure and provide the resources needed to keep up with urban growth. This means many urban areas struggle to address housing, transportation, and health care. Furthermore, the increase in urbanization and the unconfined movement of people, commodities, capital, and services have resulted in changes in lifestyle factors, such as what people eat and drink and how they behave. While the depth of these challenges and opportunities differs from one urban area to another, the impact of these factors remains and could influence health both positively and negatively. Some of these themes are not distinctly African but challenges that emerge from urbanization. The degree to which different cities engage with, and the diversity with which they navigate, these challenges differs. There are no single paths, policies, or frameworks.

Critical to urban health policy and programming is urban health research, which provides robust and context-relevant data to inform policy and action. Despite evidence that most urban residents in sub-Saharan Africa live in slums, raising intricate policy and program questions on their health and well-being, those questions remain inadequately answered following the dearth of available robust and appropriate local data across the region (Ezeh et al. 2017; Muindi 2014). Slum populations are not uniquely identified in censuses and national surveys, and current estimates rely on the definition of households that either lack certain basic amenities or live in houses with defined characteristics (Muindi 2014). Consequently, existing national estimates do not sufficiently answer questions critical to the health and livelihood status of the urban poor, who constitute the majority of city dwellers, often blurring inter- and intra-subgroup inequities and lacking disaggregation at local levels, where the needs are located (APHRC 2002;

Gallardo 2014; Vlahov et al. 2011). Urban health programming is done practically at local levels by local governments, yet evidence points to a lack of urban health statistics implementing agencies and local governments need to measure progress, identify interventions that work, and pinpoint priorities moving forward. Local data for each slum would help to address local needs more effectively and would reveal issues to prioritize in each slum (Gallardo 2014). Despite considerable efforts to address data and evidence gaps across the region in the last two decades (APHRC 2002; Mberu et al. 2016; Muindi 2014), the search for pathways to building resilient and healthy cities will require sustained investments in data systems at local levels to inform policy and action, especially in monitoring and evaluating interventions and in determining what works (Ezeh and Mberu 2019).

Related to evidence generation is the need for identifying and testing viable solutions to urban health and livelihood challenges in the region. Evidence from Kenya has chronicled interventions aimed at ensuring access to safe and affordable housing, upgrading slum settlements, and improving access to basic services and amenities, including health and education services in informal settlements, through targeted actions (Ezeh and Mberu 2019; Mberu et al. 2016). The specific case studies profiled by Ezeh and Mberu (2019) include a service delivery model that shows the power of targeted support for public-private partnerships in expanding access to high quality, accessible, and affordable maternal and child health care among the urban poor, an intervention that demonstrates the potential for improved quality of care for hypertension patients. They also study an HIV prevention intervention through nontraditional service delivery models (mobile clinics and research studies), which are convenient and adaptable to specific contexts, bridging service access and utilization deficits among disadvantaged populations. Beyond working well in improving health outcomes, each of the service delivery models has elements that can be scalable across other urban poor settings in Kenya and in low- and middle-income countries of the Global South (Ezeh and Mberu 2019). Building resilient and healthy cities will require sustained investments informed by credible local scientific evidence and validated and scalable solution models across the region.

7. Conclusion

In the chapters that follow, we seek to present a rounded view of health and factors influencing health in cities in Africa. The study of urban health in Africa is the study of the health of people. It is the study of how the complexity and heterogeneity of the urbanization process is affecting the lives of ordinary urban residents. We highlight the role of research for evidence generation to inform policy and action, pointing to urban health interventions that provide models for improving urban health outcomes in the region. In learning from current challenges and innovations that make cities in Africa work, there is immense potential for planning healthier cities.

REFERENCES

Abdoul, Mohamadou. 2005. "Urban Development and Urban Informalities: Pikine, Senegal." In *Urban Africa: Changing Contours of Survival in the City*, edited by AbdouMaliq Simone and Abouhani Abdelghani, 235. Dakar, Senegal: Zed Books.

Ades, Alberto F., and Edward L. Glaeser. 1995. "Trade and Circuses: Explaining Urban Giants." *Quarterly Journal of Economics* 110 (1): 195–227.

"African Development Report 2007." 2007. *OUP Catalogue*. Oxford: Oxford University Press. https://ideas.repec.org/b/oxp/obooks/9780199238866.html.

Ahonsi, Babatunde A. 2002. "Popular Shaping of Metropolitan Forms and Processes in Nigeria: Glimpses and Interpretations from an Informed Lagosian." *Documenta 11_Platform* 4:129–51.

Aliyu, Alhaji A., and Lawal Amadu. 2017. "Urbanization, Cities, and Health: The Challenges to Nigeria—a Review." *Annals of African Medicine* 16 (4): 149.

APHRC (African Population and Health Research Center). 2002. *Population and Health Dynamics in Nairobi's Informal Settlements*. Nairobi, Kenya: APHRC.

Artuso, Mario. 2011. "*State of the World's Cities 2010/11–Bridging the Urban Divide*, by UN Habitat." *Urban Research and Practice* 4:221.

Barrios, Salvador, Luisito Bertinelli, and Eric Strobl. 2006. "Climatic Change and Rural–Urban Migration: The Case of Sub-Saharan Africa." *Journal of Urban Economics* 60 (3): 357–71.

Bouillon, Antoine. 2002. "Between Euphemism and Informalism: Inventing the City." In *Under Siege, Four African Cities, Freetown, Johannesburg, Kinshasa, Lagos: Documenta 11, Platform 4*, edited by Okwui Enwezor, Carlos Basualdo, Ute Meta Bauer, Susanne Ghez, and Sarat Maharaj, 81–98. New York: Hatje Cantz.

Chen, Nancy, Paolo Valente, and Hania Zlotnik. 1998. "What Do We Know about Recent Trends in Urbanization." In *Migration, Urbanization, and Development: New Directions and Issues*, edited by Richard E. Bilsborrow, 59–88. Boston: Kluwer Academic.

Cheru, Fantu. 2002. *African Renaissance: Roadmaps to the Challenge of Globalization*. London: Zed Books.

Choplin, Armelle. 2012. "De-Westernising Urban Theory." Translated by Oliver Waine. *Metropolitics*, December 5. https://metropolitics.org/De-Westernising-Urban-Theory.html.

Chukwuezi, Barth. 2001. "Through Thick and Thin: Igbo Rural-Urban Circularity, Identity and Investment." *Journal of Contemporary African Studies* 19 (1): 55–66.

Cobbinah, Patrick Brandful. 2015. "Local Attitudes towards Natural Resources Management in Rural Ghana." *Management of Environmental Quality: An International Journal* 26 (3): 423–36.

Davies, G. R., and R. G. Finch. 2003. "Sales of Over-the-Counter Remedies as an Early Warning System for Winter Bed Crises." *Clinical Microbiology and Infection* 9 (8): 858–63.

De Boeck, Filip, and Marie-Françoise Plissart. 2014. *Kinshasa: Tales of the Invisible City.* Leuven, Belgium: Leuven University Press.

Enwezor, Okwui, Carlos Basualdo, Ute Meta Bauer, Susanne Ghez, and Sarat Maharaj, eds. 2002. *Under Siege: Four African Cities, Freetown, Johannesburg, Kinshasa, Lagos: Documenta 11, Platform 4.* New York: Hatje Cantz.

Ezeh, Alex, and Blessing Mberu. 2019. "Case Studies in Urban Health: Nairobi, Kenya." In *Urban Health,* edited by Sandro Galea, Catherine K. Ettman, and David Vlahov, 330–39. New York: Oxford University Press.

Ezeh, Alex, Oyinlola Oyebode, David Satterthwaite, Yen-Fu Chen, Robert Ndugwa, Jo Sartori, Blessing Mberu, Gerardo J. Melendez-Torres, Tilahun Haregu, and Samuel I. Watson. 2017. "The History, Geography, and Sociology of Slums and the Health Problems of People Who Live in Slums." *Lancet* 389 (10068): 547–58.

Fotso, Jean-Christophe, Alex Ezeh, Nyovani Madise, Abdhallah Ziraba, and Reuben Ogollah. 2009. "What Does Access to Maternal Care Mean among the Urban Poor? Factors Associated with Use of Appropriate Maternal Health Services in the Slum Settlements of Nairobi, Kenya." *Maternal and Child Health Journal* 13 (1): 130–37.

Fox, Sean. 2012. "Urbanization as a Global Historical Process: Theory and Evidence from Sub-Saharan Africa." *Population and Development Review* 38 (2): 285–310.

Gallardo, Cristina. 2014. "Health in Urban Slums Depends on Better Local Data." SciDev.Net, March 17, 5–7.

Gandy, Matthew. 2005. "Learning from Lagos." *New Left Review* 33:37.

Gberie, Lansana. 2005. "Africa: The Troubled Continent." *African Affairs* 104 (415): 337–42.

Gugler, Josef. 2002. "The Son of the Hawk Does Not Remain Abroad: The Urban–Rural Connection in Africa." *African Studies Review* 45 (1): 21–41.

Güneralp, Burak, Shuaib Lwasa, Hillary Masundire, Susan Parnell, and Karen C. Seto. 2017. "Urbanization in Africa: Challenges and Opportunities for Conservation." *Environmental Research Letters* 13 (1): 015002.

Heinrigs, Philipp. 2020. "Africapolis: Understanding the Dynamics of Urbanization in Africa." *Field Actions Science Reports: The Journal of Field Actions* 22:18–23.

Henderson, J. Vernon, Adam Storeygard, and Uwe Deichmann. 2014. "Is Climate Change Driving Urbanization in Africa?" World Bank Policy Research Working Paper, October 28.

Jedwab, Rémi. 2013. "Urbanization without Structural Transformation: Evidence from Consumption Cities in Africa." Department of Economics, George Washington University, Washington, DC, February 28.

Kessides, Christine. 2006. *The Urban Transition in Sub-Saharan Africa: Implications for Economic Growth and Poverty Reduction.* Washington, DC: Cities Alliance.

Lahariya, Chandrakant. 2008. "The State of the World Population 2007: Unleashing the Potential of Urban Growth." *Indian Pediatrics* 45 (6): 481.

Mbembe, Achille. 2001. "At the Edge of the World: Boundaries, Territoriality, and Sovereignty in Africa." In *Globalization*, 22–51. Durham, NC: Duke University Press.

Mberu, Blessing. 2015. "Migration Circulation and Rural Development in Sub-Saharan Africa: A Multi-Factor Review of the Case of Eastern Nigeria." In *Demographic Issues in Nigeria: Insights and Implications*, edited by Onipede Wusu, Ezebunwa Nwokocha, and Lorretta Ntoimo, chapter 12. Bloomington, IN: AuthorHouse.

Mberu, Blessing, Caroline W. Kabiru, Donatien Beguy, and Alex C. Ezeh. 2016. "Consolidating Research on Population Dynamics and Health of the Urban Poor in Sub-Saharan Africa: An Overview." *African Population Studies* 30 (3): 3016–21.

Montgomery, Mark R., Richard Stren, Barney Cohen, and Holly E. Reed. 2013. *Cities Transformed: Demographic Change and Its Implications in the Developing World*. London: Routledge.

Moriconi-Ebrard, François, Eric Denis, Dominique Harre-Roger, Catherine Chatel, Ousmane Thiam, and Marion Séjourné. 2008. *Africapolis*. English version. Paris: OECD.

Muindi, K. 2014. *Population and Health Dynamics in Nairobi's Informal Settlements: Report of the Nairobi Cross-Sectional Slums Survey (NCSS) 2012*. Nairobi, Kenya: APHRC.

Murray, Martin J., and Garth A. Myers. 2007. *Cities in Contemporary Africa*. Cham: Springer.

Myers, Garth A. 2011a. *African Cities: Alternative Visions of Urban Theory and Practice*. London: Zed Books.

Myers, Garth A. 2011b. "Why Africa's Cities Matter." *African Geographical Review* 30 (1): 101–6.

Myers, Garth A., and Martin J. Murray. 2006. "Introduction: Situating Contemporary Cities in Africa." In *Cities in Contemporary Africa*, edited by Martin J. Murray and Garth A. Myers, 1–25. New York: Palgrave Macmillan.

Obeng-Odoom, Franklin. 2010. "'Abnormal' Urbanization in Africa: A Dissenting View." *African Geographical Review* 29 (2): 13–40.

OECD. 2020. *Africa's Urbanisation Dynamics 2020*. OECD, Sahel and West Africa Club. https://doi.org/10.1787/b6bccb81-en.

Potts, Deborah. 2012. "Challenging the Myths of Urban Dynamics in Sub-Saharan Africa: The Evidence from Nigeria." *World Development* 40 (7): 1382–93.

Silimperi, Diana R. 1995. "Linkages for Urban Health—The Community and Agencies." In *Urban Health in Developing Countries: Progress and Prospects*, edited by Marcel Tanner and Trudy Harpham, 9. Hoboken, NJ: Taylor and Francis.

Simone, AbdouMaliq. 2004. *For the City Yet to Come: Changing African Life in Four Cities*. Durham, NC: Duke University Press.

Simone, AbdouMaliq. 2005. "Local Navigation in Douala." In *Future City*, edited by Stephen Read, Jürgen Rosemann, and Job van Eldijk, chapter 14. London: Spon Press.

Smith, Daniel Jordan. 1999. "Having People: Fertility, Family and Modernity in Igbo-Speaking Nigeria." PhD diss., Emory University.

Smith, Daniel Jordan. 2004. "Burials and Belonging in Nigeria: Rural–Urban Relations and Social Inequality in a Contemporary African Ritual." *American Anthropologist* 106 (3): 569–79.

Sow, Mariama. 2015. "Foresight Africa 2016: Urbanization in the African Context." Brookings Institution, December 30.

Sumari, Neema Simon, Patrick Brandful Cobbinah, Fanan Ujoh, and Gang Xu. 2020. "On the Absurdity of Rapid Urbanization: Spatio-Temporal Analysis of Land-Use Changes in Morogoro, Tanzania." *Cities* 107:102876.

Swilling, Mark. 1997. *Governing Africa's Cities*. Johannesburg: Wits University Press.

Tostensen, Arne, Inge Tvedten, and Mariken Vaa. 2001. "The Urban Crisis, Governance and Associational Life." In *Associational Life in African Cities: Popular Responses to the Urban Crisis*, edited by Arne Tostensen, Inge Tvedten, and Mariken Vaa, 7–26. Uppsala, Finland: Nordiska Afrikainstitutet.

Turok, Ivan. 2014. "Linking Urbanisation and Development in Africa's Economic Revival." In *Africa's Urban Revolution*, edited by Sue Parnell and E. A. Pieterse, 60–81. London: Zed Books.

UN Department of Economic and Social Affairs, Population Division. 2014. *World Urbanization Prospects, the 2011 Revision*. New York: United Nations.

UN Economic Commission for Africa. 2008. *The State of African Cities 2008: A Framework for Addressing Urban Challenges in Africa*. Nairobi, Kenya: UN-Habitat.

United Nations. 2014. *World Population Prospects, 2017*. New York: United Nations.

United Nations. 2018. *Revision of World Urbanization Prospects*. New York: United Nations.

Vlahov, David, Siddharth Raj Agarwal, Robert M. Buckley, Waleska Teixeira Caiaffa, Carlos F. Corvalan, Alex Chika Ezeh, Ruth Finkelstein, Sharon Friel, Trudy Harpham, and Maharufa Hossain. 2011. "Roundtable on Urban Living Environment Research (RULER)." *Journal of Urban Health* 88:793–857.

White, Michael J., Blessing U. Mberu, and Mark A. Collinson. 2012. "African Urbanization: Recent Trends and Implications." In *The New Global Frontier: Urbanization, Poverty, and Environment in the 21st Century*, edited by George Martine, Gordon McGranahan, Mark Montgomery, and Rogelio Fernández-Castilla, 315–30. London: Earthscan.

WHO (World Health Organization) Centre for Health Development. 2010. *Hidden Cities: Unmasking and Overcoming Health Inequities in Urban Settings*. Geneva: World Health Organization.

World Bank, Africa Region. 2011. *Africa's Future and the World Bank's Support to It*. World Bank Africa Strategy 2011. Washington, DC: World Bank.

II SOCIAL DETERMINANTS OF HEALTH

Cities attract people in search of opportunities and a better quality of life. Certain characteristics of cities, however—specifically, the conditions in the social and physical environment in which people are born, live, work, play, and learn (i.e., the social determinants of health)—can have both positive and negative effects. The chapters in this section describe features of African cities that influence individual and population health. The section starts with a chapter on informal settlements and slums, which have become important features of cities in Africa. Many factors influence the emergence and growth of slums in urban areas. In Africa, some of the relevant factors have included colonialism, marginalization, rural–urban migration, population growth, poor urban planning, and discriminatory real estate markets. People who live in slums face many challenges, including limited access to healthy housing, water, and sanitation, as well as food insecurity. The subsequent chapter argues for stronger and effective policy interventions to address food insecurity in slums. The remaining chapters discuss the challenges and policy interventions associated with other important social determinants of health that affect most residents living in cities. These include healthy housing; water, sanitation, and hygiene (WASH); air pollution; transportation; and conflict. Policy recommendations presented in each chapter could improve the health and well-being of city residents.

4

The Challenges of Informal Settlements and Slums in Urban Africa

Marylene Wamukoya and Kanyiva Muindi

1. Introduction

The world is urbanizing rapidly, with more than half of the world's population (54 percent) residing in urban areas by 2015. Different regions are urbanizing at different growth rates, and Africa has the highest (3.44 percent), with the urban population growing through natural increase, migration from rural areas to harness the urban advantage, expansion of urban areas, and reclassification of rural areas (UN-Habitat 2016b). Between 2010 and 2050, the urban population is projected to triple to 1.23 billion (UN-Habitat 2016a, 2020a).

This rapid and unplanned urbanization is characterized by an increase in slum populations, with over 50 percent of urban populations projected to live in slums by 2050 (UN-Habitat 2003, 2020; WHO 2000). Estimates indicate that globally, 1 billion people currently live in urban slums (UNDESA 2022a), with the African continent having the third largest number of slum dwellers (230 million) after central, southern, eastern, and southeastern Asia.

Slums transform the topography of cities, sustaining inequality, which is often characterized by pockets of wealthy living spaces engulfed by a sprawl of poverty (UN-Habitat 2010, 2020a). Slums, which are increasingly becoming the predominant type of living area in cities, are typified by a polluted environment, overcrowding, poor infrastructure, poor sanitation, high levels of violence, marked absence of the public sector, and debilitating poverty (APHRC 2002, 2014; Kyobutungi et al. 2008; UN-Habitat 2016a; Zulu et al. 2011). The urban advantage becomes the urban paradox in that it promotes urban residence for the economic opportunities and superior infrastructure and services, yet rapid and unplanned urbanization leads to the proliferation of slums, with the slum dwellers' lived experiences not matching the urban advantage (Owoko 2018; R. B. Patel and Burke 2009). The proliferation of slums in Africa has led to several consequences in health and other outcomes for residents of African cities.

2. Challenges of Slums

2.1. Marginalization

The marked absence of the public sector in slums often leaves the residents of these areas out of the public agenda and separated from public and social protections. They are often marginalized and stigmatized and are more likely to experience loss of property due to lack of tenure and title, destruction of their dwellings, displacement from their homes, and reduced access to basic services (A. Ezeh et al. 2017; UN-Habitat 2016a).

The inequality in cities is depicted in wealth gaps that limit interactions between the rich and poor. The result is social exclusion and marginalization of the poor, with little access to basic services and social networks. This in turn may lead poorer residents to resort to desperate measures to eke out a living, leading to further profiling, stigmatization, and marginalization of slum residents as criminals and slums as dens of criminality (Owoko 2018).

The existing segregation of slum and nonslum areas in African cities may be a sequalae of colonialism, during which the practice of racial and tribal segregation was rampant, as many of the cities in Africa began to be planned and built (Kimani-Murage, Zulu, and Undie 2007). Politics also plays a major role in driving this marginalization because the promulgation of policies around infrastructure and public services is often driven by the will of the political class and the advantages or disadvantages these policies would present to their political affiliates. As such, governments delay in recognizing slums as legal residential areas. This is reflected in civil registration and vital statistics systems (CRVS) in many countries in sub-Saharan Africa, whereby the political decision makers do not prioritize the establishment or use of CRVS in their decision-making processes. As such, marginalized groups such as slum residents may bear much more of the brunt of marginalization and exist without being counted at birth or at death; they are also not accounted for in planning and provision of services. Lack of birth registration also prevents access to certain basic services, such as education, whereby children cannot be enrolled in school without proof of birth registration (Juma, Beguy, and Mberu 2016; R. B. Patel and Burke 2009; Ye et al. 2012).

The lack of basic public services and infrastructures in slums often leads to the proliferation of private providers of public services, with very little regulation of prices and standards (Kimani-Murage, Zulu, and Undie 2007). For example, Juma, Beguy, and Mberu (2016) report that parents in two slums in Nairobi, Kenya, enrolled their unregistered children in informal and private primary schools that had waived the Kenya Ministry of Education requirements (that all children must have a registered birth to be enrolled in school and to sit national examinations that would enable them to transition to higher education). These children wound up at a disadvantage, when they were unable to transition to formal secondary schools. In another study, the authors state that residents of slums in some African cities pay five to seven times more per liter of water compared to residents of North America (Ramin 2009; Undie, John-Langba, and Kimani-Murage 2006).

2.2. Vulnerable Groups

"An individual or household is said to be vulnerable to a hazard if they are more susceptible to being harmed or killed and/or to livelihood, income or asset loss and if they have less capacity to cope and adapt. So, if the hazard to which they are vulnerable is removed, they are not vulnerable" (Satterthwaite and Bartlett 2017, 5). As such, slum residence is a hazard to its residents, and factors associated with inequality, such as gender, income levels, and age, interplay with slum conditions to increase the vulnerability of certain groups (R. B. Patel and Burke 2009).

The conditions in slums worsen morbidity and mortality outcomes in particular groups, such as children under the age of five years and older persons (A. Ezeh et al. 2006; Kyobutungi et al. 2008). Children's vulnerability arises from factors such as low immunization rates, low breastfeeding rates, under- and malnutrition, poor sanitation, stunting, and subsequent impaired cognitive development and increased mortality, with children living in slums having worse outcomes than children in rural areas (APHRC 2002, 2014; A. Ezeh et al. 2017; R. B. Patel and Burke 2009; Ramin 2009; UN-Habitat 2016a).

Slum conditions also degrade social structures because of limited access to basic services and the public sector (including law enforcement). It is common for crime to proliferate in these conditions and for it to remain unreported and unaddressed (Wa 2011; Wamukoya et al. 2020). Different groups are vulnerable to different types of crime, with women being more likely to be victims of rape and men being more likely to be victims of muggings and assault. Moreover, other demographic factors, apart from gender, are also associated with different risks; for example, the elderly are more likely to be victims of con men and road traffic accidents, while younger persons are more likely to be assaulted (Mberu et al. 2015; Wa 2011).

2.3. Socioeconomic Changes

Urbanization is accompanied by demographic, social, economic, and psychological changes. Social changes often affect family and family life patterns, which contributes to the loss of family support in caring for members as the system of extended families breaks down; economic changes are associated with industrialization and subsequent economic growth; and psychological changes are a result of the unique stressors associated with slums and slum dwelling (Okasha 2002; Srivastava 2009).

Slums dwellers experience challenges with employment opportunities, which leads to engagement in unskilled and very low-paying economic activities. Although they are able to survive from day to day, they are unable to change their living conditions. This in turn affects the economic power of the cities that contain these slums, as they are not able to harness a vibrant and youthful workforce in formal employment (UN-Habitat 2016a). Slum dwellers experience debilitating poverty and often find themselves falling into cycles of "barely surviving" and "extreme poverty" whenever they experience any type of deviation from their normal life, such as illness or death (A. Ezeh et al. 2017; UN-Habitat 2016a).

Slum dwellers also experience different forms of poverty. For example, Mowafi and Khawaja (2005) defined the chronic poor as "those whose resources are severely below established needs and so they suffer from persistent deprivation," and the transient poor as those who "cross over the poverty line frequently ('the churning poor') or only occasionally." Chronic poverty is of great concern because not only is it a symptom of prolonged deprivation in the past, it is also a cause of destitution, with lasting consequences on health (e.g., stunted growth in children and physical impairment), on access to health care and education, and on mental trauma (Arif and Bilquees 2007; Clark and Hulme 2010).

2.4. Transportation

Estimates from 2020 indicate that globally, only 37 percent of urban areas have access to public transport, and 52 percent of the urban population has convenient access to public transport. This means that they live within 500 meters' walking distance of low-capacity transport systems, such as bus stops, or within one kilometer of high-capacity transport systems, such as trains and ferries. In Africa, the figures stand at 23 percent and 31 percent, respectively (UNDESA 2022a). Convenient access to public transportation remains a major challenge in slums and their surroundings as a result of overcrowding and lack of passable or designated roads for both motorized and nonmotorized traffic. A lack of roadways for motorized traffic makes it impossible for public services such as fire engines and ambulances to reach certain parts of slum communities.

Major safety issues are associated with the lack of nonmotorized roadways, which would make walking safer, particularly as walking is the main mode of transport for slum dwellers (UN-Habitat 2016a). Mberu et al. (2015) note that deaths due to injuries in the Korogocho and Viwandani slums of Nairobi, Kenya, increased from 17 percent in 2003 to 34 percent in 2012. They further identified the main causes of injury and deaths as assault, road traffic accidents, and exposure to smoke and fire (Mberu et al. 2015).

2.5. Housing, Water, and Sanitation

Housing is a key social determinant of both physical and mental health (Bonnefoy 2007; WHO 2018). Healthy housing is defined as "shelter that supports a state of complete physical, mental and social well-being" (WHO 2018). "Healthy housing also refers to the dwelling's structural integrity, its ability to protect occupants from the elements, access to safe fuel or electricity and adequate sanitation as well as protection from pollutants, pests and injury hazards. Healthy housing also depends on the local community, which enables social interactions that support health and well-being. Finally, healthy housing relies on the immediate housing environment, and the extent to which this provides access to services, green space, and active and public transport options, as well as protection from waste, pollution and the effects of disaster, whether natural or man-made" (WHO 2018). About 20 percent of the global population resides in inadequate housing, that is, housing in "poor physical condition, overcrowded, poorly ventilated, [with] poor access to municipal services and . . . located far from employment nodes and basic facilities" (UN-Habitat 2020b). Most slum residents lack security of tenure, which contributes to their failure to invest in improving their houses and the environment in which they live, given the ever-present threat of eviction (Corburn et al. 2020).

Slums across sub-Saharan Africa are characterized by poor quality housing, usually constructed using low quality materials, exposing occupants to temperature extremes, especially during the hot and cold seasons. Given the informality surrounding slum settlements, they remain unplanned spaces, and most houses offer limited space to residents, leading to crowding. For example, most households in Nairobi slums occupy a single room that serves as the kitchen and sleeping space (Beguy et al. 2015). Crowding and poor ventilation drive the spread of infectious diseases (Corburn et al. 2020; A. Ezeh et al. 2017; Nkosi et al. 2019). In addition, poor ventilation exposes occupants to high levels of household air pollution from cooking and lighting appliances (Lam et al. 2012; Muindi et al. 2016), with implications for respiratory health (Simkovich et al. 2019) and birth outcomes (Amegah, Quansah, and Jaakkola 2014).

Access to safe drinking water and safely managed sanitation are important given the far-reaching effects these services have on health. The WHO/ UNICEF Joint Monitoring Programme (JMP) defines improved sources of drinking water as those with the following attributes: (1) easily accessible (within thirty minutes), (2) available when needed (continuously and in sufficient quantity), and (3) free from contamination. Safely managed sanitation must meet the following criteria: (1) effective containment; (2) emptying, treatment, and disposal from on-site storage facilities; and (3) transport of wastewater through sewer systems to treatment off-site (UNICEF and WHO 2018). In Africa, 42 percent of the urban population has access to safe water and safely managed sanitation (Du et al. 2019). With the relative lack of basic infrastructure and the near absence of the public sector in slum areas, access to water becomes a challenge. Furthermore, with limited sanitation, slum areas are characterized by open sewer lines that empty waste into open spaces and various waterways, as well as by open defecation because of the lack of adequate toilets (Chikozho et al. 2019; UN-Habitat 2016a; Wamukoya et al. 2020). This predisposes slum dwellers to health risks as-

The Challenges of Informal Settlements and Slums   55

sociated with the use and consumption of unsafe drinking water and poor sanitation and hygiene, including diarrhea, typhoid, and cholera (UN-Habitat 2016a).

2.6. Disasters and Disease Outbreaks

The closely spaced dwellings in slums as well as the limited living space within these dwellings increase the risk of slum dwellers being adversely affected by natural disasters associated with extreme weather, as well as other disasters, such as fires and demolitions (A. Ezeh et al. 2017; Mberu et al. 2015; UN-Habitat 2016a). These densely packed areas are also more prone to infectious diseases and remain the most unprepared to withstand such health crises because their marginalization excludes them from community-level interventions (R. B. Patel and Burke 2009; Ramin 2009; Solymári et al. 2022; UN-Habitat 2016a).

Slum areas are often located in fragile areas of cities typically affected by heavy rainfall and prone to landslides and floods. The aforementioned living conditions (i.e., overcrowded spaces with very little drainage, minimal passages, and filled with dwellings constructed from inadequate materials) usually exacerbate natural climate and weather changes, turning them into disasters and leading to disease, disability, and loss of lives, livelihoods, and homes. Extreme rainfall and rising sea levels mean that slums in African cities located in areas prone to flooding will suffer the brunt of climate change (Baker 2012; Ramin 2009).

Changes in climate drive natural events such as droughts, which are more frequent and longer in sub-Saharan Africa than in previous years. Droughts pose a challenge because (1) when they occur in rural areas, they prompt migration to urban areas, thereby burdening resources that are already overstretched; (2) urban slum residents that rely on remittances of food from rural areas see an increase in food insecurity, which in turn leads to malnutrition; and (3) water scarcity leads to consumption of water from nonimproved sources (Ramin 2009). In addition, increasing temperatures lead to discomfort, especially among slum residents who live in housing that does not protect them from heat. Further, exposure to extreme heat may lead to heat stroke, especially among older persons, who have poor thermoregulation (Millyard et al. 2020).

Furthermore, slums in African cities are often located near factories and busy roads, and the resultant emissions from the factories and motor vehicles make slums residents prone to respiratory ill health and premature mortality due to prolonged exposure to air pollution (Ramin 2009).

2.7. Mental Health and Substance Abuse

In sub-Saharan Africa, mental and substance use disorders accounted for 19 percent of years lived with disability (YLD) in 2010. An estimated 130 percent increase by 2050 is projected, which will in turn affect productivity and health (Charlson et al. 2014). Slum residents in sub-Saharan Africa are more likely to suffer from mental illnesses such as major depressive disorder than those in middle- or higher-income groups (Duthé et al. 2016). The most important mental illnesses affecting slum dwellers are affective disorders, schizophrenia, and substance abuse, such as alcoholism. These are a result of minimal livelihood opportunities as well as precarious living conditions, which lead to engagement in risky patterns of behaviors, such as substance intoxication (especially alcohol), which is associated with higher levels of interpersonal violence and therefore injuries and deaths (Ziraba, Kyobutungi, and Zulu 2011; Zulu et al. 2011). Mental illnesses also increase the risk for both communicable and noncommunicable diseases (Prince et al. 2007).

2.8. Food Insecurity

Food security exists "when all people, at all times, have physical and economic access to sufficient, safe and nutritious food that meets their dietary needs and food preferences for an active and healthy life" (FAO 2006). The United Nation's Sustainable Development Goal (SDG) 2 aspires to achieve zero hunger by the year 2030 (UNDESA 2022b); however, a recent report indicates that this may not be realized, as some regions are experiencing substantial hunger, which worsened with the COVID-19 pandemic. For example, Africa had about 20 percent prevalence of hunger in 2021 (FAO et al. 2022), and this could worsen because of climate variability across the continent (FAO 2015; Carleton 2022). In addition, ongoing global conflicts and those within Africa affect local food systems as well as international food supply chains, pushing prices of commodities beyond the reach of many households (Anderson et al. 2021; Burrier 2022; Messer and Cohen 2004).

Urban areas, which are mostly dependent on food produced in rural areas in addition to food imports, have had challenges in getting adequate food following supply chain disruptions during the COVID-19 pandemic (C. U.

Ezeh et al. 2020). Slum areas fared worse, especially when lockdowns were implemented, affecting incomes, as people lost their jobs, and limiting movement between urban and rural areas, whose linkages supplement food supply to urban households (Crush and Caesar 2017; Zimmer et al. 2022). The current global fertilizer shortages, if not addressed, will no doubt affect food production, causing shortages and further rise in food prices in the near future. The effects on food insecurity will be most severe for slum residents, owing to their low and unstable incomes, which not only affect the purchase of food but also access to energy for cooking (Shupler et al. 2020). Previous research has documented the vulnerability of Nairobi slum residents to food insecurity, with evidence that four in five households were food insecure, and nearly half had both child and adult hunger, with adults forgoing meals to prioritize their children (Faye et al. 2011).

2.9. Pollution

While urbanization is most often associated with the prosperity of cities, it is also a source of environmental pollution, with implications for human health and well-being. Poorly managed urban processes, such as manufacturing, transportation, and municipal waste, as well as inadequate sanitation services contribute to environmental pollution. Beyond ambient and household air pollution covered in chapter 8, we address other forms of pollution in this subsection.

In the African region, environmental pollution accounts for 23 percent of the disease burden (WHO AFRO 2017). The burden of environmental pollution is not evenly distributed among city residents, as slum neighborhoods tend to face higher levels of pollution because of their location, for example, near industries and along busy highways as well as near the siting of pollution sources such as dumpsites (Mberu et al. 2020; UN-Habitat 2003). In Nairobi, the Dandora dumpsite is located close to public institutions like schools and near the informal settlements of Kariobangi North and Korogocho, as well as near the Dandora and Baba Ndogo residential estates. This dumpsite poses a range of health risks to the over 250,000 people living adjacent to it, in addition to causing extensive damage to the environment.

Poor solid waste management in slums as a result of infrastructural limitations, such as lack of access roads to reach households, as well as inability of households to pay for private garbage collection services, leads to waste burning and accumulation in the settlements (B. Mberu et al. 2017). Leachate from dumpsites, in addition to wastewater from industries, fecal contamination from poor sanitation facilities, and open defecation, leads to water and soil contamination (Monney et al. 2013; Kimani and UNEP 2007). In addition, river systems adjacent to slums are polluted from industrial, domestic, and fecal waste (Vane et al. 2022), with implications for the health of residents consuming crops grown using this contaminated water. Further, an earlier study found that the close proximity of the Dandora dumpsite to the Nairobi River, whose waters are used to grow vegetables for sale at various city markets, indicates the potential exposure of almost all city residents to contaminants from the dumpsite (Kimani and UNEP 2007).

3. Opportunities

Despite the foregoing challenges, slums offer numerous opportunities; for example, the dense population within small areas provide economies of scale for rolling out interventions and programs (Lilford et al. 2017). Further, slum communities' knowledge on resilience (S. Patel 2009) could inform citywide actions in response to certain shocks. The ability of slum residents to organize is a strength that can be harnessed to bring their voices to the decision-making table before undertaking various programs such as slum upgrading.

Cities in Africa are becoming the main dwelling place of its citizens, and it is critical for policymakers to prioritize decision making toward ensuring that these cities are equipped to accommodate the rising urban population. Governments are obligated to increase the resilience of slum residents, and this is best accomplished through city planning and management that focuses on reducing risks for all citizens of the city, with a focus on service delivery and the introduction of basic infrastructure (Baker 2012). Additionally, investments in cities should be geared toward equipping urban economies to generate employment opportunities as well as investing in infrastructure, social services, and affordable housing (UN-Habitat 2020). Efforts should include policies that enable adaptation to the sequalae of climate change, that is, droughts, rising sea levels, and increased frequency of extreme precipitation (Ramin 2009). Such policies should also be cognizant of the varying dimensions of vulnerability that arise from different individual-, household-, and community-level factors by understanding the vulnerable groups, the hazards that affect the groups, why they are affected, and the appropriate actions to mitigate their vulnerability (Satterthwaite and Bartlett 2017).

The effects of slums are felt not only within the slums but also in the urban communities where they are located. Improving slums and the livelihoods of slum dwellers would also improve urban geographies as well as the lives of urban dwellers not in slums (UN-Habitat 2016a). Slums can be improved through slum upgrading efforts: enhancing housing and basic infrastructure; providing security of tenure; introducing the public sector in slums; and improving demographic, social, economic, and psychological transitions and processes. Such efforts must be collaborative and participatory, involving all stakeholders, most especially the communities that reside in these slums, and require the concerted commitment of policymakers (UN-Habitat 2016a, 2020a).

Efforts toward CRVS in slum areas would also reduce the marginalization of slum residents, who often cannot access basic services because they lack the requisite documents, which cannot be obtained without birth registration. Government contributions in this area would include sensitization drives, waiving of administrative red tape and informal fees associated with birth registrations, not requiring birth registration to access basic services, incentivizing traditional birth attendants and community health workers to participate in referral systems, among other initiatives (Juma, Beguy, and Mberu 2016).

To study the health of slum dwellers, it is important to separate slum health from urban health in national, regional, and global surveys and agendas, as well as to examine slum health outside the association between poverty and health, as slums carry with them other dynamics (such as neighborhood effects—factors that affect community health despite individual- and household-level factors) that are not associated directly with poverty (A. Ezeh et al. 2017; Zerbo, Delgado, and González 2020). It is also important to be cognizant of the fact that, although slum residents are often treated homogeneously, even slums have different poverty classes. It is often assumed that all slum residents are affected similarly by poverty; future ventures in studying the health of slum dwellers should recognize the socioeconomic heterogeneities within these populations and account for classes such as chronic poor and transient poor.

The implementation of epidemiologic and operation research will enable both government and nongovernment agencies to develop programs that

60   Social Determinants of Health

protect city dwellers, both slum and nonslum, by building a strong and vast knowledge base on slum systems, areas, and residents. This research must be dedicated to interventions that exploit the urban advantage, with the commitment of government agencies to scale up research that prevents the erosion of gains made in global health thus far and that promotes adaptation to global patterns such as climate change (R. B. Patel and Burke 2009; Ramin 2009).

REFERENCES

Amegah, Adeladza K., Reginald Quansah, and Jouni J. K. Jaakkola. 2014. "Household Air Pollution from Solid Fuel Use and Risk of Adverse Pregnancy Outcomes: A Systematic Review and Meta-Analysis of the Empirical Evidence." *PloS One* 9 (12): e113920.

Anderson, Weston, Charles Taylor, Sonali McDermid, Elisabeth Ilboudo-Nébié, Richard Seager, Wolfram Schlenker, Fabien Cottier, Alex de Sherbinin, Dara Mendeloff, and Kelsey Markey. 2021. "Violent Conflict Exacerbated Drought-Related Food Insecurity between 2009 and 2019 in Sub-Saharan Africa." *Nature Food* 2 (8): 603–15. https://doi .org/10.1038/s43016-021-00327-4.

APHRC (African Population and Health Research Center). 2002. *Population and Health Dynamics in Nairobi's Informal Settlements.* Nairobi, Kenya: APHRC.

APHRC (African Population and Health Research Center). 2014. *Population and Health Dynamics in Nairobi's Informal Settlements: Report of the Nairobi Cross-Sectional Slums Survey (NCSS) 2012.* Nairobi, Kenya: APHRC.

Arif, Ghulam M., and Faiz Bilquees. 2007. "Chronic and Transitory Poverty in Pakistan: Evidence from a Longitudinal Household Survey." *Pakistan Development Review* 46 (2): 111–27.

Baker, Judy L., ed. 2012. *Climate Change, Disaster Risk, and the Urban Poor: Cities Building Resilience for a Changing World.* Washington, DC: World Bank.

Beguy, Donatien, Patricia Elung'ata, Blessing Mberu, Clement Oduor, Marylene Wamukoya, Bonface Nganyi, and Alex Ezeh. 2015. "HDSS Profile: The Nairobi Urban Health and Demographic Surveillance System (NUHDSS)." *International Journal of Epidemiology* 44 (2): 462–71. https://doi.org/10.1093/ije/dyu251.

Bonnefoy, Xavier. 2007. "Inadequate Housing and Health: An Overview." *International Journal of Environment and Pollution* 30 (3/4): 411–29.

Burrier, Edward A. 2022. "In Africa, Putin's War on Ukraine Drives Food, Fuel and Finance Crises." US Institute of Peace, June 30.

Carleton, Elliot. 2022. "Climate Change in Africa: What Will It Mean for Agriculture and Food Security?" International Livestock Research Institute, February 28. https:// www.ilri.org/news/climate-change-africa-what-will-it-mean-agriculture-and-food -security.

Charlson, Fiona J., Sandra Diminic, Crick Lund, Louisa Degenhardt, and Harvey A. Whiteford. 2014. "Mental and Substance Use Disorders in Sub-Saharan Africa: Predictions of Epidemiological Changes and Mental Health Workforce Requirements for the Next 40 Years." *PLoS One* 9 (10): e110208. https://doi.org/10.1371/journal.pone.0110208.

Chikozho, Claudious, Damazo T. Kadengye, Marylene Wamukoya, and Benedict O. Orindi. 2019. "Leaving No One Behind? Analysis of Trends in Access to Water and Sanitation Services in the Slum Areas of Nairobi, 2003–2015." *Journal of Water, Sanitation and Hygiene for Development* 9 (3): 549–58. https://doi.org/10.2166/washdev.2019.174.

Clark, D., and D. Hulme. 2010. "Poverty, Time and Vagueness: Integrating the Core Poverty and Chronic Poverty Frameworks." *Cambridge Journal of Economics* 34 (2): 347–66.

Corburn, J., D. Vlahov, B. Mberu, L. Riley, W. T. Caiaffa, S. F. Rashid, A. Ko, S. Patel, S. Jukur, E. Martínez-Herrera, S. Jayasinghe, S. Agarwal, B. Nguendo-Yongsi, J. Weru, S. Ouma, K. Edmundo, T. Oni, and H. Ayad. 2020. "Slum Health: Arresting COVID-19 and Improving Well-Being in Urban Informal Settlements." *Journal of Urban Health* 97:348–57. https://doi.org/10.1007/s11524-020-00438-6.

Crush, J., and M. Caesar. 2017. "Food Remittances: Rural-Urban Linkages and Food Security in Africa." IIED (London) working paper, March. http://pubs.iied.org/10793IIED.

Du, Jillian, Diana Mitlin, Victoria A. Beard, and David Satterthwaite. 2019. "We're Grossly Underestimating the World's Water Access Crisis." World Resources Institute, *Insights*, August 13. https://www.wri.org/insights/were-grossly-underestimating -worlds-water-access-crisis.

Duthé, Géraldine, Clémentine Rossier, Doris Bonnet, Abdramane Bassiahi Soura, and Jamaica Corker. 2016. "Mental Health and Urban Living in Sub-Saharan Africa: Major Depressive Episodes among the Urban Poor in Ouagadougou, Burkina Faso." *Population Health Metrics* 14:18. https://doi.org/10.1186/s12963-016-0084-2.

Ezeh, Alex, Gloria Chepngeno, Abdhalah Ziraba Kasiira, and Zewdu Woubalem. 2006. "The Situation of Older People in Poor Urban Settings: The Case of Nairobi, Kenya." In *Aging in Sub-Saharan Africa: Recommendation for Furthering Research*, edited by Barney Cohen and Jane Menken, 189–213. Washington, DC: National Academies Press.

Ezeh Alex, Oyinlola Oyebode, David Satterthwaite, Yen-Fu Chen, Robert Ndugwa, Jo Sartori, Blessing Mberu, et al. 2017. "The History, Geography, and Sociology of Slums and the Health Problems of People Who Live in Slums." *Lancet* 389 (10068): 547–58. https://doi.org/10.1016/S0140-6736(16)31650-6.

Ezeh, Christopher Uche, Dakéga Saberma Ragatoa, Charles Lamoussa Sanou, and Chukwudi Nnaemeka Emeribe. 2020. "A Review of the Impacts of COVID-19: Lessons for Africa." *Parana Journal of Science and Education* 6 (4): 65–70. https://doi .org/10.5281/zenodo.3880565.

FAO (Food and Agriculture Organization of the United Nations). 2006. "Policy Brief: Food Security, Issue 2." News release, June. FAO. https://reliefweb.int/report/world /policy-brief-food-security-issue-2-june-2006.

FAO (Food and Agriculture Organization of the United Nations). 2015. *Climate Change and Food Security: Risks and Responses*. Rome: FAO.

FAO, IFAD, UNICEF, WFP, and WHO. 2022. *The State of Food Security and Nutrition in the World: Repurposing Food and Agricultural Policies to Make Healthy Diets More Affordable*. Rome: FAO.

Faye, Ousmane, Angela Baschieri, Jane Falkingham, and Kanyiva Muindi. 2011. "Hunger and Food Insecurity in Nairobi's Slums: An Assessment Using IRT Models." *Journal of Urban Health* 88 (Suppl 2): 235–55. https://doi.org/10.1007/s11524-010-9521-x.

Juma, Collins, Donatien Beguy, and Blessing Mberu. 2016. "Levels of and Factors Associated with Birth Registration in the Slums of Nairobi." *African Population Studies* 30 (2). https://doi.org/10.11564/30-2-848.

Kimani, Njoroge G., and UNEP (United Nations Environment Programme). 2007. *Environmental Pollution and Impact to Public Health: Implications of the Dandora Municipal Dumping Site in Nairobi, Kenya*. Nairobi, Kenya: UNEP.

Kimani-Murage, Elizabeth, Eliya Zulu, and Chi-Chi Undie. 2007. "Health and Livelihood Implications of the Marginalization of Slum Dwellers in the Provision of Water and Sanitation Services in Nairobi City." Paper presented to the PRIPODE workshop Urban Population, Development and Environment Dynamics in Developing Countries, June 11–13, 2007, Nairobi, Kenya.

Kyobutungi, C., A. K. Ziraba, A. Ezeh, and Y. Ye. 2008. "The Burden of Disease Profile of Residents of Nairobi's Slums: Results from a Demographic Surveillance System." *Population Health Metrics* 6:1.

Lam, Nicholas L., Yanju Chen, Cheryl Weyant, Chandra Venkataraman, Pankaj Sadavarte, Michael A. Johnson, Kirk R. Smith, et al. 2012. "Household Light Makes Global Heat: High Black Carbon Emissions from Kerosene Wick Lamps." *Environmental Science and Technology* 46 (24): 13531–38.

Lilford, Richard J., Oyinlola Oyebode, David Satterthwaite, G. J. Melendez-Torres, Yen-Fu Chen, Blessing Mberu, Samuel I. Watson, et al. 2017. " Improving the Health and Welfare of People Who Live in Slums." *Lancet* 389 (10068): 559–70. https://doi.org/10.1016/S0140-6736(16)31848-7.

Mberu, Blessing, Caroline Kabaria, Dickson Amugsi, and Kanyiva Muindi. 2017. *Solid Waste Management and Risks to Health in Urban Africa—A Study of Nairobi and Mombasa Cities in Kenya*. Nairobi, Kenya: African Population Health Research Center.

Mberu, Blessing, Michael Mutua, Caroline Kabaria, Dickson Amugsi, and Kanyiva Muindi. 2020. "Levels of Household Exposure to Solid Waste Dumpsites and Associated Loss to Health in Urban Kenya and Senegal." *Cities and Health* 6 (1): 168–79. https://doi.org/10.1080/23748834.2020.1768686.

Mberu, Blessing, Marylene Wamukoya, Samuel O. Oti, and Catherine Kyobutungi. 2015. "Trends in Causes of Adult Deaths among the Urban Poor: Evidence from Nairobi Urban Health and Demographic Surveillance System, 2003–2012." *Journal of Urban Health* 93 (3): 422–45. http://www.ncbi.nlm.nih.gov/pmc/articles/PMC4456477/.

Messer, Ellen, and Marc J. Cohen. 2004. "Breaking the Links between Conflict and Hunger in Africa." Prepared for *Assuring Food and Nutrition Security in Africa by 2020*, Kampala, Uganda, April 1–3. Washington, DC: International Food Policy Research Institute.

Millyard, Alison, Joe D. Layden, David B. Pyne, Andrew M. Edwards, and Saul R. Bloxham. 2020. "Impairments to Thermoregulation in the Elderly during Heat Exposure Events." *Gerontology and Geriatric Medicine* 6. https://doi.org/https://doi.org/10.1177/2333721420932432.

Monney, I., S. N. Odai, R. Buamah, E. Awuah, and P. M. Nyenje. 2013. "Environmental Impacts of Wastewater from Urban Slums: Case Study—Old Fadama, Accra." *International Journal of Development and Sustainability* 2 (2): 711–28.

Mowafi, Mona, and Marwan Khawaja. 2005. "Poverty." *Journal of Epidemiology and Community Health* 59:260–64. https://doi.org/10.1136/jech.2004.022822.

Muindi, Kanyiva, Elizabeth Kimani-Murage, Thaddaeus Egondi, Joacim Rocklov, and Nawi Ng. 2016. "Household Air Pollution: Sources and Exposure Levels to Fine Particulate Matter in Nairobi Slums." *Toxics* 4 (3): 12. https://doi.org/10.3390/toxics 4030012.

Nkosi, Vusumuzi, Tanya Haman, Nisha Naicker, and Angela Mathee. 2019. "Overcrowding and Health in Two Impoverished Suburbs of Johannesburg, South Africa." *BMC Public Health* 19 (1): 1358. https://doi.org/10.1186/s12889-019-7665-5.

Okasha, Ahmed. 2002. "Mental Health in Africa: The Role of the WPA." *World Psychiatry* 1 (1): 32–35. http://www.ncbi.nlm.nih.gov/pmc/articles/PMC1489826/.

Owoko, Henry. 2018. "Lies We Tell Ourselves: Urban Advantage." African Population and Health Research Center (blog), June 20. https://aphrc.org/blogarticle/lies-we-tell -ourselves-urban-advantage/.

Patel, Ronak B., and Thomas F. Burke. 2009. "Urbanization—An Emerging Humanitarian Disaster." *New England Journal of Medicine* 361 (8): 741–43. https://doi.org/10.1056 /NEJMp0810878.

Patel, Sheela. 2009. "Culture, Identity and Slum Areas: Opportunities and Challenges Seen from Slum Dwellers' Perspective." Adapted from remarks given at "The Role of Cultural Heritage in Poor Urban Settlements," panel, Oslo, October 5.

Prince, Martin, Vikram Patel, Shekhar Saxena, Mario Maj, Joanna Maselko, Michael R. Phillips, and Atif Rahman. 2007. "No Health without Mental Health." *Lancet* 370 (9590): 859–77. https://doi.org/10.1016/S0140-6736(07)61238-0.

Ramin, Brodie. 2009. "Slums, Climate Change and Human Health in Sub-Saharan Africa." *Bulletin of the World Health Organization* 87 (1564-0604): 886.

Satterthwaite, David, and Sheridan Bartlett. 2017. "Editorial: The Full Spectrum of Risk in Urban Centres: Changing Perceptions, Changing Priorities." *Environment and Urbanization* 29 (1): 3–14. https://doi.org/10.1177/0956247817691921.

Shupler, Matthew, James Mwitari, Arthur Gohole, Rachel Anderson de Cuevas, Elisa Puzzolo, Iva Čukić, Emily Nix, and Dan Pope. 2020. "COVID-19 Lockdown in a Kenyan Informal Settlement: Impacts on Household Energy and Food Security." *medRxiv*, preprint, May 29. https://doi.org/10.1101/2020.05.27.20115113.

Simkovich, Suzanne M., Dina Goodman, Christian Roa, Mary E. Crocker, Gonzalo E. Gianella, Bruce J. Kirenga, Robert A. Wise, and William Checkley. 2019. "The Health and Social Implications of Household Air Pollution and Respiratory Diseases." *Primary Care Respiratory Medicine* 29:12. https://doi.org/10.1038/s41533-019-0126-x.

Solymári, Daniel, Edward Kairu, Ráhel Czirják, and István Tarrósy. 2022. "The Impact of COVID-19 on the Livelihoods of Kenyan Slum Dwellers and the Need for an Integrated Policy Approach." *PloS One* 17 (8): e0271196.

Srivastava, Kalpana. 2009. "Urbanization and Mental Health." *Industrial Psychiatry Journal* 18 (2): 75–76. https://doi.org/10.4103/0972-6748.64028.

UNDESA (United Nations Department of Economic and Social Affairs). 2022a. "Make Cities and Human Settlements Inclusive, Safe, Resilient and Sustainable." Goal 11, UNDESA. https://unstats.un.org/sdgs/report/2022/Goal-11/.

UNDESA (United Nations Department of Economic and Social Affairs). 2022b. *The Sustainable Development Goals Report 2022*. New York: UNDESA. https://unstats.un.org/sdgs/report/2022/.

Undie, Chi-Chi, Johannes John-Langba, and Elizabeth W. Kimani-Murage. 2006. "'The Place of Cool Waters': Women and Water in the Informal Settlements of Nairobi, Kenya." *Journal of Transnational Women's and Gender Studies* 3 (1): 40–60.

UN-Habitat (United Nations Human Settlements Programme). 2003. *The Challenge of Slums: Global Report on Human Settlement 2003*. London: Earthscan.

UN-Habitat (United Nations Human Settlements Programme). 2010. *The State of African Cities 2010: Governance, Inequality and Urban Land Markets*. Nairobi, Kenya: UN-Habitat.

UN-Habitat (United Nations Human Settlements Programme). 2016a. *Slum Almanac 2015/2016: Tracking Improvement in the Lives of Slum Dwellers*. Nairobi, Kenya: UN-Habitat.

UN-Habitat (United Nations Human Settlements Programme). 2016b. *World Cities Report 2016: Urbanization and Development—Emerging Futures*. Nairobi, Kenya: UN-Habitat. https://unhabitat.org/books/world-cities-report/.

UN-Habitat (United Nations Human Settlements Programme). 2020a. *UN-Habitat Sub-Saharan Africa Atlas*. Nairobi, Kenya: UN-Habitat.

UN-Habitat (United Nations Human Settlements Programme). 2020b. *The Value of Sustainable Urbanization*. Nairobi, Kenya: UN-Habitat.

UNICEF and WHO. 2018. "JMP Methodology: 2017 Update and SDG Baselines." Joint Monitoring Programme, March. https://washdata.org/monitoring/methods.

Vane, Christopher H., Alexander W. Kim, Raquel A. Lopes dos Santos, Joel C. Gill, Vicky Moss-Hayes, Jemimah K. Mulu, Jessica R. Mackie, Antonio M. P. J. Ferreira, Simon R. Chenery, and Lydia A. Olaka. 2022. "Impact of Organic Pollutants from Urban Slum Informal Settlements on Sustainable Development Goals and River Sediment Quality, Nairobi, Kenya, Africa." *Applied Geochemistry* 146:105468. https://doi.org/10.1016/j.apgeochem.2022.105468.

Wamukoya, Marylene, Damazo Kadengye, Samuel Iddi, Claudious Chikozho, and Demographic System. 2020. "The Nairobi Urban Health and Demographic Surveillance of Slum Dwellers, 2002–2019: Value, Processes, and Challenges." *Global Epidemiology* 2:100024. https://doi.org/10.1016/j.gloepi.2020.100024.

WHO (World Health Organization). 2000. *WHO Report on Global Surveillance of Epidemic-prone Infectious Diseases*. Geneva: WHO.

WHO (World Health Organization). 2018. *WHO Housing and Health Guidelines*. Edited by World Health Organization. Geneva: WHO.

WHO-AFRO (World Health Organization Regional Office for Africa). 2017. *Regional Strategy for the Management Of Environmental Determinants of Human Health in the African Region 2017–2021*. Victoria Falls, Zimbabwe: WHO-AFRO.

Ye, Yazoume, Marilyn Wamukoya, Alex Ezeh, Jacques B. O. Emina, and Osman Sankoh. 2012. "Health and Demographic Surveillance Systems: A Step towards Full Civil Registration and Vital Statistics System in Sub-Sahara Africa?" *BMC Public Health* 12 (1): 741. https://doi.org/10.1186/1471-2458-12-741.

Zerbo, Alexandre, Rafael C. Delgado, and Pedro A. González. 2020. "Vulnerability and

Everyday Health Risks of Urban Informal Settlements in Sub-Saharan Africa." *Global Health Journal* 4 (2): 46–50. https://doi.org/https://doi.org/10.1016/j.glohj.2020.04.003.

Zimmer, Andrew, Zack Guido, Julia Davies, Nupur Joshi, Allan Chilenga, and Tom Evans. 2022. "Food Systems and Rural-Urban Linkages in African Secondary Cities." *Urban Transformations* 4 (1): 13. https://doi.org/10.1186/s42854-022-00042-8.

Ziraba, Abdhalah Kasiira, Catherine Kyobutungi, and Eliya Msiyaphazi Zulu. 2011. "Fatal Injuries in the Slums of Nairobi and Their Risk Factors: Results from a Matched Case-Control Study." *Journal of Urban Health* 88 (2): 256–65. https://doi.org/10.1007/s11524-011-9580-7.

Zulu, Eliya M., Donatien Beguy, Alex C. Ezeh, Philippe Bocquier, Nyovani J. Madise, John Cleland, and Jane Falkingham. 2011. "Overview of Migration, Poverty and Health Dynamics in Nairobi City's Slum Settlements." *Journal of Urban Health* 88 (2): 185–99. https://doi.org/10.1007/s11524-011-9595-0.

5

Urban Food Insecurity in Eastern and Southern Africa during the Era of Sustainable Development

Making a Case for Slums

Linda Beyer

1. Food Security in the Era of Sustainable Development

With a global food crisis looming, low-income urban households in sub-Saharan Africa are at particular risk for heightened levels of severe food insecurity (WFP and FAO 2022). Some of the greatest remaining global burden of food insecurity persists across eastern and southern Africa—disproportionately affecting vulnerable urban households. While food security has historically been framed as a rural development challenge (Crush and Riley, 2017), slums have emerged as areas with high levels of income poverty as well as multidimensional poverty. Social determinants particular to slums include low levels of formal employment, limited access to basic services, notable disparities in health outcomes, and poor infrastructure, which exacerbate the influence of environmental stressors and climate change (Ezeh et al. 2017; Satterthwaite, Sverdlik, and Brown 2019; Tacoli 2013).

Because food insecurity has traditionally been framed as a rural development problem in sub-Saharan Africa, the needs of vulnerable urban populations are felt to be underrepresented in academic, policy, and programmatic responses (Battersby 2012; Crush, Hovorka, and Tevera 2017; Crush and Riley, 2017; Tacoli 2017). African Urban Food Security Network (AFSUN) efforts have contributed to a body of evidence that aids in the conceptualization of urban food security—with 2009 baseline work carried out across eleven cities in southern Africa (Crush, Frayne, and Pendleton 2012; Frayne, Crush, and McCordic 2018). This chapter builds on evidence centered on food insecurity in vulnerable urban environments—making a case for why we need to pay greater attention to what is happening in slums.

The sustainability of food is essential for achieving global outcomes of

Food Insecurity in Eastern and Southern Africa 67

Table 5.1. Definition of dimensions of food security

Dimension of food security	Definition
Availability	Availability focuses on an adequate variety of nutritious foods, which is influenced by the supply of food through production, trade, and market influences (Shetty 2017).
Access	Access includes physical, sociocultural, and economic factors, with an associated importance on the entitlement to produce and procure food. Access at a household level is the "reflection of the ability to grow and retain the food grown, for consumption, to purchase the food from the market, or to acquire it by a combination of strategies that are described as representing 'entitlements to food'" (Sen 1981, as cited in Shetty 2017, 183). This is influenced by policies, incentives, access to natural resources, and agricultural inputs, including biotechnology (Shetty 2017).
Utilization	Utilization is concerned with the bioavailability of nutrients in food and is influenced by environmental factors such as clean water and good sanitation (Shetty 2017).
Stability	Stability accounts for shorter-term disruptions, such as those created by market fluctuations, conflict, and natural disasters, that may undermine food security in the immediate or near future (Clapp et al. 2021, 3).
Agency	Agency, which refers to the capacity of individuals and groups to exercise a degree of control over their own circumstances and to provide meaningful input into governance processes, is widely seen today as an important aspect of addressing widening inequities within food systems, including imbalances of power among actors within those systems (Clapp et al. 2021, 3).
Sustainability	Sustainability emphasizes the connections among ecosystems, livelihoods, society, and political economy to maintain food systems and to support food security into the distant future (Clapp et al. 2021, 5). Sustainable Development Goal 2 explicitly ties sustainability to food security in its call to "end hunger, achieve food security and improved nutrition and promote sustainable agriculture" (UNDESA 2016, n.p.).

resolving hunger, addressing social inequities, and contributing to economic development. Further, a focus on sustainability addresses critical aspects of food systems and the interface between food and nutrition security (Swinburn et al. 2019). Food security, as a nascent construct, has expanded conceptually from commonly understood pillars (table 5.1) of availability, accessibility, utilization, and stability to include a focus on agency and sustainability (Clapp et al. 2021; HLPE 2017, 2019, 2020).

A shift in the discourse on sustainability signals a major departure from aspatial and, implicitly, antiurban orientation (Parnell 2016) to what has been a renewed focus on sustainable urbanization (Pieterse, Parnell, and Haysom 2018). Attention to territorial influences includes aspects of social and structural transitions, including economic development (Henderson and Kriticos 2018), climate-related influences (Tacoli 2013; Titz and Chiotha 2019), and market-centered dynamics around food production, trade, and food losses (Sheahan and Barrett 2017).

Creating a fuller understanding of urban food security, Battersby (2019) posits the necessity of broadening the orientation from what has traditionally been centered at the household or national levels, to account for structural inequalities. Battersby and Watson (2018) submit that the expansion of supermarkets, limited governance of local food systems, and the lack of structural and market support for informal food systems are critical challenges underpinning urban food systems. As a consequence of changes in market and consumption patterns, nutrition transitions are marked by heightened levels of obesity and associated noncommunicable diseases. Syndemic patterns of food insecurity, malnutrition, and poor health following the growth of supermarkets have affected lower-income households, who are increasingly accessing foods with high energy but low nutritional quality (Battersby and Watson 2018; Wiggins et al. 2015).

While the United Nation's Sustainable Development Agenda has assisted in establishing platforms for global policy responses on food security (UNDESA 2016), this chapter highlights areas where these efforts have fallen short—lacking the needed attention to food systems in vulnerable environments such as slums. Battersby (2019) asserts that while "the framing of food security has gradually shifted from a preoccupation with food availability to the inclusion of multiple dimensions of food security, food security policy and programmatic responses have lagged behind" (56). Consistent with this assertion, Burnett et al. (2017) suggested earlier that interventions aimed at the household or individual level have several shortcomings, failing to mitigate some of the structural challenges underpinning the dominance of a private sector food system.

This chapter delineates the scale and nature of food insecurity in slum environments, integrating research undertaken in the slums of Nairobi, Kenya. Further, it contributes to an understanding of vulnerabilities specific to slum environments. Finally, this chapter identifies opportunities that strengthen an understanding of urban food systems and adaptive mechanisms in urban slums within sub-Saharan Africa—necessitating a distinct policy response under the Sustainable Development Agenda.

2. Making a Case for Food Insecurity in the Slums of Eastern and Southern Africa

A necessary starting point is to identify the scale of food insecurity estimated in slums across eastern and southern Africa. Demographic changes referenced as rapid urbanization have exhibited variability in patterns of urban growth across sub-Saharan Africa, which are paralleled by patterns of uneven economic and human development—including disparities in food insecurity. Africa's urban population has risen from estimates of 27 percent in 1950 to 40 percent in 2015 and is projected to increase to 60 percent by 2050 (Teye 2018). While underdevelopment and poverty were traditionally held as drivers of migration, socioeconomic development has contributed to migration within and outside the region (Teye 2018).

More than half of Africa's urban population live in slums (55.2 percent; The Economist 2023). About 43 million people are estimated to be living in slums across eastern and aouthern Africa, with 80 percent of these across eastern African countries, and 20 percent in southern African countries (Beyer 2023). Similar to mixed patterns of urban growth that have been shown across Sub-Saharan African countries (Potts 2012), this analysis identifies variability in patterns of populations living in slums between 1990 and 2014. While these data demonstrate a stagnation or decline in the proportion of populations living in slums, an absolute growth ensues, largely because of natural population increases.

Country estimates with more than 5 million people living in slums include Angola, Ethiopia, Kenya, Madagascar, Mozambique, South Africa, and United Republic of Tanzania. In these countries, increases in absolute numbers are largely grounded in urban primacy or growth in large centralized urban sites as well as territorial influences and growth of secondary cities. Urban primacy has notably seen the widening of social inequities, gaps in infrastructure, and inadequate access to basic services (UNICEF 2012).

Beyond the demands of population growth, uneven economic growth, limited affordable housing, and challenges centered on urban infrastructure remain as spaces of exclusion and segregation (Amado et al. 2016; Roy 2014; Smit et al. 2017). While extreme forms of income poverty have been identified as an important determinant of urban food insecurity (Satterthwaite,

McGranahan, and Tacoli 2010), multidimensional aspects of poverty have been linked with disparities in human development (Lucci, Bhatkal, and Khan 2018).

In sub-Saharan Africa, urban dwellers, particularly the urban poor, maintain strong linkages with their rural homesteads as a survival strategy (de Laat 2008; Foeken and Owuor 2008; Mberu et al. 2013; Owuor 2007; Potts 2010). Remittance flows, identified as a common feature of circular migration, link human mobility and development (Akobeng 2016; Mberu et al. 2013). Debate centered on food security and migration emphasizes that remittance flows and the expenditure of remittances on basic needs lack a needed emphasis on development outcomes (Crush and Caesar 2017; Crush and Pendleton 2009). Further, these debates have been criticized for missing the connection between food shortages and personal insecurity as drivers of migration (Crush and Caesar 2017). One important contribution of this chapter is to establish the scale and magnitude of food insecurity for populations living in slums (Amado et al. 2016; Roy 2014; Smit et al. 2017).

Advances in global policy platforms have recently explored the interconnectedness between cities and food systems, with one recent example being the Milan Urban Food Policy Pact (MUFPP)—calling for commitments from mayors on strategic food policy actions (FAO, EU, and Fondazione Cariplo 2015). As part of these commitments, the MUFPP (FAO, EU, and Fondazione Cariplo 2015) addresses the "critical need for a socially inclusive and a rights-based approach in urban food policy" (n.p.). While MUFPP (FAO, EU, and Fondazione Cariplo 2015) represents a platform to exam food security in urban contexts, this work to date has not adequately represented sub-Saharan Africa as a region that bears some of the greatest remaining burden of food insecurity globally. Analysis of the MUFPP awards from 2016 through 2020 emphasizes the lack of engagement of regions in the Global South (World Population Review 2023), with only 4 percent of total awards centered on eastern Africa. This underrepresentation of the needs of urban areas in sub-Saharan Africa accentuates a critical gap in ensuring that evidence focused on vulnerable urban populations guides global food security policy.

Vulnerable urban households have adapted ways to meet their needs for basic services and food that differ from those in rural areas. Urban populations purchase and access over 90 percent of their food from stores or local markets (Cohen and Garrett 2010), which contrasts with the prominence of producing food for consumption in rural areas. The MUFPP puts forward signature strategies of urban and peri-urban agriculture. While urban agriculture has largely been promoted through the lens of urban or peri-urban food systems (Korth et al. 2014; Lee-Smith 2010), an emerging body of research shows limited participation in urban agriculture amid rapid changes in urban food markets (Battersby 2012; Crush, Hovorka, and Tevera 2017; Frayne, McCordic, and Shilomboleni 2016; Satterthwaite, McGranahan, and Tacoli 2010).

Concerns regarding the dominance of urban agriculture as a food security strategy has been raised by lead researchers in southern Africa—identifying challenges in the transference of this rural production-centered approach "uncritically" to poor urban settings (Crush, Hovorka, and Tevera 2017). Analysis across eleven cities as part of the AFSUN initiative shows that less than one-fifth of low-income urban households produce their own food, with the majority of cities falling well below this regional average (ranging from 3 percent to 10 percent; Crush, Hovorka, and Tevera 2017). Conversely, most urban households identified obtaining food from "supermarkets (79%), the informal sector (70%) and small retail and fast food outlets" (Frayne et al. 2010, 31). The AFSUN analysis also identified that three-quarters of households undertaking urban agriculture remained food insecure (Crush, Hovorka, and Tevera 2017).

While MUFPP presents urban agriculture as a prominent strategy, AFSUN analysis suggests that urban agriculture does not contribute to improved food security among poor households—with some evidence associating it with worsening food insecurity and dietary diversity (Crush, Hovorka, and Tevera 2017). Further, systematic review of agricultural strategies identifies constraints faced by vulnerable households, including the lack of access to land, credit, and water, as well as public health concerns, particularly in relation to the safety of water and environmental contamination (Korth et al. 2014). For urban agriculture to be presented as a prominent strategy, further evidence is needed on its ability to improve food security for vulnerable populations in slums.

3. Food Insecurity in the Slums of Eastern and Southern Africa

Countries such as Ethiopia, South Africa, and Kenya have the largest incidence of food insecure populations living in slum conditions (table 5.2). With limited analysis of the scale of food insecurity in slum populations

72 Social Determinants of Health

Table 5.2. Estimates of severely food insecure populations in the slums of eastern and southern Africa

Country	Severe food insecurity in total population, 2014 to 2016 (%)[a]	Severe food insecurity/ HFIAP in cities (%)[b]	Severe food insecurity/ HFIAP in slum settlements (%)	Projected population in slum settlements (in 000s)[c]	Estimated population living in slums with severe food insecurity (in 000s)
Ethiopia	—	—	75[d]	13,570.3	10,177.7
Kenya	19	—	50[e]	6,426.6	3,213.3
Madagascar	—	—	17[f]	6,272.5	1,066.3
Malawi	52	21[b]	72[g]	1,807.6	1301.5
Mozambique	40	54[b]	38[h]	6,788.6	2,579.7
Rwanda	—	—	44[i]	1,792.3	788.6
Somalia	—	57[j]	50[j]	3108.1	1554.1
South Africa	22	27/60/68[b]	80[k]	7,858.6	6,286.9
Uganda	—	—	68[l]	3,282.5	2,232.1
United Republic of Tanzania	31	—	—	7,952.3	—
Zambia	—	69[b]	94[j]	3,282.7	3,085.7
Zimbabwe	—	72[b]	95[j]	1,191.0	1,131.5
Total	—	—	—	—	33,417.4

HFIAP = household food insecurity access prevalence,

[a] FAO 2020.

[b] African Food Security Urban Network (AFSUN) baseline studies in Blantyre, Lusaka, Harare, and Cape Town in 2008–9 (Frayne et al. 2010). In South Africa, three cities were surveyed, with variations in the proportion of severe food insecurity (HFIAP): 27% in Johannesburg, 60% in Msunduzi, and 68% in Cape Town.

[c] UNDESA 2019.

[d] Birhane et al. 2014.

[e] Kimani-Murage et al. 2014.

[f] Wambogo et al. 2018.

[g] Chilanga and Riley 2017.

[h] McCordic and Abrahamo 2019.

[i] Agho et al. 2019.

[j] WFP 2012. Severe food insecurity was assessed using food consumption scoring and not HFIAP (as per other studies referenced in this table). In Somalia, food insecurity is being measured for internally displaced populations (living in settlements) rather than slum settlements.

[k] Naicker, Mathee, and Teare 2015.

[l] Nantale et al. 2017.

across eastern and southern Africa, estimates using best available sources of data draw attention to the magnitude, with an estimated 33 million people severely food insecure (table 5.2).

The burdens of food insecurity and malnutrition in sub-Saharan Africa represent a synergy between food, nutrition, and health. Syndemic patterns of disease, conceptualized as the triple burden of HIV, TB, and food insecurity, are increasingly observed in southern African cities (Caesar and Crush. 2017; Crush et al. 2011; Fielding-Miller et al. 2014). Most recently, the influence of the COVID-19 pandemic draws attention to the interface between health and food insecurity (Béné 2020). Pandemic measures in slum settlements disrupted informal markets and significantly challenged household access to food (Wanyama, Gödecke, and Qaim 2019; Wertheim-Heck 2020; Wertheim-Heck, Raneri, and Oosterveer 2019). Further, nutrition transitions in eastern and southern Africa accentuate dichotomies in malnutrition—with the growth of obesity coexisting in the same household as children who are undernourished in many urban contexts and slums (Kimani-Murage et al. 2015; Ng et al. 2014; Swinburn et al. 2019). These dichotomies, particularly the emergence of obesity, can mask the visibility of some of the most severe forms of malnutrition, hunger, and food insecurity in slum contexts.

Complex relationships within food systems in slums, as well as interrelated social, economic, and environmental influences, remain critical for ending hunger and improving food and nutrition security (Garnett et al. 2013; Ingram, Ericksen, and Liverman 2012). In sub-Saharan Africa, climate influences the availability of food, with land degradation and natural hazards such as drought and flooding affecting production and the volatility of food price fluctuation (Swartzendruber 2014).

Alternate and informal food networks serve as main sources of food in slum environs (Haysom and Tawodzera 2018). This contrasts subsistence production supporting households in rural areas and the growth of supermarketization in urban areas (Battersby and Peyton 2014; Crush and Frayne 2018; Peyton, Moseley, and Battersby 2015). Therefore, advancing sustainability of food security for households in slums requires understanding these informal food systems in relation to the environment, the interface between food and nutrition security, as well as the need to preserve Indigenous food practices (Swinburn et al. 2019). While increasing evidence shows variability between broader urban areas and vulnerable areas such as slums (Crush, Frayne, and Pendleton 2012; Naicker, Mathee, and Teare 2015; Nantale et al, 2017), there is limited analysis contrasting dimensions of household food insecurity between these settings.

Vulnerable households in slums have heightened and sustained levels of food insecurity—influenced by social determinants of gender and employment. Thematic analysis of in-depth interviews with households in Korogocho and Mukuru slum settlements in Nairobi during 2018 identified that many households describe living on the edge of hunger—constantly restricting the amount of food consumed and eating street foods or foods from the dump (Beyer 2023). These choices involved trade-offs between access to food and the safety of the food they consumed. Households also identified begging for food—which often resulted in their children receiving some small portion that countered their inability to obtain enough food on a daily basis (Beyer 2023).

Further, a gender gap exists, with female-headed households having heightened levels of food insecurity. This gap is attributed to the variation in earning, with female-headed households averaging two-thirds the income of male-headed households (Beyer 2023). In Korogocho, one of the slum areas where research was undertaken, significantly more (65 percent) of female-headed households were severely food insecure compared with male-headed households (53 percent; p < .001; Beyer 2023). Likewise, in another slum area of Mukuru, a significantly higher proportion of female-headed households were severely food insecure (41 percent) compared with male-headed households (29 percent; p < .001; Beyer 2023). Women shared that the variability in their levels of food security were a result of income constraints and competing demands between providing food and meeting other needs, such as paying medical costs, burial costs, overdue rent to avoid eviction, and outstanding school fees so that children aren't sent home (Beyer 2023).

4. Slum-Specific Shock and Stressors on Food Insecurity

In addition to the influence of drought on food price increases, informal slum settlements also bear specific vulnerabilities, including floods and landslides and the exposure of houses to wind, heat, and water hazards (Tacoli 2013). Further, many of the food systems in slums are informal and at risk for environmental contamination—affecting access to and the safe utilization of food.

4.1. Periods of Food Price Increases

Broader literature on periods of food price increases identified that food insecurity worsened among the poorest households during periods of food price increases (Cohen and Garrett 2010). The AFSUN 2007–8 baseline analysis in eleven cities across southern Africa showed that household income was a significant predictor of the negative impact of rising food prices on household food security (McCordic and Frayne 2017). The AFSUN analysis also identified that the poorest households would have needed to raise their incomes by 22 percent to maintain the same food basket (Frayne et al. 2010).

Food prices are known to be a recurring challenge for vulnerable urban households, with a sequela of millions more people moving into more extreme forms of poverty in low- and middle-income countries (World Bank 2010). During the period following the 2009 global crisis, upward of an 8 percent increase in levels of undernourishment or hunger ensued in sub-Saharan Africa (World Bank 2011). The 2009 periods of food price increases also demonstrated a profound effect on household food insecurity in slums (Kimani-Murage et al. 2014; Ruel et al., 2010).

Two periods of March to May 2015 and June to July 2016 were periods of local food price increases in the slums of Nairobi (Beyer 2023). Subcomponents of the Household Food Insecurity and Access Scale (HFIAS) scores (table 5.3) explore dimensions of food security and more extreme measures of hunger during these periods (Beyer 2023).

During June to August 2016 (a period of food price increase), households in both slums worried more often about having enough food (noted by increases in HFIAS 1—measuring the stability of food) and reported an increase in the times they ate foods that were less preferred (HFIAS 2—measuring the acceptability of food; figure 5.1; Beyer 2023). Further, there were substantial increases in households experiencing hunger (HFIAS 7, 8, 9—measuring the quantity and stability of food) during the period of June to August 2016 compared with other months of analysis (Beyer 2023).

This period also accentuates a greater degree of hunger for households, who experienced, on average, for at least two weeks, a 2.7-fold increase in absolute hunger compared with other months of study (table 5.3; Beyer 2023). Further, periods of food price increases were also aligned with challenges in dimensions of availability and access, including the quality, quantity, and stability of food.

4.2. Environmental Shocks

While there is limited evidence on environmental shocks faced by households in slums, findings from research in Nairobi identify the influence

Table 5.3. Subcomponents of the Household Food Insecurity And Access Scale (HFIAS) scores

Number	HFIAS and HHS reference	Focus	Question	Dimension of food security being assessed
1	HFIAS	Worry about enough food	In the past 30 days, how often did you worry that your household (HH) would not have enough food?	Stability
2	HFIAS	Eating nonpreferred foods	In the past 30 days, how often were you or any HH member not able to eat the kinds of foods you preferred?	Acceptability
3	HFIAS	Limited variety of foods	In the past 30 days, how often did you or any HH member have to eat a limited variety of foods?	Quality/ diversity
4	HFIAS	Eating unwanted foods	In the past 30 days, how often did you or any HH member have to eat foods you did not want to eat?	Acceptability
5	HFIAS	Smaller meal	In the past 30 days, how often did you or any HH member have to eat a smaller meal than you felt like you needed?	Quantity
6	HFIAS	Fewer meals	In the past 30 days, how often did you or any HH member have to eat fewer meals in a day?	Quantity
7	HFIAS/ HHS	No food in house	In the past 30 days, how often was there no food in your HH?	Quantity
8	HFIAS/ HHS	Hungry at night	In the past 30 days, how often did you or any HH member go to sleep at night hungry?	Stability[*]
9	HFIAS/ HHS	Hungry day and night	In the past 30 days, how often did you or any HH member have to go a whole day without eating?	Quantity

Source: Adapted from Maxwell et al. (2013, 13).

Note: Each question is rated against frequency: 0 = never; 1 = rarely; 2 = sometimes; and 3 = often. HHS = Household Hunger Scale.

[*] This question could also be classified as a "sufficiency."

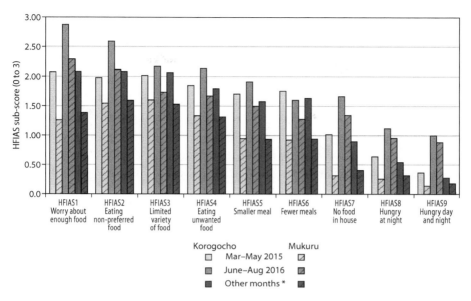

Fig. 5.1. Household Food Insecurity and Access Scale (HFIAS) scores during periods of food price increase (March to May 2015 and June to August 2016) for Korogocho and Mukuru. Source: Beyer 2023.
* "Other months" for both slums use data from July 2014–February 2015 and June 2015–May 2016.

of floods, fires, and violence on food insecurity (tables 5.4 and 5.5; Beyer 2023). Households emphasized that shocks and disturbances such as fires, water damage from heavy rains and flooding, and violence commonly affected their ability to earn a full day's income, damaged household assets, and often resulted in personal injury—indirectly affecting the ability to secure enough income to purchase food to eat. Heavy rains and flooding had a notable influence on decreasing a household's ability to earn income—with attention paid to repairing damaged structures and drying personal items that were saturated. Fires were associated with a 61 percent increase in severe hunger (tables 5.4 and 5.5). Not only did acute hunger feature in the period following fires, but households that moved into slum housing following a fire, due to increased affordability, experienced longer-term challenges in job opportunities and a notable worsening in the quality of food consumed.

Table 5.4. Shocks and food insecurity in Mukuru slum settlement (July 2014–August 2016), multivariate regression analysis

	Household Food Insecurity Access Scale (HFIAS)			Household Hunger Scale (HHS)			Severe food insecurity			Severe hunger		
	Coef.	Std. error	p value	Coef.	Std. error	p value	OR	Std. error	p value	OR	Std. error	p value
Illness in household	**1.01**[a]	0.164	0.000	**0.16**[a]	0.033	0.000	**1.41**[a]	0.097	0.000	1.23	0.219	0.245
Diarrhea in children (<5 years)	−0.02	0.290	0.954	0.02	0.058	0.721	0.95	0.109	0.638	1.06	0.276	0.833
Violence experienced by household member	**1.05**[a]	0.209	0.000	**0.25**[a]	0.042	0.000	**1.36**[a]	0.114	0.000	**2.12**[a]	0.383	0.000
Perceived personal insecurity	**1.95**[a]	0.160	0.000	**0.21**[a]	0.032	0.000	**1.72**[a]	0.121	0.000	**2.05**[a]	0.409	0.000
Fire	**1.72**[a]	0.280	0.000	**0.25**[a]	0.056	0.000	**1.65**[a]	0.186	0.000	**1.61**[b]	0.363	0.034
Flooding	**0.67**[a]	0.153	0.000	**0.08**[b]	0.030	0.009	**1.39**[a]	0.090	0.000	0.86	0.145	0.377
Sample size (households)	5,650	—	—	5,650	—	—	5,650	—	—	5,650	—	—

Source: Beyer 2023.

The estimation model of HFIAS score and HHS score against variables of SS uses ordinary least squares (OLS). OR = odds ratio. Measure of fit for HFIAS is R^2 0.31 and for HHS is R^2 0.18. A logistic regression modeled the relationship between severe household food insecurity (dummy variable based on HFIAS scores) and severe household hunger (dummy variable based on HHS scores). Analysis was controlled by a time variable (month/year). Measure of fit for HFIAS is R^2 0.25 and for HHS is R^2 0.14.

[a] $p < 0.001$
[b] $p < 0.05$

Table 5.5. Shocks and food insecurity in Korogocho slum settlement (September 2014–August 2016), multivariate regression analysis

	Household Food Insecurity Access Scale (HFIAS)			Household Hunger Scale (HHS)			Severe food insecurity			Severe hunger		
	Coef.	Std. error	p value	Coef.	Std. error	p value	OR	Std. error	p value	OR	Std. error	p value
Illness in household	**0.87**[a]	0.159	0.000	**0.27**[a]	0.037	0.000	**1.41**[a]	0.091	0.000	1.08	0.144	0.578
Diarrhea in children (<5 years)	−0.17	0.289	0.567	0.01	0.068	0.892	0.97	0.120	0.804	1.16	0.244	0.484
Violence experienced by household member	**1.94**[a]	0.182	0.000	**0.25**[a]	0.043	0.000	**1.52**[a]	0.117	0.000	**1.33**[b]	0.195	0.052
Perceived personal insecurity	**1.17**[a]	0.204	0.000	**0.10**[b]	0.048	0.041	**1.26**[b]	0.104	0.005	0.87	0.141	0.394
Fire	**0.54**[c]	0.324	0.093	**0.12**[c]	0.076	0.110	1.07	0.148	0.615	1.00	0.251	0.985
Flooding	**0.37**[b]	0.166	0.024	−0.02	0.039	0.527	1.03	0.070	0.634	0.95	0.132	0.710
Sample size (households)	5,588	—	—	5,588	—	—	5,588	—	—	5,588	—	—

Source: Beyer 2023.

The estimation model of HFIAS score and HHS score against variables of SS uses ordinary least squares (OLS). Measure of fit for HFIAS is R^2 0.31 and for HHS is R^2 0.18. A logistic regression modeled the relationship between severe household food insecurity (dummy variable based on HFIAS scores) and severe household hunger (dummy variable based on HHS scores). Analysis was controlled by a time variable (month/year). Measure of fit for HFIAS is R^2 0.24 and for HHS is R^2 0.16.

[a] $p < 0.001$
[b] $p < 0.05$
[c] $p < 0.1$

4.3. Violence

To date there is limited analysis exploring the relationship between personal insecurity or violence and food insecurity. One recent study undertaken in southern Africa examines the relationship between intimate partner violence and food insecurity (Hatcher et al. 2019).

From research in the slums of Nairobi, gendered forms of violence also had a direct influence on food security. In-depth interviews with women identified that they experienced sexual violence in their attempt to gain access to income and food (Beyer 2023). Women identified that they could always access food from the neighboring dump, but that this required sex as an exchange—either voluntary or through forced rape or gang sex. Men experience violence while moving around in the broader community and scavenging, with the severity of injuries resulting from physical assault, negatively affecting their ability to work, with some injuries resulting in the loss of employment. Households identified that having a family member experience violence, such as mugging or being assaulted while scavenging, or having their household robbed affected their ability to earn income and competed with scarce resources to replace assets. Measures taken to enhance personal security required household members to deploy strategies that reduced their ability to gain a full day's wage, including travel to work within daytime hours, returning from work early, and lengthening travel to avoid areas known to be insecure. Households that experienced violence had a significant 30 percent to twofold increase in severe hunger (tables 5.4 and 5.5).

These findings highlight social and environmental influences specific to slums and their effects on household food insecurity—with fires and violence having the most profound influence on hunger.

5. Adaptive Capacity and Food Insecurity

While food is largely available in informal food markets, households in slums face substantial challenges accessing this food and ensuring the safety and sustainability of food utilized at a household level. In slums, households predominantly purchased food items from the local market (87 percent), with the remaining purchasing cooked food from the streets (Kimani-Murage et al. 2014). Poorer households notably shared meals with neighbors or other households (44.5 percent), ate food provided by others (34.1 percent), and borrowed food (29.2 percent), with 5.5 percent receiving some of their food through remittances (Battersby 2012). Marginal income from casual employment in slum settlements resulted in individuals borrowing food or buying food in smaller amounts to address their daily needs (Githiri et al. 2016).

Food credit is used by one out of every two households in slums and more frequently by households with children under 15 years of age (Amendah, Buigut, and Mohamed 2014; Beyer 2023; Beyer, Chandhuri, and Kagima 2016). While food expenditure ideally runs at approximately 30 percent of household income, a disproportionate burden ensues when households spend 50 percent or more of their income on food. This burden is demonstrated by households in slums of Nairobi, which identified spending 70 percent to 100 percent of their income on food (Beyer 2023). As a result, households often use strategies and make trade-offs to balance household expenditures such as food, school, and rent. While food credit has been shown to significantly improve food security (Amendah, Buigut, and Mohamed 2014), research undertaken in two slums of Nairobi in 2018 advances the understanding of the use of this as well as other adaptive strategies.

5.1. Food Credit

In Korogocho and Mukuru slum settlements, obtaining and using food credit, taking additional actions to get food or income, and promoting personal security were prominent coping behaviors (figure 5.2; Beyer 2023). In Korogocho, the use of food credit and additional actions to get food or income were associated with improved levels of severe food insecurity (see tables 5.6 and 5.7). Multivariate findings for the use of various coping strategies against food security measures (such as HFIAS; Coates, Swindale, and Bilinsky 2007; Becquey et al. 2010) demonstrated that the use of food credit also had a positive relationship with improved levels of food security during one of the periods of food price increases—demonstrating a 25 percent improvement in levels of food security among the poorest households during these periods (Beyer 2023). In many respects, the influence of the use of food credit on improved food security indicates "what worked," presenting food credit as an adaptive capacity, even during periods of food price increases. Limitations in the use of food credit were identified by extremely vulnerable households, who shared that they were not able to access, negotiate, and leverage food credit—often being harassed due to their inability to repay this debt (Beyer 2023).

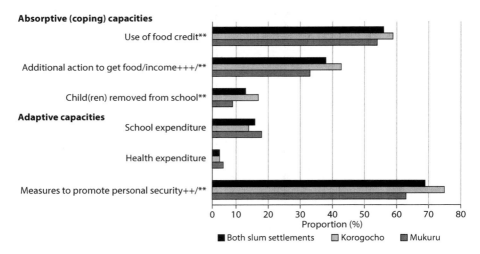

Fig. 5.2. Household absorptive and adaptive capacities (%) by slum settlement, July 2014 to August 2016. Source: Beyer 2023.
** $p < 0.001$ for variance between Korogocho and Mukuru slum settlements.
++ Measures to promote personal security include using escorts, using unusual/alternate routes, and coming home earlier than usual.
+++ Additional actions to get food or money include taking up a second job, selling an asset, taking a loan, and begging.

5.2. Hustling for Income

Another adaptive behavior centers on employment, or what many households identify as "hustling" to find work and food. While hustling or scavenging in the dump provided enough food to eat, there were substantial challenges with the safety and quality of this food—with people at times reporting having eaten "rotten" food, with a sequel of illness as a result. Hustling for women also involved sex work, which was suggested to be used by approximately one-third of younger women. In-depth interviews and focus groups stressed that after several years of sex work, women and their households were left more vulnerable, suffering related effects of sex work, such as living with AIDS and sexually transmitted infections. Further, as the result of pregnancies from lack of contraception during these years of sex work, women also carried an increased responsibility to care for higher numbers of dependents. These households described facing extreme hunger, often drinking black tea to curb hunger, and having children cry themselves to sleep

Table 5.6. Resilience capacities and food insecurity in Mukuru slum settlement (July 2014–August 2016), multivariate regression analysis

	Household Food Insecurity Access Scale (HFIAS)			Household Hunger Scale (HHS)			Severe food insecurity			Severe hunger		
	Coef.	Std. error	p value	Coef.	Std. error	p value	OR	Std. error	p value	OR	Std. error	p value
Use of food credit	**3.01**[a]	0.250	0.000	**0.26**[a]	0.054	0.000	**2.15**[a]	0.248	0.000	1.61	0.482	0.110
Additional action to get food/ income	**1.89**[a]	0.257	0.000	**0.41**[a]	0.056	0.000	**2.11**[a]	0.228	0.000	**2.87**[a]	0.800	0.000
Child(ren) removed from school	**2.71**[a]	0.542	0.000	**0.80**[a]	0.118	0.000	**4.16**[a]	1.044	0.000	**3.48**[a]	1.143	0.000
Health expenditure	**0.01**[a]	0.015	0.000	**0.01**[a]	0.003	0.000	**1.02**[a]	0.007	0.000	1.01	0.011	0.203
School expenditure	−0.08	0.139	0.586	0.01	0.030	0.650	1.06	0.067	0.354	0.91	0.143	0.542
Measures to promote personal security	**2.04**[a]	0.244	0.000	**0.13**[b]	0.053	0.014	**1.63**[a]	0.183	0.000	1.30	0.335	0.307
Sample size (households)	6,993	—	—	6,993	—	—	6,993	—	—	6,993	—	—

Source: Beyer 2023.

The estimation model of HFIAS score and HHS score against variables of resilience capacities uses ordinary least squares (OLS). Measure of fit for HFIAS is R^2 0.30 and for HHS is R^2 0.15. A logistic regression modeled the relationship between severe household food insecurity (dummy variable based on HFIAS scores) and severe household hunger (dummy variable based on HHS scores). Odds ratios are presented. Analysis was controlled for by the use of socio-economic variables (household size, equivalized monthly household income, household dependent on casual labor, female-household headship and level of education of household head) as well as a time variable (month/year). Measure of fit for HFIAS is R^2 0.31 and for HHS is R^2 0.18.

[a] $p < 0.001$
[b] $p < 0.05$

Table 5.7. Adaptive capacities and food insecurity in Korogocho slum settlement (September 2014–August 2016), multivariate regression analysis

	Household Food Insecurity Access Scale (HFIAS)			Household Hunger Scale (HHS)			Severe food insecurity			Severe hunger		
	Coef.	Std. error	p value	Coef.	Std. error	p value	OR	Std. error	p value	OR	Std. error	p value
Use of food credit	**0.37**[c]	0.206	0.070	0.02	0.048	0.604	**0.85**[c]	0.078	0.080	1.16	0.271	0.535
Additional action to get food/income	0.03	0.194	0.891	**−0.09**[b]	0.045	0.036	**0.75**[a]	0.065	0.001	1.02	0.214	0.919
Child(ren) removed from school	**1.52**[a]	0.289	0.000	**0.44**[a]	0.067	0.000	**1.76**[a]	0.242	0.000	**1.63**[c]	0.422	0.058
Health expenditure	**0.03**[b]	0.014	0.040	**0.01**[a]	0.003	0.001	**1.03**[a]	0.008	0.001	1.01	0.012	0.199
School expenditure	**0.28**[c]	0.153	0.064	**0.10**[b]	0.036	0.004	**1.26**[a]	0.087	0.001	0.98	0.175	0.929
Measures to promote personal security	**1.72**[a]	0.233	0.000	**−0.12**[b]	0.054	0.031	**1.61**[a]	0.164	0.000	**0.64**[c]	0.147	0.053
Sample size (households)	6,878	—	—	6,878	—	—	6,878	—	—	6,878	—	—

Source: Beyer 2023.

The estimation model of HFIAS score and HHS score against variables of resilience capacities uses ordinary least squares (OLS). Measure of fit for HFIAS is R^2 0.30 and for HHS is R^2 0.15. A logistic regression modeled the relationship between severe household food insecurity (dummy variable based on HFIAS scores) and severe household hunger (dummy variable based on HHS scores). Odds ratios (ORs) are presented. Analysis was controlled for by the use of socio-economic variables (household size, equivalized monthly household income, household dependent on casual labor, female-household headship, and level of education of household head) as well as a time variable (month/year). Measure of fit for HFIAS is R^2 0.20 and for HHS is R^2 0.15.

[a] $p < 0.001$
[b] $p < 0.05$
[c] $p < 0.1$

when the mother comes home empty handed, with no food, or not enough food at the end of the day.

5.3. Removal of Children from School

While removing child(ren) from school was identified by households in Nairobi as an absorptive capacity—to cope with the lack of money—it did not have an influence on improving levels of household food security. It is important to note, however, that during periods of food price increases, there was a 100 percent increase in child(ren) being removed from school (Beyer 2023). The practice of removing children from school was associated with heightened levels of severe food insecurity and nonsignificant reductions in hunger in Korogocho and Mukuru slums (tables 5.6 and 5.7). While trade-offs between debt for school fees and purchasing food were not significant, it is important to consider the depth of austerity measures households used. One question that emerges from this analysis is the mitigating influence that removing children from school played in alleviating more extreme forms of hunger and food insecurity.

5.4. Community Support and Help from Neighbors

Research analysis from Nairobi identified that help received from neighbors and assistance from community organizations made a difference, with variation among some households, stating that they did not hear about these benefits and received no support or received limited or sporadic support (Beyer 2023). Although food transfers from rural areas played an intermittent role from a week to a few weeks following food shared from a rural homestead after harvest, the incremental support provided by neighbors helped households on a daily or weekly basis.

Nairobi-based analysis identified the flow of cash in both directions, with incremental cash from households in slums given to rural households to cope with costs for funerals or medical care, and food and cash shared by rural households with households in slums to meet heightened daily needs, such as school fees and medical costs (Beyer 2023). Analysis focused on Nairobi slums found that 80 percent of older migrants maintained contact with their rural origin homes over the course of a year (Mberu et al. 2013). The AFSUN findings vary slightly, identifying more of a one-directional flow, with food transfers being mobilized from rural to urban households, and cash being shared by urban to rural households (Crush and Caesar 2016).

Some households in the slums did not provide support to members of their extended family in rural areas—stating, "I have nothing to give" (Beyer 2023). These findings contribute to the understanding of various adaptive behaviors used in slums, their influence on food insecurity, and considerations for future analysis and for shaping various policy responses.

6. Generating a Greater Understanding of Food Insecurity in Slums

Challenges in the conceptualization of urban food insecurity in regions of Africa, Latin America, and developing parts of Asia are influenced by weakness in approaches to its measurement—failing to capture disparities and underlying determinants of urban food insecurity (Patel and McMichael 2009; Satterthwaite 2011; Tacoli 2013). Critiques also identify the lack of granularity in analysis using broad rural/urban cohorts rather than analysis using sublocations (Lucci and Bhatkal 2014; Lucci, Bhatkal, and Khan 2018).

Most studies examine food insecurity in rural contexts, urban contexts, or slum contexts, with limited intergeographic comparisons. Comparisons between various geographic settings in the AFSUN cohort were undertaken in different periods, which limits the ability to interpret these findings. The most substantive gap in evidence involves the lack of comparisons of rural and slum contexts. Cross-geographic comparisons have utility for distinctions in dimensions and determinants of food insecurity, as well as in the influences of context-specific shocks and resilience capacities. Future investment in comparative studies would also enable a broader conceptualization of food insecurity.

Archer et al. (2020) identifies the utility of assets as a safety net for those "who work in the informal sector, lacking job security or social security protection," as well as their role in providing essential social and moral support (172). While certain types of shocks in slum settlements, such as floods or fires, may damage a household's assets, Moser et al. (2008) have identified that the use of assets plays a critical role in the adaptive capacity of low-income urban households. While most of the current literature focuses on areas of vulnerability or coping behaviors, future exploration could include aspects of adaptation and resilience—or what works (Alinovi, Mane, and Romano, 2009).

Measures of food insecurity that are sensitive to slum contexts need to

Food Insecurity in Eastern and Southern Africa   87

incorporate context-specific coping strategies. Much of the current measures of food insecurity, specifically the coping strategies index, have been developed and validated for use in rural contexts. Slum-specific behaviors, such as obtaining food from the dump, eating street food, and begging for food, should be incorporated as coping strategies utilized for slum-centered analysis.

A final area of consideration focuses on the measure of hunger—demonstrating opportunities for using the Household Hunger Scale (HHS) as a more extreme form of food insecurity. The HHS scores examine partial or complete lack of food in a household during a 24-hour period (Ballard et al. 2011; Deitchler et al. 2011). This measure of hunger is particularly relevant in slum contexts, where forms of severe food insecurity exist, as well as variation between different geospatial contexts, such as rural areas and slums. One opportunity that could have enhanced the use of household hunger was that of the AFSUN initiative, which gathered data but did not analyze this data in referenced publications.

Given the synergistic or cumulative influence of these shocks on household food insecurity, future analysis could establish the causal pathways from various types of slum-specific shocks on household food insecurity. Recent studies have begun to model the influence of multiple shocks as well as explore these relationships through qualitative approaches.

7. Conclusion

In an era when global efforts are focused on planetary health and how food production and consumption can be sustained within environmental limits (Friel et al. 2008; Springmann et al. 2018), commitments remain for "leaving no one behind" as part of the sustainable development aims for "zero hunger" (UNDESA 2016). Greater policy attention and programmatic response are needed to address the challenges underlying food insecurity in slums.

Policy directives aim at addressing social and environmental stressors affecting food security—such as personal insecurity and gendered forms of violence, informal sector influences on employment and food markets, and mechanisms to respond to fires and floods—mitigating the influence of these on food security. Urban analysis needs to ensure appropriate sampling and disaggregated analysis—having slum-based populations as a subset of urban as well as expanding a focus on comparative geospatial analysis. Future analysis would also benefit from validation of measures supporting food insecurity and hunger sensitive to households in slums. Analysis that supports a deeper understanding of vulnerability would examine the compounded influence of multiple shocks and stressors on food insecurity. Additionally, adaptive capacities specific to slum environments will aid in an understanding of dimensions supporting the sustainability of food security.

Over the last decade, there has been an absolute growth of slums and urban poverty (Lucci, 2014), reflecting the challenges facing an estimated 43 million people across eastern and southern Africa. Further, analysis using the best available sources of data identified that approximately 33 million people living in slums across eastern and southern Africa are food insecure.

Advances in global policy platforms have recently explored the interconnectedness between cities and food systems; a review of the MUFPP (FAO, EU, and Fondazione Cariplo, 2015) identified gaps in representation for sub-Saharan Africa as well as for more vulnerable slum environments. A review of South Africa's government-led child support grant, an unconditional social transfer, reported a positive benefit on child nutrition and food security, with food poverty among beneficiaries in the lowest quintile reduced from 27 percent to 20 percent (Leroy, Ruel, and Verhofstadt 2009). The child support grant contributed to an increase in food expenditures at the household level, with more than half of recipients citing the greatest share of income going toward purchasing food.

There is complimentary analysis on the role of social protection and cash transfer pilots from work undertaken in Nairobi, Kenya. Findings from the Nairobi Urban Health and Demographic Surveillance System (NUHDSS) show that when a household in slum settlements is engaging in some form of social protection (e.g., "merry-go-rounds" or cash transfers), they are 1.6 times less likely to go hungry and 1.9 times more likely to eat regular meals (Amendah, Buigut, and Mohamed 2014). Further, households that received the cash transfers reported an increase in meal frequency, a decrease in household food insecurity, and a doubling of dietary diversity scores over an eleven-month period (MacAuslan and Schofield 2011). With the scale of food insecurity in slum environments, it is essential for global policy efforts to establish interventions and guidance that responds to the realities of populations in slums—ensuring no one is left behind.

REFERENCES

Agho, Kingsley E., Christine Mukabutera, Monica Mukazi, Michael Ntambara, Irene Mbugua, Margy Dowling, and Joseph K. Kamara. 2019. "Moderate and Severe Household Food Insecurity Predicts Stunting and Severe Stunting among Rwanda Children Aged 6–59 Months Residing in Gicumbi District." *Maternal and Child Nutrition* 15 (3): e12767.

Akobeng, Eric. 2016. "Out of Inequality and Poverty: Evidence for the Effectiveness of Remittances in Sub-Saharan Africa." *Quarterly Review of Economics and Finance* 60:207–23.

Alinovi, L., E. Mane, and D. Romano. 2009. "Towards the Measurement of Household Resilience to Food Insecurity: Applying a Model to Palestinian Household Data." In *Deriving Food Security Information from National Household Budget Surveys: Experiences, Achievement, Challenges,* edited by R. Sibrian, 137–52. Rome: FAO.

Amado, Miguel P., Inês Ramalhete, António R. Amado, and João C. Freitas. 2016. "Regeneration of Informal Areas: An Integrated Approach." *Cities* 58:59–69.

Amendah, Djesika D., Steven Buigut, and Shukri Mohamed. 2014. "Coping Strategies among Urban Poor: Evidence from Nairobi, Kenya." *PLoS One* 9 (1): e83428.

Archer, Diane, Wijitbusaba Marome, Boonanan Natakun, Pattaradeth Mabangyang, and Nuttavikhom Phanthuwongpakdee. 2020. "The Role of Collective and Individual Assets in Building Urban Community Resilience." *International Journal of Urban Sustainable Development* 12 (2): 169–86.

Ballard, Terri, Jennifer Coates, Anne Swindale, and Megan Deitchler. 2011. *Household Hunger Scale (HHS): Indicator Definition and Measurement Guide.* Washington, DC: Food and Nutrition Technical Assistance III Project (FANTA).

Battersby, Jane. 2012. "Beyond the Food Desert: Finding Ways to Speak about Urban Food Security in South Africa." *Geografiska Annaler: Series B, Human Geography* 94 (2): 141–59.

Battersby, Jane. 2019. "The Food Desert as a Concept and Policy Tool in African Cities: An Opportunity and a Risk." *Sustainability* 11 (2): 458.

Battersby, Jane, and Stephen Peyton. 2014. "The Geography of Supermarkets in Cape Town: Supermarket Expansion and Food Access." *Urban Forum* 25 (2): 153–64.

Battersby, Jane, and Vanessa Watson. 2018. "Critically Assessing the Role of Informal Retailers." In *Integrating Food into Urban Planning,* edited by Yves Cabannes and Cecilia Marocchino, 186. London: UCL Press.

Becquey, Elodie, Yves Martin-Prevel, Pierre Traissac, Bernard Dembélé, Alain Bambara, and Francis Delpeuch. 2010. "The Household Food Insecurity Access Scale and an Index-Member Dietary Diversity Score Contribute Valid and Complementary Information on Household Food Insecurity in an Urban West-African Setting." *Journal of Nutrition* 140 (12): 2233–40.

Béné, Christophe. 2020. "Resilience of Local Food Systems and Links to Food Security–A Review of Some Important Concepts in the Context of COVID-19 and Other Shocks." *Food Security* 12 (4): 805–22.

Beyer, Linda. 2023. "Household Food Insecurity and Resilience in Slum Settlements of Nairobi, Kenya." Unpublished manuscript, University of Oxford, January 24.

Beyer, Linda, Jay Chandhuri, and Barbara Kagima. 2016. "Kenya's Focus on Urban Vulnerability and Resilience in the midst of Urban Transitions in Nairobi." *Development Southern Africa* 33 (1): 3–22.

Birhane, Tesfay, Solomon Shiferaw, Seifu Hagos, and Katia Sarla Mohindra. 2014. "Urban Food Insecurity in the Context of High Food Prices: A Community Based Cross Sectional Study in Addis Ababa, Ethiopia." *BMC Public Health* 14 (1): 1–8.

Burnett, Kristin, Kelly Skinner, Travis Hay, Joseph LeBlanc, and Lori Chambers. 2017. "Retail Food Environments, Shopping Experiences, First Nations and the Provincial Norths." *Health Promotion and Chronic Disease Prevention in Canada: Research, Policy and Practice* 37 (10): 333.

Caesar, Mary, and Jonathan Crush. 2017. "The Triple Burden of HIV, TB and Food Insecurity." In *Food and Nutrition Security in Southern African Cities*, edited by Bruce Frayne, Jonathan Crush, and Cameron McCordic, 135–55. New York: Routledge.

Chilanga, Emmanuel, and Liam Riley. 2017. *Food Insecurity in Informal Settlements in Lilongwe Malawi*. Urban Food Security Series No. 25. Southern African Migration Programme. Cape Town: African Food Security Urban Network.

Clapp, Jennifer, William G. Moseley, Barbara Burlingame, and Paola Termine. 2021. "The Case for a Six-Dimensional Food Security Framework." *Food Policy* 106:art. 102164.

Coates, Jennifer, Anne Swindale, and Paula Bilinsky. 2007. *Household Food Insecurity Access Scale (HFIAS) for Measurement of Food Access: Indicator Guide: Version 3*. Washington, DC: Food and Nutrition Technical Assistance III Project (FANTA).

Cohen, Marc J., and James L. Garrett. 2010. "The Food Price Crisis and Urban Food (in) Security." *Environment and Urbanization* 22 (2): 467–82.

Crush, Jonathan. 2013. "Linking Food Security, Migration and Development." *International Migration* 51 (5): 61–75.

Crush, Jonathan, and Mary Caesar. 2016. *Food Remittances: Migration and Food Security in Africa*. Cape Town: African Books Collective.

Crush, Jonathan, and Mary Caesar. 2017. *Food Remittances: Rural-Urban Linkages and Food Security in Africa*. London: International Institute for Environment and Development (IIED).

Crush, Jonathan, Scott Drimie, Bruce Frayne, and Mary Caesar. 2011. "The HIV and Urban Food Security Nexus in Africa." *Food Security* 3 (3): 347–62.

Crush, Jonathan, and Bruce Frayne. 2018. "The 'Supermarketization' of Food Supply and Retail: Private Sector Interests and Household Food Security." In *Food and Nutrition Security in Southern African Cities*, edited by Bruce Frayne, Jonathan Crush, and Cameron McCordic, 168–97. London: Routledge.

Crush, Jonathan, Bruce Frayne, and Wade Pendleton. 2012. "The Crisis of Food Insecurity in African Cities." *Journal of Hunger and Environmental Nutrition* 7 (2–3): 271–92.

Crush, Jonathan, Alice Hovorka, and Daniel Tevera. 2017. "Farming the City: The Broken Promise of Urban Agriculture." In *Food and Nutrition Security in Southern African Cities*, edited by Bruce Frayne, Jonathan Crush, and Cameron McCordic, 101–17. London: Routledge.

Crush, Jonathan, and Wade Pendleton. 2009. "Remitting for Survival: Rethinking the Development Potential of Remittances in Southern Africa." *Global Development Studies* 5 (3–4): 53–84.

Crush, Jonathan, and Liam Riley. 2017. "Urban Food Security, Rural Bias and the Global Development Agenda." HCP Discussion Paper No. 11. Hungry Cities Partnership, Waterloo, Ontario.

Deitchler, Megan, Terri Ballard, Anne Swindale, and Jennifer Coates. 2011. *Introducing a Simple Measure of Household Hunger for Cross-Cultural Use.* Technical Note No. 12. Washington, DC: Food and Nutrition Technical Assistance II Project.

de Laat, Joost. 2008. "Household Allocations and Endogenous Information." CIRPEE Working Paper No. 08-27, September 16.

The Economist. 2023. "Latin American Cities Are Becoming Far Nicer for Poorer Inhabitants: The World's Most Urbanised Region Holds Lessons for Developing Countries." *Economist*, January 12. https://www.economist.com/the-americas/2023/01/12/latin-american-cities-are-becoming-far-nicer-for-poorer-inhabitants.

Ezeh, Alex, Oyinlola Oyebode, David Satterthwaite, Yen-Fu Chen, Robert Ndugwa, Jo Sartori, Blessing Mberu, et al. 2017. "The History, Geography, and Sociology of Slums and the Health Problems of People Who Live in Slums." *Lancet* 389 (10068): 547–58.

FAO (Food and Agriculture Organization), EU (European Union), and Fondazione Cariplo. 2015. "Milan Urban Food Policy Pact." Food and Agriculture Organization of the United Nations.

FAO (Food and Agriculture Organization of the United Nations), ECA (United Nations Economic Commission for Africa), and AUC (African Union Commission). 2020. *Africa Regional Overview of Food Security and Nutrition 2019.* Accra: FAO.

Fielding-Miller, Rebecca, Zandile Mnisi, Darrin Adams, Stefan Baral, and Caitlin Kennedy. 2014. "'There Is Hunger in My Community': A Qualitative Study of Food Security as a Cyclical Force in Sex Work in Swaziland." *BMC Public Health* 14 (1): 1–10.

Foeken, Dick W. J., and Samuel O. Owuor. 2008. "Farming as a Livelihood Source for the Urban Poor of Nakuru, Kenya." *Geoforum* 39 (6): 1978–90.

Frayne, Bruce, Jonathan Crush, and Cameron McCordic. 2018. "Divorcing Food and Agriculture: Towards an Agenda for Urban Food Security Research." In *Food and Nutrition Security in Southern African Cities*, edited by Jonathan Crush and Cameron McCordic, 1–8. London: Routledge.

Frayne, Bruce, Cameron McCordic, and Helena Shilomboleni. 2016. "The Mythology of Urban Agriculture." In *Rapid Urbanisation, Urban Food Deserts and Food Security in Africa*, edited by Jonathan Crush and Jane Battersby, 19–31. Cham: Springer.

Frayne, Bruce, Wade Pendleton, Jonathan Crush, Ben Acquah, Jane Battersby-Lennard, Eugenio Bras, Asiyati Chiweza, et al. 2010. *The State of Urban Food Insecurity in Southern Africa.* Urban Food Security Series No. 2. Cape Town: African Food Security Urban Network.

Friel, Sharon, Michael Marmot, Anthony J. McMichael, Tord Kjellstrom, and Denny Vågerö. 2008. "Global Health Equity and Climate Stabilisation: A Common Agenda." *Lancet* 372 (9650): 1677–83.

Garnett, Tara, Michael C. Appleby, Andrew Balmford, Ian J. Bateman, Tim G. Benton, Phil Bloomer, Barbara Burlingame, et al. 2013. "Sustainable Intensification in Agriculture: Premises and Policies." *Science* 341 (6141): 33–34.

Githiri, Grace, Regina Ngugi, Patrick Njoroge, and Alice Sverdlik. 2016. "Nourishing Livelihoods: Recognising and Supporting Food Vendors in Nairobi's Informal Settlements." International Institute for Environment and Development, working paper, January. https://pubs.iied.org/pdfs/10762IIED.pdf.

Hatcher, Abigail M., Heidi Stöckl, Ruari-Santiago McBride, Mzwakhe Khumalo, and Nicola Christofides. 2019. "Pathways from Food Insecurity to Intimate Partner Violence Perpetration among Peri-urban Men in South Africa." *American Journal of Preventive Medicine* 56 (5): 765–72.

Haysom, Gareth, and Godfrey Tawodzera. 2018. "'Measurement Drives Diagnosis and Response': Gaps in Transferring Food Security Assessment to the Urban Scale." *Food Policy* 74:117–25.

Henderson, J. Vernon, and Sebastian Kriticos. 2018. "The Development of the African System of Cities." *Annual Review of Economics* 10:287–314.

HLPE (High Level Panel of Experts). 2017. *Nutrition and Food Systems*. HLPE Report 12. Rome: Committee on World Food Security. http://www.fao.org/3/a-i7846e.pdf.

HLPE (High Level Panel of Experts). 2019. *Agroecological and Other Innovative Approaches for Sustainable Agriculture and Food Systems that Enhance Food Security and Nutrition*. HLPE Report 14. Rome: Committee on World Food Security. http://www.fao.org/3/ca5602en/ca5602en.pdf.

HLPE (High Level Panel of Experts). 2020. *Food Security and Nutrition: Building a Global Narrative Towards 2030*. HLPE Report 15. Rome: Committee on World Food Security. http://www.fao.org/3/ca9731en/ca9731en.pdf.

Ingram, John, Polly Ericksen, and Diana Liverman. 2012. *Food Security and Global Environmental Change*. London: Routledge.

Kimani-Murage, Elizabeth W., Stella K. Muthuri, Samuel O. Oti, Martin K. Mutua, Steven Van De Vijver, and Catherine Kyobutungi. 2015. "Evidence of a Double Burden of Malnutrition in Urban Poor Settings in Nairobi, Kenya." *PLoS One* 10 (6): e0129943.

Kimani-Murage, Elizabeth W., Lilly Schofield, Frederick Wekesah, Shah Mohamed, Blessing Mberu, Remare Ettarh, Thaddaeus Egondi, Catherine Kyobutungi, and Alex Ezeh. 2014. "Vulnerability to Food Insecurity in Urban Slums: Experiences from Nairobi, Kenya." *Journal of Urban Health* 91 (6): 1098–1113.

Korth, Marcel, Ruth Stewart, Laurenz Langer, Nolizwe Madinga, Natalie Rebelo Da Silva, Hazel Zaranyika, Carina van Rooyen, and Thea de Wet. 2014. "What are the Impacts of Urban Agriculture Programs on Food Security in Low and Middle-Income Countries: A Systematic Review." *Environmental Evidence* 3 (1): 1–10.

Lee-Smith, Diana. 2010. "Cities Feeding People: An Update on Urban Agriculture in Equatorial Africa." *Environment and Urbanization* 22 (2): 483–99.

Leroy, Jef L., Marie Ruel, and Ellen Verhofstadt. 2009. "The Impact of Conditional Cash Transfer Programmes on Child Nutrition: A Review of Evidence Using a Programme Theory Framework." *Journal of Development Effectiveness* 1 (2): 103–29.

Lucci, Paula, and Tanvi Bhatkal. 2014. "Monitoring Progress on Urban Poverty: Are Indicators Fit For Purpose?" Overseas Development Institute (ODI), working paper, October 16. https://odi.org/en/publications/monitoring-progress-on-urban-poverty-are-current-data-and-indicators-fit-for-purpose/.

Lucci, Paula, Tanvi Bhatkal, and Amina Khan. 2018. "Are We Underestimating Urban Poverty?" *World Development* 103:297–310.

MacAuslan, Ian, and Lilly Schofield. 2011. *Evaluation of Concern Kenya's Korogocho Emergency and Food Security Cash Transfer Initiative*. Nairobi: Concern Worldwide and Oxford Policy Management.

Mberu, Blessing Uchenna, Alex Chika Ezeh, Gloria Chepngeno-Langat, James Kimani, Samuel Oti, and Donatien Beguy. 2013. "Family Ties and Urban–Rural Linkages among Older Migrants in Nairobi Informal Settlements." *Population, Space and Place* 19 (3): 275–93.

McCordic, Cameron, and Ezequiel Abrahamo. 2019. "Family Structure and Severe Food Insecurity in Maputo and Matola, Mozambique." *Sustainability* 11 (1): 267.

McCordic, Cameron, and Bruce Frayne. 2017. "Household Vulnerability to Food Price Increases: The 2008 Crisis in Urban Southern Africa." *Geographical Research* 55 (2): 166–79.

Moser, Caroline, and David Satterthwaite. 2008. "Towards Pro-Poor Adaptation to Climate Change in the Urban Centres of Low- and Middle-Income Countries." Human Settlements Working Paper, November. https://www.iied.org/10564iied.

Mougeot, Luc JA. 2000. "Urban Agriculture: Definition, Presence, Potentials and Risks." In *Growing Cities, Growing Food: Urban Agriculture on the Policy Agenda* 1:42, edited by Nico Bakker, Marielle Dubbeling, Sabine Gündel, Ulrich Sabel-Koschella, and Henk de Zeeuw, 1–42. Feldafing, Germany: German Foundation for International Development.

MUFPP (Milan Urban Food Policy Pact). 2022. "Milan Pact Awards 2022." https://www.milanurbanfoodpolicypact.org/milan-pact-awards/milan-pact-awards-2022/.

Naicker, Nisha, Angie Mathee, and June Teare. 2015. "Food Insecurity in Households in Informal Settlements in Urban South Africa." *South African Medical Journal* 105 (4): 268–70.

Nantale, Grace, Nazarius Mbona Tumwesigye, Noah Kiwanuka, and Richard Kajjura. 2017. "Prevalence and Factors Associated with Food Insecurity among Women Aged 18–49 Years in Kampala Slums Uganda; A Mixed Methods Study." *Journal of Food Security* 5 (4): 120–28.

Ng, Marie, Tom Fleming, Margaret Robinson, Blake Thomson, Nicholas Graetz, Christopher Margono, Erin C. Mullany, et al. 2014. "Global, Regional, and National Prevalence of Overweight and Obesity in Children and Adults during 1980–2013: A Systematic Analysis for the Global Burden of Disease Study 2013." *Lancet* 384 (9945): 766–81.

Owuor, Samuel O. 2007. "Migrants, Urban Poverty and the Changing Nature of Urban–Rural Linkages in Kenya." *Development Southern Africa* 24 (1): 109–22.

Parnell, Susan. 2016. "Defining a Global Urban Development Agenda." *World Development* 78:529–40.

Patel, Raj, and Philip McMichael. 2009. "A Political Economy of the Food Riot." *Review (Fernand Braudel Center)* 32 (1): 9–35.

Peyton, Stephen, William Moseley, and Jane Battersby. 2015. "Implications of Supermarket Expansion on Urban Food Security in Cape Town, South Africa." *African Geographical Review* 34 (1): 36–54.

Pieterse, Edgar, Susan Parnell, and Gareth Haysom. 2018. "African Dreams: Locating Urban Infrastructure in the 2030 Sustainable Developmental Agenda." *Area Development and Policy* 3 (2): 149–69.

Potts, Deborah. 2010. *Circular Migration in Zimbabwe and Contemporary Sub-Saharan Africa*. Suffolk: Boydell and Brewer.

Potts, Deborah. 2012. "Whatever Happened to Africa's Rapid Urbanisation?" *World Economics* 13:17.

Roy, Ananya. 2014. "Slum-Free Cities of the Asian Century: Postcolonial Government and the Project of Inclusive Growth." *Singapore Journal of Tropical Geography* 35 (1): 136–50.

Ruel, Marie T., James L. Garrett, Corinna Hawkes, and Marc J. Cohen. 2010. "The Food, Fuel, and Financial Crises Affect the Urban and Rural Poor Disproportionately: A Review of the Evidence." *Journal of Nutrition* 140 (1): 170S–176S.

Satterthwaite, David. 2011. "Why Are the Main Means by which Urban Dwellers Avoid Hunger Ignored?" *IIED Insights* (blog), October 5. https://www.iied.org/why-are-main-means-which-urban-dwellers-avoid-hunger-ignored.

Satterthwaite, David, Gordon McGranahan, and Cecilia Tacoli. 2010. "Urbanization and Its Implications for Food and Farming." *Philosophical Transactions of the Royal Society B: Biological Sciences* 365 (1554): 2809–20.

Satterthwaite, David, Alice Sverdlik, and Donald Brown. 2019. "Revealing and Responding to Multiple Health Risks in Informal Settlements in Sub-Saharan African Cities." *Journal of Urban Health* 96 (1): 112–22.

Sheahan, Megan, and Christopher B. Barrett. 2017. "Food Loss and Waste in Sub-Saharan Africa." *Food Policy* 70:1–12.

Shetty, P. S. 2017. "Food and Nutrition Security." In *Oxford Textbook of Global Public Health*, vol. 1, edited by R. Detels, M. Gulliford, Q. A. Karim, and C. C. Tan, 180–200. Oxford: Oxford University Press.

Smit, Suzanne, Josephine Kaviti Musango, Zora Kovacic, and Alan C. Brent. 2017. "Conceptualising Slum in an Urban African Context." *Cities* 62:107–19.

Springmann, Marco, Michael Clark, Daniel Mason-D'Croz, Keith Wiebe, Benjamin Leon Bodirsky, Luis Lassaletta, Wim De Vries, et al. 2018. "Options for Keeping the Food System within Environmental Limits." *Nature* 562 (7728): 519–25.

Swartzendruber, J. F. 2014. *Sustainability and Resilience for Food Security in Sub-Saharan Africa*. Washington, DC: GEF.

Swinburn, Boyd A., Vivica I. Kraak, Steven Allender, Vincent J. Atkins, Phillip I. Baker, Jessica R. Bogard, Hannah Brinsden, et al. 2019. "The Global Syndemic of Obesity, Undernutrition, and Climate Change: The Lancet Commission Report." *Lancet* 393 (10173): 791–846.

Swindale, Anne, and Paula Bilinsky. 2006. *Household Dietary Diversity Score (HDDS) for Measurement of Household Food Access: Indicator Guide*. Washington, DC: Food and Nutrition Technical Assistance Project, Academy for Educational Development.

Tacoli, Cecilia. 2013. "Urban Poverty, Food Security and Climate Change." IIED Briefing Paper 17149. London: International Institute for Environment and Development (IIED).

Tacoli, Cecilia. 2017. "Food (In)security in Rapidly Urbanising, Low-Income Contexts." *International Journal of Environmental Research and Public Health* 14:1554. https://doi.org/10.3390/ijerph14121554.

Tacoli, Cecilia. 2020. "Food (In) Security in Rapidly Urbanizing, Low-Income Contexts." In *Handbook on Urban Food Security in the Global South*, edited by Jonathan Crush, Bruce Frayne, and Gareth Haysom, 23–33. Cheltenham, UK: Edward Elgar.

Teye, Joseph. 2018. "Urbanization and Migration in Africa." In *United Nations Expert Group*

Meeting for the Review and Appraisal of the Programme of Action of the International Conference on Population and Development and Its Contribution to the Follow-Up and Review of the 2030 Agenda for Sustainable Development, 1–2. New York: United Nations Secretariat.

Titz, Alexandra, and Sosten S. Chiotha. 2019. "Pathways for Sustainable and Inclusive Cities in Southern and Eastern Africa through Urban Green Infrastructure?" *Sustainability* 11 (10): 2729.

UNDESA (United Nations Department of Economic and Social Affairs). 2016. *Sustainable Development Goals.* New York: United Nations. https://sustainabledevelopment.un .org/?menu=1300.

UNDESA (United Nations Department of Economic and Social Affairs). 2019. *World Urbanization Prospects: The 2018 Revision.* New York: United Nations. https://population .un.org/wup/Publications/Files/WUP2018-Report.pdf.

UNICEF (United Nations Children's Fund). 2012. *The State of the World's Children 2012: Children in an Urban World.* New York: United Nations.

Wambogo, Edwina A., Hala Ghattas, Kenneth L. Leonard, and Nadine R. Sahyoun. 2018. "Validity of the Food Insecurity Experience Scale for Use in Sub-Saharan Africa and Characteristics of Food-Insecure Individuals." *Current Developments in Nutrition* 2 (9): nzy062.

Wanyama, Rosina, Theda Gödecke, and Matin Qaim. 2019. "Food Security and Dietary Quality in African Slums." *Sustainability* 11 (21): 5999.

Wertheim-Heck, Sigrid. 2020. "The Impact of COVID-19 Lock-Down on the Dies of Hanoi's Urban Poor." *IIED Insights,* April 8.

Wertheim-Heck, Sigrid, Jessica Evelyn Raneri, and Peter Oosterveer. 2019. "Food Safety and Nutrition for Low-Income Urbanites: Exploring a Social Justice Dilemma in Consumption Policy." *Environment and Urbanization* 31 (2): 397–420.

WFP (World Food Programme). 2012. *Mogadishu Urban Food Security and Nutrition Assessment.* Rome: WFP.

WFP (World Food Programme) and FAO (Food and Agriculture Organization). 2022. *Hunger Hotspots: FAO-WFP Early Warnings on Acute Food Insecurity: October 2022 to January 2023 Outlook.* Rome: FAO.

Wiggins, Steve, Sharada Keats, Euna Han, Satoru Shimokawa, Joel Alberto, Vargas Hernández, and Rafael Moreira Claro. 2015. *The Rising Cost of a Healthy Diet: Changing Relative Prices of Foods in High-Income and Emerging Economies.* London: Overseas Development Institute.

World Bank. 2010. "Food Price Watch." Poverty Reduction and Equity Group and Poverty Reduction and Economic Management Network (PREM), World Bank, February. https://documents1.worldbank.org/curated/en/776591468181476052/pdf/531600 NEWS0FIN1newoseries101PUBLIC1.pdf.

World Bank. 2011. "Food Price Watch." Poverty Reduction and Equity Group and Poverty Reduction and Economic Management Network (PREM), World Bank, February. https://documents1.worldbank.org/curated/en/240161468338505130/pdf/643610 BRI0Food00Box0362535B0PUBLIC0.pdf.

World Population Review. 2023. "Global South Countries." https://worldpopulationreview .com/country-rankings/global-south-countries.

6

Housing as a Determinant of Health in African Cities

Meggie Mwoka

1. Introduction

The concept of housing has evolved over time from just the physical structure that directly provides a roof over one's head to encompassing the environment (physical, social, built) around this structure, also known as the neighborhood. The World Health Organization (WHO), with the view that housing is a public health issue, put forward the concept of healthy housing (WHO 2018). Healthy housing is defined as shelter that supports a state of complete physical, mental, and social well-being, including providing a feeling of *home*, a sense of belonging, security, and privacy (WHO 2018). It refers to the physical structure of the dwelling, and the extent to which it enables physical health, including being structurally sound, providing shelter from the elements, facilitating adequate sanitation and sufficient space, and protecting the inhabitants from pollutants, injury hazards, mold, and pests. The US Centers for Disease Control and Prevention (CDC) also recognizes that housing should provide both physiologic and psychologic needs, including but not limited to protection from the elements, an atmosphere of reasonable chemical purity, adequate privacy for the individual, and opportunities for normal family life (CDC and HUD 2006). The African Commission on Human and Peoples' Rights recognizes the right to adequate housing and legal protection from forced and arbitrary evictions (Government of Kenya 1981).

The United Nations (UN) further defines housing from a rights lens, based on the 1948 Universal Declaration of Human Rights and the 1966 International Covenant on Economic, Social and Cultural Rights, which recognizes everyone's right to an adequate standard of living, including adequate housing (UN-Habitat and UNHCR 2009). According to the UN, adequate housing must meet the following minimum criteria beyond basic supply and availability of housing:

- *Security of tenure*: housing is not adequate if its occupants do not have a degree of tenure security which guarantees legal protection against forced evictions, harassment, and other threats.
- *Availability of services, materials, facilities, and infrastructure*: housing is not adequate if its occupants do not have safe drinking water, adequate sanitation, energy for cooking, heating, lighting, food storage or refuse disposal.
- *Affordability*: housing is not adequate if its cost threatens or compromises the occupants' enjoyment of other human rights.
- *Habitability*: housing is not adequate if it does not guarantee physical safety or provide adequate space, as well as protection against the cold, damp, heat, rain, wind, other threats to health and structural hazards.
- *Accessibility*: housing is not adequate if the specific needs of disadvantaged and marginalized groups are not considered.
- *Location:* housing is not adequate if it is cut off from employment opportunities, health-care services, schools, childcare centres, and other social facilities, or if located in polluted or dangerous areas.
- *Cultural adequacy*: housing is not adequate if it does not respect and consider the expression of cultural identity. (UN-Habitat and UNHCR 2009)

Currently about 472 million people are living in urban centers in Africa (UN-Habitat and UNICEF 2020). The region is rapidly urbanizing, at rates as high as 4 percent annually in some countries. The rapid population growth in cities is being outweighed by increased demand for infrastructure, housing, and amenities such as electricity and safe reliable water and sanitation (Akande 2021; World Bank 2015). Deficits of affordable quality housing have led to a rise of informal settlements, often characterized by poor service delivery and limited access to basic amenities such as water, sanitation, and electricity (World Bank 2015). About 55 percent of African households face higher costs relative to their per capita GDP compared to households in other regions, much of it accounted for by housing (World Bank 2015). Moreover, African cities are 29 percent more expensive than cities in countries at similar income levels (World Bank 2015). Households are cost burdened if they spend more than 30 percent of their income on housing, and severely cost burdened if they spend more than 50 percent of their income on housing (Bailey et al. 2016). In Nigeria, for example, it is estimated that households are spending up to 50 percent of their annual income on rent, while in Nairobi, residents spend 40 percent of their income on rent (Abimaje, Akingbohungbe, and Baba 2014; Government of Kenya 2019). These high costs disproportionately affect the already vulnerable and low-income populations, working informal jobs and living in informal settlements, leaving them with little left to spend on other necessities, such as health care, food, utilities, and education for their children.

2. Housing as a Determinant of Health

The Adelaide Statement on Health in All Policies recognizes well-designed, accessible housing to be key in addressing fundamental determinants of health for disadvantaged individuals and communities (WHO and Government of South Australia 2010). The Sustainable Development Goals, which serve as a global blueprint and commitment by countries globally to achieve a better and more sustainable future for all, recognize in Goal 11 the need to make cities inclusive, safe, resilient, and sustainable (United Nations 2015). Housing therefore serves as a fundamental pillar to the sustainable social and economic development of cities, in addition to contributing to the physical, social, and mental health and well-being of individuals in it.

Housing directly and indirectly affects individual and population health outcomes. Literature has documented four main interconnected pathways linking housing and health (Rolfe et al. 2020; Taylor 2018). These are:

1. the stability pathway: health impacts of not having a stable home
2. housing safety and quality pathway: health effects of conditions inside the home
3. the affordability pathway: the influence on health of financial burdens resulting from high-cost housing
4. the neighborhood pathway: health impacts of neighborhoods, including both the environmental and social characteristics of where people live

These pathways demonstrate housing as a key determinant of health within the African context.

2.1. Stability

Housing instability has no standard definition (Frederick et al. 2014; Kushel et al. 2006). It ranges from difficulty paying rent, frequent relocation, and being at constant risk of eviction to the most severe form—homelessness. With the rise in rural–urban migration and the mismatch in housing demand versus supply, informal housing and homelessness are becoming common features in urban areas in Africa. Informal housing represents a spectrum of different shelter types, locations, conditions, and tenure statuses (UN-Habitat 2003). It can be defined by deviations from the laws and regulatory frameworks that govern formal access and use of land and buildings (UN-Habitat 2003.). Characteristics of informal housing include self-designed and self-built houses with local materials, nonconformity to building and land use standards, being poorly serviced by infrastructure networks and public services, absence of legal title, and often insecure tenure (World Bank 2015). These characteristics have been shown to produce and aggravate symptoms of physical and mental illness because of the high susceptibility of such housing to a lack of basic facilities, including safe reliable running water, toilet facilities, and electricity; overcrowding; lack of privacy; poor security; and endangered safety. On the other hand, formal housing is characterized by a valid legal title, is structurally sound, complies with local planning standards and building codes, and can be pledged as collateral for a long-term mortgage loan (World Bank 2015). The majority of households in urban areas, however, are unable to afford formal housing and thus are relegated to informal channels, which contribute around three-quarters of the total housing stock in Africa (World Bank 2015).

People living in informal settlements are most at risk of forced evictions and persistent harassment from authorities (Dupont 2011; United Nations 2014). Forced evictions, which have been reported across informal settlements in multiple African settings, are devastating to people's lives, often leading to loss of homes, possessions, livelihoods, and networks (United Nations 2014). The phenomenon of forced evictions stems from unequal access to land and poor regulation of the urban land market, skewed toward private developers and recognizing mainly titleholders (Mwau and Sverdlik 2020; Otiso 2002). Thus, the majority of people living on low income are forced to obtain land informally, through illegal occupancy, in a bid to provide themselves with appropriate and affordable housing (United Nations 2014). The impending risk of eviction and the actual occurrence of forced evictions only worsens the state of health (especially mental health) and well-being of people living in informal settlements.

Homelessness is housing deprivation in its most severe form. Evidence shows that people who are homeless suffer from a range of physical and mental health problems, and underutilize health care services. As a result, they face substantially higher morbidity and mortality (De-Graft Aikins and Ofori-Atta 2007; Fekadu et al. 2014; Moyo, Patel, and Ross 2015). Beijer, Wolf, and Fazel (2012) estimated that globally, the death rate among people who are homeless is about four times higher than that of the general population. People who are homeless are categorized as a high-risk group for developing tuberculosis, owing to the difficulty in accessing health care services and the likelihood to engage in risky health behaviors such as substance abuse (Heo, Min, and Lee 2012; Tankimovich 2013; Z. M. Ndlovu 2019). This has been further demonstrated by a study in Ethiopia that estimated the point prevalence of smear positive pulmonary tuberculosis in homeless individuals to be 4.67 times higher than in the general population (Semunigus et al. 2016). An assessment of the mental health of adults in Ethiopia who are homeless showed that about 90 percent had experienced some form of mental or alcohol use disorder: 41.0 percent had psychosis, 60.0 percent had hazardous or dependent alcohol use, and 14.8 percent reported attempting suicide in the previous month (Fekadu et al. 2014). Furthermore, individuals experiencing homelessness continue to have limited or no access to mental health care services, creating a cycle of impaired health and well-being.

2.2. Affordability

Closely related to the stability pathway is the issue of affordability. The affordability pathway depicts the situation by which the financial burden of housing reduces the occupant's income available for health care and health-promoting goods, including nutrition (Taylor 2018). High housing-related costs can place a particular economic burden on low-income households, forcing trade-offs between food and other basic needs, such as health care (Abimaje, Akingbohungbe, and Baba 2014; Achamwie and Danso-Wiredu 2021a; Asante et al. 2018). A study found that low-income people with difficulty paying rent, mortgage, or utility bills were less likely to have a usual source of medical care and more likely to postpone treatment and use the

Housing as a Determinant of Health   101

emergency room for treatment (Harkness and Newman 2005). Moreover, low-income households have limited capability to afford quality housing because of weaknesses in the delivery value chains on the supply and demand side. For instance, housing that has been categorized as affordable remains inaccessible to the populations it targets (Bah, Faye, and Geh 2018). Thus, housing that remains truly affordable is often informal housing. For example, in Malawi, the least expensive available formal house is almost fifty-seven times more expensive than a typical informal shelter alternative (World Bank 2015). Furthermore, across the majority of African countries, financial mechanisms to support housing finance are either not structured or not accessible to cater to low-income households, limiting their capability to access adequate housing (Bah, Faye, and Geh 2018; World Bank 2015). The design of economic and social policies can disproportionately limit access to affordable quality housing, pushing the majority of populations in urban areas into housing that is poorly constructed and disconnected from essential services and amenities such as solid waste management, posing persistent health challenges to populations that reside in these areas.

Rental housing remains an important housing option for those not ready or able to buy or build houses of their own, especially in Africa, where most people are tenants (UN-Habitat 2011). Despite this, national and local economic and political conditions and regulatory frameworks have done little to support the improvement of existing rental housing in addition to expanding affordable rental housing options. Some of the reasons rental housing is a key option is that it offers flexibility to move depending on where work is available or to manage household budgets (e.g., moving to cheaper housing when times are hard) and it offers convenience for households not ready to make the long-term financial commitment (Bah, Faye, and Geh 2018; UN-Habitat 2011; World Bank 2015). Evidence shows that renters compared to homeowners are more likely to experience conditions of poor housing because of lax policies and regulation within this sector. For example, in Liberia where 50 percent of tenant households earn less than US$10 per month, tenants pay about US$2.67–US$3.33 a month for one room in a zinc or mud brick house without a latrine, safe drinking water, or electricity (UN-Habitat 2014). A lack of tenure security due to lax rental policies is demonstrated in Ghana, where house owners or landlords typically require renters to pay about two to five years' advance for a rental unit. Failure to pay results in the tenant being evicted—a practice that is incoherent with the Rent Act in Ghana (Achamwie and Danso-Wiredu 2021). The constant threat of eviction, and the risks associated with poor quality housing conditions, has been shown to increase the risk of psychological distress among renters (Acharya, Bhatta, and Dhakal 2022; Vásquez-Vera et al. 2017).

2.3. Quality and Safety

The way housing is designed has significant implications for the health and well-being of its inhabitants. The housing safety and quality pathway refers to the link between the physical conditions inside the home and its occupants' health. Evidence shows that most housing in African cities is low quality (World Bank 2015). Below are some key components of housing quality and safety that affect health and well-being.

Lack of access to safe drinking water and clean sanitation facilities is a major contributor to the spread of infectious diseases such as diarrhea, which remains a leading cause of death among children under 5 in the region (WHO 2022). Data from the NUHDSS demonstrated that the mortality burden of children under the age of 5 years in slums was four times more than the rest of the population, mostly due to pneumonia and diarrheal diseases (Kyobutungi et al. 2008). Sub-Saharan Africa has the lowest proportion of urban population with access to piped water. Only 56 percent of city dwellers have access to piped water, down from 67 percent in 2003, and just 11 percent have a sewer connection (Eberhard 2019). Where piped water does not exist, communities are forced to use other sources of differing quality, such as dug wells, hand pumps, kiosks with public taps, ponds, and vended water (Eberhard 2019). Studies assessing water quality in urban areas across the region show high instances of tested water being unsafe for drinking and favorable for propagation of waterborne diseases such as cholera (Bwire et al. 2020; Gara et al. 2018; Kamara et al. 2022; Wolde et al. 2020). A strong indicator of the current gap in active and continuous screening and treating of water sources is needed to prevent and control the spread of infectious diseases.

Damp and moldy housing conditions in sub-Saharan Africa are much more prevalent in slums than in non-slum areas (Alaazi and Aganah 2020). Mold has been associated with a variety of respiratory conditions such as pneumonia, which is one of the leading causes of mortality among children below 5 years in informal settlements in Nairobi (Kyobutungi et al. 2008). The main contributors include the poor state of housing and crowding, in addition to the use of kerosene and charcoal stoves in poorly ventilated rooms (Kyobutungi et al. 2008).

In the absence of electricity and other cleaner sources of energy, households within informal settlements depend highly on biomass fuel (Alaazi and Aganah 2020). In Lagos, Nigeria, for example, 52.1 percent of households use gas (LPG), 50.6 percent kerosene, 15.2 percent charcoal, and 9.17 percent firewood as their fuel sources (Lagos State Ministry of Environment 2021). This dependence is a major source of indoor air pollution and its related health impacts in informal settlements. Moreover, inadequate ventilation and small dwelling space aggravates indoor air pollution. Associated health outcomes of indoor pollution include eye infections, respiratory-related infections, and deaths (Kyobutungi et al. 2008). Vulnerable groups, especially women, children, and the elderly, bear the brunt of the health effects of indoor air pollution in slums, as they typically spend most of their time indoors (Alaazi and Aganah 2020; Kyobutungi et al. 2008; World Bank 2015).

Exposure to lead (Pb) and asbestos in sub-Saharan African homes and neighborhoods is still high (Alaazi and Aganah 2020). Lead has been found in the pipes of water distribution systems and in paints in homes. It is a major source of contaminated drinking water (Makokha et al. 2008; Mghweno et al. 2008). Physicochemical analysis of pipe water samples from Kisumu, Kenya, and Kampala, Uganda, found Pb levels several times above the WHO's recommended maximum limit (10 µg/g) for drinking water (Makokha et al. 2011). Frequent exposure to Pb-contaminated water or Pb paint can contribute to cognitive disabilities, neurodevelopmental defects, and even death in young children. In South Africa, an estimated 1,428 people died from Pb poisoning in 2000 alone (Norman et al. 2007).

Exposure to asbestos is largely due to use of noncorrosive roofing material, creating a health hazard in sub-Saharan African slums (Alaazi and Aganah 2020). Moreover, in South Africa and Zimbabwe, people live in houses located on asbestos fiber dumps or in neighborhoods contaminated with asbestos (Ndlovu, Naude, and Murray 2013). Asbestos is a primary source of carcinogenic fiber, which can cause lung cancer, asbestosis, and mesothelioma when inhaled in sufficient quantity (Braun and Kisting 2006; Osinubi, Gochfeld, and Kipen 2000). Data on asbestos-related diseases and deaths in sub-Saharan African remain largely undocumented; therefore it is currently difficult to quantify the rate of exposure and related health impacts.

Physical hazards in the home and surrounding neighborhood contribute to injuries and premature deaths in informal housing. Examples include burns, scalds, accidental fires, cuts, and injuries from falls (Satterthwaite 2016). A slew of fire outbreaks across informal settlements in sub-Saharan African cities are a result of poor and flimsy construction materials and the use of candles, kerosene lamps, and open fires or unstable stoves for cooking, lighting, and heating (Alaazi and Aganah 2020; Dodman et al. 2019).

Adequate privacy has been recognized as a key contributor to psychological needs for healthy and adequate housing. Informal settlements are majorly overcrowded, however, increasing both mental and physical risks, such as disease spread, and poor psychological well-being due to lack of privacy. In Ghana, housing congestion, especially in rental housing, is common, with room occupancy rates from five to nine people in a room meant to accommodate at most three persons, in accordance with the UN-Habitat standard (Achamwie and Danso-Wiredu 2021; UN-Habitat 2018). Moreover, most of these houses lack access to basic amenities like lavatories, increasing the risk of spreading infectious diseases such as tuberculosis, meningitis, acute respiratory infections, and diarrheal diseases (Achamwie and Danso-Wiredu 2021; Nkosi et al. 2019; Norheim et al. 2014; Ofori 2020).

2.4. Neighborhood Pathway

The neighborhood pathway demonstrates that the location of one's house determines one's health. This includes access to public transportation, safety and security, food, education, health care, and public spaces, as well as social factors such as neighborhood segregation and social capital (Taylor 2018). The majority of informal settlements often have limited access to these neighborhood components, perpetuating poverty and reinforcing the lack of decent housing options. Informal settlements are typically unplanned and constructed without access routes. In case of fire outbreaks, lack of routes impedes access for firefighters and firefighting equipment (Alaazi and Aganah 2020). Waste disposal in many towns and cities in sub-Saharan Africa is inefficient or nonexistent, especially in informal settlements. About 55 percent (68 million tons) of municipal solid waste is collected, with the remaining dumped onto sidewalks, open fields, storm water drains, and rivers (Godfrey et al. 2020; Scarlat et al. 2015). This contributes to the pollution of groundwater and surface waters, which may be used as a source for drinking water. Moreover, the indiscriminate dumping and burning of waste causes significant air pollution, which not only affects human

Housing as a Determinant of Health 105

health but also contributes to environmental pollution with far-reaching effects (Wilson 2015).

3. Data on Housing

The lack of robust disaggregated housing sector data, and especially of informal housing prices, tenure types, and housing quality, presents a significant challenge to the development of appropriate housing policies and interventions (World Bank 2015). Putting in place strong data systems will be key to effectively plan and cater for the growing urban populations in the region and to ensure that their health and well-being is addressed (Tusting et al. 2019). This includes clarity on definitions and measurement of adequate housing, identifying appropriate data sources and existing platforms (if any) to leverage for appropriate data collection, interpretation, and use. An example of a definition that varies across countries, thus affecting measurement, is homelessness. In Zimbabwe, for instance, 1.2 to 1.5 million people are estimated to be homeless, defined as living in informal residential settlements. While in Nigeria an estimated 24.4 million people are homeless, defined to include both rough sleepers and internally displaced people (Chitekwe-Biti 2009; UNHCR 2010). Where existing and readily available, tapping into traditional data sources such as household surveys, population censuses, and health assessments will be key to beginning to gain an in-depth understanding of the impact of housing on health. For example, the Kenya Integrated Household Budget Survey (KIHBS) provides a rich source of data on the key socioeconomic aspects of the Kenyan population, including education, health, energy, housing, water and sanitation. Recognizing that most countries have some form of data system, it would be key to try to leverage these to fill in the gaps often presented by incomplete and not up-to-date data while working on strengthening or building these systems to be more robust.

Moreover, data systems may need to make certain that data utilization for decision making is built in as a key component to ensure translation of evidence into action. The current data revolution era provides an opportunity to utilize technology to better collect data, integrate multiple data sources, and improve data quality and management, in addition to taking advantage of new data sources where appropriate, such as satellite images of night lights, daytime satellite pictures, Google Street View, and mobile phone networks (Jean et al. 2016). Additionally, there is a need to ensure data disaggregation to capture the nuances within a population and countries to appropriately target populations over the long term. An example can be disaggregating data across the spectrum of informal housing to appropriately capture the differences in housing and health conditions that may be masked if, for example, the focus is only on slums (Mwau and Sverdlik 2020).

4. Conclusions

Housing is an integral determinant of the quality of life and welfare of urban residents. Not one solution can solve the housing challenge across urban areas in Africa, especially with regard to how it affects health. Despite data limitations, existing evidence on the impact of housing on population health and well-being provides a basis for the involvement of the health sector in the housing sector. This has been done in the United Kingdom through the Housing Health and Safety Rating System (HHSRS)—a health-based risk assessment procedure for residential properties (Stafford Borough Council 2024). The HHSRS evaluates the potential effect of any faults on the health and safety of occupants, visitors, neighbors, and passersby. Examples of hazards assessed include damp and mold growth, radiation, property security from intruders, crowding and space, noise, water supply, personal hygiene, sanitation and drainage, electrical hazards, structural collapse, and falling elements. The health sector can therefore play a critical role in technical standard setting and proactively contribute to inspection processes.

To ensure legal security of tenure for all, to protect citizens from unlawful eviction, requires both establishing and enforcing appropriate housing policies in addition to regulating the housing market to create an enabling environment for governmental and commercial forces to respond to the housing needs of the most vulnerable. This includes both supply- and demand-side interventions, such as strengthening local construction and building materials sectors to reduce the cost of formal housing; enhancing access to inclusive financial mechanisms, such as mortgages that cater to diverse socioeconomic groups; and strengthening residential rental markets, which stand to be the main housing options for the majority of urban populations (Arvanitis 2013). Considering the effect of the neighborhood, building and upgrading housing should ensure that the quality of the neighborhood is also improved. This process will be dependent on proper collection, analysis, and utilization of housing market data to better inform decisions.

Considering the key role leadership and governance plays to address such a multifaceted issue, a Health in All Policies (HiAP) approach provides a mutually beneficial, sustainable approach to promote health and equity objectives within the housing sector (WHO 2014). The HiAP approach, which builds on the concept of healthy public policies and intersectoral action for health, recognizes the critical roles all sectors including housing play in either advancing or impeding health and well-being, depending on the policies and interventions undertaken (WHO 2014). A core sector critical in building healthy, sustainable, and habitable cities is urban planning. There is increasing recognition of the role of urban policies to define the air we breathe, the quality of spaces we use, the water we drink, the way we move, our access to food, and the treatment of diseases through adequate access to health care for all (UN-Habitat and WHO 2020). This highlights the fundamental need for multisectoral collaboration between planners, city managers, health professionals, and others toward developing cities planned and built with a focus on human and environmental health. Globally, efforts driven by UN-Habitat and the WHO have sought to demonstrate the critical link between health and sustainable cities and communities and vice versa (UN-Habitat and WHO 2020). The HiAP approach requires commitment and leadership at the highest level to mobilize the whole government to develop coherent policies and to collaborate on shared solutions. This chapter draws on diverse evidence to demonstrate housing as a key determinant of health and well-being. With an estimated additional population of 950 million people in African cities in the next twenty-eight years, urgent transdisciplinary partnership is needed to tap into existing and potential resources and knowledge to prioritize adequate housing that promotes the health and well-being of the region's population.

REFERENCES

Abimaje, Joshua, Davies Akingbohungbe, and Adams Ndalai Baba. 2014. "Housing Affordability In Nigerian Towns: A Case of Idah, Nigeria." *International Journal of Civil Engineering, Construction and Estate Management* 1 (2): 31–38. https://www.researchgate.net/publication/279963903.

Achamwie, Peter Kwame, and Esther Yeboah Danso-Wiredu. 2021. "The Rental System in Ghana's Low-Income Housing Communities, Challenges and Adaptation Strategies." *Town and Regional Planning* 79:67–78. https://doi.org/10.18820/2415-0495/trp79i1.8.

Acharya, Binod, Dependra Bhatta, and Chandra Dhakal. 2022. "The Risk of Eviction and the Mental Health Outcomes among the US Adults." *Preventive Medicine Reports* 6 (29): 101981. https://doi.org/10.1016/j.pmedr.2022.101981.

Akande, Oluwafemi K. 2021. "Urbanization, Housing Quality and Health: Towards a Redirection for Housing Provision in Nigeria." *Journal of Contemporary Urban Affairs* 5 (1): 35–46. https://doi.org/10.25034/ijcua.2021.v5n1-3.

Alaazi, D. A., and G. A. M. Aganah. 2020. "Understanding the Slum-Health Conundrum in Sub-Saharan Africa: A Proposal for a Rights-Based Approach to Health Promotion in Slums." *Global Health* 27 (3): 65–72.

Arvanitis, Yannis. 2013. "African Housing Dynamics Lessons from the Kenyan Market." *Africa Economic Brief* 4 (3): 1–12.

Asante, L. A., E. K. Gavu, D. P. O. Quansah, and Derek Tutu. 2018. "The Difficult Combination of Renting and Building a House in Urban Ghana: Analysing the Perception of Low and Middle Income Earners in Accra." *GeoJournal* 83:1223–37.

Bah, El-hadj M., Issa Faye, and Zekebweliwai F. Geh. 2018. "Slum Upgrading and Housing Alternatives for the Poor." In *Housing Market Dynamics in Africa*, edited by El-hadj M. Bah, Issa Faye, and Zekebweliwai F. Geh. London: Palgrave Macmillan. https://doi.org/10.1057/978-1-137-59792-2_6.

Bailey, Kathryn T., John T. Cook, Stephanie Ettinger de Cuba, Patrick H. Casey, Mariana Chilton, Sharon M. Coleman, Diana Becker Cutts, et al. 2016. "Development of an Index of Subsidized Housing Availability and Its Relationship to Housing Insecurity." *Housing Policy Debate* 26 (1): 172–87. https://doi.org/10.1080/10511482.2015.1015042.

Beijer, Ulla, Achim Wolf, and Seena Fazel. 2012. "Prevalence of Tuberculosis, Hepatitis C Virus, and HIV in Homeless People: A Systematic Review and Meta-Analysis." *Lancet Infectious Diseases* 12 (11): 859–70. https://doi.org/10.1016/S1473-3099(12)70177-9.

Braun, Lundy, and Sophia Kisting. 2006. "Asbestos-Related Disease in South Africa: The Social Production of an Invisible Epidemic." *American Journal of Public Health* 96 (8): 1386–96. https://doi.org/10.2105/AJPH.2005.064998.

Bwire, Godfrey, David A. Sack, Atek Kagirita, Tonny Obala, Amanda K. Debes, Malathi Ram, Henry Komakech, Christine Marie George, and Christopher Garimoi Orach. 2020. "The Quality of Drinking and Domestic Water from the Surface Water Sources (Lakes, Rivers, Irrigation Canals and Ponds) and Springs in Cholera Prone Communities of Uganda: An Analysis of Vital Physicochemical Parameters." *BMC Public Health* 20 (1): 1128. https://doi.org/10.1186/s12889-020-09186-3.

CDC (Centers for Disease Control and Prevention) and HUD (Department of Housing and Urban Development). 2006. *Healthy Housing Reference Manual*. Atlanta, GA: US Department of Health and Human Services.

Chitekwe-Biti, Beth. 2009. "Struggles for Urban Land by the Zimbabwe Homeless People's Federation." *Environment and Urbanization* 21 (2): 347–66. https://doi.org/10.1177/0956247809343764.

De-Graft Aikins, Ama, and Angela L. Ofori-Atta. 2007. "Homelessness and Mental Health in Ghana: Everyday Experiences of Accra's Migrant Squatters." *Journal of Health Psychology* 12 (5): 761–78. https://doi.org/10.1177/1359105307080609.

Dodman, David, Ibidun Adelekan, Donald Brown, Hayley Leck, Mtafu Manda, Blessing Mberu, Mark Pelling, et al. 2019. "A Spectrum of Methods for a Spectrum of Risk: Generating Evidence to Understand and Reduce Urban Risk in Sub-Saharan Africa." *Area* 51 (3): 586–94. https://doi.org/10.1111/area.12510.

Dupont, Véronique. 2011. "The Challenge of Slums and Forced Evictions." In *Urban Policies and the Right to the City in India: Rights, Responsibilities and Citizenship*, edited by Marie-Hélène Zérah, Véronique Dupont, and S. T. Lama-Rewal, 76–97. New Delhi: UNESCO, CSH.

Eberhard, Rolfe. 2019. *Access to Water and Sanitation in Sub-Saharan Africa*. Bonn: Deutsche Gesellschaft für Internationale Zusammenarbeit (GIZ) GmbH.

Fekadu, Abebaw, Charlotte Hanlon, Emebet Gebre-Eyesus, Melkamu Agedew, Haddis Solomon, Solomon Teferra, Tsehaysina Gebre-Eyesus, et al. 2014. "Burden of Mental Disorders and Unmet Needs among Street Homeless People in Addis Ababa, Ethiopia." *BMC Medicine* 12 (1): 138. https://doi.org/10.1186/s12916-014-0138-x.

Frederick, Tyler, Michal Chwalek, Jean Hughes, Jeff Karabanow, and Sean Kidd. 2014. "How Stable Is Stable? Defining and Measuring Housing Stability." *Journal of Community Psychology* 42 (8): 964–79.

Gara, Takawira, Li Fengting, Innocent Nhapi, Clifton Makate, and Webster Gumindoga. 2018. "Health Safety of Drinking Water Supplied in Africa: A Closer Look Using Applicable Water-Quality Standards as a Measure." *Exposure and Health* 10 (2): 117–28. https://doi.org/10.1007/s12403-017-0249-7.

Godfrey, L., Mohamed Tawfic Ahmed, Giday Gebremedhin, Jamidu H. Y. Katima, Suzan Oelofse, Oladele Osibanjo, Henning Richter, and Arsène H. Yonli. 2020. "Solid Waste Management in Africa: Governance Failure or Development Opportunity?" In *Regional Development in Africa*, edited by Norbert Edomah, n.p. DOI: 10.5772/intechopen.86974.

Government of Kenya. 1981. "African Charter on Human and Peoples' Rights [Banjul Charter]." Nairobi, Kenya.

Government of Kenya. 2019. "Kenya's Affordable Housing Programme: Delivery Framework Overview." Centre for Affordable Housing Finance in Africa, November 20. https://housingfinanceafrica.org/documents/kenyas-affordable-housing-programme -delivery-framework-overview/.

Harkness, Joseph, and Sandra Newman. 2005. "Housing Affordability and Children's Well-Being: Evidence from the National Survey of America's Families, Housing Policy Debate." *Housing Policy Debate* 16:223–55.

Heo, Dal Joo, Hong Gi Min, and Hyun Ho Lee. 2012. "The Clinical Characteristics and Predictors of Treatment Success of Pulmonary Tuberculosis in Homeless Persons at a Public Hospital in Busan." *Korean Journal of Family Medicine* 33 (6): 372–80. https://doi.org/10.4082/kjfm.2012.33.6.372.

Jean, Neal, Marshall Burke, Michael Xie, W. Matthew Davis, David B. Lobell, and Stefano Ermon. 2016. "Combining Satellite Imagery and Machine Learning to Predict Poverty." *Science* 353 (6301): 790–94.

Kamara, Dauda, Doris Bah, Momodu Sesay, Anna Maruta, Bockarie Pompey Sesay, Bobson Derrick Fofanah, Ibrahim Franklyn Kamara, et al. 2022. "Evaluation of Drinking Water Quality and Bacterial Antibiotic Sensitivity in Wells and Standpipes at Household Water Points in Freetown, Sierra Leone." *International Journal of Environmental Research and Public Health* 19 (11): 6650. https://doi.org/10.3390/ijerph19116650.

Kushel, Margot B., Reena Gupta, Lauren Gee, and Jennifer S. Haas. 2006. "Housing Instability and Food Insecurity as Barriers to Health Care among Low-Income

Americans." *Journal of General Internal Medicine* 21 (1): 71–77. https://doi.org/10.1111/j.1525-1497.2005.00278.x.

Kyobutungi, Catherine, Abdhalah Kasiira Ziraba, Alex Ezeh, and Yazoumé Yé. 2008. "The Burden of Disease Profile of Residents of Nairobi's Slums: Results from a Demographic Surveillance System." *Population Health Metrics* 6 (March): 1. https://doi.org/10.1186/1478-7954-6-1.

Lagos State Ministry of Environment. 2021. *Lagos Informal Settlement Household Energy Survey: Final Report*. Lagos: Nigerian Slum / Informal Settlement Federation and JEI.

Makokha, Anselimo, Leonard R. Mghweno, Happy S. Magoha, Amina Nakajugo, and John M. Wekesa. 2008. "Environmental Lead Pollution and Contamination in Food Around Lake Victoria, Kisumu, Kenya." *African Journal of Environmental Science and Technology* 2 (10): 349–53.

Makokha, A. O., L. R. Mghweno, H. S. Magoha, A. Nakajugo, and J. M. Wekesa. 2011. "The Effects of Environmental Lead Pollution in Kisumu, Mwanza and Kampala." *Open Environmental Engineering Journal* 4:133–40. https://doi.org/10.2174/1874829501104010133.

Mghweno, Leonard R., Anselimo O. Makokha, Happy S. Magoha, John M. Wekesa, and Amina Nakajugo. 2008. "Environmental Lead Pollution and Food Safety around Kampala City in Uganda." *Journal of Applied Biosciences* 12:642–49.

Moyo, U., L. Patel, and E. Ross. 2015. "Homelessness and Mental Illness in Hillbrow, South Africa: A Situation Analysis." *Social Work/Maatskaplike Werk* 51 (1): 1–21.

Mwau, Baraka, and Alice Sverdlik. 2020. "High Rises and Low-Quality Shelter: Rental Housing Dynamics in Mathare Valley, Nairobi." *Environment and Urbanization* 32 (2): 481–502. https://doi.org/10.1177/0956247820942166.

Ndlovu, Ntombizodwa, Jim teWater Naude, and Jill Murray. 2013. "Compensation for Environmental Asbestos-Related Diseases in South Africa: A Neglected Issue." *Global Health Action* 6 (1): 19410. https://doi.org/10.3402/gha.v6io.19410.

Ndlovu, Zethembe Mthokozisi. 2019. "An Exploratory Study on Substance Abuse among Homeless People: A Case Study of Durban City Centre." Master's thesis, School of Applied Human Sciences, University of KwaZulu-Natal, Howard College Campus, Durban, South Africa.

Nkosi, Vusumuzi, Tanya Haman, Nisha Naicker, and Angela Mathee. 2019. "Overcrowding and Health in Two Impoverished Suburbs of Johannesburg, South Africa." *BMC Public Health* 19 (1): 1358. https://doi.org/10.1186/s12889-019-7665-5.

Norheim, Gunnstein, Manish Sadarangani, Omar Omar, Ly Mee Yu, Kåre Mølbak, Michael Howitz, Per Olcén, Margaretha Haglund, Arie van der Ende, and Andrew J. Pollard. 2014. "Association between Population Prevalence of Smoking and Incidence of Meningococcal Disease in Norway, Sweden, Denmark and the Netherlands between 1975 and 2009: A Population-Based Time Series Analysis." *BMJ Open* 4 (2): e003312. https://doi.org/10.1136/bmjopen-2013-003312.

Norman, Rosana, Angela Mathee, Brendon Barnes, Lize van der Merwe, Debbie Bradshaw, and South African Comparative Risk Assessment Collaborating Group. 2007. "Estimating the Burden of Disease Attributable to Lead Exposure in South Africa in 2000." *SAMJ* 97 (7): 773–80.

Ofori, Peres. 2020. "Housing Poverty in Developing Countries: Challenges and Implications for Decent Accommodation in Swedru, Ghana." *Acta Structilia* 27 (2): 57–92. http://dx .doi.org/10.18820/24150487/as27i2.3.

Osinubi, Omowunmi Y., Michael Gochfeld, and Howard M. Kipen. 2000. "Health Effects of Asbestos and Nonasbestos Fibers." *Environmental Health Perspectives* 108 (supp. 4): 665.

Otiso, Kefa M. 2002. "Forced Evictions in Kenyan Cities." *Singapore Journal of Tropical Geography* 23 (3): 252–67. https://doi.org/10.1111/1467-9493.00130.

Rolfe, Steve, Lisa Garnham, Jon Godwin, Isobel Anderson, Pete Seaman, and Cam Donaldson. 2020. "Housing as a Social Determinant of Health and Wellbeing: Developing an Empirically-Informed Realist Theoretical Framework." *BMC Public Health* 20 (1): 1138. https://doi.org/10.1186/s12889-020-09224-0.

Satterthwaite, David. 2016. *The Current and Potential Development Impact of Sub-Saharan Africa's Cities*. London: IIED.

Scarlat, N., V. Motola, J. F. Dallemand, F. Monforti-Ferrario, and Linus Mofor. 2015. "Evaluation of Energy Potential of Municipal Solid Waste from African Urban Areas." *Renewable and Sustainable Energy Reviews* 50:1269–86. https://doi.org/10.1016/j.rser .2015.05.067.

Semunigus, Tsedale, Belay Tessema, Setegn Eshetie, and Feleke Moges. 2016. "Smear Positive Pulmonary Tuberculosis and Associated Factors among Homeless Individuals in Dessie and Debre Birhan Towns, Northeast Ethiopia." *Annals of Clinical Microbiology and Antimicrobials* 15 (1): 50. https://doi.org/10.1186/s12941-016-0165-x.

Stafford Borough Council. 2024. "Housing Health and Safety Rating System: The 29 Hazards." Last updated March 21. https://www.staffordbc.gov.uk/housing-health -and-safety-rating-system-the-29-hazards.

Tankimovich, Mariya. 2013. "Barriers to and Interventions for Improved Tuberculosis Detection and Treatment among Homeless and Immigrant Populations: A Literature Review." *Journal of Community Health Nursing* 30:83–95.

Taylor, Lauren A. 2018. "Housing and Health: An Overview of the Literature." Health Affairs, Robert Wood Johnson Foundation, June 7. https://www.healthaffairs.org /content/briefs/housing-and-health-overview-literature

Tusting, Lucy S., Donal Bisanzio, Graham Alabaster, Ewan Cameron, Richard Cibulskis, Michael Davies, Seth Flaxman, et al. 2019. "Mapping Changes in Housing in Sub-Saharan Africa from 2000 to 2015." *Nature* 568 (7752): 391–94. https://doi.org/10 .1038/s41586-019-1050-5.

UN-Habitat. 2003. *The Challenge of Slums Global Report on Human Settlements 2003*. Nairobi, Kenya: UN-Habitat.

UN-Habitat. 2011. *Housing the Poor in African Cities*. Nairobi, Kenya: UN-Habitat.

UN-Habitat. 2014. *Liberia Housing Profile*. Nairobi, Kenya: UN-Habitat. https://unhabitat .org/sites/default/files/documents/2019-05/liberia_housing_sector.pdf.

UN-Habitat. 2018. *SDG Indicator 11.1.1 Training Module: Adequate Housing and Slum Upgrading*. Nairobi, Kenya: UN-Habitat.

UN-Habitat and UNHCR (Office of the United Nations High Commissioner for Human Rights). 2009. *The Right to Adequate Housing*. Nairobi, Kenya: UN-Habitat. https:// hlrn.org/img/publications/fs21_rev_1_housing_en.pdf.

UN-Habitat and UNICEF. 2020. *Analysis Report: Analysis of Multiple Deprivations in Second-*

ary Cities in Sub-Saharan Africa. London: Cardino. https://www.unicef.org/esa/reports/analysis-multiple-deprivations-secondary-cities-sub-saharan-africa.

UN-Habitat and WHO (World Health Organization). 2020. *Integrating Health in Urban and Territorial Planning: A Sourcebook*. Geneva: UN-Habitat and WHO.

UNHCR (Office of the United Nations High Commissioner for Human Rights). 2010. *2009 Global Trends: Refugees, Asylum-Seekers, Returnees, Internally Displaced and Stateless Peoples*. Geneva: UNHCR, Division of Programme Support and Management.

United Nations. 2014. *Forced Evictions*. Fact Sheet No. 25/Rev. 1. Geneva: United Nations.

United Nations. 2015. "Goal 11: Make Cities and Human Settlements Inclusive, Safe, Resilient and Sustainable." *Transforming Our World: The 2030 Agenda for Sustainable Development*. https://sdgs.un.org/2030agenda.

Vásquez-Vera, Hugo, Laia Palència, Ingrid Magna, Carlos Mena, Jaime Neira, and Carme Borrell. 2017. "The Threat of Home Eviction and Its Effects on Health through the Equity Lens: A Systematic Review." *Social Science and Medicine* 175:199. https://doi.org/10.1016/j.socscimed.2017.01.010.

WHO (World Health Organization). 2014. *Health in All Policies (HiAP) Framework for Country Action*. Geneva: World Health Organization.

WHO (World Health Organization). 2018. *WHO Housing and Health Guidelines*. Geneva: World Health Organization.

WHO (World Health Organization). 2022. "Child Mortality (under 5 Years)." World Health Organization, January 28. https://www.who.int/news-room/fact-sheets/detail/levels-and-trends-in-child-under-5-mortality-in-2020.

WHO (World Health Organization) and Government of South Australia. 2010. "Adelaide Statement on Health in All Policies." Government of South Australia, Adelaide, September 8.

Wilson, D. C. 2015. *Global Waste Management Outlook*. New York: United Nations Environment Programme.

Wolde, Amsalu Mekonnen, Kemal Jemal, Gebru M. Woldearegay, and Kassu Desta Tullu. 2020. "Quality and Safety of Municipal Drinking Water in Addis Ababa City, Ethiopia." *Environmental Health and Preventive Medicine* 25 (1): 9. https://doi.org/10.1186/s12199-020-00847-8.

World Bank. 2015. *Stocktaking of the Housing Sector in Sub-Saharan Africa: Challenges and Opportunities*. Washington, DC: World Bank.

7

Water, Sanitation, and Hygiene (WASH) in Urban Areas of Africa

Situational Analysis and Opportunities for Improvement

Sheillah Simiyu and Phylis Busienei

1. Introduction

Water, sanitation, and hygiene (WASH) are generally accepted as fundamental human rights. In 2010, the UN General Assembly recognized the right to water and sanitation, noting that they are essential to the realization of human rights. They are key for sustainable development and for the achievement of the Sustainable Development Goals (SDGs), including health, education, and gender equity.

Beyond the SDGs, WASH has been shown to have health benefits of reducing mortality and morbidity from leading childhood diseases, such as diarrhea and respiratory tract infections (Prüss-Ustün et al. 2019). WASH also prevents other infectious diseases and conditions such as trachoma and helminth infections, which affect childhood nutrition and overall growth and development (Russell and Azzopardi 2019). WASH is therefore an important determinant of the disease burden, especially among children under 5 years (Prüss-Ustün et al. 2019).

In addition to the health benefits, WASH has development and human well-being benefits. On the one hand, economic growth and development benefits result from and are catalyzed by WASH services; and on the other hand, economic prosperity leads to investment in WASH services and infrastructure, which leads to reduced incidence of disease, protection of the workforce, and an enabling environment for socioeconomic development (Libanio 2022). Furthermore, WASH is a determinant of educational outcomes in girls, especially in settings of limited access, when the burden of water collection is placed on girls. Improved access to sanitation and hygiene

Social Determinants of Health

services is essential for menstrual hygiene management and enables school attendance for girls (Russell and Azzopardi 2019).

The Joint Monitoring Programme (JMP) of the World Health Organization (WHO) and the United Nations Children's Fund (UNICEF) estimates that in 2020, only 39 percent of the population in Africa used safely managed drinking water, 27 percent used safely managed sanitation, and 37 percent used basic hygiene facilities (UNICEF and WHO 2022). There are significant disparities between and within countries in Africa. In rural areas, 75 percent of the population lack access to safely managed water and sanitation, and 70 percent lack basic hygiene services; and in urban areas, 40 percent of the population lack access to water, 67 percent lack access to safely managed sanitation, and 50 percent lack basic hygiene services (UNICEF and WHO 2022). Urban areas in Africa seem to have better access to WASH services than rural areas.

Except for countries within the southern African region, which have the best access to WASH in Africa, most African countries are lagging behind in achieving the SDG targets on WASH, which requires an increase of twelve to forty-two times the current rates of progress (UNICEF and WHO 2022; Zerbo, Delgado, and González 2021). This chapter assesses the WASH situation in urban Africa by analyzing current circumstances, and proposing opportunities for improvement for urban health in African cities.

2. Water in Urban Areas of Africa

Over the years, urban areas of Africa have experienced population growth and rapid urbanization, resulting in the growth of towns, urban centers, and low-income areas. The result of this growth is a higher demand for water and disparities in access to water within urban areas, with planned and higher-income areas having better access to water supply compared to unplanned low-income areas (Dos Santos et al. 2017). Water supply in low-income areas is particularly difficult because these areas are not wholly covered by the piped water network (Beard and Mitlin 2021). Residents of low-income areas that are not served by the piped network rely on other sources, such as wells, boreholes, kiosks, and private vendors (Beard and Mitlin 2021).

2.1. Access, Security, and Affordability

The JMP defines access to drinking water in terms of sources and management, with the gold standard being safely managed drinking water.

Such water should be from an improved source that is accessible on the premises, available when needed, and free from any contamination. Since the 1990s, African countries have made significant improvement in increasing access to improved water sources. In many African countries, more than half of the national population and of the urban population has access to improved water sources. This increase has been through efforts from various state and nonstate actors.

One of the major determinants of access to improved and safely managed water sources is socioeconomic status. Research indicates that households of a higher socioeconomic status in urban areas of Africa are 329 percent more likely to have access to improved water sources compared to the urban poor (Armah et al. 2018). Socioeconomic status encompasses factors such as income, education, and family size (Dos Santos et al. 2017). Residents of low-income areas who are of a lower socioeconomic status have inadequate access to safely managed water services. Further, researchers have pointed to the extra cost to the poor in society in accessing basic goods and services compared to middle- and high- income residents of the same city, called the "poverty penalty"—or sometimes the "poverty premium." This extra cost takes on different forms: a "quality penalty," when the poor pay the same price for an inferior good or service, and a "price penalty," when the poor pay more to access the same good or service, sometimes being priced out of the market (Mutinda et al. 2020).

Inadequate access to safely managed water services in low-income areas has resulted in initiatives such as the pro-poor approaches and the privatization of water supply, which were implemented in various African cities, such as Dar es Salaam, Lagos, Nairobi, and Kampala. These approaches were promoted so that households, especially those in low-income areas, can afford piped water supply (Mitlin et al. 2019). The pro-poor approach aims to alleviate barriers that consumers in low-income areas face when accessing water services, such as low income levels and lack of land tenure (Boakye-Ansah, Schwartz, and Zwarteveen 2019). In this approach, water utilities make adaptations to technological, financial, and organizational measures to improve service provision in low-income areas (see an example in box 7.1). The involvement of the private sector was meant to enable cost recovery, improve access, and increase the financial viability of the water utilities, among other purposes (Beard and Mitlin 2021). Reviews from several African cities, however, suggest that although privatization led to health benefits in

116 Social Determinants of Health

> ### Box 7.1. The Delegated Management Model for Water Supply in Low-Income Areas of Kisumu, Kenya
>
> The delegated management model for water supply is a service delivery model in which a water utility company supplies water in bulk to individuals or groups (often called master operators), who then distribute the water through individual piped networks or standpipes to community members. This model is a pro-poor strategy that targets marginalized groups and is expected to reduce water losses, improve access to safe water, and create income-generation opportunities for slum dwellers. This model was applied in Kisumu city in the Nyalenda low-income area from 2009. An evaluation of the model in 2013 showed some positive outcomes. The model provided opportunities for slum dwellers to earn income from selling water. It also resulted in reduced water cost and improved revenue collection by the water utility company. It led to reductions in payment defaulting, since individual operators collectively have to pay for the water to be in operation. The failure of one person to pay for water may lead to collective failure of the master operator and therefore losses to the group. Areas of improvement identified include the need for structural improvements in the water system and stronger coordination between the utility company and the operators.
>
> *Source:* Nzengya 2015.

some African cities, such as Nairobi and Kampala, it also resulted in increased tariffs, which further disadvantaged the poor, and has therefore not resulted in water being available or affordable (Beard and Mitlin 2021; Dos Santos et al. 2017;).

In addition, residents of low-income areas have access to informal, private water service providers. These informal providers are popular because they offer flexibility in supply arrangements and payment systems, which are often beyond the scope of the large-scale water providers (Beard and Mitlin 2021; Sarkar 2020). These initiatives to increase access to water in low-income areas, however, are faced with several challenges. Although pro-poor services may increase provision of water in low-income areas, the services risk widening the already existing inequities of water access even within the settlements, since the urban poor may have access to services of low quality, for which they pay (Boakye-Ansah, Schwartz, and Zwarteveen 2019; Dos Santos et al. 2017). Similarly, informal service providers often charge higher rates and have been known to sell low-quality water to residents of low-income areas (Sarkar 2020). Research indicates that the private water suppliers charge as much as fifty-two times the cost of piped water (Mitlin et al. 2019). In Nairobi, for example, poor urban residents living in informal settlements pay a much higher price for services such as water and electricity as well as for other basic goods and services: paying nearly four times more for water, when compared with formally housed middle- and upper-income residents (Mutinda et al. 2020).

Similarly, studies from Blantyre, Windhoek, and Dar es Salaam show that even with low-cost community water supplies, households spend up to 15 percent of their income for 20 liters of water per day. For these reasons, the cost of water in African cities has been described as unaffordable, with the water being undrinkable (Mitlin et al. 2019).

2.2. Water Quality

The quality of the water that slum residents use has equally been an area of concern. Studies from low-income areas reveal that water access, quality, and the related health risks vary, and that water quality changes over long, medium, and short time scales (Price, Adams, and Quilliam 2019). The water quality, for example, changes daily as water is collected, transported, stored, and used, and it is affected by factors such as the cleanliness of the water containers (Meierhofer, Wietlisbach, and Matiko 2019; Price et al. 2021). Such temporal changes not only directly influence the biological quality of water, but also have direct health impacts.

Insufficient and poor-quality water are part of the determinants of health outcomes, although often times, these water-related determinants combine with other factors, such as inadequate sanitation and poor hygiene practices, to produce the consequent grim outcomes. It is therefore important and logical to explore sanitation and hygiene factors in urban areas of Africa.

3. Sanitation in Urban Areas of Africa

Just like water, safely managed sanitation services are improved sanitation technologies (such as flush toilets, pour flush latrines, and dry toilets) that are not shared with other households, where excreta are treated and disposed or stored, transported, and treated off-site. Safe sanitation technologies are those that separate excreta from being in contact with humans. The sanitation sector in most countries in Africa has been considered a distasteful issue, and the government allocation of resources to address the current issues has not been fruitful (Abubakar 2017). Just like water services, there are disparities in access to safely managed sanitation services in African countries, and within cities across Africa.

3.1. Fecal Sludge Management

The JMP definition of safely managed sanitation services is drawn from the excreta (feces) flow diagram that tracks waste from different types of sanitation facilities through stages of containment, emptying, transportation, treatment, and reuse or disposal. Excreta flow diagrams have been developed for several cities in Africa.

In Blantyre (Malawi), for example, the developed excreta flow diagram showed that 34 percent of fecal waste from Blantyre city is safely managed, while 66 percent of the waste is unsafely managed. The safely managed waste goes through the fecal sludge management process until treatment, while the waste that is unsafely managed comprises open defecation, fecal sludge that is contained but not emptied, or waste that is emptied but not treated.

Fecal sludge management in African cities is mainly through on-site and off-site services. On-site sanitation services have fecal waste contained in pit latrines and septic tanks, while off-site technologies have fecal waste in sewer systems. On-site sanitation systems are more common in African cities, especially pit latrines, which serve the large population living in low-income areas (Nakagiri et al. 2016). Pit latrines often require emptying and transportation of the sludge from the containment location to the treatment site. Emptying and transportation requires services from vacuum and nonvacuum service providers. The vacuum service providers include the truck operators, while nonvacuum providers are mainly the manual pit latrine emptiers. The manual pit latrine emptiers are preferred because they can navigate through the crowded settlements, they use equipment that empties solids common in the pits, and they have flexible payment plans (Semiyaga et al. 2022; Simiyu, Chumo, and Mberu 2021). In most cases, sludge from pit latrines contains solids, and vacuum trucks and technologies may not empty the solids because the equipment can damage unlined pit latrines (Semiyaga et al. 2022).

Vacuum and nonvacuum technologies are common in African cities. Nonvacuum technologies are a potential solution in low-income settings if the right measures are put in place. Such measures may include having transfer stations closer to households, capacity building of staff involved, and provision of the right equipment (Semiyaga et al. 2022; Simiyu, Chumo, and Mberu 2021). Collection and transport of fecal sludge from low-income settlements is costly because of traffic congestion and long distances to treatment plants (Semiyaga et al. 2015).

Some research studies indicate that vacuum truck operators are more cost effective than manual emptying because these operators are faster, conducting more emptying services in a day, thereby serving a larger proportion of residents (Peletz, Feng, et al. 2020; Semiyaga et al. 2022). The main challenge with vacuum truck operators, however, is financial constraints from households, even though households may be interested in having safely managed sanitation services (Peletz, MacLeod, et al. 2020).

3.2. Access to Sanitation Services across African Cities

From 1990 to 2015, access to improved sanitation in sub-Saharan Africa (SSA) increased from 24 percent to 30 percent, making SSA the region with the lowest sanitation coverage in the world (UNICEF and WHO 2015). As noted, only 27 percent of the population in Africa in 2020 used safely managed sanitation services (UNICEF and WHO 2022). Just like access to water, various factors determine access to sanitation facilities. These factors include socioeconomic and demographic status, political factors, and geographic and environmental factors, such as loose soils and high water levels, which lead to the collapse of pit latrines. These factors limit access to population groups such as older people and persons with disabilities. The use of flying toilets (i.e., the use of plastic bags for defecation, which are then thrown into the open environment) has been reported in some African cities, such as Nairobi, Kampala, and Kisumu, and is an indication of a lack of or limited access to a latrine or toilet facility (Cherunya, Ahlborg, and Truffer 2020; Lusambili 2011; Tumwebaze 2013).

As with water services, overcrowding in informal settlements has resulted in little or no space for construction of adequate sanitation facilities. In addition to lack of space, households in low-income areas are faced with lack of land tenure and financial resources for constructing sanitation facilities. As a result of these challenges, most low-income households in urban Africa share sanitation facilities. There have been different views on the role of shared sanitation, since according to the JMP standards, it is not recognized as part of "safely managed" services. Some scholars argue, however, that shared sanitation facilities bridge the gap of lack of access to sanitation facilities in deprived settings and should be recognized and included in investment decisions as an immediate solution (Evans et al. 2017; Tidwell et al. 2021).

Studies on shared sanitation in African cities have further highlighted the need for consideration of factors such as decision-making dynamics, social relations, land tenure, social capital, gender variations, group dynamics of users, and management factors that influence the continued use of shared sanitation (see box 7.2 and table 7.1; Chipungu et al. 2018; Foggitt et al. 2019; Kwiringira et al. 2014b; Simiyu et al. 2020; Shiras et al. 2018; Tumwebaze and Mosler 2015).

3.3. Sharing and Quality of Sanitation Facilities in Urban Africa

Unlike water, whose quality can be defined by clearly established parameters, the quality of sanitation facilities is more complex to define. Several studies in African cities have therefore defined quality of sanitation using criteria such as cleanliness/hygiene, accessibility, use, sustainability, and desirability (Antwi-Agyei et al. 2022; Meili et al. 2021; Schelbert et al. 2020; Simiyu, Swilling, Cairncross, et al. 2017; Tidwell et al. 2018, 2019). Most of these studies have been conducted on shared sanitation in low-income areas where there is inadequate sanitation service and have highlighted that the "quality" of sanitation facilities affects their usage, and that quality can be influenced by factors such as number of users and sanitation technology (Meili et al. 2021; Simiyu, Swilling, Cairncross, et al. 2017). By focusing on cleanliness of shared sanitation facilities as a measure of quality, studies have indicated that shared sanitation facilities can often be unclean because users do not cooperate in their cleaning and the facilities lack defined rules for use, a leader—such as a landlord—within the compound, privacy during use, water, and regular monitoring (Chipungu et al. 2018; Antwi-Agyei et al. 2020, 2022; Simiyu et al. 2020; Hailu, Alemu, and Adane 2022; Tumwebaze and Mosler 2014; Tumwebaze et al. 2014). Unclean sanitation facilities have been shown to lead to dissatisfaction among users, which lead to poor usage or reverting to inappropriate methods, such as open defecation (Kwiringira et al. 2014a; Tumwebaze 2013).

From a city level, Daudey (2018) compares the cost of different sanitation

Box 7.2. Sharing Sanitation Facilities in Selected African Cities

Sharing sanitation facilities is common in low-income areas of African cities, such as those in the southern region of Africa (South Africa, Zambia, Mozambique), from the eastern region (Kenya, Uganda, Tanzania, Ethiopia), and from the western region (Ghana, Nigeria).

Two main sharing arrangements are common. The first entails community blocks of shared sanitation. In this arrangement, blocks with water and sanitation facilities, often called community ablution blocks (CABs), or communal blocks, are installed within the community for use. Community members can access the ablution blocks for their WASH needs (including bathing and toilet use). This model of CABs is exemplified in South Africa, Ghana, and Kenya (Ramlal et al. 2022; Wiltgen Georgi, Buthelezi, and Meth 2021; Simiyu 2016; Peprah et al. 2015). The second arrangement is the sharing of sanitation facilities among households. In this approach, sanitation facilities are mainly pit latrines or septic tank systems, shared by several households living in a plot or compound. Plots typically have two or more households and may have a landlord on-site. Other compounds or plots have absentee landlords (landlords who do not live within the plot). Landlords are often charged with the responsibility of providing the facilities, and tenants are required to be involved in daily cleaning and maintenance of the facilities. These models are exemplified in Zambia, Kenya, Uganda, Ethiopia, Nigeria, and Ghana (Aluko et al. 2018; Antwi-Agyei et al. 2020, 2022; Chipungu et al. 2018; Foggitt et al. 2019; Hailu, Alemu, and Adane 2022; Nyambe, Agestika, and Yamauchi 2020; Simiyu et al. 2020; Tumwebaze and Mosler 2014; Tumwebaze et al. 2014). In both models of shared sanitation, the challenges remain the same, as summarized in table 7.1.

options in urban areas in Africa and Asia, highlighting that the conventional sewer system is the most expensive investment, compared to other systems, such as septic tanks, pit latrines, and pour flush toilets. His sentiments are also echoed by McConville et al. (2019) from their research in Uganda. These reviews identify costs from an investment perspective, which includes the costs of capital, operation and maintenance, and direct and indirect support. From a case study in Johannesburg, Manga, Bartram, and Evans (2020) sug-

122 Social Determinants of Health

Table 7.1. Summary of sharing sanitation in several countries in Africa

	Southern Africa	East Africa	West Africa
Countries	South Africa, Zambia	Kenya, Uganda, Tanzania, Ethiopia	Ghana, Nigeria
Arrangement	Community ablution blocks (Durban); sanitation facilities shared by several households in a plot (Lusaka)	Sanitation facilities shared by several households in a plot; community ablution blocks	Sanitation facilities shared by several households in a plot; community ablution blocks
Challenges identified	Unclean facilities, lack of willingness among households to clean, lack of water, lack of regular monitoring system, operation and maintenance challenges		
Successes	Community ablution blocks in Durban, South Africa, have increased access to WASH facilities within the communities where they have been installed and have led to training and job opportunities to community members. In other countries like Kenya, where the ablution blocks have been installed with proper management, the facilities are clean, and other initiatives, such as the production of biogas from the ablution blocks, have been initiated. These initiatives have benefited the community. Similarly, studies from Kenya, Mozambique, and Zambia have identified that social dynamics and cooperation initiatives among household members who share sanitation facilities can lead to improved cleanliness, and they may improve social relations among users.		

gest that simplified sewerage is cheaper, especially for low-income settlements. These studies suggest that sewer systems may be more expensive investments, but it is also important to understand contexts (such as low-income areas) and design suitable investment options.

From a household level, studies from low-income areas have highlighted that households may be interested in safe sanitation services but often lack financial resources (Peletz et al. 2021). As such, households make use of available services, which may be of poor quality or inadequate. Studies further indicate that these residents end up paying higher rates for sanitation services, which usually include costs of managing waste from the available facilities (Simiyu, Swilling, Rheingans, et al. 2017). When household sanitation facilities are lacking, households end up using communal sanitation facilities or pay-per-use (presented in box 7.1), which present a significant economic burden to slum residents, as many of them cannot afford the costs (Doe and Aboagye 2022; Simiyu 2016). These financial constraints and socioeconomic conditions lead to sharing the available services or using unhygienic options such as open defecation.

4. Hygiene in Urban Areas of Africa

Hygiene encompasses various activities, including hand hygiene, menstrual hygiene management, and food hygiene. There is no clear, agreed-on, internationally recognized definition of hygiene (UNICEF and WHO 2021). Hand hygiene is one of the most important measures in the prevention of infectious diseases, such as diarrheal and respiratory diseases, including COVID-19 (UNICEF and WHO 2021).

Increasing urbanization coupled with extreme crowding, poor housing quality, and unsanitary environmental conditions make poor hygiene a growing problem in many African cities. Hygiene and other environmental problems in growing urban low-income settlements are tremendous, presenting high-risk environments for disease transmission. In addition, poor hygienic practices such as poor handwashing, food handling, and disposal of feces, including animal feces, have been linked to the spread of enteric disease (Bauza et al. 2020).

4.1. Hand Hygiene and Handwashing

Handwashing is one hygienic strategy that reduces infections by breaking the chain of transmissions, and studies have linked poor handwashing with a high prevalence of diseases (Freeman et al. 2014). Evidence to support the link between handwashing and enteric pathogen transmission was published as early as 1977, with results showing a reduction in diarrheal disease cases due to increased handwashing (Mirza et al. 1997).

Proper handwashing practices in African cities are threatened by inadequate water supply and water scarcity (Amuakwa-Mensah et al. 2021). In general, compared to water and sanitation, access to basic handwashing facilities is low in most African countries and cities (figures 7.1 and 7.2). Studies from low-income areas in African countries such as Ethiopia, Kenya, Uganda, Rwanda, Tanzania, and Côte d'Ivoire generally indicate that households often lack handwashing facilities at the household level (Adane et al. 2018; Davis et al. 2018; Kamau and Njiru 2018; Kisaakye, Ndagurwa, and Mushomi 2021), and therefore, the provision of functional handwashing facilities in these settings has been shown to result in improved handwashing practices (Amon-Tanoh et al. 2021).

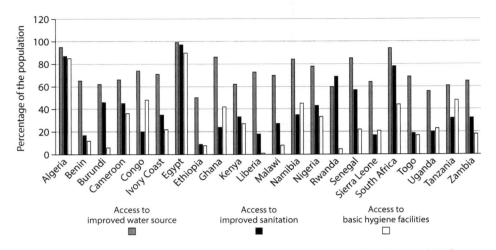

Fig. 7.1. Access to WASH services in various African countries. Source: WHO and UNICEF, 2021.

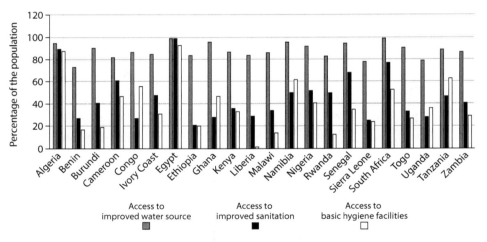

Fig. 7.2. Access to improved WASH services in urban areas of various African countries. Source: WHO and UNICEF, 2021.

Challenges to hand hygiene in low-income settlements in cities in these countries include the need to purchase soap for handwashing, which decreases the potential to wash hands even at the basic recommended times (Austrian et al. 2020; Davis et al. 2018). In general, income level is a determinant for handwashing with soap, since poorer households are less likely to afford the basic necessities for proper handwashing, especially if water costs are high (Ahamad, Burbach, and Tanin 2021; Kamau and Njiru 2018). Other determinants of soap use with handwashing include knowledge of the importance of handwashing and the presence of handwashing places within a household (Amon-Tanoh et al. 2021; Schneider 200).

4.2. Food Hygiene

The WHO estimates that in 2010, 230,000 deaths and 18 million disability-adjusted life years worldwide resulted from foodborne diarrheal diseases, and the greatest burden of these deaths were from Africa (WHO 2015). Factors that hamper food hygiene include poor quality water, poor hygiene practices, and contaminated environments. Most of the disease burden in children occurs during weaning, when children are introduced to complementary foods (Tsai et al. 2019). Studies from cities in Kenya and Mozambique have highlighted that most of the food fed to infants is contaminated with diarrheal disease-causing pathogens (Bick et al. 2020; Tsai et al. 2019). In general, food hygiene in urban Africa, especially in low-income areas, is influenced by various factors, including environmental conditions, lack of knowledge of food hygiene, low income/poverty, and caregiver behavior and practices (Bick et al. 2020; Hoffmann et al. 2022; Mumma et al. 2020; Touré et al. 2013)

4.3. Hygiene in Public Spaces

Aside from the household level, hand hygiene should be practiced in public spaces, which include markets, bus and train parks and stations, restaurants and other eateries, worship places, and public halls. A few studies (e.g., Akpabio and Udofia 2017) have documented the hygiene status in such spaces, and often times, hygiene and handwashing facilities are less than optimal. Some public spaces, however, such as public halls, may have WASH facilities to serve their clients and customers.

In many African cities, food and food products are often sold in open air spaces and public markets. Studies have shown that foods sold in these markets are sometimes contaminated with disease-causing pathogens and are therefore a potential source of disease spread (Akoachere, Tatsinkou, and Nkengfack 2018; Gwenzi 2021; Lazaro, Kapute, and Holm 2019). Such foods are often contaminated at various points in the supply chain, including during transportation and at the point of sale (Knight-Jones et al. 2016).

The causes of contamination are mainly poor handling practices, inadequate knowledge of foodborne diseases, poor hygiene practices, lack of equipment and skilled personnel, and outdated or incomplete regulatory frameworks (Akoachere, Tatsinkou, and Nkengfack 2018; Knight-Jones et al. 2016; Morse et al. 2018).

The COVID pandemic, however, led to the installation of handwashing and hygiene facilities in public spaces in most African countries (e.g., in Ghana; Asante and Mills 2020). A study evaluating the frequency of handwashing in several African countries indicated that the level of concern about the spread of COVID-19 significantly increased the frequency of handwashing more than five times a day in several African countries, including Benin, Ghana, Côte d'Ivoire, Kenya, Rwanda, South Africa, and Zambia (Amuakwa-Mensah et al. 2021). The sustainability of the practices and the facilities, however, is yet to be documented, but the findings point to concerns about water shortage and the need to invest in sustainable water infrastructure.

4.4. Environmental Hygiene and the Role of Animals in Disease Transmission

Health impacts of enteric pathogens in animal excreta is a challenge that has not been adequately researched. Like water, animal excreta also play a major role in transmitting pathogens to humans, especially children. Studies have demonstrated that households in urban areas in Africa own domestic animals for various purposes, and there has been an association between water contamination in households with animals or the presence of animal feces (Barnes, Mumma, and Cumming 2018; Barnes et al. 2018). In Kisumu, household ownership and the presence of animal waste was associated with 30–38 percent higher levels of enterococcus bacteria in drinking water and an increased rate of child contact with animal feces, especially among the urban poor, who tend to have limited space for separate animal and human living (Barnes et al. 2018). These studies indicate that animals are a potential source of enteric disease transmission.

4.5. Menstrual Hygiene Management

For women and girls to live healthy, productive, and dignified lives, they must be able to manage menses effectively. Adequate management of menses requires access to adequate WASH services (clean water, sanitation facilities) that provide enough privacy for disposal of used menstrual products, as well as access to information on the menstrual cycle and hygienic ways of managing menstruation.

Inadequate access to menstrual hygiene facilities and products, coupled with cultural beliefs around menstruation, has a significant impact on girls' access to education. Because of the lack of good sanitation facilities with enough privacy and adequate water to clean, cases of absenteeism in schools have been reported among adolescent girls, who also worry that boys would laugh at them if they soiled their clothes (Miiro et al. 2018).

5. Effects of Inadequate WASH on Health in Urban Africa

It is estimated that 7.75 percent of total deaths from diarrheal diseases across sub-Saharan Africa can be attributed to unsafe WASH practices (Zerbo, Delgado, and González 2021). Poor hygienic practices such as inadequate handwashing, poor food handling, and poor disposal of feces, including animal feces, have been linked to the spread of enteric diseases (Bauza et al. 2020; Whitley et al. 2019). Inadequate access to sanitation facilities and poor drainage can lead to wastewater leaking into drinking water or street food, thus increasing the exposure to pathogens that contribute to diarrhea and its other effects, such as malnutrition, especially in children (Miller et al. 2014). Communicable diseases from inadequate and poor quality water, such as diarrheal diseases, are common in cities, and particularly in low-income settlements, where household water treatment is minimal (Cherunya, Janezic, and Leuchner 2015; Zerbo, Delgado, and González 2020). Poor quality water has also been shown to have other health effects, such as emotional distress among households (Kangmennaang, Bisung, and Elliott 2020).

In most urban areas, children are found playing in the streets and may pick up and ingest or mouth objects that have been contaminated (Buttenheim 2009). On the other hand, children are not likely to use the available latrine facilities and may defecate in such places, thus exacerbating the transmission of enteric pathogens in street food. Long-term exposure to these pathogens hinders brain development in infants and reduces immunity. Similarly, this exposure leads to limited absorption of food in the stomach, thus leading to malnutrition and stunting.

Several studies indicate that proper hygiene is key in the prevention of under 5 diarrhea (Nguyen et al. 2021). Other contradicting studies and reports indicate that handwashing interventions have not had significant effects on diarrheal disease reduction or prevalence (Mulatya and Ochieng

2020; Null et al. 2018). These contradicting findings point to the need for a holistic approach to WASH in disease prevention, as the three determinants interact to influence disease spread.

5.1. Effects of Inadequate WASH on Women and Girls

Lack of access to sanitation facilities and poor usage have far-reaching effects on women and girls. Unclean or shared latrines mean that women are forced to clean them in order to prevent exposure to infections (Kwiringira et al. 2014a). Similarly, women and girls shun facilities that may expose them to these infections, including resorting to open defecation or walking for longer distances to look for better facilities. This is accompanied by other challenges, such as violence (Corburn and Hildebrand 2015) and rape, especially at night and when using toilets far from their households, with unlockable doors and without a proper lighting system. Furthermore, various studies have suggested a clear link between poor or inadequate menstrual hygiene and diseases such as reproductive and urinary infections (Chinyama et al. 2019; Phillips-Howard et al. 2016).

5.2. Effects of Shared Sanitation on Health

Studies on the role of shared sanitation on health have produced differing findings. Some studies have indicated that shared sanitation is associated with increased odds of disease transmission. Following an analytical review of various studies to evaluate the role of shared sanitation in disease transmission, Ramlal et al. (2019) highlight that shared sanitation leads to a significant increase in diarrheal diseases, although children under 5 were less affected. A study from CABs in Durban showed that surfaces within ablution blocks, such as cistern handles and pull latches, are potential hotspots for fecal contamination and pathways for disease spread (Ramlal et al. 2022). In Maputo, high levels of fecal contamination were noted in households with poor-quality shared sanitation facilities, which were a potential source of disease spread (Holcomb et al. 2020).

Other studies have shown insignificant associations between shared sanitation and disease spread. A study from Cape Town indicated a significantly lower risk of diarrhea among households sharing sanitation facilities with more than three other households compared to those using nonshared facilities (Nguyen et al. 2021). A study from Lusaka showed that having an improved toilet facility increased the odds of household diarrhea prevalence by 10.9 percent. The study also noted, however, that toilets used by more than ten persons (rather than households) were found to increase the risk of household diarrhea prevalence (Nyambe, Agestika, and Yamauchi 2020). A main highlight from these studies is to focus on the number of persons sharing rather than the number of households, since the former considers the formal and informal nature of toilet sharing, as some private toilets may have more users than shared toilets because of the number of household members and overall users.

6. Looking Forward: Opportunities for Improvement

Building on the WASH situation in urban Africa and the effects on health, the section below presents recommendations for improving the urban health situation in African cities.

6.1. Effective WASH Interventions

Policymakers should identify and adopt WASH interventions and implementation strategies that have been shown to be effective in Africa and other regions, especially regions with similar context. WASH interventions evaluated using randomized control trials, as well as longitudinal and other study designs, that have shown effectiveness in improving population health and reducing the incidence of diarrheal diseases are described in systematic reviews by Chirgwin et al. (2021) and Ramesh et al. (2015), among others.

6.2. Further Research

To curb the WASH challenges in cities and in low-income areas, further rigorous research is needed on gray areas identified in this review: the opportunities for cost reduction in the WASH sector while ensuring that poor households have access to good quality services, the role of the communal environment on disease spread, effective approaches for community sensitization and delivery of WASH messages, management of waste from sanitation systems, the role of shared services on health outcomes, individual and contextual factors that shape the use of WASH facilities and services, demand and attitudes toward WASH, coping mechanisms at household and community levels, and power relations that determine access and involvement in decision making. Research should take into consideration the different contexts and cultures in cities, as these provide lessons for effective policies and models.

6.3. Availability of Data

There is need for investments in quality data collection and monitoring, at the national and subnational levels. At local levels, such as secondary cities, for example, subnational governments and stakeholders should align their data collection processes for informed and collective data. In addition, research on WASH needs to be aligned with the available country gaps in WASH for more informed decision making. These data are important in identifying areas where all stakeholders, including governments, need to implement required interventions, as well as informing policy and action.

6.4. Policy and Regulations

Governments and relevant authorities may need to ensure that policies and regulations are implemented effectively. Where the policies are nonexistent, the involvement of all stakeholders in research will need to identify these gaps and by working together, co-design context-specific policies for each country. The policies will also need to ensure effective integration of the policies at the national and subnational levels, as well as across the related ministries. Implementation of WASH policies may considerably improve the overall WASH status in African cities.

6.5. Governance, Leadership, and Political Will

Good governance is achieved through a clear means of supporting or assisting the disadvantaged in society, especially the population living in low-income settlements. The presence of regulations also promotes transparency, accountability, equitability, and efficiency. Improvement approaches combined with proper leadership and the right political commitment will enable cities to exploit available opportunities. The improvements will need to also be aligned to commitments and targets such as SDGs and be anchored in African-led initiatives, such as the African Union Agenda 2063. WASH has to be much more prominent in the political agenda of most developing countries, given that there can be no solutions without political solutions (Mara and Evans 2018).

6.6. Practical and Participatory Co-design Approaches

A holistic approach to adequate WASH management will need to be adopted by drawing from all disciplines and stakeholders, for example, engineering, finance, politics, urban planning, technology and infrastructure, and public health. The stakeholders should include households and communities who propose and adopt community-based governance approaches. Such a transdisciplinary approach with the existing stakeholders will offer technical expertise while partnering with communities who offer practical and contextualized solutions. Stakeholder platforms that bring together the different actors could enable accountability and monitoring of progress, as well as aligning the needs of all concerned stakeholders. With such approaches, solutions and interventions can be designed from a systems perspective, encompassing all groups and populations (such as women, children, persons with disability, and older people)

6.7. Health Education and Awareness

In addition to co-design approaches, sensitization and awareness approaches will need to be intensified in cities, especially in regions with low service levels. Community-led sensitization approaches that involve community members will need to be adopted, as they are more likely to be sustainable. These approaches will include activities that stimulate demand for WASH and encourage positive hygiene-related behavior.

7. Conclusion

Promoting universal access to adequate WASH in urban Africa remains a challenge for all stakeholders. Whereas most urban areas in Africa seem to be better served with water, sanitation, and hygiene services, there are disparities within African cities in access to these services. Low-income areas in particular are faced with challenges of inadequacy, costs, and quality of the available services. These challenges limit access of the most disadvantaged communities and population groups, and they have serious health effects, such as the spread of infectious diseases. WASH is an important element in the achievement of SDGs, however, and governments and all stakeholders need to come to consensus on the important role played by WASH in urban health. Opportunities for improvement include further research, availability of findings to all stakeholders, and the co-design of interventions and solutions by including all stakeholders in decision making. WASH advocacy is needed so that development decisions are inclusive of the role of WASH in urban health.

REFERENCES

Abubakar, Ismaila Rimi. 2017. "Access to Sanitation Facilities among Nigerian Households : Determinants and Sustainability Implications." *Sustainability* 9 (547): 1–17. https://doi.org/10.3390/su9040547.

Adane, Metadel, Bezatu Mengistie, Worku Mulat, Girmay Medhin, and Helmut Kloos. 2018. "The Most Important Recommended Times of Hand Washing with Soap and Water in Preventing the Occurrence of Acute Diarrhea among Children under Five Years of Age in Slums of Addis Ababa, Ethiopia." *Journal of Community Health* 43 (2): 400–405.

Ahamad, Mazbahul G., Mark Burbach, and Fahian Tanin. 2021. "Relationships among Toilet Sharing, Water Source Locations, and Handwashing Places without Observed Soap: A Cross-Sectional Study of the Richest Households in Bangladesh." *Environmental Health Insights* 15. https://doi.org/10.1177/11786302211060163.

Akoachere, Jane-Francis Tatah Kihla, Bertrand Fossi Tatsinkou, and Joseph Mbapngong Nkengfack. 2018. "Bacterial and Parasitic Contaminants of Salad Vegetables Sold in Markets in Fako Division, Cameroon and Evaluation of Hygiene and Handling Practices of Vendors." *BMC Research Notes* 11 (1): 1–7. https://doi.org/10.1186s13104-018 -3175-2.

Akpabio, Emmanuel M., and Eti-ido S. Udofia. 2017. "Unsafe Water, Sanitation and Hygiene in Nigeria's Public Spaces: The Political Economy Angle." *International Journal of Water Resources Development* 33 (2): 310–25. https://doi.org/10.1080/07900627.2016 .1189814.

Aluko, O. O., E. O. Oloruntoba, U. A. Chukwunenye, E. U. Henry, and E. Ojogun. 2018. "The Dynamics and Determinants of Household Shared Sanitation Cleanliness in a Heterogeneous Urban Settlement in Southwest Nigeria." *Public Health* 165:125–35. https://doi.org/10.1016/j.puhe.2018.09.013.

Amon-Tanoh, Maud A., Jim McCambridge, Patrice K. Blon, Herman A. Kouamé, Patrick Nguipdop-Djomo, Adam Biran, and Simon Cousens. 2021. "Effects of a Social Norm-Based Handwashing Intervention Including Handwashing Stations, and a Handwashing Station-Only Intervention on Handwashing with Soap in Urban Côte d'Ivoire: A Cluster Randomised Controlled Trial." *Lancet Global Health* 9 (12): e1707–18. https://doi.org/10.1016/S2214-109X(21)00387-9.

Amuakwa-Mensah, Franklin, Rebecca Afua Klege, Philip Kofi Adom, and Gunnar Köhlin. 2021. "COVID-19 and Handwashing: Implications for Water Use in Sub-Saharan Africa." *Water Resources and Economics* 36 (October): 100189. https://doi.org/10.1016/j.wre .2021.100189.

Antwi-Agyei, Prince, Bismark Dwumfour-Asare, Kwaku Amaning Adjei, Raphael Kweyu, and Sheillah Simiyu. 2020. "Understanding the Barriers and Opportunities for Effective Management of Shared Sanitation in Low-Income Settlements—The Case of Kumasi, Ghana." *International Journal of Environmental Research and Public Health* 17 (12): 4528.

Antwi-Agyei, Prince, Isaac Monney, Kwaku Amaning Adjei, Raphael Kweyu, and Sheillah Simiyu. 2022. "Shared but Clean Household Toilets: What Makes This Possible? Evidence from Ghana and Kenya." *International Journal of Environmental Research and Public Health* 19 (7): 4271.

Armah, Frederick Ato, Bernard Ekumah, David Oscar Yawson, Justice O. Odoi, Abdul-Rahaman Afitiri, and Florence Esi Nyieku. 2018. "Access to Improved Water and Sanitation in Sub-Saharan Africa in a Quarter Century." *Heliyon* 4 (11): e00931. https://doi.org/10.1016/j.heliyon.2018.e00931.

Asante, Lewis Abedi, and Richael Odarko Mills. 2020. "Exploring the Socio-Economic Impact of COVID-19 Pandemic in Marketplaces in Urban Ghana." *Africa Spectrum* 55 (2): 170–81. https://doi.org/10.1177/0002039720943612.

Austrian, Karen, Jessie Pinchoff, James B. Tidwell, Corinne White, Timothy Abuya, Beth Kangwana, Rhoune Ochako, et al. 2020. "COVID-19 Related Knowledge, Attitudes, Practices and Needs of Households in Informal Settlements in Nairobi, Kenya." *SSRN Electronic Journal*, April 23. https://doi.org/10.2139/ssrn.3576785.

Barnes, Amber N., John D. Anderson, Jane Mumma, Zahid Hayat Mahmud, and Oliver Cumming. 2018. "The Association between Domestic Animal Presence and Ownership and Household Drinking Water Contamination among Peri-urban Communities of Kisumu, Kenya." *PLoS One* 13 (6): e0197587.

Barnes, Amber N., J. Mumma, and O. Cumming. 2018. "Role, Ownership and Presence of Domestic Animals in Urban Households of Kisumu, Kenya." *Zoonoses Public Health* 65:202–14. https://doi.org/10.1111/zph.12429.

Bauza, Valerie, Vincent Madadi, Robinson Ocharo, Thanh H. Nguyen, and Jeremy S. Guest. 2020. "Enteric Pathogens from Water, Hands, Surface, Soil, Drainage Ditch, and Stream Exposure Points in a Low-Income Neighborhood of Nairobi, Kenya." *Science of the Total Environment* 709:135344. https://doi.org/10.1016/j.scitotenv.2019.135344.

Beard, Victoria A., and Diana Mitlin. 2021. "Water Access in Global South Cities: The Challenges of Intermittency and Affordability." *World Development* 147:105625. https://doi.org/10.1016/j.worlddev.2021.105625.

Bick, Sarah, Lauren Perieres, Lauren D'Mello-Guyett, Kelly K. Baker, Joe Brown, Bacelar Muneme, Rassul Nalá, Robert Dreibelbis, and Oliver Cumming. 2020. "Risk Factors for Child Food Contamination in Low-Income Neighbourhoods of Maputo, Mozambique: An Exploratory, Cross-Sectional Study." *Maternal and Child Nutrition* 16 (4): 1–21. https://doi.org/10.1111/mcn.12991.

Boakye-Ansah, Akosua Sarpong, Klaas Schwartz, and Margreet Zwarteveen. 2019. "Unravelling Pro-Poor Water Services: What Does It Mean and Why Is It So Popular?" *Journal of Water Sanitation and Hygiene for Development* 9 (2): 187–97. https://doi.org/10.2166/washdev.2019.086.

Buttenheim, Alison M. 2009. "The Sanitation Environment in Urban Slums: Implications for Child Health." *Population and Environment* 30 (1–2): 26–47. https://doi.org/10.1007/s11111-008-0074-9.

Cherunya, Pauline C., Helene Ahlborg, and Bernhard Truffer. 2020. "Anchoring Innovations in Oscillating Domestic Spaces: Why Sanitation Service Offerings Fail in Informal Settlements." *Research Policy* 49 (1): 103841. https://doi.org/10.1016/j.respol.2019.103841.

Cherunya, Pauline C., Christine Janezic, and Michael Leuchner. 2015. "Sustainable Supply of Safe Drinking Water for Underserved Households in Kenya: Investigating the Viability of Decentralized Solutions." *Water (Switzerland)* 7 (10): 5437–57. https://doi.org/10.3390/w7105437.

Chinyama, Joyce, Jenala Chipungu, Cheryl Rudd, Mercy Mwale, Lavuun Verstraete, Charity Sikamo, Wilbroad Mutale, Roma Chilengi, and Anjali Sharma. 2019. "Menstrual Hygiene Management in Rural Schools of Zambia: A Descriptive Study of Knowledge, Experiences and Challenges Faced by Schoolgirls." *BMC Public Health* 19 (1): 1–10. https://doi.org/10.1186/s12889-018-6360-2.

Chipungu, Jenala, James B. Tidwell, Roma Chilengi, Valerie Curtis, and Robert Aunger. 2018. "The Social Dynamics around Shared Sanitation in an Informal Settlement of Lusaka, Zambia." *Journal of Water, Sanitation and Hygiene for Development* 9 (1): 102–10. https://doi.org/10.2166/washdev.2018.102.

Chirgwin, Hannah, Sandy Cairncross, Dua Zehra, and Hugh Sharma Waddington. 2021. "Interventions Promoting Uptake of Water, Sanitation and Hygiene (Wash) Technologies in Low-and Middle-income Countries: An Evidence and Gap Map of Effectiveness Studies." *Campbell Systematic Reviews* 17 (4): e1194.

Corburn, Jason, and Chantal Hildebrand. 2015. "Slum Sanitation and the Social Determinants of Women's Health in Nairobi, Kenya." *Journal of Environmental and Public Health* 2015:1–6.

Daudey, Loïc. 2018. "The Cost of Urban Sanitation Solutions: A Literature Review." *Journal of Water Sanitation and Hygiene for Development* 8 (2): 176–95. https://doi.org/10.2166/washdev.2017.058.

Davis, Emily, Oliver Cumming, Rose Evalyne Aseyo, Damaris Nelima Muganda, Kelly K. Baker, Jane Mumma, and Robert Dreibelbis. 2018. "Oral Contact Events and Caregiver Hand Hygiene: Implications for Fecal-Oral Exposure to Enteric Pathogens among Infants 3–9 Months Living in Informal, Peri-urban Communities in Kisumu, Kenya." *International Journal of Environmental Research and Public Health* 15 (2): 192. https://doi.org/10.3390/ijerph15020192.

Doe, Benjamin, and Prince Dacosta Aboagye. 2022. "The Place of Subsidy: Affordable Sanitation Service Delivery in Slums of Kumasi, Ghana." *GeoJournal* 87 (1): 295–317. https://doi.org/10.1007/s10708-020-10256-7.

Dos Santos, S., E. A. Adams, G. Neville, Y. Wada, A. de Sherbinin, E. Mullin Bernhardt, and S. B. Adamo. 2017. "Urban Growth and Water Access in Sub-Saharan Africa: Progress, Challenges, and Emerging Research Directions." *Science of the Total Environment* 607–608:497–508. https://doi.org/10.1016/j.scitotenv.2017.06.157.

Evans, Barbara, Andrés Hueso, Richard Johnston, Guy Norman, Eddy Pérez, Tom Slaymaker, and Sophie Trémolet. 2017. "Limited Services? The Role of Shared Sanitation in the 2030 Agenda for Sustainable Development." *Journal of Water Sanitation and Hygiene for Development* 7 (3): 349–51. https://doi.org/10.2166/washdev.2017.023.

Foggitt, Ella, Sally Cawood, Barbara Evans, and Patricia Acheampong. 2019. "Experiences of Shared Sanitation—Towards a Better Understanding of Access, Exclusion and 'Toilet Mobility' in Low-Income Urban Areas." *Journal of Water, Sanitation and Hygiene for Development* 9 (3): 581–90. https://doi.org/10.2166/washdev.2019.025.

Freeman, Matthew C., Meredith E. Stocks, Oliver Cumming, Aurelie Jeandron, Julian P. T. Higgins, Jennyfer Wolf, Annette Prüss-Ustün, et al. 2014. "Hygiene and Health: Systematic Review of Handwashing Practices Worldwide and Update of Health Effects." *Tropical Medicine and International Health* 19 (8): 906–16. https://doi.org/10.1111/tmi.12339.

Gwenzi, Willis. 2021. "Leaving No Stone Unturned in Light of the COVID-19 Faecal-Oral Hypothesis? A Water, Sanitation and Hygiene (WASH) Perspective Targeting Low-Income Countries." *Science of the Total Environment* 753:141751. https://doi.org/10.1016/j.scitotenv.2020.141751.

Hailu, Kidist, Zewdie Aderaw Alemu, and Metadel Adane. 2022. "Barriers to Cleaning of Shared Latrines in Slums of Addis Ababa, Ethiopia." *PLoS One* 17 (3): e0263363. https://doi.org/10.1371/journal.pone.0263363.

Hoffmann, Vivian, Sheillah Simiyu, Daniel K. Sewell, Kevin Tsai, Oliver Cumming, Jane Mumma, and Kelly K. Baker. 2022. "Influence of Milk Product Safety and Household Food Hygiene on Bacterial Contamination of Infant Food in Peri-urban Kenya." *Frontiers in Public Health* 9 (February): 772892. https://doi.org/10.3389/fpubh.2021.772892.

Holcomb, David A., Jackie Knee, Trent Sumner, Zaida Adriano, Ellen de Bruijn, Rassul Nalá, Oliver Cumming, Joe Brown, and Jill R. Stewart. 2020. "Human Fecal Contamination of Water, Soil, and Surfaces in Households Sharing Poor-Quality Sanitation Facilities in Maputo, Mozambique." *International Journal of Hygiene and Environmental Health* 226 (February): 113496. https://doi.org/10.1016/j.ijheh.2020.113496.

Kamau, Njoroge, and Haron Njiru. 2018. "Water, Sanitation and Hygiene Situation in Kenya's Urban Slums." *Journal of Health Care for the Poor and Underserved* 29 (1): 321–36. https://doi.org/10.1353/hpu.2018.0022.

Kangmennaang, Joseph, Elijah Bisung, and Susan J. Elliott. 2020. "'We Are Drinking Diseases': Perception of Water Insecurity and Emotional Distress in Urban Slums in Accra, Ghana." *International Journal of Environmental Research and Public Health* 17 (3): 890. https://doi.org/10.3390/ijerph17030890.

Kisaakye, Peter, Pedzisai Ndagurwa, and John Mushomi. 2021. "An Assessment of Availability of Handwashing Facilities in Households from Four East African Countries." *Journal of Water, Sanitation and Hygiene for Development* 11 (1): 75–90. https://doi.org/10.2166/washdev.2020.129.

Knight-Jones, Theodore J. D., M. Bernard Hang'ombe, Mwansa M. Songe, Yona Sinkala, and Delia Grace. 2016. "Microbial Contamination and Hygiene of Fresh Cow's Milk Produced by Smallholders in Western Zambia." *International Journal of Environmental Research and Public Health* 13 (7): 1–13. https://doi.org/10.3390/ijerph13070737.

Kwiringira, Japheth, Peter Atekyereza, Charles Niwagaba, and Isabel Günther. 2014a. "Descending the Sanitation Ladder in Urban Uganda: Evidence from Kampala Slums." *BMC Public Health* 14 (1): 624. https://doi.org/10.1186/1471-2458-14-624.

Kwiringira, Japheth, Peter Atekyereza, Charles Niwagaba, and Isabel Günther. 2014b. "Gender Variations in Access, Choice to Use and Cleaning of Shared Latrines: Experiences from Kampala Slums, Uganda." *BMC Public Health* 14 (1): 1180. https://doi.org/10.1186/1471-2458-14-1180.

Lazaro, Jazimoni, Fanuel Kapute, and Rochelle H. Holm. 2019. "Food Safety Policies and Practices in Public Spaces: The Urban Water, Sanitation, and Hygiene Environment for Fresh Fish Sold from Individual Vendors in Mzuzu, Malawi." *Food Science and Nutrition* 7 (9): 2986–94. https://doi.org/10.1002/fsn3.1155.

Libanio, Paulo Augusto Cunha. 2022. "WASH Services and Human Development: A Tangible Nexus for Achieving Water-Related SDGs." *International Journal of River Basin Management* 20 (1): 57–66. https://doi.org/10.1080/15715124.2021.1909603.

Lusambili, Adelaide. 2011. "'It Is Our Dirty Little Secret': An Ethnographic Study of the Flying Toilets in Kibera Slums, Nairobi." STEPS Working Paper 44. Brighton: STEPS Centre.

Manga, Musa, Jamie Bartram, and Barbara E. Evans. 2020. "Economic Cost Analysis of Low-Cost Sanitation Technology Options in Informal Settlement Areas (Case Study: Soweto, Johannesburg)." *International Journal of Hygiene and Environmental Health* 223 (1): 289–98. https://doi.org/10.1016/j.ijheh.2019.06.012.

Mara, Duncan, and Barbara Evans. 2018. "The Sanitation and Hygiene Targets of the Sustainable Development Goals: Scope and Challenges." *Journal of Water Sanitation and Hygiene for Development* 8 (1): 1–16. https://doi.org/10.2166/washdev.2017.048.

McConville, Jennifer R., Elisabeth Kvarnström, James M. Maiteki, and Charles B. Niwagaba. 2019. "Infrastructure Investments and Operating Costs for Fecal Sludge and Sewage Treatment Systems in Kampala, Uganda." *Urban Water Journal* 16 (8): 584–93. https://doi.org/10.1080/1573062X.2019.1700290.

Meierhofer, Regula, Basil Wietlisbach, and Carol Matiko. 2019. "Influence of Container Cleanliness, Container Disinfection with Chlorine, and Container Handling on Recontamination of Water Collected from a Water Kiosk in a Kenyan Slum." *Journal of Water and Health* 17 (2): 308–17. https://doi.org/10.2166/wh.2019.282.

Meili, Dario, Vasco Schelbert, Mahbub-Ul Alam, Prince Antwi-Agyei, Sheillah Simiyu, Kwaku Amaning Adjei, Bismark Dwumfour-Asare, et al. 2021. "Indicators for Sanitation Quality in Low-Income Urban Settlements: Evidence from Kenya, Ghana, and Bangladesh." *Social Indicators Research* 162:683–720. https://doi.org/10.1007/s11205-021-02855-9.

Miiro, George, Rwamahe Rutakumwa, Jessica Nakiyingi-Miiro, Kevin Nakuya, Saidat Musoke, Juliet Namakula, Suzanna Francis, et al. 2018. "Menstrual Health and School Absenteeism among Adolescent Girls in Uganda (MENISCUS): A Feasibility Study." *BMC Women's Health* 18 (1): 1–13. https://doi.org/10.1186/s12905-017-0502-z.

Miller, Mark, Angel Mendez Acosta, Cesar Banda Chavez, Julian Torres Flores, Maribel Paredes Olotegui, Silvia Rengifo Pinedo, Dixner Rengifo Trigoso, et al. 2014. "The MAL-ED Study: A Multinational and Multidisciplinary Approach to Understand the Relationship between Enteric Pathogens, Malnutrition, Gut Physiology, Physical Growth, Cognitive Development, and Immune Responses in Infants and Children up to 2 Years of Age in Resource-Poor Environments." *Clinical Infectious Diseases* 59 (suppl. 4): S193–206. https://doi.org/10.1093/cid/ciu653.

Mirza, Nazrat M., Laura E. Caulfield, Robert E. Black, and William M. Macharia. 1997. "Risk Factors for Diarrheal Duration." *American Journal of Epidemiology* 146 (9): 776–85. https://doi.org/10.1093/oxfordjournals.aje.a009354.

Mitlin, Diana, Victoria A. Beard, David Satterthwaite, and Jillian Du. 2019. *Unaffordable and Undrinkable: Rethinking Urban Water Access in the Global South.* Washington, DC: World Resources Institute.

Morse, Tracy D., Humphreys Masuku, Sarah Rippon, and Hudson Kubwalo. 2018. "Achieving an Integrated Approach to Food Safety and Hygiene—Meeting the Sustainable Development Goals in Sub-Saharan Africa." *Sustainability (Switzerland)* 10 (7): 2394. https://doi.org/10.3390/su10072394.

Mulatya, Diana Mutuku, and Caroline Ochieng. 2020. "Disease Burden and Risk Factors of Diarrhoea in Children under Five Years: Evidence from Kenya's Demographic Health Survey 2014." *International Journal of Infectious Diseases* 93:359–66. https://doi.org/10.1016/j.ijid.2020.02.003.

Mumma, Jane Awiti Odhiambo, Oliver Cumming, Sheillah Simiyu, Alexandra Czerniewska, Rose Evalyne Aseyo, Damaris Nelima Muganda, Emily Davis, Kelly K. Baker, and Robert Dreibelbis. 2020. "Infant Food Hygiene and Childcare Practices in Context: Findings from an Urban Informal Settlement in Kenya." *American Journal of Tropical Medicine and Hygiene* 102 (1): 220–22. https://doi.org/10.4269/ajtmh.19-0279.

Mutinda, Mary, Baraka Mwau, Jack Makau, and Alice Sverdlik. 2020. "Policy Briefing: Rethinking Slum Upgrading in Light of Nairobi's Poverty Penalty (SDI Kenya)." *Muungano Wa Wanavijiji*, May 1. https://www.muungano.net/publicationslibrary/2020/5/20/muungano-alliance-policy-briefing-rethinking-slum-upgrading-in-light-of-nairobis-poverty-penalty.

Nakagiri, Anne, Charles B. Niwagaba, Philip M. Nyenje, Robinah N. Kulabako, John B. Tumuhairwe, and Frank Kansiime. 2016. "Are Pit Latrines in Urban Areas of Sub-Saharan Africa Performing? A Review of Usage, Filling, Insects and Odour Nuisances." *BMC Public Health* 16 (120): 1–16. https://doi.org/10.1186/s12889-016-2772-z.

Nguyen, Thi Yen Chi, Bamidele Oladapo Fagbayigbo, Guéladio Cissé, Nesre Redi, Samuel Fuhrimann, John Okedi, Christian Schindler, et al. 2021. "Diarrhoea among Children Aged under Five Years and Risk Factors in Informal Settlements: A Cross-Sectional Study in Cape Town, South Africa." *International Journal of Environmental Research and Public Health* 18 (11): 6043. https://doi.org/10.3390/ijerph18116043.

Null, Clair, Christine P. Stewart, Amy J. Pickering, Holly N. Dentz, Charles D. Arnold Benjamin F. Arnold, Thomas Clasen Jade Benjamin-Chung, Kathryn G. Dewey, et al. 2018. "Effects of Water Quality, Sanitation, Handwashing, and Nutritional Interventions on Diarrhoea and Child Growth in Rural Kenya: A Cluster Randomised Controlled Trial." *Lancet Global Health* 6 (3): e316–29. https://doi.org/10.1016/S2214-109X(18)30005-6.

Nyambe, Sikopo, Lina Agestika, and Taro Yamauchi. 2020. "The Improved and the Unimproved: Factors Influencing Sanitation and Diarrhoea in a Peri-urban Settlement

of Lusaka, Zambia." *PLoS ONE* 15 (5): 1–19. https://doi.org/10.1371/journal.pone
.0232763.

Nzengya, Daniel M. 2015. "Exploring the Challenges and Opportunities for Master Operators and Water Kiosks under Delegated Management Model (DMM): A Study in Lake
Victoria Region, Kenya." *Cities* 46:35–43. https://doi.org/10.1016/j.cities.2015.04.005.

Peletz, Rachel, Caroline Delaire, Joan Kones, Clara Macleod, Edinah Samuel, Alicea
Easthope-Frazer, and Ranjiv Khush. 2021. "Will Households Invest in Safe Sanitation? Results from an Experimental Demand Trial in Nakuru, Kenya." *International
Journal of Environmental Research and Public Health* 18 (9): 4462. https://doi.org/10
.3390/ijerph18094462.

Peletz, Rachel, Andy Feng, Clara MacLeod, Dianne Vernon, Tim Wang, Joan Kones, Caroline Delaire, Salim Haji, and Ranjiv Khush. 2020. "Expanding Safe Fecal Sludge Management in Kisumu, Kenya: An Experimental Comparison of Latrine Pit-Emptying
Services." *Journal of Water, Sanitation and Hygiene for Development* 10 (4): 1–12. https://
doi.org/10.2166/washdev.2020.060.

Peletz, Rachel, Clara MacLeod, Joan Kones, Edinah Samuel, Alicea Easthope-Frazer, Caroline Delaire, and Ranjiv Khush. 2020. "When Pits Fill Up: Supply and Demand for Safe
Pit-Emptying Services in Kisumu, Kenya." *PLoS ONE* 15 (9): e0238003. https://doi.org
/10.1371/journal.pone.0238003.

Peprah, Dorothy, Kelly K. Baker, Christine Moe, Katharine Robb, Nii Wellington, Habib
Yakubu, and Clair Null. 2015. "Public Toilets and Their Customers in Low-Income
Accra, Ghana." *Environment and Urbanization* 27 (2): 589–604. https://doi.org/10.1177
/0956247815595918.

Phillips-Howard, Penelope A., Bethany Caruso, Belen Torondel, Garazi Zulaika, Murat
Sahin, and Marni Sommer. 2016. "Menstrual Hygiene Management among Adoles-
cent Schoolgirls in Low- and Middle-Income Countries: Research Priorities." *Global
Health Action* 9 (1): 33032. https://doi.org/10.3402/GHA.V9.33032.

Price, Heather D., Ellis A. Adams, Peter D. Nkwanda, Theresa W. Mkandawire, and Richard S. Quilliam. 2021. "Daily Changes in Household Water Access and Quality in
Urban Slums Undermine Global Safe Water Monitoring Programmes." *International
Journal of Hygiene and Environmental Health* 231:113632. https://doi.org/10.1016/j
.ijheh.2020.113632.

Price, Heather, Ellis Adams, and Richard S. Quilliam. 2019. "The Difference a Day Can
Make: The Temporal Dynamics of Drinking Water Access and Quality in Urban Slums."
Science of the Total Environment 671:818–26. https://doi.org/10.1016/j.scitotenv.2019
.03.355.

Prüss-Ustün, Annette, Jennyfer Wolf, Jamie Bartram, Thomas Clasen, Oliver Cumming,
Matthew C. Freeman, Bruce Gordon, Paul R. Hunter, Kate Medlicott, and Richard
Johnston. 2019. "Burden of Disease from Inadequate Water, Sanitation and Hygiene
for Selected Adverse Health Outcomes: An Updated Analysis with a Focus on Low- and
Middle-Income Countries." *International Journal of Hygiene and Environmental Health*
222 (5): 765–77. https://doi.org/10.1016/j.ijheh.2019.05.004.

Ramesh, Anita, Karl Blanchet, Jeroen H. J. Ensink, and Bayard Roberts. 2015. "Evidence
on the Effectiveness of Water, Sanitation, and Hygiene (WASH) Interventions on

Health Outcomes in Humanitarian Crises: A Systematic Review." *PloS One* 10 (9): e0124688.

Ramlal, P. S., T. A. Stenström, S. Munien, I. D. Amoah, C. A. Buckley, and Sershen. 2019. "Relationships between Shared Sanitation Facilities and Diarrhoeal and Soil-Transmitted Helminth Infections: An Analytical Review." *Journal of Water, Sanitation and Hygiene for Development* 9 (2): 198–209. https://doi.org/10.2166/washdev.2019.180.

Ramlal, Preshod S., Johnson Lin, Christopher A. Buckley, Thor Axel Stenström, and Isaac D. Amoah. 2022. "An Assessment of the Health Risks Associated with Shared Sanitation: A Case Study of the Community Ablution Blocks in Durban, South Africa." *Environmental Monitoring and Assessment* 194 (3): 1–13. https://doi.org/10.1007/s10661-022-09815-x.

Russell, Fiona, and Peter Azzopardi. 2019. "WASH: A Basic Human Right and Essential Intervention for Child Health and Development." *Lancet Global Health* 7 (4): e417. https://doi.org/10.1016/S2214-109X(19)30078-6.

Sarkar, Anindita. 2020. "Informal Water Vendors and the Urban Poor: Evidence from a Nairobi Slum." *Water International* 45 (5): 443–57. https://doi.org/10.1080/02508060.2020.1768022.

Schelbert, Vasco, Dario Meili, Mahbub-Ul Alam, Sheillah Simiyu, Prince Antwi-Agyei, Bismark Dwumfour-Asare, Kwaku Amaning Adjei, Mahbubur Rahman, et al. 2020. "When Is Shared Sanitation Acceptable in Low-Income Urban Settlements? A User Perspective on Shared Sanitation Quality in Kumasi, Kisumu and Dhaka." *Journal of Water, Sanitation and Hygiene for Development* 10 (4): 959–68. https://doi.org/10.2166/washdev.2020.084.

Schneider, Tommye. 2007. "Food Workers' Perspectives on Handwashing Behaviors in the Restaurant Environment." *Journal of Environmental Health* 70 (2): 36.

Semiyaga, Swaib, Gilbert Bamuhimbise, Sheilla C. Apio, Joel R. Kinobe, Allan Nkurunziza, Najib B. Lukooya, and Robinah Kulabako. 2022. "Adequacy of Vacuum and Non-Vacuum Technologies for Emptying Faecal Sludge from Informal Settlements of Kampala City." *Habitat International* 125 (August): 102596. https://doi.org/10.1016/j.habitatint.2022.102596.

Semiyaga, Swaib, Mackay A. E. Okure, Charles B. Niwagaba, Alex Y. Katukiza, and Frank Kansiime. 2015. "Decentralized Options for Faecal Sludge Management in Urban Slum Areas of Sub-Saharan Africa: A Review of Technologies, Practices and End-Uses." *Resources, Conservation and Recycling* 104 Part A: 109–19. https://doi.org/10.1016/j.resconrec.2015.09.001.

Shiras, Tess, Oliver Cumming, Joe Brown, Becelar Muneme, Rassul Nalá, and Robert Dreibelbis. 2018. "Shared Sanitation Management and the Role of Social Capital: Findings from an Urban Sanitation Intervention in Maputo, Mozambique." *International Journal of Environmental Research and Public Health* 15 (10): 2222. https://doi.org/10.3390/ijerph15102222.

Simiyu, Sheillah. 2016. "Determinants of Usage of Communal Sanitation Facilities in Informal Settlements of Kisumu, Kenya." *Environment and Urbanization* 28 (1): 241–58. https://doi.org/10.1177/0956247815616732.

Simiyu, Sheillah, Ivy Chumo, and Blessing Mberu. 2021. "Fecal Sludge Management in

Low Income Settlements: Case Study of Nakuru, Kenya." *Frontiers in Public Health* 9 (October): 1–8. https://doi.org/10.3389/fpubh.2021.750309.

Simiyu, Sheillah, Raphael Kweyu, Prince Antwi-Agyei, and Kwaku A. Adjei. 2020. "Barriers and Opportunities for Cleanliness of Shared Sanitation Facilities in Low-Income Settlements in Kenya." *BMC Public Health* 20 (1632): 1–12. https://doi.org/10.21203/rs.2.20081/v1.

Simiyu, Sheillah, Mark Swilling, Sandy Cairncross, and Richard Rheingans. 2017. "Determinants of Quality of Shared Sanitation Facilities in Informal Settlements: Case Study of Kisumu, Kenya." *BMC Public Health* 17 (1): 68. https://doi.org/10.1186/s12889-016-4009-6.

Simiyu, Sheillah, Mark Swilling, Richard Rheingans, and Sandy Cairncross. 2017. "Estimating the Cost and Payment for Sanitation in the Informal Settlements of Kisumu, Kenya: A Cross Sectional Study." *International Journal of Environmental Research and Public Health* 14 (1): 49. https://doi.org/10.3390/ijerph14010049.

Tidwell, James B., Jenala Chipungu, Roma Chilengi, and Robert Aunger. 2018. "Assessing Peri-Urban Sanitation Quality Using a Theoretically Derived Composite Measure in Lusaka, Zambia." *Journal of Water, Sanitation and Hygiene for Development* 8 (4): 668–78. https://doi.org/10.2166/washdev.2018.029.

Tidwell, James B., Jenala Chipungu, Ian Ross, Prince Antwi-Agyei, Mahbub-Ul Alam, Innocent K. Tumwebaze, Guy Norman, Oliver Cumming, and Sheillah Simiyu. 2021. "Where Shared Sanitation Is the Only Immediate Option: A Research Agenda for Shared Sanitation in Densely Populated Low-Income Urban Settings." *American Journal of Tropical Medicine and Hygiene* 104 (2): 429–32. https://doi.org/10.4269/ajtmh.20-0985.

Touré, Ousmane, Salimata Coulibaly, Aminata Arby, Farmata Maiga, and Sandy Cairncross. 2013. "Piloting an Intervention to Improve Microbiological Food Safety in Peri-urban Mali." *International Journal of Hygiene and Environmental Health* 216 (2): 138–45. https://doi.org/10.1016/j.ijheh.2012.02.003.

Tsai, Kevin, Sheillah Simiyu, Jane Mumma, Rose Evalyne Aseyo, Oliver Cumming, Robert Dreibelbis, and Kelly K. Baker. 2019. "Enteric Pathogen Diversity in Infant Foods in Low-Income Neighborhoods of Kisumu, Kenya." *International Journal of Environmental Research and Public Health* 16 (3): 506. https://doi.org/10.3390/ijerph16030506.

Tumwebaze, Innocent K. 2013. "Prevalence and Determinants of the Cleanliness of Shared Toilets in Kampala Slums, Uganda." *Journal of Public Health* 22 (1): 33–39. https://doi.org/10.1007/s10389-013-0590-7.

Tumwebaze, Innocent K., and Hans-Joachim Mosler. 2014. "Why Clean the Toilet if Others Don't? Using a Social Dilemma Approach to Understand Users of Shared Toilets' Collective Cleaning Behaviour in Urban Slums: A Review." *Journal of Water, Sanitation and Hygiene for Development* 4 (3): 359–70. https://doi.org/10.2166/washdev.2014.152.

Tumwebaze, Innocent K., and Hans-Joachim Mosler. 2015. "Effectiveness of Group Discussions and Commitment in Improving Cleaning Behaviour of Shared Sanitation Users in Kampala, Uganda Slums." *Social Science and Medicine* 147:72–79. https://doi.org/10.1016/j.socscimed.2015.10.059.

Tumwebaze, Innocent K., Charles B. Niwagaba, Isabel Günther, and Hans-Joachim Mosler. 2014. "Determinants of Households' Cleaning Intention for Shared Toilets: Case of 50 Slums in Kampala, Uganda." *Habitat International* 41 (January): 108–13. https://doi.org/10.1016/j.habitatint.2013.07.008.

UNICEF (United Nations Children's Fund) and WHO (World Health Organization). 2015. *25 Years Progress on Sanitation and Drinking Water—2015 Update and MDG Assessment.* Geneva: UNICEF and WHO.

UNICEF (United Nations Children's Fund) and WHO (World Health Organization). 2021. *State of the World's Hand Hygiene: A Global Call to Action to Make Hand Hygiene a Priority in Policy and Practice.* New York: UNICEF.

UNICEF (United Nations Children's Fund) and WHO (World Health Organization). 2022. *Progress on Drinking Water, Sanitation and Hygiene in Africa.* New York: UNICEF and WHO.

Whitley, Lucy, Paul Hutchings, Sarah Cooper, Alison Parker, Abinet Kebede, Solome Joseph, John Butterworth, Barbara Van Koppen, and Adolph Mulejaa. 2019. "A Framework for Targeting Water, Sanitation and Hygiene Interventions in Pastoralist Populations in the Afar Region of Ethiopia." *International Journal of Hygiene and Environmental Health* 222 (8): 1133–44. https://doi.org/10.1016/j.ijheh.2019.08.001.

WHO (World Health Organization). 2015. *WHO Estimates of the Global Burden of Foodborne Diseases.* Geneva: World Health Organization.

Wiltgen Georgi, Neele, Sibongile Buthelezi, and Paula Meth. 2021. "Gendered Infrastructural Citizenship: Shared Sanitation Facilities in Quarry Road West Informal Settlement, Durban, South Africa." *Urban Forum* 32 (4): 437–56. https://doi.org/10.1007/s12132-021-09421-z.

Zerbo, Alexandre, Rafael C. Delgado, and Pedro A. González. 2020. "Vulnerability and Everyday Health Risks of Urban Informal Settlements in Sub-Saharan Africa." *Global Health Journal* 4 (2): 46–50. https://doi.org/10.1016/j.glohj.2020.04.003.

Zerbo, Alexandre, Rafael C. Delgado, and Pedro A. González. 2021. "Water Sanitation and Hygiene in Sub-Saharan Africa: Coverage, Risks of Diarrheal Diseases, and Urbanization." *Journal of Biosafety and Biosecurity* 3 (1): 41–45. https://doi.org/10.1016/j.jobb.2021.03.004.

8

Ambient and Household Air Pollution in African Cities

Kanyiva Muindi

1. Introduction

Air pollution (combined ambient and household air pollution) is an important risk factor for ill health and premature mortality, ranking fourth as a leading cause of early death globally (GBD 2019 Risk Factors Collaborators 2020). Further, the global burden of disease study indicates that in Africa, household air pollution was the fifth ranked risk factor for death and disability combined, while lower respiratory illnesses were the second leading cause of death and third leading cause of premature mortality (IHME 2018). Recent analysis of risk factors indicates that globally, ambient air pollution was ranked seventh, while household air pollution ranked tenth, in percentage of attributable disability adjusted life years (DALYs) for all ages. DALYs measure the overall burden of disease and "one DALY represents the loss of the equivalent of one year of full health" (WHO 2022b). For children ages 0 to 9 years, household air pollution was ranked fourth, while ambient air pollution was ninth, and for those aged 50 to 74 years, ambient air pollution was fifth, while household air pollution was ninth, pointing to the differential impact of the same risk factor across the life course (GBD 2019 Risk Factors Collaborators 2020). Across most of Africa, the percentage of DALYs attributable to air pollution range from 8 to 15 percent (GBD 2019 Risk Factors Collaborators 2020). According to the World Health Organization (WHO), in 2019, an estimated 99 percent of the world's population lived in areas where air pollution exceeded the WHO air quality guidelines (WHO 2021). In the same year, 4.14 and 2.31 million deaths globally were due to causes attributed to ambient and household air pollution, respectively (Health Effects Institute 2020). Other more recent estimates indicate that air pollution–

related mortality is 8.8 million globally, with a corresponding loss of life expectancy of 2.9 years (Lelieveld et al. 2020).

The biggest burden of poor ambient and household air quality is borne by populations living in low- and middle-income countries, where rapid urbanization coupled with reliance on biomass fuels for cooking contribute to dangerous pollutant levels (UNEP 2016; WHO 2021). Estimates for Africa indicate that about 960,000 deaths from causes attributable to air pollution occur annually. In addition, loss of life expectancy was estimated at 3.1 years (Lelieveld et al. 2020). Lower respiratory infections, ischemic heart disease, and other noncommunicable diseases (NCDs) contribute considerably to the annual air pollution–related mortality on the continent (Lelieveld et al. 2020).

Beyond mortality and loss of life expectancy, various health outcomes are attributable to air pollution. Studies from across the globe have shown the contribution of air pollution to cerebrovascular disease, chronic obstructive pulmonary disease (COPD), ischemic heart disease, lung cancer, lower respiratory infections, and other NCDs (Guan et al. 2016; Z. Hu and Rao 2009; Lelieveld et al. 2020; Nguyen et al. 2017; WHO 2021). Other studies indicate impacts of air pollution on pregnancy outcomes, including low birth weight and stillbirths (Amegah and Jaakkola 2014; Amegah, Quansah, and Jaakkola 2014; Dadvand et al. 2013; D. P. Pope et al. 2010; Wilhelm et al. 2011). Further, there is evidence on air pollution's role in pregnancy-related health outcomes such as hypertensive disorders (H. Hu et al. 2014; Mobasher et al. 2013; Pedersen et al. 2014).

This chapter begins with a summary of the state and sources of ambient air pollution in Africa's cities, followed by a focus on household air pollution in cities, with discussion of the policy and data implications. The chapter ends with recommendations on how to improve air quality.

2. Current State and Sources of Ambient Air Pollution in Africa's Cities

More than half of the world's population (56 percent) live in urban areas (UNDESA, Population Division 2018), and about 60 percent will live in urban settlements across the world by 2030. Africa's urban growth rate is reported as the highest in the world. It is projected that by 2035, half of the African population will be urban (UNDESA, Population Division 2018). The process of urbanization is associated with demographic, environmental, and socioeconomic changes that have important impacts on the health and well-being of urban populations. A distinct feature of rapid urbanization in sub-Saharan Africa has been the rapid growth of slums and unplanned settlements. The most recent estimates indicate that in 2018, 58 percent of the region's urban population lived in slums (World Bank Group 2020). Existing evidence indicates that slum households mostly rely on kerosene or paraffin and charcoal for cooking (APHRC, n.d.; Emina et al. 2011; Sustainable Energy Africa 2014). Further, poor solid waste management in slums has led to routine burning of waste. These practices have implications for air quality and health at both the local and the city scale.

In addition, while urbanization is a key driver of economic development, urban spaces concentrate risks and hazards for health, especially where there is poor urban and transport planning, as in most cities in Africa. Generally, urbanization is accompanied by industrialization and increases in motorized transport and large-scale construction projects, which in turn negatively affect population health through various pathways, including air pollution. Although Africa has the lowest motorization rates globally at below one hundred vehicles per one thousand population, the rates are rising. For example, between 2008 and 2012, the number of motorcycles and auto-cycles in Kenya grew by 368 percent, with the overall number of registered vehicles increasing by 77 percent (Rajé, Tight, and Pope 2018). Urban ambient air pollution is mainly driven by vehicular emissions from combustion of petrol or diesel, oil, and lubricants, as well as by noncombustion-related sources, such as resuspension of dust on unpaved roads and wear and tear of vehicle parts (Gaita et al. 2014; Kinney et al. 2011; Kirago et al. 2022), industrial activities, and open burning of waste. With Africa's mostly secondhand vehicle fleet and, in some countries, high sulfur fuels, the implications of these on ambient air quality are serious.

The negative environmental consequences of human activity driving economic development, including air pollution in many cities in developing countries, represent an unprecedented threat to human health and well-being (GBD 2013 Risk Factors Collaborators 2015; McMichael 2013). In Africa, limited evidence exists on systemwide interventions to mitigate the impacts of air pollution on population health. Despite the recent increased attention by governments and development partners to the health of urban populations, especially slum dwellers, little has been done to tackle air pollution, one of

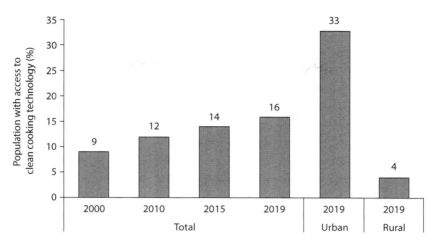

Fig. 8.1. Proportion of population with access to clean cooking technologies in sub-Saharan Africa, 2000–2019. Data source: "Household Energy Database," WHO, accessed June 4, 2024, https://www.who.int/data/gho/data/themes/air-pollution/who-household-energy-db.

the top causes of health problems around the world (International Agency for Research on Cancer 2013; WHO 2021).

In Africa, only forty-three cities in twelve countries had air quality data as of April 2022 (WHO 2022a). A recent report indicates that Africa lags behind other major regions in routine air quality monitoring (UNICEF 2019).

Given the lack of routine ambient air quality monitoring in Africa, short-term research projects conducted in various cities provide information on key pollutant levels. Global air quality studies give a view of the trend of air pollution across the region. You can see the trend in ambient particulate pollution across four world regions for the period 1990 to 2019 on the Health Effects Institute's State of Global Air website. Asia and Africa have the highest levels of particulate pollution, appearing to level off between 2017 and 2019, though they remain significantly above the WHO guidelines (Health Effects Institute 2024).

A review of studies conducted in individual cities paints a picture of high levels of particulate as well as gas-phase pollutants. For example, the "A Systems Approach to Air Pollution in East Africa" (ASAP East Africa) study, conducted in Addis Ababa, Kampala, and Nairobi, indicates that the three cities are facing poor ambient air. In Nairobi, measured annual $PM_{2.5}$ and PM_{10} levels showed exceedance of WHO recommendations of 3.7 and 4.7, respectively (F. D. Pope et al. 2018). Further, the WHO ambient air quality database indicates that most of African cities with existing data exceed the WHO guidelines for $PM_{2.5}$ and PM_{10} (WHO 2022a).

Dust from the Sahara Desert influences air pollution in many West African countries, reflecting seasonal variation in $PM_{2.5}$ levels noted in cities where air quality monitoring is ongoing. In Accra, evidence indicates that the ambient $PM_{2.5}$ levels are "typically 2 to 10 times of the WHO guideline levels depending on location and season, with the Harmattan periods resulting in very significant increases in ambient concentrations" (Odoi and Kleiman 2021). Indeed, $PM_{2.5}$ concentrations between 2015 and 2020 were found to range from 26 to 98.4 $\mu g/m^3$, with higher concentrations observed during the Harmattan period (Alli et al. 2021; Mudu 2021). Similarly, in Senegal, seasonal variation in particulate concentrations with elevated levels of both PM_{10} and $PM_{2.5}$ was observed in the dry season, while rainy seasons have lower concentrations. Data for the period 2010 to 2018 indicate that PM_{10} levels ranged between 75 and 380 $\mu g/m^3$, while $PM_{2.5}$ levels ranged between 22 and 110 $\mu g/m^3$ during the dry season. During the rainy season, PM_{10} and $PM_{2.5}$ were between 25 and 160 $\mu g/m^3$ and between 5 and 35 $\mu g/m^3$, respectively (Sow et al. 2021). Other studies have also revealed high levels of ambient air pollutants in West African cities (Doumbia et al. 2012; Val et al. 2013).

2.1. Household Air Pollution in Urban Homes in Africa

Globally, about 3 billion people are dependent on biomass for their cooking and heating needs, with the largest proportion of users being in low-income countries in Africa, Asia, and Latin America (WHO 2021a). Across Africa, households, especially in rural areas and low-income urban neighborhoods, continue to use wood and charcoal for their cooking and heating needs, with implications for the health of primary cooks and vulnerable individuals who spend most of their time indoors (i.e., children, elderly, and those living with disability, especially individuals with limited mobility). In Africa, an estimated 900 million lack access to clean cooking technologies, and 600 million have no access to grid electricity (IEA 2019). Models of energy demand for urban Africa indicate that residential users account for 22 percent of the total energy, with most of this going to cooking. The energy demand is expected to rise to 76 percent by 2040 as a result of high rates of urbanization in the region (Sustainable Energy Africa 2015). A breakdown of fuel types indicates that in 2012, cleaner cooking options accounted for only 19 percent of urban Africa demand, with biomass and kerosene taking the largest proportion (Sustainable Energy Africa 2015).

The energy demand trends observed in 2012 have changed little, and in 2019, only 33 percent (or 293 million) of sub-Saharan Africa's urban population had access to clean cooking solutions, representing the region with the lowest penetration of these technologies (World Bank Group, ESMAP, and AFREA 2015). The rate of uptake of these technologies has remained slow (see figure 8.1). This is a worrying trend for the region given the health and climate implications of low access to clean cooking. In addition, with urban areas in the region expected to be home to more than 50 percent of its population by 2050, there is a need for concerted efforts to speed up access to clean cooking to keep pace with or even outpace urban population growth. This will push the region to levels comparable to other major regions, such as Asia, which has made strides in increasing access to clean energy (IEA et al. 2021).

2.2.1. CLEAN COOKING

Sub-Saharan African countries are not on track to meet the seventh Sustainable Development Goal (SDG 7), which seeks to ensure access to affordable, reliable, sustainable, and modern energy for all (IEA et al. 2021). This is because just about a third of the urban population has access to clean cooking technologies, while rural areas are far behind (below 5 percent). Studies have demonstrated that households' failure to transition to clean cooking options is driven by low consumer willingness to adopt these options and limited ability to buy the often more expensive cleaner cooking solutions, such as liquefied petroleum gas and electricity (Muller and Yan 2016; World Bank Group 2014). In addition, market barriers, such as poor supply infrastructure, as well as poor policy direction for the clean cooking sector limit the reach of these solutions to the masses (Schlag and Zuzarte 2008; World Bank Group 2014). Other barriers include low awareness of cleaner options and sociocultural factors that affect the adoption and consistent use, for example, cooking preferences that may lead to perceived clean cookstove mismatch with household cooking needs. Tackling these barriers alongside others (Ray, Clifford, and Jewitt 2014; Rehfuess et al. 2014; World

Bank Group 2014) would ensure reasonable uptake and sustained use of clean cookstoves.

Several initiatives have been launched to increase the uptake of clean cookstoves across the region and within individual countries. In addition, there have been efforts to provide alternative lighting solutions through solar energy and electrification of slum and rural areas. Some of the initiatives targeting the clean cooking sector or lighting solutions include the Africa Renewable Energy and Access program, Clean Cooking Alliance, KOKO Networks, and Project Gaia.

- Africa Renewable Energy and Access program (AFREA): The first phase of this program was initiated in 2009 by the World Bank "to focus on the special needs of the energy sector in Africa. The program was designed to help expand access to modern energy services by improving service delivery and scaling up innovations in electricity, lighting, and cooking" (World Bank Group, ESMAP, and AFREA 2015). Under the AFREA program, the following initiatives were rolled out:
  - Biomass Energy Initiative for Africa (BEIA): This World Bank–funded initiative aims at modernizing the biomass energy sector, recognizing that biomass fuels form the largest proportion of energy for residential and some commercial uses in Africa. The initiative was launched in 2010, supporting nine biomass energy projects in eight countries. "The initiative focused on technologies ranging from charcoal to briquettes to social biofuels, and from high efficiency cookstoves to bioelectricity. It used innovative delivery models and relied on private initiatives, social enterprises, and public–private partnerships" (World Bank Group, ESMAP, and AFREA 2015). The project demonstrated the potential of modernizing biomass to protect health and the environment.
  - Africa Clean Cooking Energy Solutions (ACCES): The project was launched in 2012 by the World Bank and sought "to promote the enterprise-driven, large-scale adoption of clean cooking solutions throughout SSA [sub-Saharan Africa]," with the goal of reducing poverty, health risks, and environmental impacts associated with biomass use through encouraging uptake of highly efficient cookstoves (World Bank Group, ESMAP, and AFREA 2015). At the regional level, the program "initiated a quality assurance and tech-

nical support system to create performance standards for clean cookstoves" (World Bank Group, ESMAP, and AFREA 2015).

- Lighting Africa: An estimated 600 million people in Africa do not have access to grid electricity (IEA et al. 2021), with 110 million of these living in urban areas (Shirley 2018). Three countries in the region (Nigeria, DRC, and Ethiopia) account for the largest deficit in access to electricity, while Kenya and Uganda, which were part of the deficit countries, increased their rates of electrification between 2010 and 2019 (IEA et al. 2021). The World Bank launched the Lighting Africa initiative in 2010, seeking to bridge the region's access to electricity by providing 250 million people with solar photovoltaic lighting systems by 2030.
- Clean Cooking Alliance (CCA): Established in 2010, the CCA "works with a global network of partners to build an inclusive industry that can make clean cooking accessible to all. CCA is driving consumer demand, mobilizing investment, and supporting policies that allow the clean cooking sector to thrive" (CCA, n.d.).
- KOKO Networks: Launched in 2019 in Kenya to provide affordable clean cooking energy (bioethanol) across the country, KOKO manufactures stoves that use a smart canister (unique to each user). Fuel is dispensed from ATMs managed by over 1,400 agents across the country. With over half a million customers, this venture is enabling households to access clean cooking (Dredger and Manchester 2022). While this initiative is neither global nor continental, it has the potential to reach across the region and beyond.
- Project Gaia: This organization promotes clean, safe, efficient cookstoves powered by alcohol fuels to change the face of energy poverty. It works in countries in Africa, Asia (India), South America, and the Caribbean (Haiti). Project Gaia has been instrumental in setting up community microdistilleries in various countries to ensure easy access to alcohol fuels by consumers (Project Gaia, n.d.).

3. Challenges and Opportunities in Addressing Ambient and Household Air Pollution

Africa's fast urbanization and attendant motorization and industrial growth contribute to the continent's poor ambient air quality. The situation is compounded by low deployment of ground-level monitors and lack of air quality legislation in many countries, leading to nonattention on this challenge. On the household energy front, concerted efforts are needed to bring the region closer toward achieving SDG 7. The SDG 7 tracking report recommends, "Clean cooking fuels and technologies must be made a top political priority with targeted policies. To achieve the universal target, a multisectoral and a coordinated effort is needed. All household energy needs, including cooking energy and electricity access, should be integrated into a national energy plan" (IEA et al. 2021, 7).

The following challenges have been identified as contributing toward poor ambient air quality in the region. There is limited routine assessment of the state of ambient air quality (UNICEF 2019). Many governments have not invested in monitoring networks to provide time-series data on the state of air, amid competing priorities for often-limited resources. Second, many countries in the region lack national and local air quality policies and guidelines, and where these exist, enforcement is often weak. A recent global assessment of air quality legislation indicates that only seventeen states in Africa have ambient air quality legislation in place (UNEP 2021). Without legislation in place, it becomes difficult to implement air pollution controls. Third, rising motorization rates (Rajé, Tight, and Pope 2018) combined with poor road networks (which contribute to traffic congestion) in most African cities compound the air pollution problem. Fourth, solid waste management challenges in most African cities have led to air pollution, owing to reliance on open dumpsites, where combustion of waste often takes place either automatically or through human activities. In addition, citizens' habitual burning of solid waste in efforts to reduce it contributes to air pollution (Godfrey et al. 2019; UNEP 2018).

Regarding household air pollution, the following challenges have been identified; first, financial constraints, especially among users of traditional cooking technologies, remain a huge barrier to the adoption of clean cookstoves (Rehfuess et al. 2014). Biomass use among urban residents is prevalent in slum communities, whose precarious financial situation makes it difficult for them to transition to cleaner energy sources. Second, infrastructural challenges in the clean cookstove supply chain have led to concentration of the technologies in major urban centers, leaving poorly connected cities and towns underserved (Schlag and Zuzarte 2008). Third, unfavorable policy directions have made it difficult for stakeholders in the clean cooking sector to lower the cost of their products. For example, the imposition of taxes on imports of materials needed to assemble stoves as well as taxes levied on cleaner fuels force the transfer of these costs to consumers (CCA, Duke Energy Access Project, and EED Advisory 2021). This, alongside the financial constraints indicated above, leaves households willing to shift to cleaner household energy without options, as prices remain prohibitive. Fourth, long-held customs around cooking, with preference for wood- or charcoal-cooked meals, contribute to low uptake or inconsistent use of clean cooking technologies in the region (Rehfuess et al. 2014). Last, there is low awareness of the implications of biomass use on both human and environmental health. This coupled with paucity of data on indoor air pollutant levels and the health impacts of this across the region, in addition to other factors above, contribute to persistent biomass use.

Despite these challenges, there are opportunities for the region to correct course and ensure that urban residents are afforded the best ambient and household air quality possible. First, the Internet of Things (IoT) provides an opportunity for citizen involvement in the development and deployment of sensors (Penza 2020) to bridge the data gap through the design of sensors that are lightweight and wearable. These can be carried or worn by individuals to provide continuous and localized data on both ambient and indoor air quality. Citizen participation as data collectors (citizen science) provides an opportunity for raising awareness about air pollution and its impacts on health. The advent of low-cost sensor technologies (Penza 2020) offers governments the opportunity to set up air quality monitoring (AQM) networks at a fraction of the cost of the more expensive monitors, to provide data for decision making at national and local levels (Awokola et al. 2020). Perhaps for comparability, countries could invest in a few standard AQM stations to provide reference points for the low-cost sensors. Second, national and local governments in the region need to speed up passing legislation on air quality to guide emissions and remediation (UNEP 2021). Third, investing in mass transit and light rail as well as having dedicated cycling and walking lanes would go a long way in decongesting cities. This should go hand in hand with proper urban planning as well as the rollout of disincentives for driving personal vehicles. Fourth, adoption of more efficient ways of solid waste management would contribute to reduction in air pollution (and other forms of environmental pollution).

Fifth, household air pollution largely remains invisible to decision makers, perhaps because it happens in private spaces. Policies, however, especially energy policies, have a huge role to play in mitigating household air pollution. Current energy policies in the region are too electricity focused and leave out other, cleaner options that would be affordable to low-income households. While electricity is generally a clean energy source, its use for cooking in the region remains low, mostly because of prohibitive costs. For poorer households, even with cheaper tariffs, the capital needed to purchase cooking appliances would remain a critical barrier in switching to electricity for cooking. There is therefore a need to broaden the energy reach of policies while also ensuring that clean cooking and lighting technologies with proven health and environmental benefits remain affordable to the poorest, if the region is to achieve SDG 7. In addition, governments in the region need to focus on policies that will lead to the development of their economies to lift more households out of poverty. This would not only ensure access to cleaner cooking and lighting technologies but also have an impact on the educational, social, and health outcomes of citizens (Rehfuess et al. 2014; Schlag and Zuzarte 2008).

Further, partnerships between the public and private sectors (i.e., public-private partnerships, or PPPs) have been shown to work well in the delivery of services. These need to be embraced to ensure the diffusion of clean cooking technologies to areas beyond the primate cities. The partnerships should include awareness raising to provide education to potential users of these technologies, covering the health and environmental impacts of cooking under business as usual and the benefits of transitioning to existing cleaner options. The partnerships must also address the supply chain challenges in different markets to ensure uninterrupted supply of devices and fuels for sustained use. Embracing technologies such as PayGo would ensure inclusivity of the PPPs, since consumers could acquire the devices and fuels for the cash at hand. Last, to ensure the region speeds up the adoption of clean cooking technologies, governments would need to consider tax incentives to manufacturers as well as consumer subsidies where possible. These would keep the cost of clean cooking appliances and fuels affordable and therefore increase uptake when carried out alongside education and awareness-raising activities.

4. Conclusions

Data and policy are critical in the push toward cleaner air in African cities. Embracing a culture of routine monitoring of ambient air quality backed by strong policies and guidelines on emissions and remediation would ensure that governments tackle the air pollution challenge. This should run concurrently with capacity building of city management teams to enable them to analyze and interpret the data as well as manage the AQM networks. Cities that have not started routine monitoring could learn from efforts in South Africa (Gwaze and Mashele 2018), Dakar (Sow et al. 2021), and Accra (Mudu 2021), among others, where governments have deployed ambient air pollution sensors.

In addition to routine monitoring, addressing the traffic congestion witnessed across cities in the region, as well as better planning of upcoming cities, would ensure reduction in transport-related emissions. For household air pollution, governments across the region need to increase efforts to ensure more households make the transition to clean cooking and lighting. These efforts must go hand in hand with awareness creation to educate the public on the implications of cooking with biomass on both human and environmental health and the benefits of making the energy transition. Given the challenge inherent in routine monitoring of household air quality at scale, governments could take advantage of existing networks, such as community health volunteers who can be trained to assess household air pollution and educate communities on actions to mitigate it. Energy policies beyond that which are largely electricity focused would need to be pro-poor in pushing for household energy options that are affordable to the poorest citizens to ensure equitable access to clean energy by all.

REFERENCES

APHRC (African Population and Health Research Center). n.d. "Nairobi Urban Health and Demographic Surveillance System (NUHDSS)." Accessed June 3, 2024. https://aphrc .org/project/nairobi-urban-health-and-demographic-surveillance-system-nuhdss/.

Alli, Abosede S., Sierra N. Clark, Allison Hughes, James Nimo, Josephine Bedford-Moses, Solomon Baah, Jiayuan Wang, et al. 2021. "Spatial-Temporal Patterns of Ambient Fine Particulate Matter ($PM_{2.5}$) and Black Carbon (BC) Pollution in Accra." *Environmental Research Letters* 16 (7): 074013. https://doi.org/10.1088/1748-9326/ac074a.

Amegah, Adeladza K., and Jouni J. K. Jaakkola. 2014. "Work as a Street Vendor, Associated Traffic-Related Air Pollution Exposures and Risk of Adverse Pregnancy Outcomes in Accra, Ghana." *International Journal of Hygiene and Environmental Health* 217:354–62.

Amegah, Adeladza K., Reginald Quansah, and Jouni J. K. Jaakkola. 2014. "Household Air Pollution from Solid Fuel Use and Risk of Adverse Pregnancy Outcomes: A Systematic Review and Meta-Analysis of the Empirical Evidence." *PLoS One* 9 (12): e113920.

Awokola, Babatunde, I., Gabriel Okello, Kevin J. Mortimer, Christopher P. Jewell, Annette Erhart, and Sean Semple. 2020. "Measuring Air Quality for Advocacy in Africa (MA3): Feasibility and Practicality of Longitudinal Ambient $PM_{2.5}$ Measurement Using Low-Cost Sensors." *International Journal of Environmental Research and Public Health* 17 (19): 7243. https://doi.org/10.3390/ijerph17197243.

CCA (Clean Cooking Alliance). n.d. "Our Mission and Impact." Accessed June 3, 2024. https://cleancooking.org/mission-impact/.

CCA (Clean Cooking Alliance), Duke Energy Access Project, and EED Advisory. 2021. *Value-Added Tax on Cleaner Cooking Solutions in Kenya: Costs Outweigh Benefits and Impede National Climate and Sustainable Development Goals.* Washington, DC: CCA.

Dadvand, Payam, Jennifer Parker, Michelle L. Bell, Matteo Bonzini, Michael Brauer, Lyndsey A. Darrow, Ulrike Gehring, et al. 2013. "Maternal Exposure to Particulate Air Pollution and Term Birth Weight: A Multi-Country Evaluation of Effect and Heterogeneity." *Environmental Health Perspectives* 121 (3): 367–73. https://doi.org/http://dx.doi.org/10.1289/ehp.1205575.

Doumbia, El Hadji Thierno, Catherine Liousse, Corinne Galy-Lacaux, Seydi Ababacar Ndiaye, Babacar Diop, Marie Ouafo, Eric Michel Assamoi, et al. 2012. "Real Time Black Carbon Measurements in West and Central Africa Urban Sites." *Atmospheric Environment* 54:529–37.

Dredger, Dan, and Katherine Manchester. 2022. "KOKO Networks: Delivering Solutions, Expanding Trust." CCA Leadership Series, August 10. https://cleancooking.org/news/koko-networks-delivering-solutions-expanding-trust/.

Emina, Jacques, Donatien Beguy, Eliya M. Zulu, Alex C. Ezeh, Kanyiva Muindi, Patricia Elung'ata, John K. Otsola, and Yazoumé Yé. 2011. "Monitoring of Health and Demographic Outcomes in Poor Urban Settlements: Evidence from the Nairobi Urban Health and Demographic Surveillance System." *Journal of Urban Health* 88:200–218.

GBD 2013 Risk Factors Collaborators. 2015. "Global, Regional, and National Comparative Risk Assessment of 79 Behavioural, Environmental and Occupational, and Metabolic Risks or Clusters of Risks in 188 Countries, Analysis for the Global Burden of Disease Study 2013." *Lancet* 386:2287–2323.

GBD 2019 Risk Factors Collaborators. 2020. "Global Burden of 87 Risk Factors in 204 Countries and Territories, 1990–2019: A Systematic Analysis for the Global Burden of Disease Study 2019." *Lancet* 396:1223–49.

Godfrey, Linda, Mohamed Tawfic Ahmed, Kidane Giday Gebremedhin, Jamidu H. Y. Katima, Suzan Oelofse, Oladele Osibanjo, Ulf Henning Richter, and Arsène H. Yonli. 2019. "Solid Waste Management in Africa: Governance Failure or Development Opportunity?" In *Regional Development in Africa*, edited by Norbert Edomah. London: IntechOpen. https://doi.org/10.5772/intechopen.86974.

Guan, Wei-Jie, Xue-Yan Zheng, Kian Fan Chung, and Nan-Shan Zhong. 2016 "Impact of Air Pollution on the Burden of Chronic Respiratory Diseases in China: Time for Urgent Action." *Lancet* 388 (10054): 1939–51. https://doi.org/10.1016/S0140-6736(16)31597-5.

Gwaze, Patience, and Sindisiwe H. Mashele. 2018. "South African Air Quality Information

System (SAAQIS) Mobile Application Tool: Bringing Real Time State of Air Quality to South Africans." *Clean Air Journal* 28 (1). https://doi.org/10.17159/2410-972X/2018/v28n1a1.

Health Effects Institute. 2020. *State of Global Air 2020*. Boston, MA: Health Effects Institute.

Health Effects Institute. 2024. "Explore the Data." State of Global Air. https://www.stateofglobalair.org/data/.

Hu, Hui, Sandie Ha, Jeffrey Roth, Greg Kearney, Evelyn O. Talbott, and Xiaohui Xu. 2014. "Ambient Air Pollution and Hypertensive Disorders of Pregnancy: A Systematic Review and Meta-Analysis." *Atmospheric Environment* 97:336–45. http://www.sciencedirect.com/science/article/pii/S1352231014006219.

Hu, Zhiyong, and K. Ranga Rao. 2009. "Particulate Air Pollution and Chronic Ischemic Heart Disease in the Eastern United States: A County Level Ecological Study Using Satellite Aerosol Data." *Environmental Health* 8:26.

IEA (International Energy Agency). 2019. *Africa Energy Outlook 2019*. Paris: IEA. https://www.iea.org/reports/africa-energy-outlook-2019

IEA (International Energy Agency), IRENA (International Renewable Energy Agency), UNSD (United Nations Statistics Division), World Bank, and WHO (World Health Organization). 2021. *Tracking SDG 7: The Energy Progress Report*. Washington, DC: World Bank.

IHME (Institute for Health Metrics and Evaluation). 2018. *Findings from the Global Burden of Disease Study 2017*. Seattle, WA: IHME.

International Agency for Research on Cancer. 2013. "Outdoor Air Pollution a Leading Environmental Cause of Cancer Deaths." Press release, October 17. WHO International Agency for Research on Cancer.

Kinney, Patrick L., Michael Gatari Gichuru, Nicole Volavka-Close, Nicole Ngo, Peter K. Ndiba, Anna Law, Anthony Gachanja, et al. 2011. "Traffic Impacts on $PM_{2.5}$ Air Quality in Nairobi, Kenya." *Environmental Science and Policy* 14 (4): 369–78.

Kirago, Leonard, Michael J. Gatari, Örjan Gustafsson, and August Andersson. 2022. "Black Carbon Emissions from Traffic Contribute Substantially to Air Pollution in Nairobi, Kenya." *Communications Earth and Environment* 3:74. https://doi.org/10.1038/s43247-022-00400-1.

Lelieveld, Jos, Andrea Pozzer, Ulrich Poschl, Mohammed Fnais, Andy Haines, and Thomas Munzel. 2020. "Loss of Life Expectancy from Air Pollution Compared to Other Risk Factors: A Worldwide Perspective." *Cardiovascular Research* 116:1910–17.

McMichael, A. J. 2013. "Globalization, Climate Change, and Human Health." *New England Journal of Medicine* 368:1335–43.

Mobasher, Zahra, Muhammad T. Salam, T. Murphy Goodwin, Frederick Lurmann, Sue A. Ingles, and Melissa L. Wilson. 2013. "Associations between Ambient Air Pollution and Hypertensive Disorders of Pregnancy." *Environmental Research* 123:9–16. http://www.sciencedirect.com/science/article/pii/S0013935113000108.

Mudu, Pierpaolo. 2021. *Ambient Air Pollution and Health in Accra, Ghana*. Geneva: World Health Organization.

Muller, Christophe, and Huijie Yan. 2016. *Household Fuel Use in Developing Countries: Re-*

view of Theory and Evidence. AMSE working paper, March 18. https://halshs.archives -ouvertes.fr/halshs-01290714/document.

Nguyen, T. K., T. H. Tran, C. L. Roberts, G. J. Fox, S. M. Graham, and B. J. Marais. 2017. "Risk Factors for Child Pneumonia—Focus on the Western Pacific Region." *Paediatric Respiratory Reviews* 21:95–101. https://doi.org/10.1016/j.prrv.2016.07.002.

Odoi, Justice, and Gary Kleiman. 2021. *Strengthening Air Quality Management in Accra, Ghana.* Washington, DC: World Bank. https://openknowledge.worldbank.org/handle /10986/37493.

Pedersen, Marie, Leslie Stayner, Rémy Slama, Mette Sørensen, Francesc Figueras, Mark J. Nieuwenhuijsen, Ole Raaschou-Nielsen, and Payam Dadvand. 2014. "Ambient Air Pollution and Pregnancy-Induced Hypertensive Disorders: A Systematic Review and Meta-Analysis." *Hypertension* 64:494–500.

Penza, Michele. 2020. "Low-Cost Sensors for Outdoor Air Quality Monitoring." In *Advanced Nanomaterials for Inexpensive Gas Microsensors*, edited by Eduard Llobet, 235–88. Amsterdam: Elsevier.

Pope, Daniel P., Vinod Mishra, Lisa Thompson, Amna R. Siddiqui, Eva A. Rehfuess, Martin Weber, and Nigel G. Bruce. 2010. "Risk of Low Birth Weight and Stillbirth Associated with Indoor Air Pollution from Solid Fuel Use in Developing Countries." *Epidemiologic Reviews* 32 (1): 70–81. https://doi.org/10.1093/epirev/mxq005.

Pope, Francis D., Michael Gatari, David Ng'ang'a, Alexander Poynter, and Rhiannon Blake. 2018. "Airborne Particulate Matter Monitoring in Kenya Using Calibrated Low-Cost Sensors." *Atmospheric Chemistry and Physics* 18:15403–418. https://doi.org/10.5194 /acp-18-15403-2018.

Project Gaia. n.d. Home page. Accessed September 2. https://projectgaia.com/.

Rajé, Fiona, Miles Tight, and Francis D. Pope. 2018. "Traffic Pollution: A Search for Solutions for a City like Nairobi." *Cities* 82:100–107.

Ray, Charlotte, Mike Clifford, and Sarah Jewitt. 2014. "The Introduction and Uptake of Improved Cookstoves: Making Sense of Engineers, Social Scientists, Barriers, Markets and Participation." *Boiling Point* 64:2–5.

Rehfuess, Eva A., Elisa Puzzolo, Debbi Stanistreet, Daniel Pope, and Nigel G. Bruce. 2014. "Enablers and Barriers to Large-Scale Uptake of Improved Solid Fuel Stoves: A Systematic Review." *Environmental Health Perspectives* 122:120–30.

Samuel, M. Gaita, Johan Boman, Michael J. Gatari, Jan B.C. Pettersson, and Sara Janhäll. 2014. "Source Apportionment and Seasonal Variation of $PM_{2.5}$ in a Sub-Saharan African City: Nairobi, Kenya." *Atmospheric Chemistry and Physics* 14 (18): 9977–91. https://doi.org/10.5194/acp-14-9977-2014.

Schlag, Nicolai, and Fiona Zuzarte. 2008. *Market Barriers to Clean Cooking Fuels in Sub-Saharan Africa: A Review of Literature.* Stockholm: SEI.

Shirley, Rebekah. 2018. "Millions of Urban Africans Still Don't Have Electricity: Here's What Can Be Done." *Conversation*, April 19.

Sow, Baïdy, Bertrand Tchanche, Ibrahima Fall, Saliou Souaré, and Aminata Mbow-Diokhané. 2021. "Monitoring of Atmospheric Pollutant Concentrations in the City of Dakar, Senegal." *Open Journal of Air Pollution* 10:18–30.

Sustainable Energy Africa. 2014. *Tackling Urban Energy Poverty in South Africa*. Cape Town: Sustainable Energy Africa.

Sustainable Energy Africa. 2015. "Modelling the Urban Energy Future of Sub-Saharan Africa." Working paper, Sustainable Energy Africa, Cape Town. https://www.african cityenergy.org/uploads/resource_26.pdf.

UNDESA (United Nations Department of Economic and Social Affairs), Population Division. 2019. *World Urbanization Prospects: The 2018 Revision*. New York: United Nations.

UNEP (United Nations Environment Programme). 2016. "Air Pollution: Africa's Invisible, Silent Killer." https://www.unep.org/news-and-stories/story/air-pollution-africas -invisible-silent-killer-0.

UNEP (United Nations Environment Programme). 2018. *Africa Waste Management Outlook*. Nairobi, Kenya: United Nations Environment Programme.

UNEP (United Nations Environment Programme). 2021. *Regulating Air Quality: The First Global Assessment of Air Pollution Legislation, Nairobi*. Nairobi, Kenya: United Nations Environment Programme.

UNICEF (United Nations Children's Fund). 2019. *Silent Suffocation in Africa: Air Pollution Is a Growing Menace, Affecting the Poorest Children the Most*. New York: UNICEF. https:// www.unicef.org/media/55081/file/Silent_suffocation_in_africa_air_pollution_2019 .pdf.

Val, Stéphanie, Cathy Liousse, El Hadji Thierno Doumbia, Corinne Galy-Lacaux, Hélène Cachier, Nicolas Marchand, Anne Badel, Eric Gardrat, Alexandre Sylvestre, and Armelle Baeza-Squiban. 2013. "Physico-Chemical Characterization of African Urban Aerosols (Bamako in Mali and Dakar in Senegal) and Their Toxic Effects in Human Bronchial Epithelial Cells: Description of a Worrying Situation." *Particle and Fibre Toxicology* 10:10. http://www.particleandfibretoxicology.com/content/10/1/10.

WHO (World Health Organization). 2021a. "Ambient (outdoor) Air Pollution." https:// www.who.int/news-room/fact-sheets/detail/ambient-(outdoor)-air-quality-and -health.

WHO (World Health Organization). 2021b. "Population with Primary Reliance on Polluting Fuels and Technologies for Cooking." In *The global Health Observatory*. Geneva, Switzerland.

WHO (World Health Organization). 2022a. "Ambient Air Quality Database, WHO, April 2022." https://www.who.int/data/gho/data/themes/air-pollution/who-air-quality -database.

WHO (World Health Organization). 2022b. "Disability-adjusted life years (DALYs)." https://www.who.int/data/gho/indicator-metadata-registry/imr-details/158# :~:text=Definition%3A-,One%20DALY%20represents%20the%20loss%20of%20 the%20equivalent%20of%20one,health%20condition%20in%20a%20population.

Wilhelm, Michelle, Jo Kay Ghosh, Jason Su, Myles Cockburn, Michael Jerrett, and Beate Ritz. 2011. "Traffic-Related Air Toxics and Preterm Birth: A Population-Based "Case-Control Study in Los Angeles County, California." *Environmental Health* 10 (89).

158   Social Determinants of Health

World Bank Group. 2014. *Clean and Improved Cooking in Sub-Saharan Africa: A Landscape Report*. Washington, DC: World Bank.

World Bank Group. 2020. *Population Living in Slums (% of Urban Population)—Sub-Saharan Africa*. Washington, DC: World Bank.

World Bank Group, ESMAP (Energy Sector Management Assistance Program), and AFREA (Africa Renewable Energy and Access Program). 2015. *Energizing Africa: Achievements and Lessons from the Africa Renewable Energy and Access Program (AFREA) Phase I*. Washington, DC: World Bank Group.

9

Transportation and Urban Health Risks in Africa

Peter Elias and Femi Ola Aiyegbajeje

1. Introduction

Transport shapes the character and pattern of cities. A variety of transportation options are available in African cities, including motorcycles and tricycle taxis, which have different names in different cities and regions. These different modes of transportation allow many benefits, including increased access to employment, education, health services, and recreational opportunities. Yet transportation systems also have negative impacts on health in African cities, causing road traffic injuries, air and noise pollution, and increased prevalence of noncommunicable diseases partly due to an increase in sedentary lifestyles. For example, it is estimated that 91 percent of urban populations breathe in polluted air, resulting in about 780,000 deaths annually (WHO 2018). Similarly, the World Bank (2022) report on urban mobility in Africa indicates that travelers do not have access to dependable, affordable, and safe transport services, resulting in traffic congestion, increased costs, pollution, accidents, noise, intrusion, and long delays for both users and nonusers.

This chapter examines transport systems and their urban health risks and benefits in African cities, first interrogating the relationship between transport development and urban health risks in African cities. This is followed by a section on strategies to improve transport systems and health benefits in African cities, concluding with major recommendation for improving transport systems and health in urban Africa.

2. Transport Systems in African Cities: Challenges and Benefits

Transport systems in African cities are characterized by both challenges and benefits. The types of vehicles used for public transport shape the features of transport systems in African cities. Transport systems and types of vehicles are further associated with different challenges and benefits in African cities.

2.1. Transport Vehicles in African Cities

Transportation in urban Africa, as in most urban areas in the world, is characterized by the dominant use of vehicles. African cities have unique but similar vehicles used for transportation. They are unique because they are not commonly found in cities in other regions of the world. Some examples of these vehicles are motorcycle taxis (called *boda bodas* in Kampala and *okadas* in Lagos) and commuter buses, such as minibuses, which are referred to as *danfo* in Lagos, *poda-poda* in Freetown, *trotro* in Accra, *daladala* in Dar es Salaam, *matatu* in Kenya, *car rapides* in Dakar, *kamuny* in Kampala, *gbaka* in Abidjan, *esprit de mort* in Kinshasa, *candongueiros* in Luanda, *sotrama* in Bamako, *songa kidogo* in Kigali, and *kombi* in Cape Town. The continent's transit sector is evolving with the emergence of newer transport modes, such as Bus Rapid Transit (BRT) in Lagos, which is known as City Bus in Johannesburg. Other transportation options used in some African cities are light rail systems and e-ridesharing.

2.1.1. MOTORCYCLES

The use of motorcycles as a means of transport, such as commercial motorcycles or motorcycle "taxis" in public transport, is popular in many African cities (Marija et al. 2022). Commercial motorcycles (figure 9.1) are mainly used to carry passengers for hire. They complement other modes of transportation, such as minibuses, taxis, and light rail, by taking commuters to their doorstep, thereby making motorcycle transport more accessible. The decline in organized public transport systems coupled with the flexibility and accessibility of using commercial motorcycles has increased the adoption of this mode of transportation in various cities, including Lagos, Kampala, Ouagadougou, Monrovia, Cotonou, Douala, Ndjamena, Niamey, Lomé, Bamako, and Nairobi.

Fig. 9.1. Commercial motorcycles, or motorcycle taxis, in Lagos. Source: Courtesy of Peter Elias and Femi Ola Aiyegbajeje.

This mode of transportation is unregulated in most cities, however, and efforts to regulate the market have had the contrary effect of distorting the operational market structures of the transport system. In Lagos, after the general ban on Okada use for passenger service, its usage for goods delivery increased, and regulations improved (Christie and Ward 2023).

Despite the dominant role played by commercial motorcycles in public transport, little is known about the political economy, service patterns, ridership characteristics, cost structure, or environmental, health, and other impacts. The toll associated with road traffic crashes in developing countries is very high, with the burden of injury disproportionately borne by riders—largely motorcycle riders and pedestrians (Konlan et al. 2020; Peng et al. 2017). The Global Burden of Disease Study estimates that years of life lost due to road injuries is 415.7 (291.0–590.1) per 100,000 people (Angell et al. 2022). Motorcycle riders represent more than 380,000 annual deaths worldwide, which accounted for over 28 percent of the global crash fatalities in 2016 (Ospina-Mateus et al. 2019). The rate of commercial motorcycle (Okada) accidents is higher during rainy seasons in Nigeria (FRSC 2007). In Kenya's Mwea town, excessive speed, alcohol intake, and lack of helmet use were identified as major factors responsible for accidents (Ndiwiga, Mbakaya, and Kiiyukia 2019).

162   Social Determinants of Health

In addition, because the transport system is largely unregulated, motorcycles are being used for criminal activities (such as robbery and theft) in cities such as Lagos, Monrovia, and Nairobi. Some gated neighborhoods in these cities do not allow access to motorcycles. The carbon emissions from motorcycles also pose many health risks to the populace and the environment.

2.1.2. TRICYCLES

A tricycle is a three-wheel vehicle designed to carry three to four passengers. It has emerged as a mode of transportation in most underdeveloped and developing cities of the world. In Africa, this mode of transport has different names across the continent. It is one of the most dominant means of urban transportation in cities such as Lagos, Douala, Monrovia, Bamako, Ouagadougou, Monrovia, Nairobi, Niamey, and Cotonou. Unlike motorcycle transport, it carries more than one passenger, yet like motorcycles, tricycles are accessible because they can reach most streets. This mode of transport also serves as a major source of employment for youths and middle-aged men and women.

As with motorcycles, reckless driving, disregard for traffic rules, and overloading increase the risk of accidents. Due to a lack of regulation, tricycles can also produce emissions that can harm the health of passengers and other urban residents.

2.1.3. TAXIS (CONVENTIONAL AND E-HAILING)

Taxis in African cities are like taxis in other parts of the world. They serve as a form of employment that contributes to the economy based on services rendered. Taxi operation is highly regulated in some African cities, such as Cairo, Marrakesh, Johannesburg, Algiers, Accra, and so forth, whereas in some other cities, the regulation is not comprehensive. In cities where the activities of taxi operators are not well regulated, taxis pose more challenges than where they are regulated.

Taxi operations can be divided into two categories: conventional taxi operators and the e-hailing, or e-ridesharing, taxi operations. Conventional taxis are those that do not allow for booking via phone or mobile app, while e-ridesharing involves booking using a mobile app or other digital platforms.

Conventional taxi operation can be found in many African cities, such as Lagos, Cape Town, Ibadan, Accra, Legon, Cotonou, Port-Novo, Lomé, Abidjan, Douala, Nairobi, Harare, Johannesburg, Marrakesh, Cairo, Lusaka, Kinshasa,

Niamey, and others. A major challenge of this mode of operation is poor monitoring of car quality, resulting in many rickety taxis on the roads. Traffic congestion, safety and security, and high carbon emissions are other issues facing taxi operators and commuters in major cities.

As of 2016, Africa had fifty-six e-ridesharing services, with most homegrown apps launched between 2015 and 2016. Real-time e-hailing is gradually disrupting the transportation industry and includes major companies, such as Uber, Bolt (formerly known as Taxify), TaxiDiali, Ousta, and Careem. The ride-sharing app Uber operates in fifteen African countries, with Lagos having the largest ride-sharing services among all African cities (Oreva 2016). About twenty-one African countries use ride-sharing apps (Oreva 2016). With fourteen known ride-sharing services, Lagos has the most ridesharing services in Africa. The top five cities are Lagos (14 apps), Nairobi (11), Cape Town (7), Casablanca (5), and Cairo (4) (Oreva 2016). One important advantage of an e-hailing taxi service is the flexibility and transparency in payment methods, allowing passengers to know the fare upfront. Another important aspect of e-hailing is that it provides the opportunity to share your ride with another rider heading in the same direction. It is also convenient, since the pickup can be done at location of choice. E-hailing is considered more efficient and acceptable than conventional, particularly among higher income city residents. Challenges associated with e-ridesharing taxi services, however, include safety, security, unhealthy rivalry from conventional taxi operators, and inconsistent government policies.

2.1.4. COMMUTER BUSES

Commuter bus service includes the use of minibuses, large buses, and BRT for public transportation (figure 9.2). The commuter buses are used for both intra- and intercity transport services. They are also used for chartered services. BRTs are used only for intracity services and charter services.

In many cities in Africa, public transport is dominated by *informal transport*, including, most importantly, minibus systems, which are operated by many private actors. These systems are often called *paratransit* because of their flexible schedules, stops, and routes; low levels of regulation over competition; and formal business practices (Behrens, McCormick, and Mfinanga 2016). This form of bus service can be found in most sub-Saharan African cities, unlike the North African cities, where trams and BRTs are more likely to be found.

Fig. 9.2. Commuter buses, specifically minibuses, in Lagos. Source: Courtesy of Peter Elias and Femi Ola Aiyegbajeje.

Commuter buses provide cheaper transport services for city commuters, as well as covering longer distances and major points within the city. The BRT also provides cheaper services and runs through dedicated lanes. The major advantage of using BRT is that the buses are faster, reducing travel time from one point to the other. BRT buses can be found in Lagos, Addis Ababa, Johannesburg, Nairobi, and Marrakesh. Lagos and Johannesburg were the first BRT adopters in Africa. Lagos created a "BRT-Lite system" after extensive negotiations with the minibus sector through the National Union of Road Transport Workers (NURTW). In contrast, Johannesburg replaced the minibuses with BRT and compensated the minibus owners. Nairobi has been in a protracted BRT planning phase but is now under increasing political pressure to deliver; this has led to procuring buses and painting a lane of one major highway as a BRT only corridor without clear planning or an institutional framework.

2.1.5. NONMOTORIZED TRANSPORTATION (CYCLING AND WALKING)

Nonmotorized transportation (NMT) includes all forms of transportation or movement that do not rely on an engine or motor. This form of transportation includes walking, cycling, and using small-wheeled transport (skates, skateboards, push scooters, and hand carts) or wheelchairs. Most city

Transportation and Health Risks   165

Table 9.1. Mobility and mode choices in selected African cities

City	Country	Mobility (trips per person per day)	Mode choice, % of total trips			
			Walk	Bicycle	Public transport	Private motorized transport
Morogoro	Tanzania	1.7	67	23	12	4
Dar es Salaam	Tanzania	1.9	47	3	43	7
Nairobi	Kenya	2.2	47	1	42	7
Eldoret	Kenya	2.7	48	12	24	16
Kinshasa	Congo	2.2	70	—	20	10
Addis Ababa	Ethiopia	4.9	70	—	26	4
Bamako	Mali	3.1	60	2	17	21
Ouagadougou	Burkina Faso	3.8	42	10	3	45
Harare	Zimbabwe	N/A	63	1	16	20
Niamey	Niger	N/A	60	2	9	32
Dakar	Senegal	3.2	81	1	17	1

residents in sub-Saharan Africa are from low-income households, dependent on NMT (see table 9.1), and their urban transport expenditures account for 10 percent (in the smaller cities) to 20 percent of their household incomes (Diaz, Plat, and Pochet 2008). There is also inadequate infrastructure, such as walkways, pedestrian bridges, and bicycle lanes, and this has contributed to high rate of injuries and fatalities, including among pedestrians (Elias, Babatola, and Omojola 2016). Pedestrians are the most endangered among all road users in African cities, particularly in sub-Saharan Africa (Vissoci et al. 2017).

2.1.6. LIGHT RAIL SYSTEMS

In Lagos, the light rail system is known as the blue line, starting from Okokomaiko and Marina corridors. The other corridor is known as the red line, which will commence operation by the end of 2024. The red line links Agbado and Marina corridors. In 2016, the Addis Ababa Metro, the first modern light rail system in Africa, was launched. It runs from Addis Ababa's main industrial area on the southern fringe through Merkato district to the center of Piazza. Light rail systems can also be found in Tangiers in Morocco, Algiers in Algeria, Tunis in Tunisia, and Cairo in Egypt.

2.2. Transportation Challenges in Urban Africa

Transportation in Africa has unique features that contribute to the state of urban health risks. This section describes some of the profound features and their implications for urban health risks in Africa.

2.2.1. RAPID URBANIZATION AND INTENSITY OF VEHICULAR (ROAD) TRANSPORT

The growth in urban population has dovetailed with the use of transport vehicles and the expansion of road networks across cities in Africa. Traffic congestion is a normal phenomenon and one of the major results of urbanization that can increase energy consumption and escalate air and noise pollution. For example, automobile exhaust causes elevated lead levels in cities, and pollution has major impacts on the quality of life in urban areas.

2.2.2. THE DOMINANCE OF THE INFORMAL SECTOR

Part of the challenge facing transport systems in African cities is the high dominance of the informal sector. Cities in Africa are notorious for informal modes of transport, especially minibuses, but also motorbikes, tricycles, and shared taxis. The absence or unreliability of government-owned mass transportation services has encouraged the growth and popularity of the informal and largely unregulated sector. On one hand, a lack of adherence to design standards and specifications as well as poor maintenance affect the efficiency of transportation services in African cities. On the other hand, informal modes of transportation account for most motorized trips. For example, minibuses account for an estimated four-fifths of Africa's total motorized trips. Minibuses are notorious for their usual squealing brakes, bald tires, and rattling exhaust pipes, which emit thick black smoke as a result of poor maintenance and the lack of government regulation.

2.2.3. LOW INVESTMENT

With competing demands for funds, governments are often unable to give adequate attention to building new roads or maintaining existing ones in cities (Elias, Babatola, and Omojola, 2016). In addition, low investment outlay poses serious constraints on government-owned transport systems and the attendant low access to sustainable urban transport systems in African cities. This partly explains the dominance of the informal sector. The African Development Bank Group report (2010) shows that road infrastructure in sub-Saharan Africa is only 204 km per 1,000 km^2 of land area, and only about 25 percent is paved, compared to the world average of 944 km per 1,000 km^2 of land area. Similarly, the same report indicates that Africa's private investments in roads were only US$1.4 billion between 1990 and 1999 and US$21 billion between 2000 and 2005, which fall below the demand.

2.2.4. POOR PRICING SYSTEMS

Studies suggest that road transport prices are high and may lead to low access to sustainable urban transport systems in Africa. For example, a comparative study by Rizet and Hine (1993) found that road transport prices in three Francophone countries, Cameroon, Côte d'Ivoire, and Mali, were six times more expensive than in Pakistan and about 40 percent more expensive than in France. In a related study by Rizet and Gwet (1998), comparing seven countries in three continents, reported that for distances up to 300 kilometers, the unit prices of road transport in Africa were 40–100 percent more than the rates in Southeast Asia.

2.2.5. ABSENCE OF TRANSPORT POLICY, STRONG INSTITUTIONAL CAPACITY, AND METROPOLITAN TRANSPORT AUTHORITY

Research on transport in Africa has shown weak financial performance due to inappropriate system plan specifications, which result in high initial capital costs, exaggerated demand, and poor revenue generation (Fan and Beukes 2021). For example, weak financial management of the BRT systems has been linked to a lack of political will, interagency rivalries, and the absence of dedicated and functional transport authorities. Furthermore, without enabling legal and regulatory frameworks and with ineffective coordination, institutions limit the commercial viability of public transport in Africa. This clearly contributes to low or poor implementation of mass transit and effective traffic management systems, with resultant severe negative health risks in Africa.

2.2.6. LOW ADOPTION OF DIGITAL PLATFORMS TO IMPROVE URBAN TRANSPORTATION

Emerging initiatives and platforms in Lagos, Nigeria, such as GONA, a new payment platform to support cashless operations on a fleet of buses, are being threatened by low acceptability of the payment platform. The absence of road maps and standard routing systems are a constraint for sustainable transport systems in many African cities.

2.2.7. NO MECHANISMS FOR MEASURING AND MONITORING TRANSPORT-RELATED POLLUTION

Effective air and noise quality measurement and assessment affect transport systems and help minimize health risks in African cities. When air and noise qualities are being monitored, policies can be implemented to reduce the health impact of pollution and to improve transport systems.

3. Health Risks Posed by Public Transport in African Cities

Health risks associated with public transport include motor vehicle crashes, physical inactivity, climate change, social exclusion, traffic-related environmental exposures (i.e., air and noise pollution), green space reduction, and the rise in local temperature.

3.1. Road Traffic Accidents/Crashes

The causes of road traffic accidents (RTAs) are multifactorial and involve the interaction of several precrash factors, such as the types of road users; the number, type, and condition of vehicles; and the road environment. Road traffic accidents are a global menace, leading to about 1.3 million recorded deaths annually, and these incidents are more prevalent in developing countries (World Economic Forum et al. 2015). Additionally, as many as 50 million people suffer nonfatal RTA injuries every year (Schlottmann et al. 2017).

In Africa, road injury was responsible for 297 deaths per 100,000 in 2019 and is considered a leading cause of death. Nigeria and South Africa have the highest road fatality rates, followed by five countries (Democratic Republic of Congo, Ethiopia, Kenya, Tanzania, and Uganda), all accounting for 64 percent of all road deaths in the region. Adeloye et al. (2016) reported an estimated rate for road traffic injury of 65.2 per 100,000 population and a death rate of 16.6 per 100,000 population. This situation is largely so because most countries in Africa do not have strong policies for protecting road users and lack investment in public transportation. Additionally, in most countries, there is little or no postaccident care, which is grossly inadequate when it exists.

Available data show that Nigeria has an average of 23 accidents per 1,000 vehicles. Between January and August 2021, about 101 deaths and 625 injuries were recorded in Lagos alone due to road accidents (FRSC 2021). Also, in the second quarter of 2020, Lagos recorded 92 road crashes, one of the highest rates among Nigerian cities (NBS 2020). Lagos accounts for the highest number of injuries and deaths from motorcycle crashes in Nigeria between 2010 and 2019, with much noticeable decline between 2017 and 2019 because of new legislation (Emiogun et al. 2022). The Federal Road Safety Corps (FRSC; 2020) shows that motor vehicle crashes are on the rise and the leading cause of death in Nigeria, and according to this report, between 2013 and 2019, about 41,709 deaths resulted from RTAs. Similarly, according to WHO (2020), RTA deaths in Morocco reached 6,185, or 2.71 percent of total deaths. This number is higher in the Democratic Republic of the Congo, reaching 30,256, or 4.60 percent of total deaths. The age-adjusted death rate is 39.80 per 100,000 of population in the Democratic Republic of the Congo. Furthermore, in Kenya, road traffic accidents are among the top five causes of death for Kenyans between the ages of 5 and 70, and the leading killer of boys aged 15 to 19 (WHO 2022). In Ghana, 72 persons out of every 100,000 suffered grievous bodily injury, and close to 8 of the same population died from RTAs over the last ten years (Blankson 2020).

Road traffic accidents also have important economic and disability consequences in Africa. Juillard et al. (2010) found that road traffic injuries resulted in disability for 29.1 percent, while 13.5 percent were unable to return to work. Among those with disability, 67.6 percent were unable to perform their daily activities, 16.7 percent consequently lost their jobs, and 88.6 percent had a reduction in earnings. Glazener et al. (2021) argue that most people affected by road crashes are vulnerable road users such as pedestrians, cyclists, and motorcyclists, who account for about 50 percent of all traffic deaths worldwide.

3.2. Physical Inactivity

International health experts have recommended a minimum of 150 minutes of moderate exercise per week or 75 minutes of vigorous activity weekly (CDC 2021). Globally, physical inactivity is the fourth leading risk factor for mortality, accounting for about 4 to 5 million deaths that could have been prevented. Glazener et al. (2021) observed that a lack of modal diversity for transportation among populations living in low-income countries, including Africa, leads to an increase in physical inactivity and consequently an increase in the rate of obesity and death.

High-density traffic congestion also leads to physical inactivity, since commuters spend more hours on journeys than normal. Human physical inactivity is high in African cities where most of the residents rely on motorized transport to move around. For instance, Olasunkanmi (2019) observed that 1.6 million vehicles ply Lagos roads daily, with between 200,000 and 250,000 vehicles each in Accra, Nairobi, Cotonou, Lomé, Kinshasa, and Harare. The report also indicates that about 226 cars run Lagos roads per kilometer, compared to the national average of 16 cars per kilometer. Other modes, such as motorcycles and tricycles, provide another means of door-to-door transport service that further reinforces human physical inactivity among urban residents.

3.3. Climate Change

Road transportation is the leading contributor to global warming and will continue to be for the next fifty years (NASA / Goddard Institute for Space Studies 2010). Globally, transportation accounts for about 15 to 23 percent of global greenhouse gas emissions yearly. The US Environmental Protection Agency (2024) lists the greenhouse gases as carbon dioxide (CO_2), methane, nitrous oxide, and fluorinated gases, which trap heat in the atmosphere. Passenger transport vehicles are a major contributor to transport-related greenhouse gas emissions..

According to a World Health Organization (WHO 2018) report, climate change is responsible for about 150,000 deaths annually, and this number is expected to double by 2030. The report also shows that climate change is expected to worsen health conditions of populations living in tropical regions, such as Africa, especially those living in Lagos, Cotonou, Lomé, Accra, Douala, and Abidjan. The alterations in vector-pathogen relations due to global warming result in adverse mental and physical health, as well as premature mortality (Patz et al. 2014).

3.4. Social Exclusion

Mackett and Thoreau (2015) explain that social exclusion occurs when individuals or groups of people are denied access to participate in certain activities. Social exclusion was first recognized by Rene Lenoir in 1974 and has long been identified as a problem connected to poor or restricted access to resources that may possibly lead to personal and physical harm (Glazener et al. 2021; Julien et al., 2015). Transport-related social exclusion affects some groups more than others, and the most vulnerable groups include low-income populations, disabled people, the elderly, adolescents, women, and minorities (Mackett and Thoreau 2015). One-way transport has contributed immensely to social exclusion in low-income populations, who are denied access to full transport because households cannot afford public transportation due to high cost and are subsequently denied access to jobs, education, health services, and leisure activities (Mackett and Thoreau 2015).

Another contributing factor to social exclusion is the fear of crime among women, people living with disabilities, and other minorities (Madriaza and Shaw 2016). Those who cannot afford to use public transport may be forced to walk through unsafe areas, which may increase their risk for assault. The fear of sexual harassment has negatively affected women's experience of public transportation, with increased mobility restriction and risk of social exclusion (Turdalieva and Edling, 2018). Saito et al. (2012) argue that people who are prevented from using public transport because of fear of crime suffer from the consequences of being socially excluded and are at higher risk of premature mortality.

3.5. Traffic-Related Environmental Exposures

Traffic-related environmental exposures include air pollution, noise, and increase in local temperature.

3.5.1. AIR POLLUTION

Atmospheric air pollution is caused by the presence of dangerous pollutants, such as nitrogen oxides, sulfur oxides, ozone, air toxins, and particulate matter with an aerodynamic diameter of less than 2.5 micrometers ($PM_{2.5}$), which can enter the bloodstream with an increase in mortality and morbidity (WHO 2017). Air pollution also contributes to the depletion of the ozone layer. In Africa motor vehicle traffic is known to be the main source of urban concentrations of air pollutants with identifiable hazardous properties that have serious effects on human health (East African 2021; Jancsek-Turóczi et al. 2013; Lindgren et al. 2009; Nhung et al. 2017; Shah et al. 2013). The exhaust from motor vehicles contributes to almost all carbon monoxide in the air, about 75 percent of the nitrogen oxides (NO_2), and 40 percent of particulate matter (PM_{10}).

Ozone and $PM_{2.5}$ were estimated to be responsible for 385,000 deaths

172   Social Determinants of Health

globally in 2015, and these deaths were said to have increased globally by 9.4 percent between 2010 and 2015 (Anenberg et al. 2019). Air pollution is responsible for increased premature mortality in twenty-one of the fast-growing cities in Africa (Vohra and Marais 2022). It rose from 84,000 in 2005 to 110,000 in 2018 (Khan and Strand 2018). This is on average about 2,000 avoidable deaths each year. Around one-third of these deaths are found in five of the ten cities that are signatory to the Clean Air Cities Declaration (C40).

3.5.2. NOISE

Traffic noise poses a serious health problem as it is the main source of noise pollution in cities and is the highest external cost of transport, that is, an indirect cost affecting third parties (WHO 2000, 2011). The effect of noise pollution is more pervasive and extreme in African cities compared to other urban areas. Transportation-related factors that determine the level of noise within an area include road networks, junctions, traffic flow, and speed, but the noise level is often associated with the dominant mode of transportation in the area (Hong, Shen, and Zhang 2014; Oguntunde et al. 2019; Zhao 2014).

Van Kempen et al. (2018) observed that noise pollution causes an increase in blood pressure, suppression of the central nervous system, and changes in breathing and heart rate, which may lead to cardiovascular diseases such as stroke, heart attack, and ischemic heart disease, as well as increased risks of mortality. Further negative affects of noise pollution include disruption of sleep, reduction in deep resting sleep, and untoward increased awakenings during sleep, which may cause fatigue and a corresponding decrease in performance. For example, a study on Abuja municipal conducted by Ibekwe et al. (2016) showed that daily exposure of more than five hours to noise pollution can result in cardiovascular disorders and hearing loss.

3.5.3. RISE IN LOCAL TEMPERATURE

The use of fossil fuels releases carbon dioxide and other greenhouse gases like methane (CH_4), nitrous oxide (N_2O), and hydrofluorocarbons (HFCs) into the atmosphere, thereby causing Earth's atmosphere to warm significantly and much more rapidly (EPA 2024). Scientific evidence has shown that human-caused increases in greenhouse gas are responsible for and have already created a 1.5°C temperature rise (Abraham et al. 2012). Gordon (2010) observed that air pollutants—such as the ozone-forming nitrogen oxides and hydrocarbon, carbon monoxide, particulate matter, and sulfur oxides—affect the global climate directly and indirectly.

Transportation is a direct contributor of the second most abundant greenhouse gas, carbon dioxide, which has an atmospheric lifetime of one hundred years, surpassing other direct greenhouse gas emissions from transportation. Heat is becoming common because of the built environment and transportation infrastructure, including heat-absorbing concrete. As transportation has continued to expand, it encourages tree felling while discouraging open and green spaces (Khreis et al. 2017). Anderson and Bell (2011) observe a 4.5 percent mortality risk for every 1°C increase in heat wave intensity. High temperature can contribute to respiratory diseases such as COPD and asthma (Bunker et al. 2016). A rise in temperature is also responsible for motor vehicle crashes due to vehicle overheating (Basagaña et al. 2015).

4. Improving Public Transportation and Its Health Benefits in African Cities

There are developments in transportation that are enhancing health benefits in cities in Africa. Some of these strategies include dedicated lanes with BRT, installation of road signs, provision of pedestrians' infrastructure (pedestrian bridges, walkways, zebra-crossing signs), road traffic education and advocacy, reduction in travel time, reduction of greenhouse gas emissions, and improvement on travel safety. A World Bank (2022) survey of strategies to improve transport systems and health benefits are shown in table 9.2. These include smart land use and transport policy, allocation of adequate land for green spaces, improved multimodal transport systems, road hierarchy arrangement and management, regularization of informal public transport, reduced fuel consumption and greenhouse gas emissions, among others.

4.1. Smart Land Use and Transport Policy

Smart land use and policy include the use of priority lanes, which enhances the inherent flexibility of mass transit systems such as BRT (Cervero 2013; Wright and Hook 2007). BRT operates using dedicated lanes in Lagos (Nigeria), Johannesburg (South Africa), Dar es Salaam (Tanzania), Marrakech (Morocco), Pretoria (South Africa), and Accra (Ghana). More than 150 countries have implemented the BRT system worldwide, which carries an estimated 28 million passengers each weekday. There are about 280 BRT

Table 9.2. Countries with strategies to improve public transport and health in Africa

Strategies	Countries
Smart land use and transport policy	Benin, Burkina Faso, Côte d'Ivoire, Ethiopia, Kenya, Mali, Rwanda, Togo
Allocation of adequate land for green spaces	Rwanda
Improved multimodal transport systems	Rwanda
Road hierarchy arrangement and management	Burkina Faso, Rwanda
Effective transport governance supported by institutions, frameworks, and funding commitments	Ethiopia, Burkina Faso, Mali, Nigeria, Senegal, Togo
Regularization of informal public transport	Ghana, Kenya
Efficient travel and traffic management system with real-time data and digital mapping	Ghana, Kenya, Nigeria, Senegal
Use of smartcard ticketing systems	Nigeria, Rwanda, Senegal
Reduction of fuel consumption and greenhouse gas emissions	Burkina Faso, Togo

Source: World Bank, 2022

corridors worldwide, networked on 4,800 km routes with about 6,700 stations and approximately 30,000 buses (BRTDATA.org).

4.2. Reduction in Travel Time

The benefit of dedicated lanes for transportation systems is that they encourage a preboarding payment and a level platform, which allows quicker access to the bus, together with a well-spaced metro station rather than traditional bus stops, making boarding the bus easier and faster for passengers. These features benefited residents of African cities such as Accra, Addis Ababa, Lagos, Marrakech, Dar es Salaam, Johannesburg, and others where the BRT system is operated. Commuters have seen a significant reduction in travel time between locations. With the increased number of cars and traditional buses, which have exceeded the carrying capacity of roads, many commuters have spent hours moving between two points less than two kilometers apart. Data show that with the introduction of dedicated lanes for the BRT in Lagos, commuters now save an average of thirty to forty-five minutes every day (Otunola, Kriticos, and Harman 2019). In Johannesburg, BRT users report 10–20 percent travel time savings during one-way travel to work (Vaz and Venter 2012). The time-saving capacity of the BRT is made possible by the operating speed of the buses, around 35 kph, which is possible because of the lack of interference from other vehicles on the road. The BRT bus also saves time with fast boarding techniques, enabled by an off-board electronic payment and multidoor boarding.

4.3. Road Hierarchy Arrangement and Management

Road hierarchy arrangement and management is a strategy that is transforming public transportation and governance. African governments adopt road hierarchy arrangement and management policy to enhance road infrastructure financing and governance. Allocating road infrastructure to different administrative levels allows multilevel governance and inclusive revenue generation, which can go toward poverty alleviation and sustainable development.

4.4. Effective Transport Governance Supported by Institutions, Frameworks, and Funding Commitments

Transport governance in Africa faces enormous institutional, legal, and political complexity, which influences the governance framework and funding. There are strategies to promote transparency, accountability, and inclusiveness through partnerships for effective public transport governance. The Lagos Metropolitan Transport Management Authority is a good example of effective public transport governance established through public-private partnership based on the principles of transparency, accountability, and inclusiveness supported by the World Bank.

4.5. Regularization of Informal Transport Systems

In most African cities, the private sector is at the forefront of transport service provision, which is largely informal because it is unregulated. From routing to pricing to funding, there is a marked lack of regularization, which makes informal transport service provision far from desirable. Given the volume of passengers conveyed by the informal transport system and its contributions to the economy in terms of employment creation, income generation, and mobility supports, several African cities are beginning to integrate sustainable urban transport systems.

4.6. Efficient Travel and Traffic Management System with Real-Time Data and Digital Mapping

Traffic congestion is a clear implication of rapid and unplanned urbanization, a common feature of African cities. Different governments are adopting real-time data and digital mapping as key strategies for efficient travel and traffic management. This will over time reduce wasted labor hours, air pollution, and the associated health challenges in African cities.

4.7. Use of Smartcard Ticketing Systems

The introduction of smartcard ticketing on public transport has increased the efficiency of transport service providers and enhanced the convenience of commuters in African cities (Arroyo-Arroyo, van Ryneveld, and Finn 2021). The use of smartcards has eliminated the need for commuters to queue for tickets and reduced the burden of fare transactions by transport service providers. Smartcard ticketing implementation has recorded varying degrees of successes, but its gains far outweigh the price. Lagos has implemented cowry card for its public transport, which has enhanced revenue generation and reduced long queues for tickets at bus stations.

4.8. Reduction of Fuel Consumption and Greenhouse Gas

The use of clean diesel and other low-emission fuels in African cities can reduce greenhouse gas emission. This reduction is further supported by the introduction of higher-capacity buses for public transportation. According to Carrigan et al. (2013), the shift of commuters to higher-capacity vehicles with the introduction of BRT, with a capacity of 160 passengers, can reduce the number of vehicle kilometers traveled (VKT) in a city. Increasing the number of buses carrying the same large number of passengers will help to reduce traffic and present opportunities to replace the older, polluting vehicles. Fuel efficiency technologies incorporated into the mass transit buses also help to lower fuel consumption and consequently lower emissions and passengers' exposure to pollution, either inside the bus or at the bus station.

5. Conclusions

This chapter enumerates the risks and benefits of transportation in African cities. The issues raised in this chapter relate to transport-oriented development, overdependence on motorized transportation, physical inactivity, poor modal diversity, and transport-related environmental exposures, which are increasing health burdens in African cities. Strategies to enhance health benefits should focus on maintaining the functioning of public transport systems, reducing travel time, enhancing modal diversity, reducing dependency on motorized transportation, and increasing safe walking and cycling. Conscious efforts toward sustainable urban transport systems and development should prioritize review of land use design and management policies to promote pedestrianization and cycling; facilitate investments and financial incentives to support the purchase and maintenance of bicycles and other zero-emission vehicles; encourage continuous use of mass transit over private car; improve the use of smartcard ticketing systems; and design and plan to address heavily congested roads in African cities.

REFERENCES

Abraham, Sarin, K. Ganesh, A. Senthil Kumar, and Yves Ducqd. 2012. "Impact on Climate Change due to Transportation Sector: Research Perspective." *Procedia Engineering* 38:3869–79. http://doi:10.1016/j.proeng.2012.06.445.

Adeloye, Davies, Jacqueline Y. Thompson, Moses A. Akanbi, Dominic Azuh, Victoria Samuel, Nicholas Omoregbe, and Charles K. Ayo. 2016. "The Burden of Road Traffic Crashes, Injuries and Deaths in Africa: A Systematic Review and Meta-analysis." *Bulletin of the World Health Organization* 94 (7): 510–21A.

Africa Development Bank Group. 2010. "Statistics Department Annual Report." Tunis Belvedere, Tunis, Tunisia: African Development Bank. https://www.afdb.org/en/documents/document/afdb-group-annual-report-2010-23608

Anderson, G. Brooke, and Michelle L. Bell. 2011. "Heat Waves in the United States: Mortality Risk during Heat Waves and Effect Modification by Heat Wave Characteristics in 43 U.S. Communities." *Environmental Health Perspectives* 119 (2): 210–18. https://ehp.niehs.nih.gov/doi/abs/10.1289/ehp.1002313.

Anenberg, Susan, Joshua Miller, Daven Henze, Ray Minjares. 2019. "A Global Snapshot of the Air Pollution-Related Health Impacts of Transportation Sector Emissions in 2010 and 2015." The International Council on Clean Transportation, February 26. https://theicct.org/publication/a-global-snapshot-of-the-air-pollution-related-health-impacts-of-transportation-sector-emissions-in-2010-and-2015/.

Angell, Blake, Olutobi Sanuade, Ifedayo M. O. Adetifa, Iruka N. Okeke, Aishatu Lawal Adamu, Muktar H. Aliyu, Emmanuel A. Ameh, et al. 2022. "Population Health Outcomes in Nigeria Compared with Other West African Countries, 1998–2019: A Systematic Analysis for the Global Burden of Disease Study." *Lancet* 399:1117–29.

Arroyo-Arroyo, Fatima, Philip van Ryneveld, and Brendan Finn. 2021. *Innovation in Fare Collection Systems for Public Transport in African Cities*. Washington, DC: World Bank Group.

Basagaña, Xavier, Juan Pablo Escalera-Antezana, Payam Dadvand, Òscar Llatje, Jose Barrera-Gómez, Jordi Cunillera, Mercedes Medina-Ramón, Katherine Pérez. 2015. "High Ambient Temperatures and Risk of Motor Vehicle Crashes in Catalonia, Spain: A Time-Series Analysis." *Environmental Health Perspective* 123:1309–16. https://ehp.niehs.nih.gov/doi/abs/10.1289/ehp.1409223.

Behrens, Roger, Dorothy McCormick, and David Mfinanga, eds. 2016. *Paratransit in African Cities: Operations, Regulation and Reform*. London: Routledge.

Blankson, P. K. 2020. "Road Traffic Accidents in Ghana: Contributing Factors and Economic Consequences." *Ghana Medical Journal* 54 (3): 131.

Bunker, Aditi, Jan Wildenhain, Alina Vandenbergh, Nicholas Henschke, Joacim Rocklöv, Shakoor Hajat, and Rainer Sauerborn. 2016. "Effects of Air Temperature on Climate-Sensitive Mortality and Morbidity Outcomes in the Elderly: A Systematic Review and Meta-analysis of Epidemiological Evidence." *EBioMedicine* 6:258–68. https://doi.org/10.1016/j.ebiom.2016.02.034.

Carrigan, Aileen, Robin King, Juan Miguel Velasquez, Matthew Raifman, and Nicolae Duduta. 2013. *Social, Environmental and Economic Impacts of BRT Systems: Bus Rapid Transit Case Studies from Around the World*. Washington, DC: World Resources Institute, EMBARQ.

CDC (Centers for Disease Control and Prevention). 2021. *Physical Activity Guidelines for Americans*. https://health.gov/our-work/nutrition-physical-activity/physical-activity-guidelines.

Cervero, Robert. 2013. "Bus Rapid Transit (BRT): An Efficient and Competitive Mode of Public Transport." Institute of Urban and Regional Development, Working Paper 2013-01.

Christie, Nicola, and Heather Ward. 2023. "Delivering Hot Food on Motorcycles: A Mixed Method Study of the Impact of Business Model on Rider Behaviour and Safety." *Safety Science* 158 (2023): 105991.

Diaz Olvera, Lourdes, Didier Plat, and Pascal Pochet. 2008. "Household Transport Expenditure in Sub-Saharan African Cities: Measurement and Analysis." *Journal of Transport Geography* 16:1–13. https://doi.org/10.1016/j.jtrangeo.2007.04.001.

Edubirdie. 2022. "Commercial Motorcycle Use as the Type of Transportation." Edubirdie, February 17. https://edubirdie.com/examples/commercial-motorcycle-use-as-the-type-of-transportation/.

Elias, Peter, Olatunji Babatola, and Ademola Omojola. 2016. "Effective Urban Infrastructure Governance in Africa: Resolving the Wealth-Poverty Paradox." In *Population Growth and Rapid Urbanization in the Developing World*, edited by Umar G. Benna and Shaibu B. Garba, 125–48. Hershey, PA: Information Science Reference.

Emiogun, Edobor F., Daniel Ayodele Sanni, Sunday Sokunle Soyemi, Francis Adedayo Faduyile, and John Oladapo Obafunwa. 2022. "Trends in Motorcycle Accident Mortality in Lagos: Consequences of Government Policy Changes." *Medicine, Science and the Law* 62 (4): 269–74. https://doi.org/10.1177/00258024221082341.

EPA (Environmental Protection Agency). 2024. "Overview of Greenhouse Gases." Environmental Protection Agency, last updated April 11. https://www.epa.gov/ghgemissions/overview-greenhouse-gases.

Fan, Hongye, and Edward Andrew Beukes. 2021. *Enhancing Financial Sustainability and Commercial Viability of BRTs in Sub-Saharan Africa: The Factor Analysis Report*. Washington, DC: World Bank.

FRSC (Federal Road Safety Corps). 2007. "FRSC Establishment Act." FRSC, December 15.

FRSC (Federal Road Safety Corps). 2020. "FRSC Annual Reports." National Headquarters, Abuja.

FRSC (Federal Road Safety Corps). 2021. "FRSC Annual Reports." National Headquarters, Abuja.

Glazener, Andrew, Kristen Sanchez, Tara Ramani, Josias Zietsman, Mark J. Nieuwenhuijsen, Jennifer S. Mindell, Mary Fox, and Haneen Khreis. 2021. "Fourteen Pathways between Urban Transportation and Health: A Conceptual Model and Literature Review." *Journal of Transport and Health* 21:101070. https://doi.org/10.1016/j.jth.2021.101070.

Gordon, Deborah. 2010. "The Role of Transportation in Driving Climate Disruption." Carnegie Endowment for International Peace, December 16. https://carnegieendowment.org/research/2010/12/the-role-of-transportation-in-driving-climate-disruption.

Hong, Jinhyun, Qing Shen, and Lei Zhang. 2014. "How Do Built-Environment Factors Affect Travel Behavior? A Spatial Analysis at Different Geographic Scales." *Transportation* 41:419–40. https://doi.org/10.1007/s11116-013-9462-9.

Ibekwe, T., D. Folorunso, A. Ebuta, J. Amodu, M. Nwegbu, Z. Mairami, and I. Liman, et al. 2016. "Evaluation of the Environmental Noise Levels in Abuja Municipality Using Mobile Phones." *Annals of Ibadan Postgraduate Medicine* 14 (2): 58–64.

Jancsek-Turóczi, Beatrix, András Hoffer, Ilona Nyírő-Kósa, and András Gelencsér. 2013. "Sampling and Characterization of Resuspended and Respirable Road Dust." *Journal of Aerosol Science* 65:69–76. http://www.sciencedirect.com/science/article/pii/S0021850213001584.

Juillard, Catherine, Mariam Labinjo, Olive Kobusingye, Adnan A. Hyder. 2010. "Socioeconomic Impact of Road Traffic Injuries in West Africa: Exploratory Data from Nigeria." *Injury Prevention* 16 (6): 389–92.

Khan, Raihan K., and Mark A. Strand. 2018. "Road Dust and Its Effect on Human Health: A Literature Review." *Epidemiology and Health* 40:e2018013. https://doi.org/10.4178/epih.e2018013.

Khreis, Haneen, Charlotte Kelly, James Tate, Roger Parslow, Karen Lucas, and Mark Nieuwenhuijsen. 2017. "Exposure to Traffic-Related Air Pollution and Risk of Development of Childhood Asthma: A Systematic Review and Meta-analysis." *Environment International* 100:1–31.

Konlan, Kennedy Diema, Abdul Razak Doat, Iddrisu Mohammed, Roberta M. Amoah, Joel A. Saah, Kennedy Dodam Konlan, and Juliana Asibi Abdulai. 2020. "Prevalence and Pattern of Road Traffic Accidents among Commercial Motorcyclists in the Central Tongu District, Ghana." *Scientific World Journal* 2020:9493718. https://doi.org/10.1155/2020/9493718.

Lindgren, Anna, Emilie Stroh, Peter Montnémery, Ulf Nihlén, Kristina Jakobsson, and Anna Axmon. 2009. "Traffic-Related Air Pollution Associated with Prevalence of Asthma and COPD/Chronic Bronchitis: A Cross-Sectional Study in Southern Sweden." *International Journal of Health Geographics* 8:2. https://doi.org/10.1186/1476-072X-8-2.

Mackett, Roger L., and Roselle Thoreau. 2015. "Transport, Social Exclusion and Health." *Journal of Transport and Health* 2 (4): 610–17. http://www.sciencedirect.com/science/article/pii/S2214140515006775.

Madriaza, Pablo, and Margaret Shaw, eds. 2016. *Crime Prevention and Community Safety: Cities and the New Urban Agenda.* 5th International Report. Montreal: International Centre for the Prevention of Crime. https://cipc-icpc.org/wp-content/uploads/2019/08/CIPC_5th_IR5_Final.pdf.

Marija, Jodingam, Owusu Amponsah, Henry Mensah, Stephen Appia Takyi, and Imoro Braimah. 2022. "A View of Commercial Motorcycle Transportation in Sub-Saharan African Cities through the Sustainable Development Lens." *Transportation in Developing Economies* 8:13. https://doi.org/10.1007/s40890-022-00149-4.

NASA/Goddard Space Flight Center. 2010. "Road Transportation Emerges as Key Driver of Warming in New Analysis from NASA." *ScienceDaily*, February 26. https://www.sciencedaily.com/releases/2010/02/100224214653.htm.

NBS (National Bureau of Statistics). 2020. *National Bureau of Statistics Report* 1 (2).

Ndiwiga, S. M., C. Mbakaya, and C. Kiiyukia. 2019. "Factors Associated with Road Traffic Accidents Involving Motorcyclists in Mwea Town, Kirinyaga County, Kenya." *African Journal of Health Sciences* 32 (1): 74–81.

Nhung, Nguyen Thi Trang, Heresh Amini, Christian Schindler, Meltem Kutlar Joss, Tran Minh Dien, Nicole Probst-Hensch, Laura Perez, Nino Künzli. 2017. "Short-Term Association between Ambient Air Pollution and Pneumonia in Children: A Systematic Review and Meta-analysis of Time-Series and Case-Crossover Studies." *Environmental Pollution* 230:1000–1008. http://www.sciencedirect.com/science/article/pii/S0269749117323412.

Oguntunde, Olugbenga, Jabulani Nyenwa, Farouk Musa Yusuf, Dauda Sulaiman Dauda, Abdulsamad Salihu, and Irit Sinai. 2019. "Factors Associated with Knowledge of Obstetric Danger Signs and Perceptions of the Need for Obstetric Care among Married Men in Northern Nigeria: A Cross-Sectional Survey." *BMC Pregnancy and Childbirth* 19 (1): art. 123. https://doi.org/10.1186/s12884-019-2271-1.

Olasunkanmi, O. 2019. "Transport Commissioner Says 1.6M Vehicles Ply Lagos Roads Daily." Lagos State Government Official Website, August 29. https://lagosstate.gov.ng/transport-commissioner-says-over-1-6m-vehicles-ply-lagos-roads-daily/.

Oreva, O. 2016. "The State of Ridesharing in Africa." *Techcabal*, November 16. https://techcabal.com/2016/11/16/the-state-of-ridesharing-in-africa/.

Ospina-Mateus, Holman, Leonardo A. Quintana Jiménez, Francisco J. Lopez-Valdes, and Katherinne Salas-Navarro. 2019. "Bibliometric Analysis in Motorcycle Accident Research: A Global Overview." *Scientometrics* 121 (2): 793–815. https://doi.org/10.1007/s11192-019-03234-5.

Otunola, Biodun, Sebastian Kriticos, and Oliver Harman. 2019. "The BRT and the Danfo: A Case Study of Lagos' Transport Reforms from 1999–2019." IGC Cities that Work Case Study. International Growth Centre, London.

Patz, Jonathan A., Howard Frumkin, Tracey Holloway, Daniel J. Vimont, and Andrew

Haines. 2014. "Climate Change: Challenges and Opportunities for Global Health." *Journal of the American Medical Association* 312 (15): 1565. https://doi.org/10.1001/jama.2014.13186.

Peng, Yinan, Namita Vaidya, Ramona Finnie, Jeffrey Reynolds, Cristian Dumitru, Gibril Njie, Randy Elder, et al. 2017. "Universal Motorcycle Helmet Laws to Reduce Injuries: A Community Guide Systematic Review." *American Journal of Preventive Medicine* 52 (6): 820–32.

Rizet, Christophe, and Henri Gwet. 1998. "Freight Transport: An International Comparison of Trucking Prices Africa, South-East Asia, Central America." *Research–Transport–Security* 60:68–88.

Rizet, Christophe, and John Hine. 1993. "A Comparison of Costs and Productivity of Road Freight Transport in Africa and Pakistan." *Transport Reviews* 13 (2): 151–65.

Saito, Masashige, Naoki Kondo, Katsunori Kondo, Toshiyuki Ojima, and Hiroshi Hirai. 2012. "Gender Differences on the Impacts of Social Exclusion on Mortality among Older Japanese: AGES Cohort Study." *Social Science and Medicine* 75 (5): 940–45. http://www.sciencedirect.com/science/article/pii/S0277953612003449.

Schlottmann, F., A. F. Tyson, B. A. Cairns, C. Varela, and A. G. Charles. 2017. "Road Traffic Collisions in Malawi: Trends and Patterns of Mortality on Scene." *Malawi Medical Journal* 29 (4): 301–5.

Shah, Anoop S. V., Jeremy P. Langrish, Harish Nair, David A. McAllister, Amanda L. Hunter, Ken Donaldson, David E. Newby, Nicholas L. Mills. 2013. "Global Association of Air Pollution and Heart Failure: A Systematic Review and Meta-analysis." *Lancet* 382:1039–48. https://doi.org/10.1016/S0140-6736(13)60898-3.

Van Kempen, Elise, Maribel Casas, Göran Pershagen, and Maria Foraster. 2018. "WHO Environmental Noise Guidelines for the European Region: A Systematic Review on Environmental Noise and Cardiovascular and Metabolic Effects: A Summary." *International Journal of Environmental Research and Public Health* 15 (2): 379. https://www.mdpi.com/1660-4601/15/2/379.

Vaz, Eunice, and Christo Venter. 2012. "The Effectiveness of Bus Rapid Transit as Part of a Poverty-Reduction Strategy: Some Early Impacts in Johannesburg." A Paper Presented at the 31st Southern African Transport Conference (SATC 2012), Pretoria, South Africa, July 9–12, 2012.

Vissoci, João Ricardo N., Daniel J. Shogilev, Elizabeth Krebs, Luciano de Andrade, Igor Fiorese Vieira, Nicole Toomey, Adelia Portero Batilana, Michael Haglund, and Catherine A. Staton. 2017. "Road Traffic Injury in Sub-Saharan African Countries: A Systematic Review and Summary of Observational Studies." *Traffic Injury Prevention* 18 (7): 767–73. https://doi.org/10.1080/15389588.2017.1314470.

Vohra, Karn, and Eloise Marais. 2022. "Air Pollution in Fast-Growing African Cities Presents a Risk of Premature Death." *Conversation*, June 14. https://theconversation.com/amp/air-pollution-in-fast-growing-african-cities-present-a-risk-of-premature-death-183944.

WHO (World Health Organization). 2011. *Global Plan for the Decade of Action for Road Safety, 2011–2020*. Geneva: WHO.

WHO (World Health Organization). 2017. *Air Quality Guidelines Global Update 2005:*

Particulate Matter, Ozone, Nitrogen Dioxide and Sulfur-Dioxide. Institutional Repository for Information Sharing. Copenhagen: WHO Regional Office for Europe. https://apps.who.int/iris/handle/10665/107823.

WHO (World Health Organization). 2018. "Physical Inactivity: A Global Public Health Problem." WHO. http://www.who.int/dietphysicalactivity/factsheet_inactivity/en/.

WHO (World Health Organization). 2000. "The World Health Report 2000. Health Systems: Improving Performance." Geneva: WHO. https://www.who.int/publications/i/item/924156198X.

WHO (World Health Organization). 2020. "World Health Statistics 2020: Monitoring Health for the SDGs." Geneva: WHO. https://www.who.int/publications/i/item/9789240005105

WHO (World Health Organization). 2022. "For a Safer, Healthier and Fairer World: Results Reports." Geneva: WHO. https://www.who.int/about/accountability/results/who-results-report-2020-2021

World Bank. 2022. *Urban Mobility in African Cities: Developing National Urban Mobility Policy and Delivering at the City Level: Summary Report*. Washington, DC: World Bank.

World Economic Forum, World Bank, African Development Bank, and OECD (Organisation for Economic Co-operation and Development). 2015. *Africa Competitiveness Report 2015: Transforming Africa's Economies*. Geneva: World Economic Forum.

Wright, L., and W. Hook. 2007. *Bus Rapid Transit Planning Guide*. New York: Institute of Transportation and Development.

Zhao, Pengjun. 2014. "The Impact of the Built Environment on Bicycle Commuting: Evidence from Beijing." *Urban Studies* 51 (5): 1019–37. https://journals.sagepub.com/doi/abs/10.1177/0042098013494423.

10

Road Access and Health Care Inequality in Urban Africa

Mansoureh Abbasi, Aissata Boubacar Moumouni, Marie Christelle Mabeu, and Roland Pongou

1. Introduction

In most countries, urban locations are the epicenter of economic production. They differ from rural settings in part because of the availability of better public infrastructures. Although improved infrastructures (such as transportation) are believed to drive urban economies, our knowledge of their real impact is still limited. Transportation is discussed as a social determinant of health in the previous chapter. Here we focus on a specific example showing transportation as a social pathway to health by discussing the association between road access and perinatal health outcomes.

We know very little about how urban road access affects early life human capital, including prenatal health. Early life human capital has been demonstrated to significantly affect later life outcomes, including health, economic productivity, and wealth accumulation. We also have little knowledge about whether and the extent to which the health benefits of urban road access are distributed across different population subgroups. Unfortunately, this lack of knowledge limits our ability to design effective policies to address access to infrastructures and the consequences for population health. To add to the limited evidence on this topic, this chapter is a review of current research and analysis of available data. We discuss the effect of road access on maternal health care use in urban sub-Saharan Africa. We also examine how the impact of road access on prenatal care might differ based on parental and child socioeconomic and demographic characteristics.

2. Maternal Care and Prevention of Perinatal Morbidity and Mortality

Health care practices routinely performed during pregnancy are associated with better perinatal outcomes (Alexander and Kotelchuck 1996; Carroli, Rooney, and Villar 2001). Maternal infections can increase the risk of pregnancy complications and are a significant cause of perinatal morbidity and mortality, especially in sub-Saharan Africa and South Asia (McClure et al. 2022). They are estimated to cause up to one-half of stillbirths and one in four neonatal deaths (Thwaites, Beeching, and Newton 2015; WHO 2019). For example, tetanus remains one of the leading causes of maternal and neonatal morbidity, especially in low-income countries (Yaya et al. 2019). Once the disease develops, it is almost uncontrollable, especially when appropriate medical care is unavailable (WHO 2019). Mortality rates are the highest in patients not admitted to the hospital, while delayed hospital admission is associated with adverse outcomes in neonatal tetanus (Thwaites, Beeching, and Newton 2015). In developing countries, perinatal mortality due to tetanus infection approaches 100 percent. This rate decreases to 10–60 percent with clinical care and access to intensive care facilities (WHO 2017). Furthermore, tetanus is entirely preventable by immunizing pregnant women with the tetanus vaccine and practicing hygienic delivery and cord care (Fry, Edwards, and Taylor 1998). Maternal immunization reduces neonatal tetanus mortality by an estimated 94 percent (Blencowe et al. 2010).

Antenatal care visits operate as an entry point to offer opportunities to reach pregnant women with information and interventions on many health practices, including tetanus immunization. For example, pregnant women with antenatal care follow-up have increased awareness about the importance of tetanus vaccine uptake. As a result, they are more likely to get vaccinated and immunized against tetanus, resulting in fetal protection against this disease. Not only is the number of prenatal contacts essential, but also the timing of the first visit. The first antenatal visit is crucial to optimize health outcomes for women and children. Early antenatal visits amount to 82 percent in high-income countries, compared to only 24 percent in low-income countries (Moller et al. 2017; Thwaites, Beeching, and Newton 2015).

Despite the known health benefits of prenatal care, one woman in three had fewer than four antenatal visits globally, although the World Health Organization (WHO) recommendation is at least eight prenatal care visits.

This figure is even higher in sub-Saharan Africa, where only one in two African pregnant women attends fewer than four prenatal visits (UNICEF 2022). Moreover, access to prenatal care varies a great deal across regions in Africa, with West and Central Africa recording the lowest level of access compared to the rest of the continent. To study these variations, we use data from the Demographic and Health Surveys (DHS). The DHS program has collected data on demographic outcomes and maternal and child health in most developing and middle-income countries since the mid-1980s. For our analysis, we use data on prenatal care from twenty-eight countries in Africa. Next, we define an index for maternal health care based on three binary components, which are antenatal tetanus injections, prenatal visits, and skilled care deliveries. Each of these components is known to affect maternal outcomes. Access to each component earns a respondent one point, and the index is obtained by summing the scores obtained on the three components. It follows that the index takes values between 0 and 3. Value 0 for the index means that a child was born to a mother who did not use any of the three maternal health care services during pregnancy or child delivery, and a value of 3 means that a child was born to a mother who received all three services.

There are significant temporal and spatial variations in the use of maternal health care services within the continent. During the last three decades, the use of maternal health services has significantly increased. Yet the increasing use witnessed between 1990 and 2010 has since wavered. This is true particularly for tetanus vaccine and prenatal visits. The increase in the probability of having professional delivery has been sustained. The cross-country distribution of the maternal health care index is mapped in figure 10.1. The dark brown countries, such as Burkina Faso, Cameroon, and South Africa, have the highest level of maternal health care use (ranging between 2.71 and 2.90), whereas countries such as Chad and Tanzania have the lowest level of maternal health care use (ranging between 0.01 and 2.30).

3. Road Access and Maternal Health Care in Urban Africa

Road infrastructures are a key factor likely to improve access to health services (Kanuganti et al. 2015). Roads allow easy access to health services by reducing travel time and transportation costs, as well as enabling health care providers (including ambulances) to reach populations living in remote areas. In addition, roads can enhance income, which could benefit health. Indeed, by reducing travel time and providing quick access to mar-

Social Determinants of Health

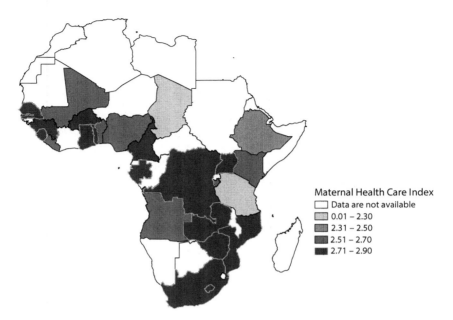

Fig. 10.1. Maternal health care use in Africa. Main findings: Maternal health care use appears to be higher in Burkina Faso, Cameroon, and South Africa. See p. 185 for our methodology.

kets, roads allow individuals living in remote areas to sell their products and participate in the labor market at competitive prices and wages (Abbasi, et al. 2022). Roads also create new employment opportunities by facilitating the creation and expansion of businesses. The combined effects of income generation and access to health services make roads an important contributor to population health.

Lack of road access is among the most important constraints in accessing a health facility in Africa. Overall, the road networks in African countries have steadily expanded from 239,018 km in 1971 to 334,391 km in 2012. We draw spatial data on road networks using Berg, Blankespoor, and Selod (2018); Jedwab and Storeygard (2021); and Nelson and Deichmann (2004). From 1971 to 2012, main roads evolved from dirt roads to paved roads, improved roads, and highways. We consider the last three types to constitute "main roads" today. We measure an individual's accessibility to the road network by calculating the distance between the centroid of that individual's cluster (i.e., participating household groupings) and the main road. The av-

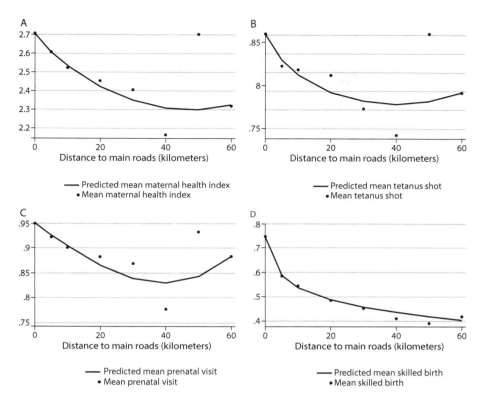

Fig. 10.2. Road access and maternal health care use. Main findings: The figure highlights the positive association between maternal health care use and proximity to main roads.

erage distance to the main road is 11.84 km. In urban areas, the average distance to a main road is 5 km, compared to 14.5 km in rural areas.

How maternal health care use is linked to proximity to main roads is shown in figure 10.2. In this figure, we draw the average value of the maternal health care index as well as its component variables against the distance to the main road, where distance is measured in bins of 10 km. We then fit the prediction of each variable. As the figure shows, when access to the main road decreases, people mainly rely on traditional maternal health care and child delivery methods. For example, people who live within 10 km of the main road have a 90 percent probability of having a prenatal visit during their pregnancy. This probability declines to 5 percent for people living within

40 km of the main road. Overall, the larger the distance to the main road, the lower the use of maternal health care services, the lower the probability of receiving the tetanus vaccine during pregnancy, the lower the probability of having antenatal health care, and the lower the probability of professional child delivery.

3.1. Effects of Road Access on Maternal Health Care Use

Studies suggest a strong association between living in an urban setting and perinatal morbidity and mortality. Road infrastructures may be one of the driving forces behind these effects. Urban mothers are more likely than rural mothers to access health care facilities because of road infrastructures (Gage and Calixte 2006). Road connectivity could effectively promote prenatal care by easing mobility. These networks allow easy access to health services by enabling populations to quickly access health care services and get the lifesaving help they may need. They also enable health care providers or ambulances to reach populations living in remote areas. We sought to empirically assess the effect of road access on the utilization of maternal health care services. To do so, we implement an ordinary least square (OLS) regression approach to examine the association between road access and the composite index of maternal health care use as well as its three component variables.

We find a significant positive relationship between road access and maternal health care use in urban Africa (figure 10.2). Our estimate indicates that getting one kilometer closer to the main road significantly increases the health care use index by 0.0180 points. This highlights the need for policymakers to foster road access. This effect is robust to controlling the socioeconomic characteristics of the mother and the child as well as geographic variables, including occupation, household wealth, child sex, proximity to the capital city, and proximity.

Furthermore, road access is positively associated with the probability of receiving a tetanus injection prior to pregnancy. Living one kilometer closer to the main road increases the possibility of receiving at least one dose of the tetanus vaccine by 0.29 percentage points. Similarly, road access fosters antenatal care visits. Being one kilometer closer to the main road increases the probability of having at least one antenatal care visit by 0.31 percentage points. Finally, road access increases the chance that child delivery will be performed by a health professional. Living one kilometer closer to the main road increases the probability of professional child delivery by 1.3 percentage points. Interestingly, these estimates show that the positive effects of road access vary significantly across health outcomes, with the effect being over four times larger on professional child delivery than on tetanus vaccine and antenatal visit. As people live closer to main roads, they shift from traditional methods of child delivery to adopt more professional methods.

3.2. Unequal Effects of Road Access on Maternal Health Care Use

While road access reduces travel time and costs, this effect might not be uniformly distributed across individuals and population subgroups in Africa's urban areas. The ability to extract the economic benefits of access to infrastructures depends on individual and contextual characteristics (Abbasi et al. 2022). As these economic benefits are likely to affect health outcomes, we expect roads to heterogeneously affect the use of maternal health care services. Also, if individual characteristics affect health care use, investments in infrastructure will likely have differential effects, depending on the characteristics of different individuals. Our results suggest that this is the case, as road access increases health care access unequally across different individuals in urban Africa. We show the heterogeneous effects of road access by mother's age, educational attainment, employment status, household wealth, and child's gender in figure 10.3.

It is generally argued that advanced maternal age is associated with adverse pregnancy outcomes. Therefore, road access could foster older women's maternal health care use (Frick 2021; Khalil et al. 2013). Testing this hypothesis, we find that the effect of access to the main road on health care use is significant for all children, but the effect is larger for children born to older mothers. Living one kilometer closer to the main roads increases health care use by 0.0185 points for mothers above 25 years old compared to 0.0135 points for mothers younger than 25 years. These results suggest older mothers are more likely to use transportation infrastructures to access health care services.

We also find that road access has larger effects on children born to more educated mothers. Indeed, being one kilometer closer to the main road increases the health care use index among children born to mothers with a higher education around three times more than among children born to mothers with only a primary education. This finding is in line with previous

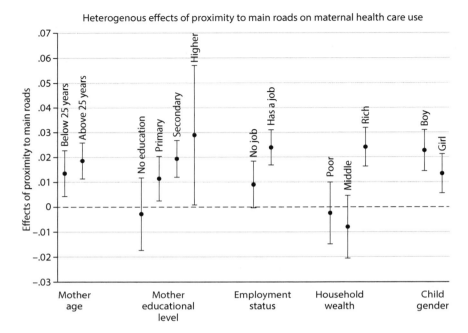

Fig. 10.3. Heterogenous effects of proximity to main roads on maternal care use. Main findings: The figure shows that road access has a more significant effect on the use of maternal health care services when a mother is older than 25 years old, highly educated, employed, wealthy, and pregnant with a male child.

studies suggesting that a mother's education positively affects the use of health care services (Amwonya, Kigosa, and Kizza 2022; Barman, Saha, and Chouhan 2020; Elo 1992); educated women are more likely than uneducated women to take advantage of medical care and comply with recommended treatments because education changes the mother's knowledge and perception of the importance of modern medical technologies in the care of children. Educated women are therefore more likely to take advantage of road availability to gain access to health services. Also, because educated women tend to be richer than their less educated counterparts, they are more able to afford the cost associated with the use of roads, which may explain the greater impact that road access has on their children.

As with education, the effect of road access on health care use varies by employment status. Women's employment is closely related to antenatal visits and skilled birth attendance (Yadav, Sahni, and Jena 2020). Employed women have higher economic status and are empowered. They can spend part of their income on health care, and they have a higher level of health care use compared to unemployed women (Adu et al. 2018; Gautam and Jeong 2019). They are also more able to afford the cost of road access. This implies that road access is more likely to benefit the children of employed mothers. To study how the effect of road access on maternal health care use depends on the mother's employment status, we split the sample based on whether a mother had a job during the twelve months preceding the survey. The results show a positive and highly significant effect for children born to both employed and unemployed women. The effect is more substantial, however, for children born to employed mothers. Living one kilometer closer to the road network increases the health care use index by 0.024 points for children born to employed women and by 0.01 points for children born to women without any job.

In line with the heterogeneous effect of road access by employment status, we find that road access has a greater effect on children born to wealthier mothers. After splitting our sample into children born to poor, middle-income, and rich households based on the wealth quintile variable available in DHS surveys, we observed that living one kilometer closer to the main road increases health care use by 0.024 points for children born in rich households compared to a nonsignificant effect for children born in middle-income and a zero effect for children born in poor households. Wealthier households have a greater ability to purchase both transportation and health services. This implies that the effect of road access is likely to be greater for these households.

Finally, we show how road access affects male and female children differently. Child sex affects a range of health outcomes, with male children being generally more fragile and more likely to die prematurely than female children (Pongou 2013). It has also been shown that shocks occurring during pregnancy affect male and female fetuses differently (Kuate, Pongou, and Rivers 2021). We know little, however, about whether pregnant mothers respond differently to improvements in infrastructure depending on the sex of the fetus. Suppose male fetuses and children require a greater amount of care and resources to survive, as the literature tends to suggest. In that case, road access may have a greater effect on the use of maternal health care services when a mother is pregnant with a male child. To assess this hypothesis, we estimate the effect of road access on maternal health care utilization separately for males and females. Living one kilometer closer to the main road increases the use of prenatal health services by 0.0218 points for males compared to 0.0151 points for females. This shows that the health benefits of roads accrue more to males than females. This finding is consistent with other studies showing that improvement in political institutions reduces infant mortality more for males than females (Mabeu and Pongou 2020; Pongou, Defo, and Dimbuene 2017).

4. Conclusion

Access to health care services for pregnant women is an important challenge for developing countries. Road networks and transportation systems play a crucial role in a mother's access to health services during pregnancy and child delivery. We have combined child-level data on the use of maternal health care services during pregnancy and delivery with data on road networks and health care facilities from twenty-eight sub-Saharan African countries to show that road access is positively associated with prenatal health care utilization in urban areas. Interestingly, the magnitude of the effect of road access varies across health services. The positive association is stronger for professional child delivery than for antenatal visits and tetanus vaccination during pregnancy. We also find that the health benefits of roads are unequally distributed across individuals and population subgroups. The effect is more pronounced for children born to mothers who are older than 25 years old, educated, employed, and wealthier. The impact is also larger for male than for female children. Overall, the findings then suggest that roads do not benefit all mothers and children equally. Though useful, they exacerbate existing socioeconomic inequalities. Poor parents may lack the necessary financial power to purchase both transportation and health services, which implies that living closer to the main transportation networks is not highly useful for them or their children.

REFERENCES

Abassi, Mansoureh, Mathilde Sylvie Maria Lebrand, Arcady Bluette Mongoue, Roland Pongou, and Fan Zhang. 2022. "Roads, Electricity, and Jobs: Evidence of Infrastructure Complementarity in Sub-Saharan Africa." Policy Research Working Paper 9976. Washington, DC: World Bank.

Adu, Joseph, Eric Tenkorang, Emmanuel Banchani, Jill Allison, and Shree Mulay. 2018. "The Effects of Individual and Community-Level Factors on Maternal Health Outcomes in Ghana." *PLoS ONE* 13 (11): e0207942.

Alexander, Greg R., and Milton Kotelchuck. 1996. "Quantifying the Adequacy of Prenatal Care: A Comparison of Indices." *Public Health Reports* 111 (5): 408–18.

Amwonya, David, Nathan Kigosa, and James Kizza. 2022. "Female Education and Maternal Health Care Utilization: Evidence from Uganda." *Reproductive Health* 19 (1): 1–18.

Barman, Bikash, Jay Saha, and Pradip Chouhan. 2020. "Impact of Education on the Utilization of Maternal Health Care Services: An Investigation from National Family Health Survey (2015–16) in India." *Children and Youth Services Review* 108:104642.

Berg, Claudia N., Brian Blankespoor, and Harris Selod. 2018. "Roads and Rural Development in Sub-Saharan Africa." *Journal of Development Studies* 54 (5): 856–74.

Blencowe, Hannah, Joy Lawn, Jos Vandelaer, Martha Roper, and Simon Cousens. 2010. "Tetanus Toxoid Immunization to Reduce Mortality from Neonatal Tetanus." *International Journal of Epidemiology* 39 (supp. 1): 102–9.

Carroli, Guillermo, Cleone Rooney, and José Villar. 2001. "How Effective Is Antenatal Care in Preventing Maternal Mortality and Serious Morbidity? An Overview of the Evidence." *Paediatric Perinatal Epidemiology* 15 (supp. 1): 1–42.

Elo, Irma T. 1992. "Utilization of Maternal Health-Care Services in Peru: The Role of Women's Education." *Health Transition Review* 2:49–69.

Frick, Alexander P. 2021. "Advanced Maternal Age and Adverse Pregnancy Outcomes." *Best Practice and Research Clinical Obstetrics and Gynaecology* 70:92–199.

Fry, Margaret, Gail Edwards, and Annette Taylor. 1998. "Tetanus—the Silent Killer: How Safe Are You?" *Australian Critical Care* 11:82–85.

Gage, Anastasia J., and Marie Guirlène Calixte. 2006. "Effects of the Physical Accessibility of Maternal Health Services on Their Use in Rural Haiti." *Population Studies* 60:271.

Gautam, Sujan, and Hyoung-Sun Jeong. 2019. "The Role of Women's Autonomy and Experience of Intimate Partner Violence as a Predictor of Maternal Healthcare Service Utilization in Nepal." *International Journal of Environmental Research and Public Health* 16 (5): 895.

Jedwab, Rémi, and Adam Storeygard. 2021. "The Average and Heterogeneous Effects of Transportation Investments: Evidence from Sub-Saharan Africa 1960–2010." *Journal of the European Economic Association* 20 (1): 1–38.

Kanuganti, Shalini, Ashoke Kumar Sarkar, Ajit Pratap Singh, and Shriniwas S. Arkatkar. 2015. "Quantification of Accessibility to Health Facilities in Rural Areas." *Case Studies on Transport Policy* 3 (3): 311–20.

Khalil, A., A. Syngelaki, N. Maiz, Y. Zinevich, and K. H. Nicolaides. 2013. "Maternal Age and Adverse Pregnancy Outcome: A Cohort Study." *Ultrasound in Obstetrics and Gynecology* 46 (6): 634–43.

Kuate, Landry, Roland Pongou, and Nicholas Rivers. 2021. "Timing Matters: Prenatal Climate Shocks, Sex Ratio, and Human Capital." Working paper, University of Ottawa.

Mabeu, Marie Christelle, and Roland Pongou. 2020. "Democracy, Genes, and the Male Survival Disadvantage." Working paper. http://dx.doi.org/10.2139/ssrn.4392234.

McClure, Elizabeth M., Robert M. Silver, Jean Kim, Imran Ahmed, Mangala Kallapur, Najia Ghanchi, Mahantesh B. Nagmoti, et al. 2022. "Maternal Infection and Stillbirth: A Review." *Journal of Maternal-Fetal and Neonatal Medicine* 35:4442–50.

Moller, Ann-Beth, Max Petzold, Doris Chou, and Lale Say. 2017. "Early Antenatal Care Visit: A Systematic Analysis of Regional and Global Levels and Trends of Coverage from 1990 to 2013." *Lancet* 5 (10): e977–e983.

Nelson, Andy, and Uwe Deichmann. 2004. "African Population Database Documentation." CIESIN Columbia University, UNEP, September. rhttp://na.unep.net/siouxfalls/global pop/africa/Africa_index.html.

Pongou, Roland. 2013. "Why Is Infant Mortality Higher in Boys than in Girls? A New Hypothesis Based on Preconception Environment and Evidence from a Large Sample of Twins." *Demography* 50 (2): 421–44.

Pongou, Roland, Barthelemy Kuate Defo, and Zacharie Tsala Dimbuene. 2017. "Excess Male Infant Mortality: The Gene-Institution Interactions." *American Economic Review* 107 (5): 541–45.

Thwaites, C. Louise, Nicholas J. Beeching, and Charles R. Newton. 2015. "Maternal and Neonatal Tetanus." *Lancet* 385 (9965): 362–70.

WHO (World Health Organization). 2017. *Tetanus Vaccines: WHO Position Paper.* Geneva: WHO.

WHO (World Health Organization). 2019. *Protecting All Against Tetanus.* Geneva: WHO.

Yadav, Arvind Kumar, Bhavna Sahni, and Pabitra Kumar Jena. 2020. "Education, Employment, Economic Status and Empowerment: Implications for Maternal Health Care Services Utilization in India." *Journal of Public Affairs* 21 (3): e2259.

Yaya, Sanni, Komlan Kota, Amos Buh, and Ghose Bishwajit. 2019. "Antenatal Visits Are Positively Associated with Uptake of Tetanus Toxoid and Intermittent Preventive Treatment in Pregnancy in Ivory Coast." *BMC Public Health* 19 (1): 1–12.

11

Conflict in Urban Areas in Africa and Implications for Urban Health

Eme T. Owoaje and Edward Asemadahun

1. Introduction

As in other parts of the world, the rapid rate of urbanization in Africa has been partly attributed to people migrating from rural to urban areas searching for better social and economic conditions (Albert and Lawanson 2019). Additionally, recurrent violent ethnic and religious conflict in the rural areas of some African countries has resulted in people fleeing to more secure urban areas. For example, the rapid population increases in cities such as Freetown, Maputo, Luanda, and Kinshasa in recent decades have been a result of conflicts (Hove, Ngwerume, and Muchemwa 2013; UNHCR and World Bank Group 2016). This massive influx of people from various ethnic, religious, cultural, social, and political orientations to the cities has increased the level of heterogeneity, which in turn has contributed to intracity conflict.

The huge population growth, however, has not been accompanied by commensurate social and economic developments. Consequently, African cities are experiencing the adverse effects of burgeoning populations, such as overcrowding, increasing poverty, and lack of access to housing, transport, essential services, and employment opportunities (Nwanna 2019; Hove, Ngwerume, and Muchemwa 2013; Abuya 2019). Therefore, millions of people in urban areas are living in informal settlements and urban sprawls, where there is limited social cohesion and increasing tension that may enhance conflict and violence. The tensions are further heightened by existing poor governance and weak administrative institutions, which promote corruption, high costs of doing business, social and geographic inequalities, and exclusion (Abuya 2019; Cockayne, Bosetti, and Hussain 2017).

Despite the significant adverse consequences of conflict on urban population health, most of the previous literature on urbanization has focused on the sociological and economic impacts. There is limited literature on the public health impacts of conflict and urbanization on residents in African cities. This chapter reviews the definition of conflict, outlines the different types, and discusses the interaction between urbanization and conflict in Africa and vice versa, as well as the impacts on the health of populations. We discuss the different types of conflicts at all levels in urban Africa, the precipitating factors, and the effects on health.

2. Definitions and Types of Conflict

Conflict is a struggle or a contest between individuals and groups with opposing needs, ideas, beliefs, values, or goals. It is endemic in human societies and usually not problematic. Unresolved conflict, however, often degenerates into violence, which is the use of physical force against another person, group, or community, resulting in coercion, injury, damage, and death (Elfversson and Höglund 2019). Despite these distinctions, the two terms, conflict and unresolved conflict, are often used interchangeably by most scholars. Factors that have been identified as contributory to conflict in urban areas include poverty, insecurity, socioeconomic inequalities, and poor governance (Abuya 2019).

2.1. Types of Conflict

Beall, Goodfellow, and Rodgers (2013) proposed an analytical framework for understanding the implications of violent conflicts in African urban areas, which consists of three broad categories of *sovereign*, *civil*, and *civic* conflict. We adopt these terms for the remainder of this chapter.

Sovereign conflict occurs in situations when international actors directly intervene in warfare or conflict between two or more countries. The war between Ethiopia and Eritrea in the late 1990s is a classic example of this form of conflict between two African countries. An example of an international intervention into existing wars in other countries is that of the United States in the Somalian war in 1993. During these conflicts, the opposing forces targeted cities because of their importance as centers of governance and wealth. Furthermore, during the postconflict period, the capital cities play critical roles because they serve as points of international engagement in reconstruction activities (Beall, Goodfellow, and Rodgers 2013). Overall, this form of urban conflict in Africa has declined since the 1990s.

Civil conflict refers to a violent confrontation between two or more armed groups within the same country, led by political, religious, or military actors within the nation for territorial control, political purposes, and public power (Büscher 2018). In these situations, rebels, local warlords, organized criminal groups, and private militias control part of the national territory (Beall, Goodfellow, and Rodgers 2013). Civil conflict in these cities may also result in insurgency and constant combat. Civil disputes can also result in rapid urbanization, as was the case in the northern Ugandan town of Gulu, which was a haven for people during the civil war in Uganda perpetrated by the Lord's Resistance Army (LRA) rebels and the Ugandan military. After the civil war, many displaced persons moved to Gulu and established slum communities. There was resultant unemployment, increasing desperation and frustration, rising social inequalities, and high crime rates (Branch, 2013).

In West Africa, the civil conflict between Charles Taylor's National Patriotic Front of Liberia (NPFL) and Samuel Doe's Armed Forces of Liberia (AFL) resulted in a civil war that lasted for fourteen years, between 1989 and 2003. During this period, there was widespread killing, abductions, torture, rape, and other human rights violations, which resulted in mass movement of people within Liberia and to neighboring countries, including Côte d'Ivoire, Sierra Leone, and Ghana. Hundreds of thousands of people were displaced from the rural areas to Liberia's capital city, Monrovia. Consequently, almost one-third of the country's population ended up migrating to Monrovia. This influx of displaced persons overburdened the limited urban infrastructure and destabilized the predominantly agrarian livelihood of the Liberians (Shilue and Fagen 2014). Similarly, Sierra Leone experienced a civil war between 1991 and 2002, led by the Revolutionary United Front (RUF) backed by Charles Taylor, which attempted to topple the government in Freetown. The war resulted in the loss of tens of thousands of lives and the displacement of over two million people from rural to urban areas without accompanying urban development. About 400,000 people fled from Sierra Leone to Guinea and Liberia as refugees (Amowitz et al. 2002). More recently, the emergence of the Islamic Boko Haram sect in northeast Nigeria has resulted in the movement of people from urban and rural areas in northern Nigeria to many cities in the southern part of the country and in surrounding countries in the Lake Chad region (UNHCR and World Bank Group 2016).

Civic conflict is the expression of the populace's social, political, or economic grievances against the state by nonviolent or violent protests, often against the inadequacy of physical and social infrastructure, such as adequate housing, employment, and social services. Protests are usually reactive processes with the intention to reconfigure power relations and not necessarily take control of governance structures. The prevailing conditions of high population density, diversity, and inequalities in most African cities provide ready platforms for significant mobilization of people for antigovernment opposition. This form of conflict may include spontaneous protests, organized violent crime, terrorism, or religious and secular uprisings (Beall, Goodfellow, and Rodgers 2013). Since the late 1990s, various forms and patterns of urban civic conflict related to the political environment have occurred in different parts of Africa. These include militia activities in Benghazi, Libya; riots and protests in Cairo, Egypt; and rebel/militia activities in Kismayo, Somalia, and Bangui, Central African Republic. There have also been episodes of election-related violence in urban areas of Kenya, Zimbabwe, Côte d'Ivoire, and Nigeria (Raleigh 2015).

2.2. Examples of Conflicts in African Cities

Land disputes that result in land evictions have been another cause of civic conflict common in many African urban areas as a result of the shortage of affordable housing. Millions of poor people reside and conduct their businesses in slum communities, which are often deemed illegal informal settlements. The buildings in these areas do not comply with municipal physical planning regulations and regulatory controls and are considered by municipal governments to be environmental hazards (Commins 2018). With the limited availability of land in urban areas and the growing demand for housing for people in higher socioeconomic groups, these informal settlements are frequently targeted for demolition by government officials and real estate developers without any prior notice to the residents (Nwanna 2019). In some countries, governments and developers have forcefully evicted tens of thousands of people from these settlements, thus causing massive ruins, shattered communities, disrupted family ties, and ruptured lives (Nwanna 2019). An example of this occurred in 2016 when the Lagos state government, in Nigeria, conducted a violent demolition of the Otodo Gbame slum. The initial protests of residents were resisted by the authorities, who used teargas and opened fire with live ammunition to dismiss the protesters. Thirty thousand people lost their homes, several people were injured, and thirteen people were killed by the end of the demolition exercise (Ekeanyanwu 2017).

Additionally, the absence of water, sanitation, and hygiene (WASH) services, including solid waste management (SWM) services, by municipal governments has been implicated in increased crime and conflict in some African cities. In the late 1990s and early 2000s, the implementation of structural adjustment programs and the informalization of the economy resulted in diminished service provision by the SWM of the City Council of Nairobi and the emergence of private service providers. These private businesses were predominantly controlled by criminal groups consisting of unemployed young men. Subsequently, there was competition for the clientele and control of the profitable business, with the emergence of armed cartels to protect interests of individual groups. This led to SWM-related extortion and illegal taxation of users of dumpsites, violent acts such as fights between rival gangs, robbery, rape, and murder in Nairobi and Mombasa (Muindi, Mberu, and Sverdlik 2019).

In recent years, xenophobic violence has become an emerging form of urban civic conflict in densely populated urban marginalized centers. These attacks are targeted toward other ethnic groups, mainly African foreigners. For example, in South Africa, migrants from other African countries have experienced conflict incited by citizens (Commins 2018; Misago and Landau 2023). There has been an influx of immigrants into South Africa from other African countries following the relaxation of the country's immigration policy in the 1990s. The migrants, who are mainly from Mozambique, Malawi, the Democratic Republic of Congo, Nigeria, Somalia, and Ethiopia, have settled in major cities such as Johannesburg, Cape Town, and Durban. They have been employed in the service sector and have opened their own informal businesses. Over the years, however, urban South Africa has experienced increasing poverty, high unemployment rates, growing racial tensions, and the perception that other Africans are taking the jobs meant for South Africans. These frustrations have resulted in repeated brutal xenophobic attacks in major cities occurring in 2008, 2015, 2018, and 2019 (Mamabolo 2015; Roth 2020).

Another form of civic conflict occurring in African cities is embodied in demonstrations by youths targeted at challenging government institutions considered incompetent at addressing the needs of urban residents. These have been on the increase in parts of Africa since the Arab Spring in 2010 (Maganga 2020). A recent example was the EndSARS demonstrations, which involved thousands of young people in many cities across Nigeria in October 2020. The main goal of the protests was to increase awareness about the brutality and extrajudiciary acts perpetrated by the State Anti-Robbery Squad (SARS) against civilians, especially Nigerian youths. The protests were abruptly truncated when the Nigerian Army and Nigerian Police Force fired live ammunition at the peaceful EndSARS demonstrators at the Lekki toll gate in Lagos (Ayandele 2021; Iwuoha and Aniche 2021; Uwazuruike 2020).

Electoral violence, defined as any act of violence perpetrated during political activities, including pre-, mid-, and postelection periods, is another type of conflict reported in urban Africa. This may include any of the following acts: use of force to disrupt political meetings or voting at polling stations; the use of dangerous weapons to intimidate voters and others during the electoral process; or causing bodily harm or injury to any person connected with electoral processes (Nwolise 2007). Electoral violence is perpetrated by state and nonstate actors to purposefully influence the outcome of elections (Birch and Muchlinski 2020). The electoral process in many African countries has most often been characterized by violence at various stages, before, during, and after elections. This violence includes physical assaults, arson, snatching of ballot boxes, and murder (Frimpong 2012). In recent years, elections in Kenya, Nigeria, and Zimbabwe have been associated with high levels of conflict. The urban areas are usually the targets of electoral violence because large populations reside in these areas (Birch, Daxecker, and Höglund 2020).

Last, terrorism is another form of conflict reported in urban areas. Boko Haram, which literally means "Western education is forbidden," is a militant Islamic terrorist organization that has been operating since 2002 as a nonstate armed group (NSAG) in Maiduguri, the capital city of Borno state and the largest city in northeastern Nigeria. The group promotes a version of Islam that forbids Muslims from participating in any Western political or social activity, including education. The ideology is based on the belief that politics in northern Nigeria has been hijacked by corrupt and false Muslims. Therefore, the organization seeks to impose sharia law in the northeastern states of the country. Boko Haram commenced insurgency attacks in northeastern Nigeria in 2009, but over the years, the attacks have spread to include other states in the north and other countries in the Lake Chad region: Cameroon and Chad. The terrorists have conducted repeated terror attacks, such as mass shootings, bombings, kidnappings, and assassinations. These have resulted in tens of thousands of deaths, displacement of hundreds of thousands, and tremendous suffering to the people in the northern part of Nigeria, particularly in Borno and Adamawa states (MacEachern 2020).

Similarly, the Islamic terrorist group al-Shabaab emerged in Somalia over twenty years ago with the aim of establishing the Islamic State in Somalia based on sharia law (Klobucista, Masters, and Sergie 2022). Due to the weakness of the central government of the country, the group has controlled Mogadishu, the capital city, and the surrounding rural areas for over three decades. Several violent conflicts caused by al-Shabaab and counter attacks by international forces have resulted in the displacement of hundreds of thousands of people from other parts of the country to cities, which are safer, thus resulting in rapid urbanization in these areas. Mogadishu and Bosaaso are typical examples of cities that have experienced rapid growth as a result of the massive population of internally displaced persons in several nearby camps (Bakonyi, Chonka, and Stuvøy 2019). Apart from the attacks conducted in Somalia, al-Shabaab has carried out hundreds of deadly attacks across East Africa, particularly in Nairobi, Kenya. In 2013, al-Shabaab was responsible for the attack of the Westgate Mall in Nairobi, which killed sixty-seven people and injured several more. The group also attacked a university in Garissa in 2015 and killed 148 people (Klobucista, Masters, and Sergie 2022).

3. Impact of Conflict on Urban Health

The different types of conflict in the African region have had multifaceted direct and indirect social, physical, and mental health impacts on the populations in urban areas. Since the turn of the century, the increased intensity of conflicts has resulted in deaths and injuries, destruction of infrastructure, displacement, disruption in livelihoods, impeded human capital development, as well as political instability and uncertainty in many African countries (Fang et al. 2020; Kaldor and Vincent 2006).

3.1. Social Impact

The social impacts of conflicts vary depending on the type of conflict. Prolonged armed conflict often results in deaths, insecurity, unemployment, and humanitarian crises characterized by unmet food, WASH, and shelter needs. Social connections are disrupted; people experience forced displacement and are insecure. Furthermore, displaced children have limited access to education during conflicts and may experience homelessness or be trafficked for the purposes of forced labor, domestic service, forced begging, or commercial sexual exploitation. In addition, adverse economic impacts disproportionately affect poor households and the unemployed, thus exacerbating preexisting conditions of chronic poverty (Amowitz et al. 2002; Kaldor and Vincent 2006; Shilue and Fagen 2014; UNHCR and World Bank Group 2016).

Episodes of electoral violence, xenophobia, and civil protests are often sporadic and have short-lived consequences, which may include extensive destruction of property, arson attacks, looting, robbery, displacement, and temporary disruption of commercial activities and services in urban areas (Ayandele 2021; Mamabolo 2015; Misago 2017).

3.2. Physical Health Impact

In the past three decades, civil conflicts in Liberia, Sierra Leone, and the countries around the Horn of Africa and Lake Chad have caused millions of people to be displaced into cities from rural areas. Forced displacement results in loss of homes, families, jobs, properties, and social networks, causing destitution (Kaldor and Vincent 2006; Lynch, Nel, and Binns 2020; Shilue and Fagen 2014; UNHCR and World Bank Group 2016). Generally, urban internally displaced persons (IDPs) tend to live in overcrowded informal houses in the poorest neighborhoods, with limited access to potable water and sanitation. These conditions are further worsened by the destruction of infrastructure, resulting in poor environmental sanitation and waste management, often resulting in contamination of food and drinking water. Thus, there is heightened risk of transmission of waterborne infectious diseases and occurrence of epidemics such as cholera and typhoid among the residents of these neighborhoods. Conflict adversely affects the delivery of health services, including disease prevention and control activities such as routine immunization services; thus, outbreaks of meningitis and measles have been reported in conflict-affected areas (Omole, Welye, and Abimbola 2015).

Persistent conflict in African cities has caused social disruption, decreased access to food markets, food scarcity, and higher food prices in the affected areas. These conditions have resulted in reduced dietary diversity, household food insecurity, decreased food intake, and ultimately malnutrition, particularly among women and children. Prolonged starvation, particularly in children, is a major contributor to high mortality, especially when there are coexistent infectious diseases like measles, typhoid, and cholera (Bendavid et al. 2021; Iacoella and Tirivayi 2020). Furthermore, the prevalence of stunting in older children is increased (Gbakiama et al. 2012).

3.3. Nonfatal Physical Injuries, Disabilities, and Mortality

In African cities, incidents of electoral violence, civil protests like the EndSARS movement, and xenophobic attacks have resulted in several injuries and mortalities among residents (Ayandele 2021; Birch and Muchlinski 2020; Mamabolo 2015). The data on the exact numbers of those injured and dead, however, are often not available or are inaccurate for many reasons, including political propaganda and lack of reports by medical officials. In one example, Misago (2017) reports that tens of thousands of people have been harassed and displaced, hundreds injured or killed, and dozens raped during xenophobic attacks in South Africa. During the civil war in Sierra Leone, people experienced amputation of limbs, lips, and ears (Kaldor and Vincent 2006). Hospital data from Niger Republic indicated that limb injuries resulting from firearms and explosives are quite common among male civilians (Sani et al. 2018). Hundreds of thousands of people in African cities are killed during armed conflicts, especially women, children, and the elderly (Amowitz et al. 2002; Kaldor and Vincent 2006; Lynch, Nel, and Binns 2020; UNHCR and World Bank Group 2016). Yet the precise figures are not readily available. Overall, countries experiencing conflict in Africa have recorded a higher mortality among children and women.

3.4. Chronic and Noncommunicable Diseases

Rapid urbanization has been associated with the increased burden of noncommunicable diseases (NCDs) in Africa (Juma et al. 2019). Many refugees and IDPs, prior to departure from their original locations, may have significant preexisting NCDs, including cardiovascular diseases, chronic obstructive airway diseases, diabetes, or mental health disorders. These conditions are exacerbated by the disrupted and weakened health systems in their previous residences and their stressful conflict-related experiences. Moreover, in the course of their journey, some experience trauma, injuries, and

204 Social Determinants of Health

sexual and physical violence. The risk of developing NCDs is also increased by residence in urban areas that expose them to behavioral risk factors such as tobacco and alcohol use, poor diet, and physical inactivity. Despite the burden and risk of NCDs, there is limited access to health care services for refugees in urban areas because of inadequate funds and lack of formal documentation of their immigrant status. This results in lack of continuity of care for refugees and the risk of the complications of their NCDs (Muindi, Mberu, and Sverdlik 2019).

3.5. Sexual and Reproductive Health

Conflict in urban areas in Africa harms the reproductive health of the population directly and indirectly. Gender-based violence is more prevalent in conflict-affected cities because of insecurity, disruption of family and social structures, and economic downturns (Amowitz et al. 2002; Wirtz et al. 2014). Reports from urban areas in Somalia and Nigeria indicate that women and girls are usually disproportionately affected by urban conflict. They experience sexual and gender-based violence, including rape, unwanted pregnancy, abortion, forced marriage, and human trafficking. Because of the absence of male relatives, women and girls confined in urban IDP camps located in cities are more vulnerable to sexual abuse. which may occur when they leave the camp areas to fetch water and collect firewood. The acts are allegedly committed by soldiers and terrorists from groups like Boko Haram (Ajayi 2020; Keita 2021). Women and children also experience sexual assault by family members, civilians, and friends (Amowitz et al. 2002). These abuses result in adverse effects on the physical and mental health of the victims, such as injuries from rape, sexually transmitted infections, and HIV (Wirtz et al. 2018). Furthermore, there is limited access to good quality reproductive health services, including family planning, maternal health care, and emergency obstetric services, due to deteriorated health infrastructure, insecurity, and staff shortages. Consequently, conflict in cities results in increased risk of maternal morbidity and mortality in women of reproductive age (Chi et al. 2015; Tunçalp et al. 2015).

3.6. Mental and Emotional Health

Researchers have reported that exposure to armed conflict in African cities, including Mogadishu in Somalia, Juba in South Sudan, and Maiduguri in Nigeria, has significant adverse mental health consequences for residents and displaced persons in those areas (Ali et al. 2023; Aluh, Okoro, and Zimboh 2020; Roberts et al. 2009). In particular, direct exposure to prolonged armed conflict has been associated with increased risk of anxiety disorders such as post-traumatic stress disorder (PTSD) and depression during and after the conflict. The burden is further heightened among people who have experienced violence, loss of a family member, disruption of family structure, social disintegration, and prolonged confinement in IDP or refugee camps (Roberts et al. 2008; Sheikh et al. 2015). The presence of stressors such as difficulties in accessing food, shelter, education, health care, finance, and employment, as well as discrimination in the host communities, also contributes to the risk of developing mental health disorders (Kemei et al. 2023; Madoro et al. 2020). In terms of gender and age distribution, some authors have reported higher prevalence of PTSD, depression, separation anxiety, and psychological symptoms among young girls and women (Roberts et al. 2008; Sheikh et al. 2015). This has been attributed to their vulnerability and the likelihood of their being victims of warring factions and violence from males.

Substance abuse is also prevalent among urban residents in conflict-affected areas. People who fled their homes because of conflicts are more likely to abuse alcohol and drugs as a coping mechanism to deal with psychosocial impacts and boredom. Young people are particularly vulnerable to this risk due to underemployment and unemployment (UNHCR and World Bank Group 2016).

4. Conclusion

Conflict in urban areas in Africa usually results from multiple socioeconomic, cultural, political, and ethnic factors. Sovereign conflict across the continent is decreasing, but civil and civic conflicts are on the rise in select African cities. The impacts on urban health vary depending on the nature and duration of the conflict; therefore, universal responses and preventive strategies cannot be uniformly applied. Nevertheless, there are overarching strategies involving multiple stakeholders that could be applied, such as sound urban governance targeted at ensuring sustainable development and security.

Even though conflict and urbanization have been increasing in many African cities in the past three decades, along with attendant health problems, research on the extent of the impacts is limited. Most of the literature available is from research conducted among refugees and IDPs in the Middle East and in refugee camps in Europe. To develop specific programs to address conflict in urban areas in sub-Saharan Africa and the consequences, multidisciplinary research addressing these issues must be conducted and the findings disseminated promptly to the relevant audiences through policy briefs, dissemination workshops, and peer-reviewed publications.

Regarding populations affected by humanitarian crises, national governments, nongovernmental organizations, and aid agencies should collaborate to provide essential preventive and curative health care and basic amenities, including food, shelter, and adequate WASH infrastructure, to meet the immediate needs of internally displaced persons. Programmatic interventions and responses for addressing the needs of IDPs should be incorporated into national and local government development plans. Additionally, efforts should be made to facilitate postdisplacement settlement of IDPs and those from refugee camps to stable, secure locations, with low-cost housing in communities that have adequate infrastructure and access to essential health care services. For civic conflicts, there is a need for policy reforms targeted at establishing oversight for law enforcement agencies to control the repressive activities of the state. This would ultimately keep security agents in check and preserve the human rights of people to protest peacefully. Furthermore, the various stakeholders in cities should be engaged in ensuring peaceful resolution of conflicts in communities to prevent large-scale violence resulting from perceived or actual communal grievances.

Intersectoral strategies that address the mental health challenges of residents in conflict-affected cities should be developed. These include the provision of equitable access to quality mental health services and adequate psychosocial support and proper follow-up programs for individuals experiencing mental health problems, as well as targeting the root causes of the conflict, such as social inequalities and poverty. Socioeconomic development initiatives that provide access to educational and employment opportunities for young people would contribute to reducing economic stressors through poverty reduction in these urban populations. Local governments and international partners should develop effective and sustainable interventions for families and communities in partnership with the various stakeholders to support conflict-affected persons.

Accessible reproductive health services that address the population's needs across the lifespan should be provided. These should include the full

Conflict in Urban Areas 207

range of family planning services, safe abortion care, and prenatal, delivery, and postnatal services. Multisectoral interventions involving community members, policymakers, the police, and health workers, including mental health specialists, should be developed to address the prevention, care, and legal aspects of gender-based violence.

REFERENCES

Abuya, J. 2019. "A Crossroads at Rural-Urban Interface: The Dilemma of Tenure Types and Land Use Controls in Housing Provision and Urban Development in Kenya." In *Urban Crisis and Management in Africa: A Festschrift for Akin Mabogunje*, edited by Isaac Olawale Albert and Taibat Lawanson, 215–25. Austin, TX: Pan-African University Press.

Ajayi, Titilope F. 2020. "Women, Internal Displacement and the Boko Haram Conflict: Broadening the Debate." *African Security* 13 (2): 171–94. https://doi.org/10.1080 /19392206.2020.1731110.

Albert, Isaac Olawale, and Taibat Lawanson. 2019. "Africa: The Rapidly Urbanizing Continent." In *Urban Crises and Management in Africa*, edited by Isaac Olawale Albert and Taibat Lawanson, 3–11. Austin, TX: Pan-African University Press.

Ali, M., T. Mutavi, J. M. Mburu, and M. Mathai. 2023. "Prevalence of Posttraumatic Stress Disorder and Depression Among Internally Displaced Persons in Mogadishu-Somalia." *Neuropsychiatric Disease and Treatment* 19:469–78. https://doi.org/10.2147/NDT .S398423.

Aluh, Deborah O., Roland N. Okoro, and Adamu Zimboh. 2020. "The Prevalence of Depression and Post-Traumatic Stress Disorder among Internally Displaced Persons in Maiduguri, Nigeria." *Journal of Public Mental Health* 19 (2): 159–68. https://doi.org/10 .1108/JPMH-07-2019-0071.

Amowitz, Lynn L., Chen Reis, Kristina H. Lyons, Beth Vann, Binta Mansaray, Adyinka M. Akinsulure-Smith, Louise Taylor, and Vincent Iacopino. 2002. "Prevalence of War-Related Sexual Violence and Other Human Rights Abuses among Internally Displaced Persons in Sierra Leone." *JAMA* 287 (4): 513–21.

Ayandele, Olajumoke. 2021. "Lessons from the #EndSARS Movement in Nigeria." Armed Conflict Location and Event Data Project (ACLED), February 9.

Bakonyi, Jutta, Peter Chonka, and Kirsti Stuvøy. 2019. "War and City-Making in Somalia: Property, Power and Disposable Lives." *Political Geography* 73:82–91. https://doi.org /10.1016/j.polgeo.2019.05.009.

Beall, Jo, Tom Goodfellow, and Dennis Rodgers. 2013. "Cities and Conflict in Fragile States in the Developing World." *Urban Studies* 50 (15): 3065–83.

Bendavid, Eran, Ties Boerma, Nadia Akseer, Ana Langer, Espoir Bwenge Malembaka, Emelda A. Okiro, Paul H. Wise, et al. 2021. "The Effects of Armed Conflict on the Health of Women and Children." *Lancet* 397 (10273): P522–32.

Birch, Sarah, Ursula Daxecker, and Kristine Höglund. 2020. "Electoral Violence: An Introduction." *Journal of Peace Research* 57 (1): 3–14. https://doi.org/10.1177/0022 343319889657.

Birch, Sarah, and David Muchlinski. 2020. "The Dataset of Countries at Risk of Electoral

Violence." *Terrorism and Political Violence* 32 (2): 217–36. https://doi.org/10.1080/09546553.2017.1364636.

Branch, Adam. 2013. "Gulu in War . . . and Peace? The Town as Camp in Northern Uganda." *Urban Studies* 50 (15): 3152–67. https://doi.org/10.1177/0042098013487777.

Büscher, Karen. 2018. "African Cities and Violent Conflict: The Urban Dimension of Conflict and Post Conflict Dynamics in Central and Eastern Africa." *Journal of Eastern African Studies* 12 (2): 193–210.

Chi, Primus C., Patience Bulage, Henrik Urdal, and Johanne Sundby. 2015. "Perceptions of the Effects of Armed Conflict on Maternal and Reproductive Health Services and Outcomes in Burundi and Northern Uganda: A Qualitative Study." *BMC International Health and Human Rights* 15 (1): 1–15. https://doi.org/10.1186/S12914-015-0045-Z.

Cockayne, James, Louise Bosetti, and Nazia Hussain. 2017. "Preventing Violent Urban Conflict: A Thematic Paper for the United Nations–World Bank Study on Conflict Prevention." United Nations University Centre for Policy Research, New York.

Commins, Stephen K. 2018. *From Urban Fragility to Urban Stability*. Washington, DC: Africa Center for Strategic Studies.

Ekeanyanwu, Ogechi. 2017. "Nigeria's Relentless Real Estate Developers Destroy Entire Slum." *TRT World*, August 2.

Elfversson, Emma, and Kristine Höglund. 2019. "Violence in the City that Belongs to No One: Urban Distinctiveness and Interconnected Insecurities in Nairobi (Kenya)." *Conflict, Security and Development* 19 (4): 347–70. https://doi.org/10.1080/14678802.2019.1640493.

Fang, Xiangming, Siddharth Kothari, Cameron McLoughlin, and Mustafa Yenice. 2020. "The Economic Consequences of Conflict in Sub-Saharan Africa." IMF Working Paper 2020/221. International Monetary Fund, Washington, DC.

Frimpong, Paul. 2012. "Electoral Violence in Africa: Causes, Implications and Solutions." *Modern Ghana*, December 14.

Gbakiama, A., R. Konteh, N. Kramer, F. Sahr, T. George, and A. Luckay. 2012. "Nutritional Status of Children in Displacement Camps in Sierra Leone." *Sierra Leone Journal of Biomedical Research* 4 (1): 22–31.

Hove, Mediel, Emmaculate T. Ngwerume, and Cyprian Muchemwa. 2013. "The Urban Crisis in Sub-Saharan Africa: A Threat to Human Security and Sustainable Development." *Stability* 2 (1): 7. https://doi.org/10.5334/sta.ap.

Iacoella, F., and N. Tirivayi. 2020. "Child Nutrition during Conflict and Displacement: Evidence from Areas Affected by the Boko Haram Insurgency in Nigeria." *Public Health* 183:132–37. https://doi.org/10.1016/J.PUHE.2020.03.012.

Iwuoha, Victor C., and Ernest Toochi Aniche. 2022. "Protests and Blood on the Streets: Repressive State, Police Brutality and #EndSARS Protest in Nigeria." *Security Journal* 35:1102–24. https://doi.org/10.1057/s41284-021-00316-z.

Juma, Kenneth, Pamela Juma, Constance Shumba, Peter Otieno, and Gershim Asiki. 2019. "Non-Communicable Diseases and Urbanization in African Cities: A Narrative Review." *Public Health in Developing Countries—Challenges and Opportunities* 15:31–50.

Kaldor, Mary, and James Vincent. 2006. *Case Study Sierra Leone: Evaluation of UNDP*

Assistance to Conflict-Affected Countries. New York: United Nations Development Programme.

Keita, Diene. 2021. "Women and Conflict in West Africa and Beyond." OECD Development Matters, April 22. https://oecd-development-matters.org/2021/04/22/women-and -conflict-in-west-africa-and-beyond/.

Kemei, Janet, Bukola Salami, Matiwos Soboka, Hayat I. M. Gommaa, Philomina Okeke-Ihejirika, and Tina Lavin. 2023. "The Forms and Adverse Effects of Insecurities among Internally Displaced Children in Ethiopia." *BMC Public Health* 23 (1): 1–12. https://bmcpublichealth.biomedcentral.com/articles/10.1186/s12889-023-15109-9.

Klobucista, Claire, Jonathan Masters, and Mohammed Aly Sergie. 2022. "Al-Shabaab." Council on Foreign Relations, December 6.

Lynch, Kenneth, Etienne Nel, and Tony Binns. 2020. "'Transforming Freetown': Dilemmas of Planning and Development in a West African City." *Cities* 101:102694. https://doi .org/10.1016/j.cities.2020.102694.

MacEachern, Scott. 2020. "Boko Haram, Bandits and Slave-Raiders: Identities and Violence in a Central African Borderland." *Canadian Journal of African Studies* 54 (2): 247–63. https://doi.org/10.1080/00083968.2019.1700142.

Madoro, D., H. Kerebih, Y. Habtamu, M. G. Tsadik, H. Mokona, A. Molla, T. Wondie, K. Yohannes. 2020. "Post-Traumatic Stress Disorder and Associated Factors among Internally Displaced People in South Ethiopia: A Cross-Sectional Study." *Neuropsychiatric Disease and Treatment* 16:2317–26. https://doi.org/10.2147/NDT.S267307.

Maganga, Tafadzwa. 2020. "Youth Demonstrations and Their Impact on Political Change and Development in Africa." *Conflict Trends* 2020/2, ACCORD, August 20.

Mamabolo, Malemela. 2015. "Drivers of Community Xenophobic Attacks in South Africa: Poverty and Unemployment." *Journal for Transdisciplinary Research in Southern Africa* 11 (4): 143–50. https://doi.org/10.4102/td.v11i4.49.

Misago, Jean Pierre. 2017. "Politics by Other Means? The Political Economy of Xenophobic Violence in Post-Apartheid South Africa." *Black Scholar* 47 (2): 40–53. https://doi.org /10.1080/00064246.2017.1295352.

Misago, Jean Pierre, and Loren B. Landau. 2023. "'Running Them Out of Time': Xenophobia, Violence, and Co-Authoring Spatiotemporal Exclusion in South Africa." *Geopolitics* 28 (4): 1611–31. https://doi.org/10.1080/14650045.2022.2078707.

Muindi, Kanyiva, Blessing Mberu, and Alice Sverdlik. 2019. "Dismantling Barriers to Health and Wellbeing for Nairobi's Refugees." *IIED Briefing*, June.

Nwanna, C. R. 2019. "Right to the City: Lagos, an Emerging Revanchist City in Nigeria?" In *Urban Crisis and Management in Africa: A Festschrift for Akin Mabogunje*, edited by Isaac Olawale Albert and Taibat Lawanson, 279–94. Austin, TX: Pan-African University Press.

Nwolise, Osisioma B. C. 2007. "Electoral Violence and Nigeria's 2007 Elections." *Journal of African Elections* 6 (2): 155–79. https://doi.org/10.20940/jae/2007/v6i2a9.

Omole, Oluwatosin, Hamira Welye, and Seye Abimbola. 2015. "Boko Haram Insurgency: Implications for Public Health." *Lancet* 385 (9972): 941. https://doi.org/10.1016/S0140 -6736(15)60207-0.

Raleigh, Clionadh. 2015. "Urban Violence Patterns across African States." *International Studies Review* 17 (1): 90–106. https://doi.org/10.1111/misr.12206.

Roberts, Bayard, Eliaba Y. Damundu, Olivia Lomoro, and Egbert Sondorp. 2009. "Post-Conflict Mental Health Needs: A Cross-Sectional Survey of Trauma, Depression and Associated Factors in Juba, Southern Sudan." *BMC Psychiatry* 9 (1): 1–10. https://doi.org/10.1186/1471-244X-9-7.

Roberts, Bayard, Kaducu F. Ocaka, John Browne, Thomas Oyok, and Egbert Sondorp. 2008. "Factors Associated with Post-Traumatic Stress Disorder and Depression amongst Internally Displaced Persons in Northern Uganda." *BMC Psychiatry* 8 (1): 1–9. https://doi.org/10.1186/1471-244X-8-38.

Roth, Kenneth. 2020. *World Report 2020: Events of 2019.* New York: Human Rights Watch.

Sani, R., H. Adamou, H. Daddy, M. I. Amodou, M. B. Adoulaye, L. D. James, I. Garba, K. Idé, Y. Hama, and S. Sanoussi. 2018. "Injuries of Boko Haram Insurgency in South-East Niger Republic." *Journal of the West African College of Surgeons* 8 (3): 22.

Sheikh, Taiwo L., Mohammed Abdulaziz, Samuel Agunbiade, Ike Joseph, Bill Ebiti, and Oluwatosin Adekeye. 2015. "Correlates of Depression among Internally Displaced Persons after Post-Election Violence in Kaduna, North Western Nigeria." *Journal of Affective Disorders* 170:46–51. https://doi.org/10.1016/J.JAD.2014.08.050.

Shilue, James S., and Patricia Fagen. 2014. *Liberia: Links between Peacebuilding, Conflict Prevention and Durable Solutions to Displacement.* Washington, DC: Brookings-LSE.

Tunçalp, Özge, Ibrahima S. Fall, Sharon J. Phillips, Inga Williams, Massambou Sacko, Ousmane B. Touré, Lisa J. Thomas, and Lale Say. 2015. "Conflict, Displacement and Sexual and Reproductive Health Services in Mali: Analysis of 2013 Health Resources Availability Mapping System (HeRAMS) Survey." *Conflict and Health* 9 (1): 1–9. https://doi.org/10.1186/S13031-015-0051-8.

UNHCR (United Nations High Commissioner for Refugees) and World Bank Group. 2016. *Forced Displacement by the Boko Haram Conflict in the Lake Chad Region.* Geneva: UNHCR and World Bank.

Uwazuruike, Allwell R. 2020. "#EndSARS: The Movement against Police Brutality in Nigeria." *Harvard Human Rights Journal*, November 12. https://journals.law.harvard.edu/hrj/2020/11/endsars-the-movement-against-police-brutality-in-nigeria/.

Wirtz, Andrea L., Nancy A. Perrin, Amelie Desgroppes, Verena Phipps, Ali A. Abdi, Brendan Ross, Francesco Kaburu, et al. 2018. "Lifetime Prevalence, Correlates and Health Consequences of Gender-Based Violence Victimisation and Perpetration among Men and Women in Somalia." *BMJ Global Health* 3 (4): 773. https://doi.org/10.1136/bmjgh-2018-000773.

Wirtz, Andrea L., Kiemanh Pham, Nancy Glass, Saskia Loochkartt, Teemar Kidane, Decssy Cuspoca, Leonard S. Rubenstein, Sonal Singh, and Alexander Vu. 2014. "Gender-Based Violence in Conflict and Displacement: Qualitative Findings from Displaced Women in Colombia." *Conflict and Health* 8:10. https://doi.org/10.1186/1752-1505-8-10.

III DEMOGRAPHIC IMPACTS AND HEALTH BEHAVIORS

African cities are youthful. This means that young people are shaping cities and being shaped by them. The urban environment can affect the emotional, physical, social, and cognitive development of children and youths, positively or negatively, by providing or limiting access to necessary resources, such as educational and medical services, and strong social networks. The first chapter in this section focuses on the sexual and reproductive health of young people. The authors describe challenges faced by youths and present examples of policy interventions that have focused on improving the health of this population. The second chapter focuses more broadly on the urban environment and healthy behaviors, as well as the threat of chronic disease epidemics in African cities, which have seen an increase in the prevalence of chronic diseases and conditions (such as obesity, diabetes, and hypertension). This has been noted alongside increases in the prevalence of risk factors, such as poor diet and physical inactivity. The authors discuss these challenges and make recommendations for policy actors, implementers, and researchers.

12

Sexual and Reproductive Health of Young People in Urban Africa

Donatien Beguy, Blessing Mberu, and Kevin Nyamai

1. Introduction

The latest estimates from the United Nations (UN) suggest that in 2020, approximately 40 percent of Africans were younger than 15 years, and almost 60 percent of the population were younger than 25 years, the highest proportion of youth anywhere in the world (UNDESA 2022). The high youth proportion in Africa is due to several factors, including persistent high fertility levels, improved life expectancy, and decline in child mortality. United Nations projections suggest that the number of young people aged 10–24 will rise to 537 million (31 percent of Africa's population) by 2030 and almost 710 million (29 percent of Africa's population) by 2050 (UNDESA 2022). In comparison, young people will represent about 15 percent of the total population of high-income countries and 20 percent of the world population by 2050. In high-income countries, this translates into a reduction of the youth population from 208 million in 2030 to about 187 million in 2050. Given the projected urbanization trends, the bulk of these young people in Africa will be living in urban areas. Therefore, their behaviors not only can affect the development and performance of cities but can also be adversely or positively affected by the city environment.

While Africa's rapid urbanization presents extensive opportunities for growth, employment, and innovation, it portends enormous challenges in terms of demands for employment, social amenities and services, and infrastructure in urban areas. As such, the adoption in September 2015 of Sustainable Development Goal (SDG) 11, "Make cities and human settlements inclusive, safe, resilient and sustainable," is critical to Africa, as it emphasizes the catalytic role cities and urban areas will play in achieving sustainable development by 2030. In particular, health challenges have been highlighted as a key problem in urban areas in Africa (Mberu et al. 2014; Zulu, Nii-Amoo Dodoo, and Ezeh 2002). The so-called urban advantage has often been questioned in the context of Africa, where evidence has shown that many urban dwellers living in poor neighborhoods, such as slums or informal settlements, often exhibit worse health outcomes than rural populations (APHRC 2002; Beguy et al. 2017; Brockerhoff and Brennan 1998). As rapid urbanization continues relentlessly in African countries, the health and well-being of young urban Africans will be key in achieving national development goals and other global development agendas, such as the 2030 for Sustainable Development Agenda, the New Urban Agenda, and the Africa Union Commission's Agenda 2063—The Africa We Want (Satterthwaite 2016). As ensuring healthy lives at all ages is essential to sustainable development, it goes without saying that achieving development agendas will depend mainly on how the health-related goals are achieved. How the health of urban young people, including sexual and reproductive health, is addressed will determine the pace at which African countries will achieve their development agendas. In either searching for pathways to reap the demographic dividend or enabling successful transition to healthy and productive adulthood, it is important to find ways to ensure healthy lives during this period of life in cities, especially among the growing number of those living in poor neighborhoods, such as urban slum settlements in African cities.

The main objective of this chapter is to provide insights into the sexual and reproductive health of young people in urban areas in Africa, including the challenges and opportunities that cities can leverage to create optimal conditions for them to thrive and to successfully transition to adulthood. In the remainder of this chapter, we discuss existing evidence on health outcomes among urban young people and relevant policies and actions needed to ensure optimal health outcomes for this important population subgroup across bourgeoning urban(izing) Africa.

2. Sexual and Reproductive Health for Urban Young People

Since the 1994 International Conference on Population and Development (ICPD), many governments and nongovernmental organizations have taken actions and developed programs and policies to address the issue of adolescent sexual and reproductive health in sub-Saharan Africa (Institute of Medicine et al. 2005; WHO 2011). Following the ICPD, the international community fully recognized the need for addressing sexual and reproductive health challenges, especially in countries with high fertility levels, as a precondition for achieving global development goals, including the SDGs. Sexual and reproductive health is explicitly mentioned in Target 3.7 under Goal 3 on health—"By 2030, ensure universal access to sexual and reproductive health-care services, including for family planning, information and education, and the integration of reproductive health into national strategies and programmes"—and in Target 5.6 under Goal 5 on gender equality: "Ensure universal access to sexual and reproductive health and reproductive rights" (UN 2015). In addition, numerous UN reports, the 2013 Lancet Commission on Adolescent Health and Well-Being, the 2016 Guttmacher-Lancet Commission on Sexual and Reproductive Health and Rights, the adoption of the UN's Global Strategy for Women's, Children's, and Adolescent's Health, and other international commitments are concrete examples of the international community's recognition of these issues (Patton et al. 2016; UN 2016; UNFPA 2014).

Although childbearing is a natural part of the transition to adulthood, it can affect people's emotional, physical, and social life if it happens in difficult conditions, which is often the case for many young people in Africa. Sexual and reproductive life is one of the key changes that characterize the transition to adulthood across the world (Beguy et al. 2011; Kabiru et al. 2010). Latest estimates show that sub-Saharan Africa continues to have the highest lifetime average of births per woman (total fertility rate of 4.3 in 2021), which is mainly caused by the highest level of adolescent fertility in the world (Ezeh, Kodzi, and Emina 2010; Singh and Darroch 2000). Although adolescent fertility among 15- to 19-year-old women has declined recently, it remains high at 101 births per 1,000 women in 2021 (UNDESA 2022). Because of women having children at young ages, the childbearing window of African women is long, which is further compounded by their often unmet needs for contraception, resulting in larger family sizes. Recent data show that, on average, about a quarter of young women aged 20 to 24 in Africa have given birth before age 18, with great disparities between countries in the region (UNICEF 2021). In 2021, in Central Africa, 30 percent of 20- to 24-year-old females were in this situation, compared with only 24 percent of their counterparts in eastern Africa.

This situation may be due to early entry into marriage and low levels of contraceptive use. For example, despite recent progress, some countries in

West and Central Africa have the highest rate of child marriage and the highest level of unmet needs for modern contraception among adolescents (Melesse et al. 2020). Specifically, 4 in 10 young women were married before the age of 18 in West and Central Africa, which represents the highest proportion in sub-Saharan Africa and globally. The child marriage rate has declined by ten percentage points, between 1990 and 2015, in the two regions, with countries making varied progress, in comparison to the rest of sub-Saharan Africa. A high prevalence and slow rate in decline of child marriage have impeded the progress of eradicating the practice, which is estimated to take at least one hundred more years at the current rate (UNICEF 2018).

Evidence shows that many births at young ages, especially during adolescence, are unintended—either unwanted or mistimed (Singh, Sedgh, and Hussain 2010), which poses clear public health challenges given that conceiving and carrying a baby at a young age poses huge health risks for the mother and her newborn child. Early motherhood is associated with high risks of morbidity and mortality for mother and child. This is because young mothers who did not want to get pregnant are often not keen on seeking prenatal care, placing them at high risk of pregnancy-related complications. In addition, young mothers are also more likely to undergo clandestine and unsafe abortions—due to restrictive laws, untrained or poorly trained providers, and limited knowledge and access to services—or to contract HIV and other sexually transmitted infections (Bankole et al. 2006; Mensch, Singh, and Casterline 2005; WHO 2011).

In Africa, about a quarter of deaths among girls and young women aged 10 to 24 are due to causes related to maternity, as suggested by Patton and colleagues (2009). Children born to adolescent mothers are more likely to have low weight, be born prematurely, die at birth, or die within the first 28 days of life. Apart from the health consequences, early childbearing adversely affects educational and employment prospects for young mothers, who in turn are more likely to fall into and remain in poverty (Gupta and Mahy 2003). Young women who become pregnant are often forced to drop out of school or have poor performance because of their inability to reconcile school and childcare responsibilities. In the long run, early childbearing and motherhood lead to marital instability, single parenthood, social stigma, and high risk of poverty. Indeed, early age at marriage and early pregnancy and motherhood are not demographic factors consistent with young women's participation in the labor force, especially working outside the home (APHRC 2014).

Compared to their rural counterparts, young people living in urban areas are more likely to engage in risky sexual behaviors, including those that expose them to HIV, with those living in poor neighborhoods, such as slums and informal settlements, having worse sexual and reproductive health and rights outcomes. Those living in urban areas, however, may have better access to modern methods of contraception and may be more prone to delay their entry into marriage and reproductive life.

Causes of pregnancy among young people, especially during teen ages, vary and can relate to sexual violence, marriage at young ages (below age 18), lack of access to sexual and reproductive health services, and lack of access to education (World Vision 2019). More than 20 percent of adolescents in sub-Saharan Africa experience some form of intimate partner violence, with high prevalence in eastern and southern Africa regions (Decker et al. 2015). In South Africa, adolescent girls and young women who experience sexual violence are more likely to report unplanned pregnancy (Ajayi et al. 2019). Young people in particular are highly vulnerable to sexual violence and may have difficulty accessing services set up to curb violence against young women (Gomez 2011).

2.1. Migration

An important dimension of youth sexual and reproductive health challenges in urban Africa relates to the strong linkages between youth geographic mobility, problematic sexual behaviors, and health outcomes. Studies have historically emphasized the social disruptions that migration entails (Mberu and White 2011), together with the relationships between migration and behavioral change. Accordingly, the much higher HIV seroprevalence levels observed in urban compared to rural areas in Africa were historically linked to the large numbers of young and unmarried adult migrants from presumably conservative rural environments to more sexually permissive African cities. Further, according to Keygnaert, Vettenburg, and Temmerman (2014), migrants are less likely to have regular screening for reproductive conditions such as cervical cancer, but more likely to get pregnant, face sexual violence, and have a high unmet need for contraception.

Closely linked to youth migration and sexual and reproductive health

(SRH) outcomes in urban Africa are the high numbers of urban refugees, internally displaced persons and asylum seekers, emanating from intractable conflicts and natural disasters in the region. Reaching these groups of distressed migrants and mobile populations poses particular logistic challenges in terms of administering targeted interventions, "more so in contexts where poor socio-economic situations of countries do not provide them opportunities to become self-reliant and less dependent on humanitarian assistance" (Mutombo et al. 2016). Most of such distressed migrants rarely have health insurance to access necessary health care during their initial or entire period of stay in the new destination. Moreover, their vulnerabilities become more complicated if they are illegal or undocumented migrants, unable to approach public health institutions out of fear that they will be repatriated or prosecuted. The International Organization for Migration estimated that 44 percent of migrants in the southern Africa region are female, and 20 percent are under 19 years old and increasingly susceptible to sexually transmitted infections, including HIV, tuberculosis, and malaria, as well noncommunicable diseases, such as mental and occupational health and safety challenges (IOM 2014, 2019). Available evidence on young migrants, with an emerging focus on male victims as well as women, shows that many are victims of sexual violence while in transit, with a number of young women arriving at their destinations pregnant (Tan and Kuschminder 2022).

An important dimension of urban health challenges attracting increasing focus in recent years is the mental health of young people. Some mental health issues are related to being young mothers, while others are linked to the poor working and living conditions of migrant workers and psychosocial distress or social isolation, including the stressors associated with distressed migration or displacements due to conflicts or natural disasters. The risk for major mental illness (e.g., anxiety or psychotic, mood, or additive disorders) is generally higher in cities compared to rural areas (Gruebner et al. 2017). Mental health problems such as depression are rated among the main causes of disability among young people globally. According to the World Health Organization (WHO), 1 in 7 adolescents (10- to 19-year-olds) experience mental disorder, accounting for nearly a quarter of the global burden of disease, with the majority of cases unrecognized and untreated (WHO 2021). In sub-Saharan Africa, 1 out of every 7 adolescents suffers from considerable mental health disorder, with 10 percent having a specific psychiatric disorder (Cortina et al. 2012).

Failure to address adolescent mental health conditions extends them into adulthood, impairing physical and mental health, and thus reducing the chances of living fulfilling adult lives. The most recent systematic review from sub-Saharan Africa estimated that 4 in 10 young people aged 10–19 (40.8 percent) suffered from emotional and behavioral problems, roughly 30 percent suffered from anxiety disorders or depression (29.8 percent and 26.9 percent), while a fifth suffered from post-traumatic stress disorder (PTSD) or suicidal thoughts (21.5 percent and 20.8 percent). In total, a documented fifty-seven mental health intervention techniques have been applied across sub-Saharan Africa among adolescents. More than 50 percent of the techniques were applied only in Kenya, Uganda, and South Africa, potentially pointing to low coverage and prioritization of mental health interventions across sub-Saharan African countries (Jörns-Presentati et al. 2021; Mabrouk et al. 2022).

3. Young People Living in Urban Slums

Slums are urban spaces characterized by overcrowding; few economic opportunities; poor environmental conditions; insecurity; lack of or poor basic social services; high levels of gender-based violence, including sexual violence; and substance abuse (APHRC 2002, 2014; Fotso et al. 2009). These living conditions are likely to adversely affect the health and well-being of the growing number of residents, including an increasing number of adolescents (Kabiru et al. 2010; UN-Habitat 2010; Zulu, Nii-Amoo Dodoo, and Ezeh 2011). Yet there is a dearth of evidence on the sexual and reproductive health and rights challenges that the growing number of young people face while living in slum environments, although significant progress was made over the past twenty years. Recent research helped shed light on the sexual and reproductive health and rights challenges and needs of young men and women who live in extremely poor urban settings in sub-Saharan Africa. Findings from South Africa and Kenya indicate that young girls living in informal settlements face heightened risks of unplanned motherhood and other socioeconomic challenges, as they are likely to be poorly educated, live in insecurity, lack autonomy because of social norms, and live in abject poverty (Beguy et al. 2013; Ezeh, Kodzi, and Emina 2010; Kabiru et al. 2010; Bolarinwa and Boikhutso 2022; Govender 2012).

In Kenya, evidence in the last two decades has highlighted the sexual and reproductive health and rights challenges faced by young people, especially adolescents, living in slum settlements. For example, research has demonstrated that adolescents living in Nairobi slums are more likely to engage in risky sexual behaviors than their counterparts living in nonslum areas of the city due to deteriorating economic conditions. These risky behaviors include early sexual debut, transactional sex, and multiple sexual partnerships (APHRC 2002, 2014; Zulu, Nii-Amoo Dodoo, and Ezeh 2002).

In Cape Town, South Africa, evidence suggests that the built environment, primarily defined by access to key basic services, is highly linked with sexual risk-taking behavior among youth. Young people living in urban environments characterized by structural poverty of access to basic services were more likely to be involved in risky sexual behavior leading to HIV/AIDS (Burns and Snow 2012). Given the inadequate knowledge about contraception and limited use of modern methods of contraception among young people in slum communities, their early sexual debut is often unprotected, which puts them at high risk of adverse sexual and reproductive health outcomes, including sexually transmitted diseases and unintended pregnancies. In such slum communities, young girls have little control over their reproductive life, including deciding on the timing of sexual debut and when to start childbearing, mainly because of the many challenges they face while growing up—poor livelihood opportunities; high risk of gender-based violence; insufficient basic services, including poor schooling facilities; high levels of substance use; and so forth (Ezeh, Kodzi, and Emina 2010).

It is widely recognized that because of social networking, migration, unemployment, and social and economic inequalities, people living in urban areas are more vulnerable to HIV/AIDS infection. Evidence shows that an increasing proportion of people living with HIV and associated diseases are urban residents. Furthermore, Pongou and Serrano (2009, 2013, 2016) showed that ethnic heterogeneity within urban areas creates cultural boundaries that encourage multiple sexual partners and create an enabling environment for infidelity, which brings mostly urban women into existing sexual networks, accounting for the higher HIV/AIDS infection rates in cities than in rural areas and among women than among men. As such, the fact that the majority of the region's population currently live in cities reinforces the need to put a special emphasis on urban areas in ending AIDS by 2030 (UN 2016).

Furthermore, young people living in slums are exposed to many economic and social stressors that increase their vulnerability to mental health problems. Strong social pressures in slums can affect drug use and teenage sexual behavior at the community level (Ezeh, Kodzi, and Emina 2016). Many studies have documented that the tenuous living conditions of slums negatively affect young people's relationships with their family and peers and likely slow their growth and cognitive abilities, worsening their self-confidence (Bhatia and Bhatia 2011; Goswami 2020). The lack of data on the burden of disease morbidity and mental health status in slums in low- and middle-income countries hampers the efficient allocation of health care initiatives and the provision of appropriate disease prevention services (Gruebner et al. 2017). This is further exacerbated by the multiple complexities embedded in studying slums and the justifiable fact that they need to be contextualized and represented in both social and physical constructs (Mahabir et al. 2016).

4. Conclusion

It is well known that cities offer inherent opportunities to tackle the challenges faced by countries, including health, poverty, inequality, unemployment, environmental degradation, and climate change. But the growth and emergence of cities have not always been beneficial to city residents and countries in general, especially in Africa. In the continent, uncontrolled urbanization has pushed many countries into an underdevelopment quagmire, characterized by poor governance and planning; lack of basic social services, such as water and sanitation; and abject poverty and consequent poor health outcomes. This means that many young people grow up in a hostile environment, where they are often exposed to health hazards, including mental health challenges, and do not have access to the necessary basic services when they fall ill. Because of these conditions, many of these young people will continue exhibiting poor health outcomes at later stages of their lives, highlighting the importance of life course approaches in seeking pathways to address youth sexual and reproductive health challenges in the region.

Further, the slum situation has called into question the so-called urban advantage, further stressing the urgent need to address the unique poor health status, including poor sexual and reproductive health outcomes, of young people, especially those living in slum settlements and shantytowns, who constitute a substantial proportion of urban residents across Africa. Doing so is central to the attainment of development goals, as it is evident that national development indicators will increasingly be driven by the well-being of urban dwellers, especially those living in poor neighborhoods. To improve the well-being of their residents, most notably those living in urban slums, national and city authorities need to develop and implement policies and programs that address comprehensively the structural, economic, behavioral, and service-oriented barriers that endanger the health of their urban residents. For example, in many countries in sub-Saharan Africa, investments in reducing early childbearing and unintended pregnancies among urban adolescents living in slums will not only minimize their adverse health effects but also contribute to slowing urbanization rates through reduction of natural population growth. Evidence shows that in some sub-Saharan African countries, high fertility among urban poor women mainly stems from unintended fertility (Ezeh, Kodzi, and Emina 2010). Beyond transforming the lives of young people, investing in adolescent health and well-being will generate high economic returns for African countries.

On migrants, especially distressed migrants fleeing to urban centers in a region, a corpus of relevant literature has highlighted the need for national and regional policies and program interventions targeting such vulnerable groups. Beyond urban refugees, other groups in urban areas of eastern and southern Africa requiring interventions include slum residents, street children, child-headed households, people with disabilities, IDPs, and cross-border migrants. Research efforts aimed at understanding the composition and characteristics of these groups, their particular health vulnerabilities, and appropriate intervention models, as well as new and innovative approaches geared toward meeting their health needs, should be an important future development investment in the region (Mberu and Pongou 2012; Mutombo et al. 2016). Migrants' access to sexual and reproductive health and rights services will be an important focus, given that their sexual and reproductive health can be at disproportionate risk given the circumstances of the migration process (Mutombo et al. 2016). Further, the health needs of migrants can also be enhanced by promoting decent work and reducing health risks, including addressing poor working and living conditions, addressing exploitation, and ensuring equitable access to health services, together with migrants' right-based policy options across the region.

Some countries in Africa are making efforts to address young people's health challenges, including policies and interventions. For example, regarding sexual violence, Sierra Leone's president declared rape and sexual violence a national emergency in 2019. This was followed by the development and launch in 2020 by the Ministry of Gender and Children's Affairs of the National Male Involvement Strategy for the Prevention of Sexual and Gender-Based Violence in Sierra Leone. By taking these actions, together with other sectorial measures and laws, such as the free access to medical treatment for victims of rape and sexual violence, the Domestic Violence Act, the Registration of Customary Marriage and Divorce Act, and the Gender Equality and Women's Empowerment Act, the country has demonstrated its resolve to address gender-based violence, but it remains to be seen whether such policies and laws will make a lasting impact on the health outcomes of children and adolescents. Recent evidence shows that while the percentage of women aged 25–49 who first got married by age 18 dropped from 58 percent in 2008 to 38 percent in 2019, the gender-based violence prevalence remains high, with the percentage of women aged 15–49 who have experienced physical, sexual, or emotional violence from their husband/ partner during the twelve months preceding the survey increasing from 34 percent in 2008 to 50 percent in 2019 (Stats SL and ICF 2020).

In Malawi, where child marriage was rife with disastrous consequences for young girls and their families, the government adopted in 2017 legislation to make under-18 marriage illegal with harsh fines for violators. A national strategy on Ending Child Marriage (ECM) was also launched in 2018. Given that child marriage is driven by poverty and out-of-wedlock childbearing, the success of such a law will also depend on changing social norms on access to family planning methods, ensuring universal access to youth-friendly sexual and reproductive health services, and providing long-lasting economic empowerment interventions for girls (e.g., keeping girls at school and providing livelihood opportunities).

In Kenya, although the adolescent reproductive health and development policy adopted in 2013 has provided guidance for priority needs and target populations, as well as strengthening approaches to improve sexual and reproductive health and rights outcomes among adolescents, the policy has not been fully implemented because of a nonsupportive multisectoral political, social, and financial environment. In 2022, the government adopted a national reproductive health policy for the period 2022–32, with one of the aims being to improve sexual and reproductive health outcomes among young people. Given the new devolution system, the extent to which the policy will improve sexual and reproductive health outcomes in the country will depend on how the various county governments will adopt and contextualize the policy in their areas of jurisdiction.

Further, recent research and policy initiatives targeting the most marginalized and vulnerable subpopulations in Nairobi slums are beginning to emerge with local data-driven evidence that promises not only the visibility of the once invisible urban subpopulations but supplies abundant hope for the future of adolescent health in the city. The ARISE program (https://www.ariseconsortium.org) is seeking to catalyze change for improving accountability and promoting well-being and health in informal settlements. Building on community-based participatory research approaches, the ARISE identified child-headed households (CHHs) among the three topmost marginalized slum resident groups in Nairobi (the two other groups identified were older persons and persons with disability). The study team highlighted the critical needs of CHHs as health care, hygiene, water, sanitation, solid waste management, help preventing high-risk behavior, accommodation, access to education and skills training, and self-esteem support (Chumo et al. 2023a, 2023b). Further engagement by the city and county government with the data has resulted in a CHH motion passed by the city's legislative assembly, with specific focus on the development of a comprehensive policy that will promote sustainable solutions for CHHs and programs to address the needs of children in CHHs, including skills training on issues of reproductive health, children's rights, drug abuse, home management, and conflict resolution. While such efforts are in their infancy, they point to progress being made and hope for the future, especially the potential of policy and intervention scale-up to other cities in Kenya's devolved county governments and to national government levels, as well as to address other youth-related challenges in the region. They promise a future not far away, when youth-focused policy and programming will be informed by local data and constitute a permanent feature of urban governance in Kenya and the region.

In Nigeria, high fertility is linked to high levels of economic dependency and descent into poverty in poor urban households, following childbirth and childcare expenditures and the opportunity costs of pregnancy and childbirth vis-à-vis young mothers' participation in the labor force (Mberu and Ezeh 2017). To address this challenge, investment in reproductive health and family planning has been identified as policy and program intervention priorities for the country to achieve lower population growth consistent with national development agendas. On the related critical challenge of early marriage, there is vital support for the provisions and full implementation of policies and strategies to end child marriage through the Child's Rights Act across all thirty-six states of the country. The act will provide the legal policy framework for seeking justice for children when their rights are denied or abused (Save the Children 2021), with positive implications for child poverty, educational advancement, and the training needed for gainful participation in the labor force. In strengthening reproductive health outcomes by addressing harmful reproductive practices among Nigerian youth, the government of Nigeria enacted the Violence Against Persons (Prohibition) Act 2015, which criminalizes female circumcision, or genital mutilation, as well as other forms of gender-based violence. While implementation challenges and weak law enforcement remain a key hindrance, and there is no specific focus on urban areas, a recent scoping review identified policy and program issues moving forward, recommending focused, multipronged, and nuanced approaches to interventions, research, and evaluations (Mberu 2017).

In general, obtaining high returns on investing in young people's health and well-being will not be possible without investments in improving production and use of data on urban residents, including youth across the continent. In many sub-Saharan countries, the lack of sound urban data affects the formulation of evidence-based policies and the design of programs to respond to urban dynamics and related challenges. Also, lack of good quality, disaggregated, relevant, accessible, and timely data on cities is a key element impeding progress in monitoring and reporting on development agenda goals, such as SDG 3, in African cities. It is therefore paramount that countries and cities invest in tools and capacities to improve their data collection, analysis, and monitoring, as well as their learning and evaluation practices, to make the necessary connection between policies and actions when it comes to sexual and reproductive health and rights.

REFERENCES

Ajayi, Anthony Idowu, Elmon Mudefi, Mohammed Sanusi Yusuf, Oladele Vincent Adeniyi, Ntombana Rala, and Daniel Ter Goon. 2019. "Low Awareness and Use of Pre-exposure Prophylaxis among Adolescents and Young Adults in High HIV and Sexual Violence Prevalence Settings." *Medicine* 98 (43): e17716. https://10.1097/MD.0000000000017716.

Ajayi, Anthony Idowu, and Henrietta Chinelo Ezegbe. 2020. "Association between Sexual Violence and Unintended Pregnancy among Adolescent Girls and Young Women in South Africa." *BMC Public Health* 20 (1): 1370. https://doi.org/10.1186/s12889-020 -09488-6.

APHRC (African Population and Health Research Center). 2002. *Population and Health Dynamics in Nairobi's Informal Settlements: Report of the Nairobi Cross-Sectional Slums Survey (NCSS) 2000.* Nairobi: APHRC.

APHRC (African Population and Health Research Center). 2014. *Population and Health Dynamics in Nairobi's Informal Settlements: Report of the Nairobi Cross-Sectional Slums Survey (NCSS) 2012.* Nairobi: APHRC.

Bankole, Akinrinola, Boniface A. Oye-Adeniran, Susheela Singh, Isaac F. Adewole, Deirdre Wulf, Gilda Sedgh, and Rubina Hussain. 2006. *Unwanted Pregnancy and Induced Abortion in Nigeria: Causes and Consequences.* New York: Guttmacher Institute.

Beguy, Donatien, Alex C. Ezeh, Blessing U. Mberu, and Jacques B. O. Emina. 2017. "Changes in Use of Family Planning among the Urban Poor: Evidence from Nairobi Slums." *Population and Development Review* 43 (S1): 216–34. https://doi.org/10.1111/padr.12038.

Beguy, Donatien, Caroline W. Kabiru, Eliya M. Zulu, and Alex C. Ezeh. 2011. "Timing and Sequencing of Events Marking the Transition to Adulthood in Two Informal Settlements in Nairobi, Kenya." *Journal of Urban Health* 88 (S2): 318–40. https://doi.org/10.1007/s11524-011-9547-8.

Beguy, Donatien, Joyce Mumah, Salome Wawire, Kanyiva Muindi, Lindsey Gottschalk, and Caroline W. Kabiru. 2013. "Status Report on the Sexual and Reproductive Health of Adolescents Living in Urban Slums in Kenya." Africa Population Health Research Centre and UKAid Working Paper, September.

Bhatia, Shashi Kant, and Subhash Bhatia. 2011. "Childhood and Adolescent Depression." *American Family Physician* 75:73. https://doi.org/10.1037/e552642011-001.

Bolarinwa, Obasanjo Afolabi, and Tlou Boikhutso. 2022. "A Mixed-Method Analysis of Inequalities Associated With Adverse Sexual and Reproductive Health Outcomes and the Requisite Interventions Among Young Women in Durban Informal Settlements, South Africa." *Frontiers in Public Health* 10:810216. https://doi.org/10.3389/fpubh.2022.810216.

Brockerhoff, Martin, and Ellen Brennan. 1998. "The Poverty of Cities in Developing Regions." *Population and Development Review* 24 (1): 75. https://doi.org/10.2307/2808123.

Burns, Paul A., and Rachel C. Snow. 2012. "The Built Environment and the Impact of Neighborhood Characteristics on Youth Sexual Risk Behavior in Cape Town, South Africa." *Health and Place* 18 (5): 1088–1100. https://doi.org/10.1016/j.healthplace.2012.04.013.

Chumo, Ivy, Caroline Kabaria, Alex Shankland, and Blessing Mberu. 2023a. "Drivers of Vulnerability to Health and Wellbeing Challenges in Informal Settlements." *Frontiers in Sustainable Cities* 5:1057726. https://doi.org/10.3389/frsc.2023.1057726.

Chumo, Ivy, Caroline Kabaria, Alex Shankland, and Blessing Mberu. 2023b. "Unmet Needs and Resilience: The Case of Vulnerable and Marginalized Populations in Nairobi's Informal Settlements." *Sustainability* 15 (1): 37. https://doi.org/10.3390/su15010037.

Cortina, Melissa A., Anisha Sodha, Mina Fazel, and Paul G. Ramchandani. 2012. "Prevalence of Child Mental Health Problems in Sub-Saharan Africa." *Archives of Pediatrics and Adolescent Medicine* 166 (3): 276. https://doi.org/10.1001/archpediatrics.2011.592.

Decker, Michele R., Amanda D. Latimore, Suzumi Yasutake, Miriam Haviland, Saifuddin Ahmed, Robert W. Blum, Freya Sonenstein, and Nan Marie Astone. 2015. "Gender-Based Violence against Adolescent and Young Adult Women in Low- and Middle-Income Countries." *Journal of Adolescent Health* 56 (2): 188–96. https://doi.org/10.1016/j.jadohealth.2014.09.003.

Ezeh, Alex C., Ivy Kodzi, and Jacques Emina. 2010. "Reaching the Urban Poor with Family Planning Services." *Studies in Family Planning* 41 (2): 109–16. https://doi.org/10.1111/j.1728-4465.2010.00231.x.

Fotso, Jean-Christophe, Alex Ezeh, Nyovani Madise, Abdhallah Ziraba, and Reuben Ogollah. 2009. "What Does Access to Maternal Care Mean among the Urban Poor? Factors Associated with Use of Appropriate Maternal Health Services in the Slum Settlements of Nairobi, Kenya." *Maternal and Child Health Journal* 13 (1): 130–37. https://doi.org/10.1007/s10995-008-0326-4.

Gomez, Anu Manchikanti. 2011. "Sexual Violence as a Predictor of Unintended Pregnancy, Contraceptive Use, and Unmet Need among Female Youth in Colombia." *Journal of Women's Health* 20 (9): 1349–56. https://doi.org/10.1089/jwh.2010.2518.

Goswami, Diya. 2020. "An Analysis of Mental Health in Slums of India." *International Journal of Policy Sciences and Law* 1 (1): 1–7. http://ijpsl.in/wp-content/uploads/2021/10/Analysis-of-Mental-Health-in-Slums-of-India_Diya-Goswami.pdf.

Govender, Carminee. 2012. "Experiences of Teenage Mothers in the Informal Settlements: An Analysis of Young Females' Reproductive Health Challenges, a Case Study of Siyanda Informal Settlement." Masters' thesis, University of KwaZulu-Natal. http://146.230.128.141/jspui/bitstream/10413/6467/1/Govender_Carminee_2011.pdf.

Gruebner, Oliver, Michael A. Rapp, Mazda Adli, Ulrike Kluge, Sandro Galea, and Andreas Heinz. 2017. "Cities and Mental Health." *Deutsches Ärzteblatt International* 114:121–27. https://doi.org/10.3238/arztebl.2017.0121.

Gupta, Neeru, and Mary Mahy. 2003. "Sexual Initiation among Adolescent Girls and Boys: Trends and Differentials in Sub-Saharan Africa." *Archives of Sexual Behavior* 32 (1): 41–53. https://doi.org/10.1023/a:1021841312539.

Institute of Medicine, National Research Council, Division of Behavioral and Social Sciences and Education, Board Youth on Children, Committee on Population, Panel on Transitions to Adulthood in Developing Countries, and Cynthia Lloyd. 2005. *Growing Up Global: The Changing Transitions to Adulthood in Developing Countries*. Washington, DC: National Academies Press.

IOM (International Organization for Migration). 2014. *International Organization for Migration Regional Strategy for Southern Africa 2014–2016*. Pretoria: International Organization for Migration. http://www.iom.int/sites/default/files/country/docs/AUP00579-RO-Pretoria-Regional-Strategy.pdf.

IOM (International Organization for Migration). 2019. *IOM Regional Strategy for Southern Africa 2019–2023*. Pretoria: International Organization for Migration. https://publications.iom.int/system/files/pdf/iom_regional_strategy_for_southern_africa.pdf.

Jörns-Presentati, Astrid, Ann-Kathrin Napp, Anja S. Dessauvagie, Dan J. Stein, Deborah Jonker, Elsie Breet, Weslin Charles, et al. 2021. "The Prevalence of Mental Health Problems in Sub-Saharan Adolescents: A Systematic Review." *PLoS ONE* 16 (5): e0251689. https://doi.org/10.1371/journal.pone.0251689.

Kabiru, Caroline, Donatien Beguy, Chi-Chi Undie, Eliya Msiyaphazi Zulu, and Alex C. Ezeh. 2010. "Transition into First Sex among Adolescents in Slum and Non-Slum Communities in Nairobi, Kenya." *Journal of Youth Studies* 13 (4): 453–71. https://doi.org/10.1080/13676261003801754.

Keygnaert, Ines, Nicole Vettenburg, and Marleen Temmerman. 2012. "Hidden Violence Is Silent Rape: Sexual and Gender-Based Violence in Refugees, Asylum Seekers and Undocumented Migrants in Belgium and the Netherlands." *Culture, Health and Sexuality* 14:505–20. https://doi.org/10.1080/13691058.2012.671961.

Kimani-Murage, Elizabeth, Jean-Christophe Fotso, Thaddaeus Egondi, Benta Abuya, Patricia Elung'ata, Abdhala Ziraba, Caroline Kabiru, and Nyovani Madise. 2014. "Trends in Childhood Mortality in Kenya: The Urban Advantage Has Seemingly Been Wiped Out." *Health and Place* 29:95–103. https://doi.org/10.1016/j.healthplace.2014.06.003.

Mabrouk, Adam, Gideon Mbithi, Esther Chongwo, Ezra Too, Ahmed Sarki, Mary Namuguzi, Joseph Atukwatse, Derrick Ssewanyana, and Amina Abubakar. 2022. "Mental Health Interventions for Adolescents in Sub-Saharan Africa: A Scoping Review." *Frontiers in Psychiatry* 13937723. https://doi.org/10.3389/fpsyt.2022.937723.

Mahabir, Ron, Andrew Crooks, Arie Croitoru, and Peggy Agouris. 2016. "The Study of Slums as Social and Physical Constructs: Challenges and Emerging Research Opportunities." *Regional Studies, Regional Science* 3 (1): 399–419. https://doi.org/10.1080/21681376.2016.1229130.

Mberu, Blessing U. 2017. "Female Genital Mutilation/Cutting in Nigeria: A Scoping Review." *Evidence to End FGM/C: Research to Help Women Thrive.* New York: Population Council. https://knowledgecommons.popcouncil.org/cgi/viewcontent.cgi?article=1596&context=departments_sbsr-rh

Mberu, Blessing U., James M. Ciera, Patricia Elung'ata, and Alex C. Ezeh. 2014. "Patterns and Determinants of Poverty Transitions among Poor Urban Households in Nairobi, Kenya." *African Development Review* 26 (1): 172–85. https://doi.org/10.1111/1467-8268.12073.

Mberu, Blessing U., and Alex C. Ezeh. 2017. "The Population Factor and Economic Growth and Development in Sub-Saharan African Countries." *African Population Studies* 31 (2): 3833–44. https://doi.org/10.11564/31-2-1056.

Mberu, Blessing U., and Roland Pongou. 2012. "Crossing Boundaries: Internal, Regional and International Migration in Cameroon." *International Migration* 54 (1): 100–18. https://doi.org/10.1111/j.1468-2435.2012.00766.x.

Mberu, Blessing U., and Michael White. 2011. "Internal Migration and Health: Premarital Sexual Initiation in Nigeria." *Social Science and Medicine* 72 (8): 1284–93.

Melesse, Dessalegn Y., Martin K. Mutua, Allysha Choudhury, Yohannes D. Wado, Cheikh M. Faye, Sarah Neal, and Ties Boerma. 2020. "Adolescent Sexual and Reproductive Health in Sub-Saharan Africa: Who Is Left Behind?" *BMJ Global Health* 5 (1): e002231. https://doi.org/10.1136/bmjgh-2019-002231.

Mensch, Barbara, Susheela Singh, and John B. Casterline. 2005. "Trends in the Timing of First Marriage among Men and Women in the Developing World." Policy Research Division Working Paper No. 202. New York: Population Council.

Mutombo, Namuunda, Blessing Mberu, Donatien Beguy, Kanyiva Muindi, Mike Mutua, Cheikh Faye, Nkechi Obisie-Nmehielle, and Erick Ventura. 2016. "Health Vulnerabilities among Migrant/Mobile Populations in Urban Settings of East and Southern

Africa: A Regional Synthesis of Evidence from Literature." *African Population Studies* 30 (3): 3047–59. https://doi.org/10.11564/30-3-920.

Patton, George C., Carolyn Coffey, Susan M. Sawyer, Russell M. Viner, Dagmar M. Haller, Krishna Bose, Theo Vos, Jane Ferguson, and Colin D. Mathers. 2009. "Global Patterns of Mortality in Young People: A Systematic Analysis of Population Health Data." *Lancet* 374 (9693): 881–92. https://doi.org/10.1016/s0140-6736(09)60741-8.

Patton, George C., Susan M. Sawyer, John S. Santelli, David A. Ross, Rima Afifi, Nicholas B. Allen, Monika Arora, et al. 2016. "Our Future: A Lancet Commission on Adolescent Health and Wellbeing." *Lancet* 387 (10036): 2423–78. https://doi.org/10.1016/s0140-6736(16)00579-1.

Pongou, Roland, and Roberto Serrano. 2009. "A Dynamic Theory of Fidelity Networks with an Application to the Spread of HIV/AIDS." Department of Economics, Brown University, Working Paper, April.

Pongou, Roland, and Roberto Serrano. 2013. "Fidelity Networks and Long-Run Trends in HIV/AIDS Gender Gaps." *American Economic Review* 103 (3): 298–302. https://doi.org/10.1257/aer.103.3.298.

Pongou, Roland, and Roberto Serrano. 2016. "Volume of Trade and Dynamic Network Formation in Two-Sided Economies." *Journal of Mathematical Economics* 63:147–63.

Satterthwaite, David. 2016. "A New Urban Agenda?" *Environment and Urbanization* 28 (1): 3–12. https://doi.org/10.1177/0956247816637501.

Save the Children. 2015. *State of the World's Mothers 2015: The Urban Disadvantage*. Fairfield, CT: Save the Children. https://www.savethechildren.org/content/dam/usa/reports/advocacy/sowm/sowm-2015.pdf.

Save the Children. 2021. "78% of Girls in the Northern Region of Nigeria Marry before the Age of 18, a New Report by Save the Children International Reveals." Save the Children, November 16. https://nigeria.savethechildren.net/news/78-girls-northern-region-nigeria-marry-age-18-new-report-save-children-international-reveals.

Singh, S., and J. E. Darroch. 2000. "Adolescent Pregnancy and Childbearing: Levels and Trends in Developed Countries." *Family Planning Perspectives* 32 (1): 14–23.

Singh, S., G. Sedgh, and R. Hussain. 2010. "Unintended Pregnancy: Worldwide Levels, Trends, and Outcomes." *Studies in Family Planning* 41 (4): 241–50. https://doi.org/10.1111/j.1728-4465.2010.00250.x.

Stats SL (Statistics Sierra Leone) and ICF. 2020. *Sierra Leone Demographic and Health Survey 2019*. Freetown, Sierra Leone: Stats SL and ICF.

Tan, Sze E., and Katie Kuschminder. 2022. "Migrant Experiences of Sexual and Gender Based Violence: A Critical Interpretative Synthesis." *Global Health* 18:68. https://doi.org/10.1186/s12992-022-00860-2.

UNDESA (United Nations Department of Economic and Social Affairs), Population Division. 2022. *World Population Prospects 2022*. New York: UNDESA.

UNFPA (United Nations Population Fund). 2014. *The Power of 1.8 Billion: Adolescents, Youth, and the Transformation of the Future*. New York: UNFPA

UNICEF (United Nations Children's Fund). 2018. *Accelerating Efforts to Eliminate Child Marriage in Africa*. New York: UNICEF.

UNICEF (United Nations Children's Fund). 2021. *The State of the World's Children 2021: On My Mind—Promoting, Protecting, and Caring for Children's Mental Health*. New York: UNICEF.

United Nations. 2015. *Transforming Our World: The 2030 Agenda for Sustainable Development*. A/RES/70/1. New York: United Nations.

United Nations. 2016. *Political Declaration on HIV and AIDS: On the Fast Track to Accelerating the Fight against HIV and Ending the AIDS Epidemic by 2030*. New York: United Nations.

WHO (World Health Organization). 2011. *The Sexual and Reproductive Health of Younger Adolescents: Research Issues in Developing Countries*. Geneva: WHO.

WHO (World Health Organization). 2021. *Mental Health of Adolescents*. Geneva: WHO.

World Vision. 2019. "The Violent Truth about Teenage Pregnancy." World Vision, September 20. https://www.wvi.org/publications/report/it-takes-world/violent-truth-about-teenage-pregnancy.

Zulu, Eliya M., Francis Nii-Amoo Dodoo, and Alex C. Ezeh. 2002. "Sexual Risk-Taking in the Slums of Nairobi, Kenya, 1993–98." *Population Studies* 56 (3): 311–23. https://doi.org/10.1080/00324720215933.

13

Urban Environments and Healthy Behaviors

Preventing the Epidemic of Chronic Diseases in African Cities

Meelan Thondoo, Feyisayo A. Wayas, and Tolu Oni

1. Introduction

1.1. Urbanization and Health

Undoubtedly, global urbanization is on the rapid increase. As of 2020, an estimated 56 percent of the population live in urban areas, and it is projected that this proportion will increase to 70 percent by 2045 (World Bank Group 2023). Most new urbanites will dwell in low- and middle-income countries (LMICs; UNDESA 2014), where deaths related to noncommunicable diseases (NCDs) are expected to increase from 30.8 million in 2015 to 41.8 million by 2030 (WHO 2013). Although Africa is currently not the world's most urbanized continent, it has the fastest urban growth rate in the world. In 2012, it was estimated that the number of cities in Africa with more than half a million people will have increased by 80 percent by 2030 (Schwela 2012). Urbanization is an important global health issue, as it brings along with its merits several health-related demerits (Hiremath 2021). Rapid and often unplanned urbanization across the continent is resulting in overcrowded housing, air pollution, inadequate transportation systems, unsafe working conditions, inadequate water supply, and poor sanitation. This is accompanied by a rise in access to processed foods, physical inactivity, and social exclusion. The nature of urbanization in many African cities exacerbates health inequalities within and between countries, with a disproportionate disease burden borne by the poorest. These rapidly growing cities are characterized by lower per capita incomes, high reliance on biomass fuels, and growing informality, with weak services and infrastructure. These exposures threaten health, while depleting environmental assets and increasing vulnerability to climate disasters (e.g., floods). As such, urban environments play, and will increasingly play, a pivotal role in the health and well-being of people.

1.2. Urbanization and NCD Risk in Africa

Evidence suggests a strong correlation between the increase in NCD burden and the rapid rate of urbanization in Africa (Hobbs and Ramsay 2015; Juma et al. 2019; Motala et al. 2022; Owolade et al. 2022; van de Vijver et al. 2014). The burden of NCDs in the WHO's African Region is greater than in high-income countries, and it is expected to exceed that of communicable disease by 2030 (Turner-Moss et al. 2021). For example, the probability of dying between the ages of 30 and 70 years from an NCD is 12 percent in the United Kingdom of Great Britain and Northern Ireland, whereas in Kenya, Cameroon, and South Africa, it is 18 percent, 20 percent, and 27 percent (WHO 2014). The likelihood that the rise in NCDs is positively correlated with urbanization is high due to the strong influence of urban environments on NCD risk factors, such as the lack of safe spaces to practice physical activity in cities and sedentary behaviors in urban populations (Guthold et al. 2018; Munyati and Drummond 2020; Nieuwenhuijsen 2018; Thondoo et al. 2020). Evidence also shows that food consumption and diet patterns in cities can lead to higher risk of NCDs (Albuquerque et al. 2022; Frumkin and Haines 2019; WHO 2019). Indeed, evidence shows that an unhealthy diet and physical inactivity are the leading modifiable behavioral risk factors for the four primary NCDs: type 2 diabetes, cardiovascular disease, cancer, and chronic respiratory diseases (WHO 2014). This is also true for African populations as, according to the 2019 Global Burden of Disease Study, the percentage of deaths from NCDs directly attributable to diet was 15.6 percent in Africa, and the percentage directly attributable to low physical activity was 2.2 percent (Payne et al. 2019). Therefore, clarifying the interactions between urban environments and health behaviors in general, but especially diet and physical activity, is crucial to bending the curve of the impending epidemic of chronic diseases in cities across African countries.

1.3. The NCD, Urbanization, and Climate Change Syndemic

Given the interaction of climate change with the pace and character of urbanization in many LMICs, it is important to consider the role that climate change plays on health. In cities most vulnerable to climate disasters, populations are at higher risk of living in precarious life conditions and suffering from bad health (Baker 2012; Myers 2021). Cities cover 3 percent of the planet yet emit 78 percent of all global greenhouse gas emissions, absorb 80 percent of final global energy use, and consume 60 percent of domestic water. Because of this, cities also contribute to climate change variation patterns while being hotspots for disease and death. These effects have stronger consequences on urbanites in LMICs who carry higher degrees of vulnerability and suffer an inequitable burden of deaths due to environmental hazards (Thondoo and Gupta 2021). LMICs claim about 80 percent of global NCD deaths (Alwan 2011), 92 percent of pollution-related deaths, and 90 percent of traffic-related deaths (Fisher et al. 2021; Landrigan et al. 2018). Such disease burden will increase as cities face high climate-related risks as a result of low levels of preparedness, capacity, and capability to absorb or prepare for increased numbers of climate disasters and fast-paced inadequately planned urbanization. Climate disasters pose great threats to public health by inducing food and water insecurity, water- and vector-borne diseases, malnutrition, decreases in natural resources, and threats to biodiversity. Sub-Saharan Africa is among the most affected regions, suffering particularly from extreme weather events related to climate change, as well as recurrent episodes of drought, wildfires, floods, landslides, extreme temperature, fog, and storms. According to the international disasters database from the Centre for Research on the Epidemiology of Disasters in Brussels, the increase in extreme weather events affected 195 percent more Africans in 2019 compared to the previous year (CRED, n.d.; Pandey 2019).

As climate disasters in Africa increase in severity, frequency, intensity, and impact (Ayal 2021; Dike et al. 2022), cities should stand prepared to safeguard health. For this reason, the nexus among urbanization, climate change, and health are crucial in the African context (figure 13.1). This enables us to consider what urbanization and climate change mean for health and how African cities are dealing with the epidemic of NCDs in terms of environments that can encourage certain health behaviors given the climate reality. We consider this nexus as a syndemic, with these synergistic epidemics posing a challenge for future-proofing health but also presenting a unique opportunity to shape and health-proof urban environments in rapidly growing cities. Synergistic epidemics can be defined as two or more epidemics of diseases or health-related problems in the context of socioenvironmental conditions that enhance their mutual impact and interactions, increasing

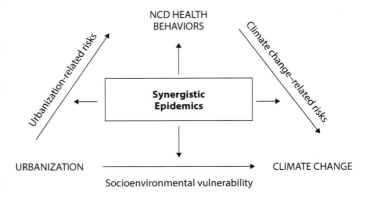

Fig. 13.1. Synergistic epidemics of noncommunicable diseases, climate change, and urbanization.

the burden of diseases (Hayran and Ataç 2019). A localized approach to health in this case considers climate change and urbanization as global drivers of disease. Hence, this chapter provides a unique opportunity to examine different categories of environments that strongly influence NCD risk in urban Africa, looking closely at the interactions between these environments and health behaviors (with a focus on diet and physical activity), and finally, considering how climate change, in the context of urbanization, influences these interactions.

Premature death from chronic diseases in cities can be avoided by promoting healthy behaviors and tackling modifiable behavioral risk factors that increase NCD prevalence. A significant portion of the NCD global burden, especially in Africa, is attributable to modifiable behavioral risk factors, such as poor diets (high consumption of sugar, fats, and salt, and low consumption of fruits and vegetables) and physical inactivity. Both behaviors are associated with malnutrition (either overnutrition or undernutrition), a metabolic risk factor for NCDs (GBD 2015 Risk Factors Collaborators 2017). Hence, interventions to prevent NCDs require an understanding of the different factors that influence diet and physical activity and the different environments in which they subsist. In this section, we describe three broad elements of the urban environment that strongly influence NCD risk via diet and physical activity in cities of Africa: built environment, food environment, and social environment.

We consider healthy behavior to be an outcome of a healthy urban environment, where people adopt a modifiable behavior that lowers the risk of early death or chronic disease. Such behavior may include healthy eating, adequate physical activity, adequate sleep, reduced substance use (tobacco and alcohol), and emotional and physical well-being. We recognize that these urban environment elements influence health through multiple pathways not covered in this chapter, such as through air pollution caused by human activities in the built environment, which affects NCD risk directly, increasing the risk of lung cancer (Loomis et al. 2013), and indirectly, reducing conduciveness of public space for physical activity (Tainio et al. 2021). Nonetheless, we have chosen to focus primarily on diet and physical activity as modifiable behavioral risk factors related to NCDs to limit the scope of the chapter. Healthy and unhealthy behaviors are shaped by socioecological factors, which are often interlinked and multifaceted. These socioecological factors are also subject to a complex interplay of influencers occurring at individual (intrapersonal), relationship (interpersonal), community, societal, and policy levels (Dahlberg and Krug 2006; Scarneo et al. 2019). Consequently, to properly understand the association between behavioral risk factors and health, and their distribution across different population groups, it is important to consider individual, social, and environmental exposures of socioecological levers, and to examine the interplay between micro-, meso- and macro-level factors that influence healthy behaviors within environments.

1.4. Built Environment

The built environment consists of human-made surroundings where people live, work, and recreate. These include density of development, mixed land uses, scale of streets, aesthetic qualities of place, connectivity of street networks, access to green space and biodiversity, urban infrastructure, housing, open spaces, sidewalks, transportation options, public transportation, walkability, playgrounds, traffic safety, residential density, and others.

Limited but robust evidence from Africa shows that the built environment can significantly influence health by providing spaces and opportunity for physical activity (Smit et al. 2011). Additionally, increased motorization, associated with growing urbanization, increases sedentary lifestyles and decreases physical activity (Nieuwenhuijsen et al. 2016). Physical activity can be practiced across different domains of daily life: transport (walking, cycling), work, school, household chores, and leisure. The participation levels of people across these different domains in the African context are influenced by socioecological factors such as age, gender, relationships, and socioeconomic status (Muthuri et al. 2016). This is true for built, food, and social environments.

Physical activity can be facilitated by different features of the built environment, such as street connectivity and the availability of parks, lower levels of crime, and the aesthetic qualities of neighborhoods (Muthuri et al. 2016). Equally, features of the built environment can also discourage the practice of physical activity in urban populations. A study conducted in a low-income area in Cape Town showed that the built environment was not conducive for physical activity in adults, especially leisure-related physical activity, because of the lack of facilities and places to exercise, low perceptions of personal safety, the absence of sidewalks or those available being used by informal street traders, and the lack of a litter-free (clean and aesthetic) environment (Odunitan-Wayas et al. 2020). A study on children and adolescents similarly showed that having few and less conducive spaces for outdoor physical activity in urban Africa is causing increasing levels of physical inactivity, leading to overweight and obesity (Barakat et al. 2022). Other systematically reported built environment features affecting physical activity are lack of traffic safety, crime (Adebusoye et al. 2022), and air pollution exposure (Coker and Kizito 2018).

In addition to physical infrastructure, mental and social perceptions of the built environment have also been reported to influence physical activity. A study in South Africa showed that physical activity levels of children and adolescents are influenced by parental perception of the built environment, especially females in relation to safety within the built environment (De Wet, Somefun, and Rambau 2018). Social disparities and gender inequalities reflected in built environment attributes are known to be critical barriers to physical activity uptake, especially among socially and economically disadvantaged populations (Barr et al. 2020; Ozodiegwu et al. 2019). This is particularly relevant for urban poor populations who lack opportunity to practice physical leisure activity (Barr et al. 2020). This is an important source of health inequality, as it is well established that leisure-time physical activity (compared to other domains of physical activity) provides added benefits to social and mental health and well-being, increasing quality of life and reducing the vulnerabilities of urban poor populations to chronic disease (Mikkelsen et al. 2010).

1.5. Food Environment

The food environment consists of spaces in which people make decisions about food, as well as what type of food is made available, accessible, affordable, and desirable in those spaces (Pingault et al. 2017). This environment consists of food stores, food service, and any physical entity by which food may be obtained, including social, economic, and cultural access to and preference for food and food systems (the interconnected systems and processes that influence nutrition). It encompasses food proximity and affordability; food promotion, advertising, and information; and food quality and safety (Pingault et al. 2017).

Increasing evidence has established linkages between food environments and diet-related NCDs on the African continent (Demmler and Qaim 2020; Laar et al. 2022; Osei-Kwasi et al. 2021). Studies show that the increasing prevalence of malnutrition- and diet-related NCDs is caused by unhealthy food purchase behavior and preferences. Factors such as more shelf space allocated to unhealthy foods than healthy foods in supermarkets and accessibility to cheap unhealthy foods to meet preference, cost, and time demands exacerbate unhealthy food behaviors (Odunitan-Wayas et al. 2021). There has been an increase in fast-foods outlets, particularly in urban(izing) contexts, which are promoting bigger unhealthy portion sizes at competitive prices and through promotions. This in turn increases the demand for these unhealthy foods, particularly in urban populations, who are more likely to purchase food for consumption than produce or cook it. These trends are further influenced by extended travel time due to traffic congestion, people having multiple jobs to meet the high cost of living in cities, and the expense of healthy foods compared to junk food. For example, the cost of a healthy quality diet is quadruple that of an energy-sufficient diet in sub-Saharan Africa (UNICEF 2020), which is beyond the affordability spectrum of the majority, given the high levels of income inequality in Africa. In addition, for many lower-income households without access to refrigeration or frequent access to electricity to power the refrigeration, storage of perishable foods such as fruits and vegetables remains a challenge, further affecting their ability to reliably access such healthy foods (Neven et al. 2006; Oluwafemi et al. 2015).

To effectively shift from an obesogenic food environment in African cities to a healthy environment as envisaged and encouraged by the United Nations and other organizations, both the formal and the informal food environment must be vital parts of the intervention targets. While the spread of formal retail stores such as supermarkets has been spurred on by urbanization, as seen in countries in the Global North, the resilience and increase in the informal food environment alongside that of the formal food environment is uniquely apparent in cities across Africa. For instance, the informal food environment (Micklesfield et al. 2013) still accounts for about 45 percent of food sales in South Africa, with about 70 percent of the urban poor purchasing food from informal outlets because of easy access, convenience, and the availability of credit facilities (Frayne et al. 2010). Informal market food environments are those that are often not regulated through formal governance structures and include street food vendors and hawkers, kiosks, and mobile vendors. They are also known to promote more unhealthy food behaviors while satisfying the needs and cultural preferences of local populations, regardless of socioeconomic status (Ambikapathi et al. 2021).

1.6. Social Environment

The social environment includes society's beliefs, customs, practices, and behaviors; social connectedness; spatial segregation; and social capital. Examples include neighborhood perception, safety, crime, traffic, social cohesion, social norms, family relationships, and peer pressure (Casper 2001; Teh and Otman 2018). Populations in urban settings of Africa are experiencing an important shift in nutrition and physical activity patterns toward higher consumption of energy-dense, nutrient-poor diets and decreasing physical activity (Yiga et al. 2020). These patterns are compounded by common social perceptions that unhealthy activities are a "sign of good living" and "wealth," and that being overweight can satisfy the cultural and social norm to fit the "standard size" of an African urbanite (Batnitzky 2008; Micklesfield et al. 2013; Pradeilles et al. 2022).

In urban settings of Africa, the influence of social environments on diet and physical activity is high, partly due to strong gender norms. Studies show that males in Africa tend to be more physically active than females as a result of predominant social and gender roles (Harkness and Hongsermeier 2015; Mudekunye 2018; Yiga et al. 2020). Leisure activities particularly, with the exception of structured physical activity in schools, are highly dependent on socioeconomic, cultural, and safety factors, which influence physical inactivity in females (Harkness and Hongsermeier 2015; Sedibe et al. 2014). With unprecedented urbanization, the increase in motorization has established more widespread social and behavioral trends toward sedentary lifestyles. These trends are caused by time constraints from traffic congestion; limited slots for planning physical activity; technologies such as elevators and virtual platforms for entertainment; increased labor time to sustain the financial requirements of urban life; cheap processed instant meals in stores; and instant home delivery options. A systematic review in the Middle East and North Africa showed that lack of suitable sports facilities, time, social support, and motivation; gender and cultural norms; harsh weather; and hot climate are common barriers to physical activity (Gissing et al. 2017). In that study, sociodemographic factors negatively associated with physical activity participation include advanced age, being female, having less education, and being married.

Regarding social factors influencing the food environment, studies show that home dietary habits and perceptions are often obstacles to healthy eating. In the African context, unhealthy food choices and household preference for cheaper and unhealthy products are often driven by culturally and socially promoted food options (Osei-Kwasi et al. 2020). This is particularly true for populations of low socioeconomic status (Reardon et al. 2021). Individual preference for junk food and negative peer pressure influencing food choices combined with physical inactivity are common in children and adolescents, regardless of gender and socioeconomic status (Brown et al. 2015; Ssewanyana et al. 2018). Evidence from South Africa demonstrates the high impact of media advertisement on diet, with almost half of all television advertisements related to food, of which almost two-thirds promoted unhealthy foods and sweetened drinks (Mchiza et al. 2013).

2. Opportunities and Challenges

Having explored how three broad categories of the urban environment influence diet and physical activity, we now turn to challenges faced in preventing NCDs in the context of urbanization and climate change, opportunities that can be leveraged, and suggested actions that can be taken by policy actors, implementers, and researchers (box 13.1).

During extreme weather events due to climate change, disruptions to food environments, particularly to food supply, can occur. This in turn increases nutrition insecurity, which directly affects social environments by

Box 13.1. Recommendations for Policy Actors, Implementers, and Researchers

Policy actors

- Rethink systems and approaches to support integrated and multisectoral action to increase urban health in Africa.
- Align key performance indicators of all policies with the explicit goal of health creation to address incoherence between policies. For instance, policies that result in increased access to unhealthy processed foods, particularly in more deprived communities, counteract policies that increase access to NCD treatment and NCD prevention awareness.
- Enforce policies for mandatory physical activity opportunities in schools adapted to gender and the socioeconomic realities of students.
- Budget and invest in active travel (walking and cycling) infrastructure aligned with strategic climate finance plans.
- Place health at the center of urban development and use health as an opportunity to address structural inequities within societies.

Implementers

- Incentivize actors involved in financing and implementing urban infrastructure projects to build walking and cycling infrastructure to increase physical activity, decrease exposure to pollutants, and increase exposure to green and blue spaces.
- Encourage commercial actors to promote healthy food awareness, improve shelf space allocation and visibility of healthy foods, and ease access to quality and affordable healthy foods.
- Foster greater collaboration between nongovernmental, public, and private sectors on public health programs to create healthy built, food, and social environments.
- Invest more in freely accessible platforms and initiatives that facilitate shared learning and knowledge exchange between communities on approaches to institutionalize youth participation in decision making as well as approaches to evaluating the health impact of interventions in the urban environment.

Researchers and research institutions

- Seek out opportunities for meaningful partnerships with nonacademic

> experts (e.g., community and policy actors) to coproduce knowledge from research design to implementation.
> - Nurture multisectoral partnerships to build a better appreciation of policy contexts (opportunity and timing).
> - Create institutional structures to support responsive research that leverages academic expertise in service of society: for example, adaptive funding that enables academic policy partnerships on natural experimental projects to evaluate the health impact of urban or climate interventions implemented by public and private sectors.

exacerbating economic inequality. As a growing proportion of people in African cities currently reside in overcrowded informal settlements, the effects of climate change aggravate built environment issues through land scarcity and lack of infrastructure for distribution of transport and sanitation services. Informal activities also tend to happen in contexts of sociopolitical unrest, hence creating a vicious cycle of societal disruption, poverty, and insecurity during extreme weather events.

Rapid and unplanned urbanization can have many negative social and environmental health impacts, which hit the poorest and most vulnerable the hardest. Health inequities are most stark in urban areas, sometimes varying from street to street. The urban poor face disproportionate risks of climate events and neighborhood-level deprivation, such as poor access to healthy food and a quality built environment. They often reside in particularly exposed areas, occupy low-quality housing, have limited education, lack financial protection, and lack opportunities for employment (Gasper, Blohm, and Ruth 2011). They are therefore most vulnerable to environmental injustice as they suffer from the hazards often generated by their wealthier counterparts. The disparities they face are consequences of social marginalization and poverty traps that feed cycles of food, financial, and housing insecurity. Hence, because the urban poor are exposed to a higher risk of unhealthy environments, health inequity is a key driver of the NCD epidemic in cities.

In addition to climate events that push ecological boundaries, hinder safe active living, and increase the risk of emerging diseases, urban populations in Africa face important socioeconomic, income, and gender inequalities due to unemployment, gender-based violence, and rises in food prices (Ben Hassen et al. 2022; Matsungo and Chopera 2020). All these factors challenge the adoption and sustenance of healthy behaviors, especially for the urban poor. They highlight the critical need for evidence-informed NCD prevention interventions that are cognizant of potential ecological vulnerabilities exacerbated by urbanization processes and accelerated by climate change, while directly affecting built, food, and social environments in ways that influence diet and physical activity. Furthermore, such interventions should also have the potential to synergistically contribute to a reduction in climate risks while mitigating the negative impacts of climate change and urbanization on diet and physical activity.

In the context of climate vulnerability, there are various opportunities to address the growing epidemic of chronic diseases in urban settings of Africa. First, the involvement of the youth in the design of NCD prevention interventions is an opportunity to develop contextually relevant future-forward interventions. Currently, sub-Saharan Africa has the largest cohort of young people in history—405 million people aged 0–14 years in 2014 (Oni et al., n.d.). This young population has the potential for economic productivity and development, particularly in cities. If current patterns persist, however, most of this population will have an NCD in their middle age (Oni et al., n.d.). Indeed, NCDs strike people during their economically productive years, with significant implications on the earning ability of individuals, and by extension their families. Additionally, the cost implications of treating and managing them will be crippling to households, health systems, and governments. Achieving this will require institutionalized mechanisms for meaningful youth participation in decision-making processes that shape the form of cities. For example, a recently published participatory intervention study design, informed in part by data collected from adolescent citizen scientists, also involved these citizen scientists in identifying important and feasible intervention options to support healthy eating and active living among children and adolescents in Cameroon and South Africa (Erzse et al. 2022).

Second, NCDs are driven by multifaceted factors that stem beyond the health care sector and are scattered across built, social, and food environments. Behavioral risk factors for NCDs are influenced by commercial determinants of health, such as tobacco, alcohol, sugar-sweetened beverages, and fast-food industries that interfere with NCD prevention and control strategies. For this reason, intersectoral policy integration is key to ensure the positive impact of NCD interventions. For instance, whether people engage in physical activity is heavily dependent on access to infrastructure that encourages an active lifestyle. This depends on built environment features and policies that promote walking, cycling, and green spaces but also socioeconomic norms around travel behavior and transit affordances. For transport systems to be sustainable in the context of urbanization and climate change, they should be safe, clean, functional, equitable, and affordable. This requires multisectoral action from many actors (e.g., technical experts, government ministries, financing structures), an integrated approach to producing health, and the leveraging of cobenefits across sectors (e.g., urban planning, waste management, air pollution, road safety). Critically, this will require platforms that support intersectoral collaboration with integration of data across sectors to facilitate evaluation of the health impact of interventions focused on elements of the urban environment or as part of climate action. An example of this is a flagship project in Riverlea, one of Johannesburg's poorest townships, focusing on intersectoral action to treat diabetes while considering environmental vulnerability and action across sectors of physical activity, nursing, sustainable development, and medical and radiation sciences (University of Johannesburg 2021). Another example is the study on the perceptions and experiences of intersectoral collaborators for healthier human settlements in Douala, Cameroon, identifying the importance of community participation in intersectoral interventions for health (Nguendo-Yongsi et al. 2022).

Finally, NCD interventions can benefit from cities being hotspots for health innovation led by communities. The efficiency of community-led action in urban spaces is becoming more common despite the lack of recreational spaces in crowded urban areas of Africa. Several initiatives have been successfully deployed in which policymakers and community actors work together to promote events or opportunities in communities in safe, healthy, and adequate spaces. For instance, the success of the Open Street program in Cape Town encouraged many African cities to engage in citizen-led movements for health-driven behavior change in cities. In 2018, an Open Streets Exchange in Cape Town was attended by representatives from African countries such as Egypt, Uganda, Kenya, Ghana, Ethiopia, Angola, Zambia (TUMI and UN-Habitat 2020). Since then, evidence of initiatives to promote safe places and increase physical activity and community togetherness has shown that they directly and indirectly alleviate social ills and risk for chronic diseases in local communities (King et al. 2016; Umstattd Meyer et al. 2019; Zieff et al. 2022).

3. Conclusion

African cities are engines for economic growth and social progress, but they are also hotspots for unhealthy behaviors and vulnerability to climate hazards, diseases, and death, all of which are interlinked. Premature death from chronic diseases in cities can be avoided by ensuring that these urban environments are supportive of healthy behaviors. Unhealthy diets and physical inactivity are behavioral risk factors for NCDs and are shaped by complex ecological drivers intersecting in local social, cultural, environmental, policy, and economic contexts. Behavioral risk factors can be mitigated by understanding the multidimensional influence of urban environments (food, built, and social) on health. For example, the practice of physical activity depends on different features of the built environment such as connectivity, availability, and safety but is also influenced by sedentary behaviors encouraged through unhealthy food advertisements and social perceptions of body size.

As the urban poor are often more likely to be exposed to unhealthy environments, health inequity is a key driver of the NCD epidemic in cities. Hence, there is critical need for evidence-informed NCD prevention interventions that are cognizant of potential socioecological vulnerabilities exacerbated by urbanization processes and accelerated by climate change. Tackling these structural determinants of health through direct action on built, food, and social environments is therefore critical to creating health-generating cities that make the healthy choice the easy choice. Interventions to prevent the epidemic of chronic diseases will benefit from explicit involvement of youth, intersectoral policy integration, and community-led action to promote healthy behaviors and safeguard the health of populations in urban environments in Africa.

REFERENCES

Adebusoye, Busola, Kaushik Chattopadhyay, Winifred Ekezie, Revati Phalkey, and Jo Leonardi-Bee. 2022. "Association of Built Environment Constructs and Physical Activity among Children and Adolescents in Africa: A Systematic Review and Meta-analysis." *JBI Evidence Synthesis*: 20 (10): 2410–44. https://doi.org/10.11124/JBIES-21-00295.

Albuquerque, Gabriela, Nuno Lunet, João Breda, and Patrícia Padrão. 2022. "Food, Nutrition and Diet in Urban Areas from Low and Middle-Income Countries in the WHO European Region." *Public Health Nutrition* 26 (S1): 1–12.

Alwan, Ala. 2011. *Global Status Report on Noncommunicable Diseases 2010*. Geneva: World Health Organization.

Ambikapathi, Ramya, Gerald Shively, Germana Leyna, Dominic Mosha, Ally Mangara, Crystal L. Patil, Morgan Boncyk, Savannah L. Froese, Cristiana K. Verissimo, and Patrick Kazonda. 2021. "Informal Food Environment Is Associated with Household Vegetable Purchase Patterns and Dietary Intake in the DECIDE Study: Empirical Evidence from Food Vendor Mapping in Peri-urban Dar es Salaam, Tanzania." *Global Food Security* 28:100474.

Ayal, Desalegn Yayeh. 2021. "Climate Change and Human Heat Stress Exposure in Sub-Saharan Africa." *CABI Reviews* 16:1.

Baker, Judy L. 2012. *Climate Change, Disaster Risk, and the Urban Poor: Cities Building Resilience for a Changing World*. Washington, DC: World Bank.

Barakat, Caroline, Susan Yousufzai, Samah Mohammed, and Rania Dghaim. 2022. "Physical Activity and Sport Participation among Adolescents from MENA." In *Adolescent Health in the Middle East and North Africa*, edited by Caroline Barakat, Rania Dghaim, and Fatme Al Anouti, 51–69. Cham: Springer.

Barr, Anna Louise, Uttara Partap, Elizabeth H. Young, Kokou Agoudavi, Naby Balde, Gibson B. Kagaruki, Mary T. Mayige, Benjamin Longo-Mbenza, Gerald Mutungi, and Omar Mwalim. 2020. "Sociodemographic Inequities Associated with Participation in Leisure-Time Physical Activity in Sub-Saharan Africa: An Individual Participant Data Meta-analysis." *BMC Public Health* 20 (1): 1–13.

Batnitzky, Adina. 2008. "Obesity and Household Roles: Gender and Social Class in Morocco." *Sociology of Health and Illness* 30 (3): 445–62.

Ben Hassen, Tarek, Hamid El Bilali, Mohammad S. Allahyari, Islam Mohamed Kamel, Hanen Ben Ismail, Hajer Debbabi, and Khaled Sassi. 2022. "Gendered Impacts of the COVID-19 Pandemic on Food Behaviors in North Africa: Cases of Egypt, Morocco, and Tunisia." *International Journal of Environmental Research and Public Health* 19 (4): 2192.

Brown, Corbett, Sheila Shaibu, Segametsi Maruapula, Leapetswe Malete, and Charlene Compher. 2015. "Perceptions and Attitudes towards Food Choice in Adolescents in Gaborone, Botswana." *Appetite* 95:29–35.

Casper, Michele. 2001. "A Definition of 'Social Environment.'" *American Journal of Public Health* 91 (3): 465–70.

Coker, Eric, and Samuel Kizito. 2018. "A Narrative Review on the Human Health Effects of Ambient Air Pollution in Sub-Saharan Africa: An Urgent Need for Health Effects Studies." *International Journal of Environmental Research and Public Health* 15 (3): 427.

CRED (Centre for Research on the Epidemiology of Disasters). n.d. EM-DAT International Disaster Database. Accessed June 15, 2024. https://www.emdat.be.

Dahlberg, Linda L., and Etienne G. Krug. 2006. "Violence a Global Public Health Problem." *Ciência and Saúde Colectiva* 11:277–92.

De Wet, Nicole, Oluwaseyi Somefun, and Ndivhuwo Rambau. 2018. "Perceptions of Community Safety and Social Activity Participation among Youth in South Africa." *PLoS One* 13 (5): e0197549.

Demmler, Kathrin M., and Matin Qaim. 2020. "Africa's Changing Food Environments and Nutritional Effects on Adults and Children." *Hidden Hunger and the Transformation of Food Systems* 121:31–41.

Dike, Victor Nnamdi, Zhao-Hui Lin, Chenglai Wu, and Colman Chikwem Ibe. 2022. "Advances in Weather and Climate Extremes." In *Climate Impacts on Extreme Weather*, edited by Victor Ongoma and Hossein Tabari, 49–63. Amsterdam: Elsevier.

Erzse, Agnes, Teurai Rwafa-Ponela, Petronell Kruger, Feyisayo A. Wayas, Estelle Victoria Lambert, Clarisse Mapa-Tassou, Edwin Ngwa, Susan Goldstein, Louise Foley, and Karen J. Hofman. 2022. "A Mixed-Methods Participatory Intervention Design Process to Develop Intervention Options in Immediate Food and Built Environments to Support Healthy Eating and Active Living among Children and Adolescents in Cameroon and South Africa." *International Journal of Environmental Research and Public Health* 19 (16): 10263.

Fisher, Samantha, David C. Bellinger, Maureen L. Cropper, Pushpam Kumar, Agnes Binagwaho, Juliette Biao Koudenoukpo, Yongjoon Park, Gabriella Taghian, and Philip J. Landrigan. 2021. "Air Pollution and Development in Africa: Impacts on Health, the Economy, and Human Capital." *Lancet Planetary Health* 5 (10): e681–e688.

Frayne, Bruce, Wade Pendleton, Jonathan Crush, Ben Acquah, Jane Battersby-Lennard, Eugenio Bras, Asiyati Chiweza, et al. 2010. *The State of Urban Food Insecurity in Southern Africa*. Urban Food Security Series 2. Cape Town: AFSUN and Queen's University.

Frumkin, Howard, and Andy Haines. 2019. "Global Environmental Change and Noncommunicable Disease Risks." *Annual Review of Public Health* 40:261–82.

Gasper, Rebecca, Andrew Blohm, and Matthias Ruth. 2011. "Social and Economic Impacts of Climate Change on the Urban Environment." *Current Opinion in Environmental Sustainability* 3 (3): 150–57.

GBD 2015 Risk Factors Collaborators. 2017. "Global, Regional, and National Comparative Risk Assessment of 79 Behavioural, Environmental and Occupational, and Metabolic Risks or Clusters of Risks, 1990–2015: A Systematic Analysis for the Global Burden of Disease Study 2015 (vol 388, pg 1659, 2016)." *Lancet* 389 (10064): E1.

Gissing, Stefanie C., Rebecca Pradeilles, Hibbah A. Osei-Kwasi, Emmanuel Cohen, and Michelle Holdsworth. 2017. "Drivers of Dietary Behaviours in Women Living in Urban Africa: A Systematic Mapping Review." *Public Health Nutrition* 20 (12): 2104–13.

Guthold, Regina, Gretchen A. Stevens, Leanne M. Riley, and Fiona C. Bull. 2018. "Worldwide Trends in Insufficient Physical Activity from 2001 to 2016: A Pooled Analysis of 358 Population-Based Surveys with 1.9 Million Participants." *Lancet Global Health* 6 (10): e1077–e1086.

Harkness, Geoff, and Natasha Hongsermeier. 2015. "Female Sports as Non-movement Resistance in the Middle East and North Africa." *Sociology Compass* 9 (12): 1082–93.

Hayran, Osman, and Ömer Ataç. 2019. "Syndemics or Synergistic Epidemics." *Journal of Health Systems and Policies* 1 (3): 174–88.

Hiremath, Sumanth S. 2021. "Impact of Urbanisation on Mental Health: A Critical Appraisal." *Journal of Alzheimer's Parkinsonism and Dementia* 5 (1):2.

Hobbs, Angela, and Michèle Ramsay. 2015. "Epigenetics and the Burden of Noncommunicable Disease: A Paucity of Research in Africa." *Epigenomics* 7 (4): 627–39.

Juma, Kenneth, Pamela A. Juma, Constance Shumba, Peter Otieno, and Gershim Asiki. 2019. "Non-communicable Diseases and Urbanization in African Cities: A Narrative Review." In *Public Health in Developing Countries—Challenges and Opportunities*, Edlyne Eze Anugwom and Niyi Awofeso, 31–50. London: IntechOpen.

King, Abby C., Sandra J. Winter, Jylana L. Sheats, Lisa G. Rosas, Matthew P. Buman, Deborah Salvo, Nicole M. Rodriguez, et al. 2016. "Leveraging Citizen Science and Information Technology for Population Physical Activity Promotion." *Translational Journal of the American College of Sports Medicine* 1 (4): 30–44. https://www.ncbi.nlm.nih.gov/pubmed/27525309.

Laar, Amos K., Phyllis Addo, Richmond Aryeetey, Charles Agyemang, Francis Zotor, Gershim Asiki, Krystal K. Rampalli, Gideon S. Amevinya, Akua Tandoh, and Silver Nanema. 2022. "Perspective: Food Environment Research Priorities for Africa—Lessons from the Africa Food Environment Research Network." *Advances in Nutrition* 13 (3): 739–47.

Landrigan, Philip J., Richard Fuller, Nereus J. R. Acosta, Olusoji Adeyi, Robert Arnold, Abdoulaye Bibi Baldé, Roberto Bertollini, Stephan Bose-O'Reilly, Jo Ivey Boufford, and Patrick N, Breysse. 2018. "The Lancet Commission on Pollution and Health." *Lancet* 391 (10119): 462–512.

Loomis, Dana, Yann Grosse, Béatrice Lauby-Secretan, Fatiha El Ghissassi, Véronique Bouvard, Lamia Benbrahim-Tallaa, Neela Guha, Robert Baan, Heidi Mattock, and Kurt Straif. 2013. "The Carcinogenicity of Outdoor Air Pollution." *Lancet Oncology* 14 (13): 1262.

Matsungo, Tonderayi Mathew, and Prosper Chopera. 2020. "Effect of the COVID-19-Induced Lockdown on Nutrition, Health and Lifestyle Patterns among Adults in Zimbabwe." *BMJ Nutrition, Prevention and Health* 3 (2): 205.

Mchiza, Zandile J., Norman J. Temple, Nelia P. Steyn, Zulfa Abrahams, and Mario Clayford. 2013. "Content Analysis of Television Food Advertisements Aimed at Adults and Children in South Africa." *Public Health Nutrition* 16 (12): 2213–20.

Micklesfield, Lisa K., Estelle V. Lambert, David John Hume, Sarah Chantler, Paula R. Pienaar, Kasha Dickie, Julia H. Goedecke, and Thandi Puoane. 2013. "Socio-cultural, Environmental and Behavioural Determinants of Obesity in Black South African Women: Review Articles." *Cardiovascular Journal of Africa* 24 (9): 369–75.

Mikkelsen, Stine S., Janne S. Tolstrup, Esben M. Flachs, Erik L. Mortensen, Peter Schnohr, and Trine Flensborg-Madsen. 2010. "A Cohort Study of Leisure Time Physical Activity and Depression." *Preventive Medicine* 51 (6): 471–75. https://doi.org/10.1016/j.ypmed.2010.09.008.

Motala, Ayesha A., Jean Claude Mbanya, Kaushik Ramaiya, Fraser J. Pirie, and Keneth Ekoru. 2022. "Type 2 Diabetes Mellitus in Sub-Saharan Africa: Challenges and Opportunities." *Nature Reviews Endocrinology* 18 (4): 219–29.

Mudekunye, Janet. 2018. "Culture and Participation in Physical Education and Sport: The Case of Tertiary Female Students in Masvingo, Zimbabwe." *Journal of Pan African Studies* 11 (8): 221–41.

Munyati, C., and J. H. Drummond. 2020. "Loss of Urban Green Spaces in Mafikeng, South Africa." *World Development Perspectives* 19:100226.

Muthuri, Stella K., Lucy-Joy M. Wachira, Vincent O. Onywera, and Mark S. Tremblay. 2016. "Associations between Parental Perceptions of the Neighborhood Environment and Childhood Physical Activity: Results from ISCOLE-Kenya." *Journal of Physical Activity and Health* 13 (3): 333–43.

Myers, Garth. 2021. "Urbanisation in the Global South." In *Urban Ecology in the Global South*, edited by C. M. Shackleton, Sarel S. Cilliers, Elandrie Davoren, and Marié J. Du Toit, 27–49. Cham: Springer.

Neven, David, Thomas Reardon, Jonathan Chege, and Honglin Wang. 2006. "Supermarkets and Consumers in Africa: The Case of Nairobi, Kenya." *Journal of International Food and Agribusiness Marketing* 18 (1–2): 103–23.

Nguendo-Yongsi, Blaise, Trish Muzenda, Yves Bertrand Djouda Feudjio, Daline Nora Kenfack Momo, and Tolu Oni. 2022. "Intersectoral Collaboration for Healthier Human Settlements: Perceptions and Experiences from Stakeholders in Douala, Cameroon." *Cities and Health* 6:1–14.

Nieuwenhuijsen, Mark J. 2018. "Influence of Urban and Transport Planning and the City Environment on Cardiovascular Disease." *Nature Reviews Cardiology* 15 (7): 432–38.

Nieuwenhuijsen, Mark J., Haneen Khreis, Ersilia Verlinghieri, and David Rojas-Rueda. 2016. "Transport and Health: A Marriage of Convenience or an Absolute Necessity." *Environment International* 88:150–52.

Odunitan-Wayas, Feyisayo A., Nicola Hamann, Nandipha A. Sinyanya, Abby C. King, Ann Banchoff, Sandra J. Winter, Sharief Hendricks, Kufre J. Okop, and Estelle V. Lambert. 2020. "A Citizen Science Approach to Determine Perceived Barriers and Promoters of Physical Activity in a Low-Income South African Community." *Global Public Health* 15 (5): 749–62.

Odunitan-Wayas, Feyisayo A., Kufre J. Okop, Robert V. H. Dover, Olufunke A. Alaba, Lisa K. Micklesfield, Thandi Puoane, Naomi S. Levitt, Jane Battersby, Shelly T. Meltzer, and Estelle V. Lambert. 2021. "Food Purchasing Behaviour of Shoppers from Different South African Socio-economic Communities: Results from Grocery Receipts, Intercept Surveys and In-Supermarkets Audits." *Public Health Nutrition* 24 (4): 665–76.

Oluwafemi, F., S. Akpoguma, T. Oladiran, and A. Kolapo. 2015. "Microbiological Quality of Household Refrigerators in Three Cities South-West of Nigeria." *Journal of Microbial and Biochemical Technology* 7 (4): 206–9.

Oni, Tolu, Ebele Mogo, Aliko Ahmed, Charles Ebikeme, Yonette Thomas, Amy Weimann, and Justine Davies. n.d. *Bolder Action for Health in Africa.* https://www.mrc-epid.cam .ac.uk/wp-content/uploads/2019/03/NEF-BOLDER-ACTION-FOR-HEALTH-IN -AFRICA.pdf.

Osei-Kwasi, Hibbah, Amos Laar, Francis Zotor, Rebecca Pradeilles, Richmond Aryeetey, Mark Green, Paula Griffiths, Robert Akparibo, Milkah Njeri Wanjohi, and Emily Rousham. 2021. "The African Urban Food Environment Framework for Creating Healthy Nutrition Policy and Interventions in Urban Africa." *PLoS One* 16 (4): e0249621.

Osei-Kwasi, Hibbah, Aarti Mohindra, Andrew Booth, Amos Laar, Milkah Wanjohi, Fiona Graham, Rebecca Pradeilles, Emmanuel Cohen, and Michelle Holdsworth. 2020. "Factors Influencing Dietary Behaviours in Urban Food Environments in Africa: A Systematic Mapping Review." *Public Health Nutrition* 23 (14): 2584–2601.

Owolade, Adedoyin, Hope Mashavakure, Abdulhammed Opeyemi Babatunde, and Abdullahi Tunde Aborode. 2022. "Time to Relook into Non-communicable Diseases (NCDs) in Africa: A Silent Threat Overwhelming Global Health in Africa." *Annals of Medicine and Surgery* 82:104522.

Ozodiegwu, Ifeoma D., Mary Ann Littleton, Christian Nwabueze, Oluwaseun Famojuro, Megan Quinn, Richard Wallace, and Hadii M. Mamudu. 2019. "A Qualitative Research Synthesis of Contextual Factors Contributing to Female Overweight and Obesity over the Life Course in Sub-Saharan Africa." *PLoS One* 14 (11): e0224612.

Pandey, Kiran. 2019. "195% More Africans Affected Due to Extreme Weather Events in 2019." *Down to Earth*, December 26. https://www.downtoearth.org.in/news/climate -change/195-more-africans-affected-due-to-extreme-weather-events-in-2019-68573.

Payne, Thomas H., Christian Lovis, Charles Gutteridge, Claudia Pagliari, Shivam Natara-jan, Cui Yong, and Lue-Ping Zhao. 2019. "Status of Health Information Exchange: A Comparison of Six Countries." *Journal of Global Health* 9 (2): 1–16.

Pingault, Nathanaël, Patrick Caron, Carol Kalafatic, Amadou Allahoury, Louise O. Fresco, Eileen Kennedy, Muhammad Khan, et al. 2017. *Nutrition and Food Systems: A Report by the High Level Panel of Experts on Food Security and Nutrition of the Committee on World Food Security*. HLPE Report 12. Rome: FAO.

Pradeilles, Rebecca, Michelle Holdsworth, Oluwabukola Olaitan, Ana Irache, Hibbah A. Osei-Kwasi, Christian B. Ngandu, and Emmanuel Cohen. 2022. "Body Size Preferences for Women and Adolescent Girls Living in Africa: A Mixed-Methods Systematic Review." *Public Health Nutrition* 25 (3): 738–59.

Reardon, Thomas, David Tschirley, Lenis Saweda O. Liverpool-Tasie, Titus Awokuse, Jessica Fanzo, Bart Minten, Rob Vos, Michael Dolislager, Christine Sauer, and Rahul Dhar. 2021. "The Processed Food Revolution in African Food Systems and the Double Burden of Malnutrition." *Global Food Security* 28:100466.

Scarneo, Samantha E., Zachary Y. Kerr, Emily Kroshus, Johna K. Register-Mihalik, Yuri Hosokawa, Rebecca L. Stearns, Lindsay J. DiStefano, and Douglas J. Casa. 2019. "The Socioecological Framework: A Multifaceted Approach to Preventing Sport-Related Deaths in High School Sports." *Journal of Athletic Training* 54 (4): 356–60.

Schwela, Dieter. 2012. *Review of Urban Air Quality in Sub-Saharan Africa Region*. Washing-ton, DC: World Bank.

Sedibe, Modiehi H., Alison Bridget Feeley, P. L. Griffiths, S. A. Norris, Carlijn Voorend, and C. M. Doak. 2014. "Narratives of Urban Female Adolescents in South Africa: Dietary and Physical Activity Practices in an Obesogenic Environment." *South African Journal of Clinical Nutrition* 27 (3): 114–19.

Smit, Warren, Trevor Hancock, Jacob Kumaresen, Carlos Santos-Burgoa, Raúl Sánchez-Kobashi Meneses, and Sharon Friel. 2011. "Toward a Research and Action Agenda on Urban Planning/Design and Health Equity in Cities in Low and Middle-Income Coun-tries." *Journal of Urban Health* 88 (5): 875–85.

Ssewanyana, Derrick, Amina Abubakar, Anneloes Van Baar, Patrick N. Mwangala, and Charles R. Newton. 2018. "Perspectives on Underlying Factors for Unhealthy Diet and Sedentary Lifestyle of Adolescents at a Kenyan Coastal Setting." *Frontiers in Public Health* 6:11.

Tainio, Marko, Zorana Jovanovic Andersen, Mark J. Nieuwenhuijsen, Liang Hu, Audrey De Nazelle, Ruopeng An, Leandro M. T. Garcia, Shifalika Goenka, Belen Zapata-Diomedi, and Fiona Bull. 2021. "Air Pollution, Physical Activity and Health: A Mapping Review of the Evidence." *Environment International* 147:105954.

Teh, Mat, and Mohd Shahril Otman. 2018. "Influence of Social Environment on Student's Behaviour." *International Journal of Academic Research in Business and Social Sciences* 8 (7): 930–39.

Thondoo, Meelan, and Joyeeta Gupta. 2021. "Health Impact Assessment Legislation in Developing Countries: A Path to Sustainable Development?" *Review of European, Comparative & International Environmental Law* 30 (1): 107–17.

Thondoo, Meelan, Natalie Mueller, David Rojas-Rueda, D. de Vries, Joyeeta Gupta, and Mark J. Nieuwenhuijsen. 2020. "Participatory Quantitative Health Impact Assessment of Urban Transport Planning: A Case Study from Eastern Africa." *Environment International* 144:106027.

TUMI (Transformative Urban Mobility Initiative) and UN-Habitat. 2020. *Open Streets: A Catalyst for Active Mobility in Cape Town*. Cape Town: UN-Habitat.

Turner-Moss, Eleanor, Ahmed Razavi, Nigel Unwin, and Louise Foley. 2021. "Evidence for Factors Associated with Diet and Physical Activity in African and Caribbean Countries." *Bulletin of the World Health Organization* 99 (6): 464.

Umstattd Meyer, M. Renée, Christina N. Bridges, Thomas L. Schmid, Amelie A. Hecht, and Keshia M. Pollack Porter. 2019. "Systematic Review of How Play Streets Impact Opportunities for Active Play, Physical Activity, Neighborhoods, and Communities." *BMC Public Health* 19 (1): 1–16.

UNDESA (United Nations Department of Economic and Social Affairs), Population Division. 2014. *World Urbanization Prospects: The 2014 Revision*. New York: UNDESA. https://population.un.org/wup/publications/files/wup2014-report.pdf.

UNICEF. 2020. *The State of Food Security and Nutrition in the World 2020*. New York: UNICEF. https://www.unicef.org/reports/state-of-food-security-and-nutrition-2020.

University of Johannesburg. 2021. *Partnership Proposal*. Johannesburg: University of Johannesburg.

van de Vijver, Steven, Hilda Akinyi, Samuel Oti, Ademola Olajide, Charles Agyemang, Isabella Aboderin, and Catherine Kyobutungi. 2014. "Status Report on Hypertension in Africa-Consultative Review for the 6th Session of the African Union Conference of Ministers of Health on NCD's." *Pan African Medical Journal* 16 (1): 38.

WHO (World Health Organization). 2013. *Projections of Mortality and Causes of Death 2015 and 2030*. Geneva: WHO.

WHO (World Health Organization). 2014. *Global Status Report on Noncommunicable Diseases 2014*. Geneva: WHO. https://www.who.int/publications/i/item/9789241564854.

WHO (World Health Organization). 2019. *Healthy Diet*. Geneva: WHO, Regional Office for the Eastern Mediterranean.

World Bank Group. 2023. "Urban Development." World Bank Group. Last updated April 3, 2023. https://www.worldbank.org/en/topic/urbandevelopment/overview.

Yiga, Peter, Jan Seghers, Patrick Ogwok, and Christophe Matthys. 2020. "Determinants of Dietary and Physical Activity Behaviours among Women of Reproductive Age in Urban Sub-Saharan Africa: A Systematic Review." *British Journal of Nutrition* 124 (8): 761–72.

Zieff, Susan G., Elaine Musselman, Claudia Guedes, Daniel Chin, Alexandria Ferrey, Carolina Overton, Nelva Rivera, Anjali Sundararaman, and Olivia Walesch. 2022. "Neighborhood Social Environment at an Open Streets Initiative." *Journal of Community Practice* 30 (1): 20–33.

IV CASE STUDIES

The case study section builds on and supports the longer chapter narratives in the previous sections by highlighting specific examples, cities, solutions, and emerging challenges. Each chapter in this section centers on a specific city and specific determinant of health. The authors spotlight the use of participatory data-driven approaches to improve urban air quality in Kampala, Uganda; the increasing interest in mental health and illness in Yaoundé, Cameroon; the use of machine learning methods in the co-design of solutions to improve education in Arusha, Tanzania; integrated planning as a pathway to improving health in informal settlements in Nairobi, Kenya; and opportunities for digital health adoption with a focus on Nairobi, Kenya.

14

Case Study of Participatory Data-Driven Approaches to Improve Urban Air Quality in Kampala, Uganda

Deo Okure, Engineer Bainomugisha, Daniel Ogenrwot, Richard Sserunjogi, Priscah Adrine, and Gabriel Okello

1. Introduction

Air pollution is a major environmental and public health risk in many African cities (Brunekreef and Holgate 2002; WHO 2018). Africa has one of the fastest-growing urban populations in the world, and populations living in African urban spaces are among the most vulnerable to exposure to dangerous levels of air pollution (Petkova et al. 2013; WHO 2018), with a scale higher than other known environmental health challenges, such as sanitation and malnutrition (Roy 2016). Available evidence shows populations in selected African urban spaces are persistently exposed to pollution levels (especially particulate matter, $PM_{2.5}$) that exceed the recommended health guidelines (Gaita et al. 2014; Petkova et al. 2013; Okure et al. 2022), often higher than levels recommended by the World Health Organization (WHO 2021).

The challenge of urban air pollution is disproportionate among different urban communities, and the magnitude of the impacts can be closely associated with socioeconomic and demographic stratifications, with lower-income countries being more vulnerable to pollution exposure (Brunekreef and Holgate 2002; WHO 2018). Implicitly, localized pollution-generating activities, including open burning, domestic cooking (Liousse et al. 2014), and transportation, predominate air pollution in African cities, a progressive shift from the traditional footprint emanating from industrial activities previously experienced in developed countries. This presents unique opportunities for community-driven initiatives to tackle air pollution in fast-growing urban spaces.

To effectively tackle air pollution in African cities, city authorities, governments, the private sector, and the population must begin to see air pollution as a priority challenge. For this to happen, data and contextual evidence are required to show the scale and magnitude of air pollution as well as its impacts on urban health. Unfortunately, air pollution in many cities in Africa are undermonitored. There are very few monitoring initiatives and hence a scarcity of data on the continent, in part due to the logistic constraints of setting up and maintaining a monitoring network, coupled with the expertise to process and analyze data. Community-driven low-cost sensing initiatives such as AirQo (n.d.) provide opportunities for closing the air quality management gaps in a growing number of African cities.

This chapter presents a progressive case study of advancing community-centric and participatory air quality management in Kampala, one of Africa's fastest-growing urban centers. We highlight how stakeholder synergies from diverse interests, including academia, civil society, the private sector, and the policy arena, have harnessed data to improve the air quality management landscape in Kampala and Uganda, focusing on increased awareness and policy. Scalable models for new approaches to air quality management have the potential to revolutionize air quality management in African urban spaces, as well as in resource-strained countries where the resource basket to invest in environmental conservation is diminished by other competing priorities. The Kampala case study is a unique test case for other African cities.

First, we provide a contextual overview of the challenges of air pollution in the African context, and in Kampala as a fast urbanizing city. We then discuss the existing air quality management situation, and how a new paradigm is conceptualized within the existing institutional setting, then follow with insights of the key components from existing engagements in Kampala city. The chapter concludes with scalability prospects for policymaking and opportunities for future research to contribute to improving the understanding of air quality management in resource-strained settings in Africa.

1.1. Air Pollution in Kampala: A Brief Profile

Kampala, the capital city of Uganda, is one of the fastest-growing cities in Africa, with a population (transient and resident) of over 4.5 million and an annual urban population growth rate estimated at 5.6 percent (Uganda Bureau of Statistics 2020). The ever-growing dense population is shared by transient and residential settlements because of the distinctive social-economic activities in the city's neighboring municipalities within and outside the Greater Kampala Metropolitan Area (GKMA). The economic activities in the city span both local and international trade in goods and services. The 2019 survey report by the Uganda Bureau of Statistics (UBOS) on international trade in services indicates an annual growth in services exports of 5.8 percent (Uganda Bureau of Statistics 2020), although the majority of the population (more than 55 percent) in Kampala depends heavily on informal businesses and trade.

Uganda, like many developing economies, recognizes the importance of urbanization as a driver for socioeconomic transformation across the country. As such, the urbanization rate within the cities is compelling and evidenced by the astronomical increase in the number of local industries (e.g., GKMA accounts for over 32 percent of Uganda's manufacturing businesses) and improved road networks and economic and communication infrastructure, among other improvements. Despite fast economic growth, however, the Kampala population still suffers from challenges, such as high poverty levels, poor waste management, traffic congestion, and air pollution, among others, which exacerbate the negative impacts on the environment, the livelihood of residents, and more generally, urban health.

The city and metropolitan areas act as a nexus of Uganda's economic growth, contributing to over 30 percent of the country's gross domestic product (GDP). Essentially, Kampala is observed as a fundamental pillar for the success of Uganda's vision 2040 and the third National Development Plan (NDP III) of transforming the country from predominantly agricultural to modern and prosperous within thirty years. The enormous economic agglomeration of activities places the city at the forefront of harboring the highest pollution-generating activities and concentration in Uganda. Rapid urbanization unmatched with proper urban planning results in scattered growth and settlement patterns, creating clusters of local pollution-generating activities, resulting in localized and sectoral-driven air pollution impacts and clustered airsheds (Green et al. 2022).

Kampala air quality ($PM_{2.5}$) is estimated to be consistently 8 to 12 times the WHO annual guidelines (WHO 2021) by various studies, including Coker et al. (2021) and Okure et al. (2022), indicative of the increased health burdens from both long-term and short-term exposures. A general outlook for Kampala's air quality is shown in figure 14.1. The aggregated average $PM_{2.5}$ concentration from the air quality network in Kampala is approximately

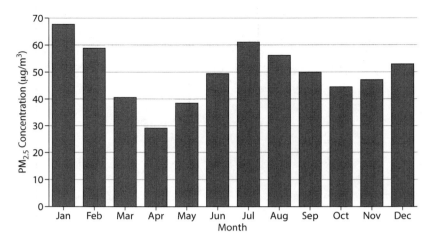

Fig. 14.1. Aggregated average monthly PM$_{2.5}$ concentration in Kampala.

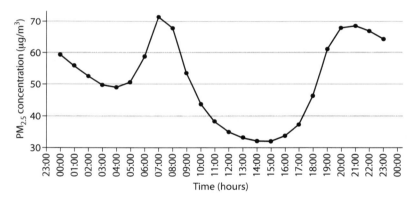

Fig. 14.2. Aggregated average diurnal PM$_{2.5}$ concentration in Kampala.

50.33 µg/m³, although there are sharp seasonal variations between 32 µg/m³ and 79 µg/m³. Higher PM$_{2.5}$ levels are generally observed in January, February, July, and December, and the lowest concentrations are observed in April, which corresponds to the dry and wet seasons, respectively. Consistent diurnal variation patterns are observed in Kampala, with higher pollution levels manifesting from 19:00 to 00:00 and from 06:00 to 09:00; while the periods from 09:00 to 17:00 have the lowest levels (figure 14.2), although this diurnal outlook is typically characteristic of PM in many cities across the world (Okure et al. 2022).

Key contributors to air pollution include domestic solid biomass burning, with over 90 percent of households depending on firewood and charcoal (CREEC 2020; Nsamba et al. 2021); outdoor waste burning; vehicle emissions; and dust from unpaved roads. While Kampala has the largest fraction of grid connections, it also remains one of the largest markets for charcoal in Uganda (Nabukalu and Gieré 2019).

2. Approaches to Air Quality Management

An explicit air quality management program that embodies a government policy framework is yet to be fully operationalized in Uganda. Because air quality is multisectoral and multifaceted, interventions have been largely through cobenefits from existing institutional, policy, and regulatory regimes relevant to urban air quality. These include advancing affordable and clean energy options; improving the national road network and traffic management systems; promoting greener mobility initiatives; establishing environmental regulations and progressive urban planning and public health policies, among others, all implemented through designated institutional establishments. Uganda's institutional framework is structured as ministries, departments, and agencies (MDAs), all aligned to specific sectors of the economy. A high-level visual overview of the existing institutional and regulatory frameworks consistent with air quality governance are shown in figure 14.3.

The Kampala Capital City Authority (KCCA) is the corporate body es-

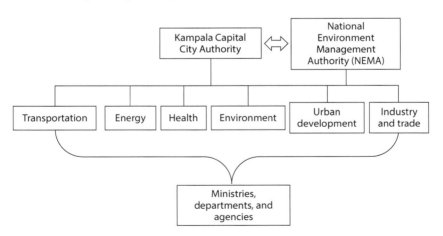

Fig. 14.3. Existing institutional landscape for air quality governance.

tablished by an act of parliament (Republic of Uganda 2019) to manage the capital city on behalf of the central government, and as such, it has the primary responsibility for managing air quality in the city; while the National Environmental Management Authority (NEMA) (Uganda Parliament 2019) is the lead agency mandated to "coordinate, regulate and supervise environmental management" nationally. In practice, NEMA works hand-in-hand with KCCA and other institutions to implement their oversight mandate.

While the current institutional framework provides avenues for improving urban air quality, an explicit regulatory framework is particularly necessary to scale up intervention initiatives and to provide adequate resources for interventions, including monitoring and evaluation, while creating opportunities for investment in air quality management.

3. Framing a New Model for City Air Quality Management: The AirQo Experience

AirQo was initiated in 2015 at Makerere University, Uganda, to close the gaps in air quality management in an African city setting. AirQo develops and deploys an end-to-end smart city air quality solution that comprises academia-government-industry-community partnerships, a locally developed air quality network built to achieve high-resolution air quality monitoring, custom community-aware digital platforms, and education and awareness. The stakeholder landscape includes decision makers and local leaders on top of the policy agenda, education establishments, civil society organizations, regulated emitters, and diplomatic missions, among others.

Community-centric and citizen science projects often fall short of combining high quality data with deep citizen engagement for policy advocacy (Van Brussel and Huyse 2019). This localized model, however, promotes leadership and community engagement, ensures focus on local issues, and offers greater prospects for sustainability and impact.

The AirQo model utilizes quality-assured air quality data and stakeholder synergies and is currently being implemented in Kampala and other cities in Uganda, as well as across selected African cities. The model particularly leverages the high convening power of air quality as a multisectoral issue to build stakeholder synergies across different interest groups. Diverse multistakeholder actions have the potential to amplify collective interventions (Ahmed and Sánchez-Triana 2008) and are consistent with the required policy levers. This scalable approach targets designated urban areas (i.e., small city or a division of a large city with populations of at least 300,000) and is conceptualized on the basis that citizen behavioral response and policy intervention are complementary and can enhance participatory policy development.

3.1. Optimized City-Specific Air Quality Monitoring Network

Varied pollution profiles from diverse and clustered sources (typical for many African cities) require a hyperlocal monitoring system for precise contextual evidence. In essence, monitoring sites should have distinct characteristics of population distribution, proximity to emission sources (e.g., domestic, industries, traffic), topography, receptors, and land use characteristics (e.g., urban, background, residential, etc.), which are considered significant for allocating optimum sites for air quality monitoring (Alsahli and Al-Harbi 2018; Raffuse et al. 2007).

First, a cloud-based artificial intelligence (AI) powered tool is deployed to provide recommendations of the probable or eligible administrative boundaries in the form of parishes. Okure et al. (2022) provides contextual details on parishes and how they fit within the administrative boundaries of Uganda. Then a multicriteria protocol is coordinated and implemented, involving diverse stakeholders, to align the proposed monitoring locations with local air quality needs, such as physical planning, legislative regimes, vulnerability risk profiles of a city, and so forth. These stakeholders are drawn from city governments, education communities (i.e., schools, advocacy groups, researchers, etc.), the private sector, and others, who contribute to prescribing additional air quality monitoring needs, including volunteering to host the devices. The proposed locations are then physically validated by the domain experts through field visits to inform the installation sites. Additional volunteers are identified and onboarded as voluntary hosts for monitoring devices; they are then engaged further to discuss the logistic requirements for installation, such as power, security, and capacity to do simple maintenance routines on the monitoring devices, such as restarting and cleaning.

Consequently, a continuous monitoring network comprising over sixty low-cost monitors and three reference monitors has been collaboratively deployed in Kampala city. Uniquely, the Kampala network includes over forty locally developed low-cost air monitors customized to the local context (Sserunjogi et al. 2022), with the capabilities to cope with the challenges of higher levels of dust, intermittent power and internet connectivity, tropical weather conditions, and other factors not seen in Northern Hemisphere settings (Coker et al. 2021; Okure et al. 2022). This addresses the technological and logistic constraints associated with most available monitoring devices, including data transmission, power, costs, and data management infrastructure. The network of low-cost sensors is routinely (monthly) calibrated against the reference grade monitors (also part of the high-resolution air quality monitoring network in the city), and deployed following the same principle, specifically to depict spatial diversity. A machine learning calibration protocol (Adong et al. 2022) with a public interface has been developed for continuous low-cost sensor calibration in Kampala and other African cities.

The Kampala monitoring network has been central in providing actionable information to raise the profile of air quality. Having a locally managed continuous data infrastructure has aided evidence-based mainstreaming of air quality management initiatives, such as the first clean air action plan for the city, making a case for investments in green mobility infrastructure, for example, the pilot nonmotorized transport corridor; providing data to inform the development of national air quality regulations and East African standards; statutory reporting of air quality through the national state of the environment report; and enhancing research and policy collaborations, among others.

3.2. Community-Aware Digital Platforms for Data Access

Awareness of air quality and the dangers of air pollution requires access to timely and reliable air quality data and information, and yet this information is not always readily available. Moreover, ordinary citizens and the general public do not have the capacity to appreciate complex datasets, which are often published long after exposure to dangerous levels of air pollution (Kosmidis et al. 2018), and there is the inherent inability to link poor air quality to individual footprints. Although open data sharing catalyzes and motivates citizen and public participation, many initiatives and prospective data providers struggle to make air quality data available to the general public and different stakeholder groups, largely attributable to the lack of robust, reliable, and accessible data management infrastructure.

The AirQo initiative has developed a custom digital platform infrastructure that attempts to address the data access challenges and to consolidate and disseminate available information on air quality in the city. These platforms are disaggregated into the data platform and dashboard as foundational infrastructure, mobile application, and website tailored to different stakeholder data needs. The digital platforms provide the ability for decision makers, for example, at city government, national, or local level, and the public to have access to actionable air quality information.

Researchers and innovators interested in air quality issues have access to the data through the dashboard and export functions, as well as programmatically through an application programming interface (API) and public-facing tools, such as air quality data visualizations, for detailed insights targeting decision makers, community leaders, stakeholders, and local "champions" who regularly engage with air quality issues. City authorities, government agencies, and decision makers are supported through periodic hands-on data access training to enhance their capacity, empower them with evidence and digital tools for air quality management, and increase data uptake for policy, while fostering advocacy to tap into the potential of citizen science.

Further access and engagement with air quality is provided through mobile channels and web tools. The AirQo air quality mobile application (the first in the African context) was developed to make air quality information available to the public and to ensure that users monitor and know the quality of the air they are breathing in order to protect themselves. The app provides timely access to air quality for the current time along with the air quality index risk level and associated advice on how to respond, depending on vulnerability. AirQo is continuously engaging various actors, including businesses, policymakers, academia, civil society organizations, and different communities to raise awareness of available resources and to deliver basic training on the interpretation of air quality information, especially using user-aware documented resources made publicly available on blogs and websites. These also act as additional outlets for disseminating information to the public, in addition to acting as central repositories for information. Employing cloud-based platforms leverages the increasing rate of internet access in Uganda (Uganda Communications Commission 2021), particularly in major urban areas, while the targeted training engagements are aimed at equipping local champions and ambassadors with basic transferable knowledge to educate their respective communities. This need-based approach is scalable and can be replicated in other African cities with similar contexts.

3.3. Education and Awareness

Limited public awareness of air pollution and its dangers remains a challenge for many urban areas in Africa, and continuous education and awareness are vital in promoting public participation and building civic competence for policy advocacy. There is universal consensus on the need to raise awareness of air pollution; for example, the European Union Air Quality Directives (Official Journal of the European Union 2005) explicitly recognize the need for deliberate dissemination of air quality information to the public by member states. The existing awareness strategy harnesses diverse stakeholder synergies with government MDAs, community-based organizations, civil society organizations (CSOs), diplomatic missions, and the private sector, among others, to raise awareness about air pollution. This is a step toward developing an African city-focused approach to public engagement to enhance participatory air quality management. Diverse media outlets and communication channels are employed to disseminate tailored information for various audiences (figure 14.4), which ensures different audiences receive timely and relevant information. This is a demand-driven model that uses existing public dissemination forums and resources on related public interest issues to ensure cost-effective and sustained campaigns. The annual air quality awareness week, which has been mainstreamed, continues to attract different key players with demonstrable roles and contributions to public health and environmental conservation.

3.4. Targeted Community and Sector-Specific Engagement

In this section, we present an example of targeted community engagement for a specific sectoral pollution driver in Uganda. This example demonstrates the scalability potential of sector-specific approaches for tackling air pollution. Community campaigns engage community members and increase awareness of the dangers of air pollution, empowering them with knowledge on actions they can take to reduce air pollution exposure. These community-led campaigns leverage community leadership structures and influential members of the community to guarantee community acceptance and ownership. The engagement sessions are held in community centers, for example, a hall, a school, or a local university, and are conducted in local languages to ensure inclusivity. These sessions are particularly tailored to address a specific pollution driver within a community, for example, waste,

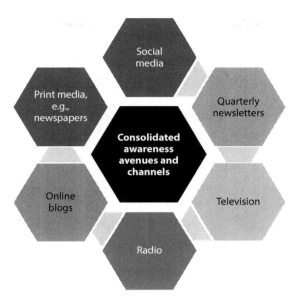

Fig. 14.4. Media and awareness avenues for disseminating tailored air quality information.

energy transport, or the like. Existing community-driven initiatives include automobile technicians in Kampala targeting the transport sector, and communities in Jinja industrial city (WEHUBIT 2022) aiming at waste and domestic energy.

3.4.1. INSIGHTS ON TACKLING TRANSPORT POLLUTION FROM THE SOURCE

Motorized transport-related pollution in Kampala comes from both exhaust and nonexhaust sources, further exacerbated by the uneven distribution of road networks, resulting in hotspots within central business districts during peak hours. Commuters along major roads and commercial centers are exposed to much higher levels of pollution relative to recommended health guidelines (Okure et al. 2022).

Although there is no precise estimate on the fleet database within Kampala, fourteen-seater commercial buses (taxis) and motorcycles (*boda*) could constitute over 75 percent of the daily rides (KCCA 2018), and the annual growth rate of traffic is over 11 percent (Ministry of Works and Transport 2009, 2010). These are largely preowned vehicles, often with a poor maintenance history. In attempting to directly address aspects of transport pollution, we implemented an engagement strategy targeting automobile technicians (mechanics) and synergized with a community-based organization (Wanyama AutoSafety) and the Ministry of Works and Transport—a government sector leader on top of the policy agenda. Vehicle maintenance practices in Kampala and in many African cities are largely informal; most mechanics learn on the job from other experienced colleagues, who would have also learned on the job, and so on. Very few attain formal education and therefore lack textbook skills on best practices for vehicle maintenance, and yet maintenance practices have a direct impact on motorized air pollution. These technicians form an integral part of a unique constituency because of the power and influence they wield within the sector, that is, "every driver in town has their mechanic," and therefore, they can be an important part of the intervention puzzle.

We targeted eighty mechanics aged between 16 and 35 who were recruited from Makindye Division, with the aim of building a community of champions and ambassadors for the sector. Makindye Division is one of the five urban divisions of Kampala, with a population of about 400,000 settled in twenty-one parishes and 884 villages over an area of 49 km². The key research objectives explored were (1) increasing awareness of air quality and improving understanding of pollution risks by involving the community in the scientific experience; (2) inducing a change in opinion about the benefits of sustainable maintenance practices and mobility options; and (3) generating contextual evidence for policy while building the civic competence of mechanics for advocacy.

Four focus group discussions were conducted with fifty-one mechanics, comprising leaders and representatives from selected automobile workshops. This was done to generate consensus on the dangers of air pollution and to understand the knowledge landscape on motorized air pollution. Two training sessions were then conducted with all eighty mechanics recruited to (1) provide understanding of the basics and the dangers of air pollution and how to access air quality data for action; (2) equip participants with the knowledge of inbuilt emissions control systems and the benefits of best maintenance practices; (3) understand the regulatory implications of transport emissions and opportunities for standardization; and (4) collaboratively develop a policy brief as a toolkit for institutionalized continual engagement of mechanics on sustainable vehicle maintenance for pollution control.

4. Conclusion: Transforming Air Quality Management in Uganda and Africa

This chapter advances the need for a community-aware and data-driven approach to air quality management in African cities, using Kampala as a test case. The work presented draws from the experience of AirQo building an end-to-end air quality management framework involving different players, disciplines, and stakeholder engagement. Such engagement should include at least four major objectives: (1) to establish city-specific partnerships and policy engagement, (2) to deploy an inclusive air quality network, (3) to build community-aware digital platforms, and (4) to boost citizen-centric air quality education and awareness. Central to this is the use of data and evidence approaches. Technology advances from the Internet of Things, machine learning, and data science have made it possible to collect data at granular levels not possible previously. Data science methods have made it possible to create insights that help set the prioritization agenda for air quality issues and guide feasible actions and target health outcomes for African cities.

The air quality network has catalyzed air quality research, increased the body of evidence on air quality in indoor and outdoor spaces, and increased public awareness and advocacy on the health impacts of air pollutants. These platforms enabled a wide range of initiatives, from correlation studies of low-cost particulate matter ($PM_{2.5}$) monitors, which have been used to develop scalable calibration protocols against gravimetric or reference monitors, to targeted citizen science projects focused on city communities, for example, automobile technicians in Kampala and communities in Jinja industrial city. The air quality information, including forecasting air pollution levels, has been disseminated to citizens through various digital channels. Through data, the city of Kampala is on a pathway to mainstreaming evidence-informed actions, and one of the long-term goals is to scale up utilization of continuous data and evidence to support the development of rigorous evidence-based national and supranational public health policies, as well as locally based interventions like creating lower emission zones in cities, fleet regulation, and so forth.

The work presented in this chapter serves as a foundation for other disciplines to contribute new knowledge and solutions to air pollution challenges. Further studies are needed on the impact of air pollution on health outcomes specific to urban spaces and households, as well as long-term impacts on economic outcomes and other attributes of quality of life. Education and awareness require future studies on effective methods to effectively monitor community air pollution and achieve sustainable behavior change. The monitoring scope also needs to be further broadened to cover sector-specific criteria pollutants beyond particulate matter.

Beyond informing formulation of regulations, air quality initiatives such as AirQo need to be sustained for a long term to measure the progress made on air quality improvement and the urban health benefits realized. Last, adopting a holistic paradigm that links all facets of tackling air pollution has the potential to accelerate action through increased awareness and participatory and inclusive advocacy; strengthening collaborations and stakeholder synergies; and improving institutional capacity for targeted interventions and policy mainstreaming. This scalable model is a great step toward building an Africa-focused solution for air quality management.

Acknowledgments

We appreciate the feedback and discussions from the AirQo team and partners from government, academia, the private sector, and civil society. We also acknowledge our formal partnerships with lead government institutions, including KCCA, NEMA, Ministry of Works and Transport, and Ministry of Lands, Housing and Urban Development, that contribute to supporting air quality research in Kampala; as well as contributions from data providers, including the Trans-African Hydro-Meteorological Observatory, AutoSafety Uganda, and the US Mission in Kampala. This work was supported by Google.org grant 1904-57882; EPSRC/GCRF grant EP/T00343X/1; Belgium through the Wehubit program implemented by Enabel Wehubit Grant Agreement BEL1707111-AP-05-2; International Development Research Centre, Ottawa, Canada, and the Swedish International Development Cooperation Agency Grant No.109630-001/002; and the US Mission grant SUG50021CA3041.

REFERENCES

Adong, Priscilla, Engineer Bainomugisha, Deo Okure, and Richard Sserunjogi. 2022. "Applying Machine Learning for Large Scale Field Calibration of Low-Cost $PM_{2.5}$ and PM_{10} Air Pollution Sensors." *Applied AI Letters* 3 (3): 1–16. https://doi.org/10.1002/ail2.76.

Ahmed, Kulsum, and Ernesto Sánchez-Triana, eds. 2008. *Strategic Environmental Assessment for Policies: An Instrument for Good Governance*. Environment and Development series. Washington, DC: World Bank.

AirQo. n.d. "Clean Air for All African Cities." Accessed June 21, 2024. https://www.airqo.africa/.

Alsahli, Mohammad M., and Meshari Al-Harbi. 2018. "Allocating Optimum Sites for Air Quality Monitoring Stations Using GIS Suitability Analysis." *Urban Climate* 24:875–86. https://doi.org/10.1016/j.uclim.2017.11.001.

Brunekreef, Bert, and Stephen T. Holgate. 2002. "Air Pollution and Health." *Lancet* 360 (9341): 1233–42. https://doi.org/10.1016/S0140-6736(02)11274-8.

Coker, Eric S., A. Kofi Amegah, Ernest Mwebaze, Joel Ssematimba, and Engineer Bainomugisha. 2021. "A Land Use Regression Model Using Machine Learning and Locally Developed Low Cost Particulate Matter Sensors in Uganda." *Environmental Research* 199:111352. https://doi.org/10.1016/j.envres.2021.111352.

CREEC (Centre for Research in Energy and Energy Conservation). 2020. "Cooking with Electricity in Uganda: Barriers and Opportunities." MECS Programme Working Paper, September.

Gaita, S. M., J. Boman, M. J. Gatari, J. B. C. Pettersson, and S. Janhäll. 2014. "Source Apportionment and Seasonal Variation of $PM_{2.5}$ in a Sub-Saharan African City: Nairobi, Kenya." *Atmospheric Chemistry and Physics* 14 (18): 9977–91. https://doi.org/10.5194/acp-14-9977-2014.

Green, Paul, Deo Okure, Priscilla Adong, Richard Sserunjogi, and Engineer Bainomugisha. 2022. "Exploring $PM_{2.5}$ Variations from a Low-Cost Sensor Network in Greater Kampala, during COVID-19 Imposed Lockdown Restrictions: Lessons for Policy." *Clean Air Journal* 32 (1): 1–14. https://doi.org/10.17159/caj/2022/32/1.10906.

KCCA (Kapala Capital City Authority). 2018. "Public Transport a Challenge: Does KCCA Care?" KCCA, September 10, 2018. https://www.kcca.go.ug/news/308/#.YwvON3ZBy3A.

Kosmidis, Evangelos, Panagiota Syropoulou, Stavros Tekes, Philipp Schneider, Eleftherios Spyromitros-Xioufis, Marina Riga, Polychronis Charitidis, et al. 2018. "HackAIR: Towards Raising Awareness about Air Quality in Europe by Developing a Collective Online Platform." *ISPRS International Journal of Geo-Information* 7 (5): 187. https://doi.org/10.3390/ijgi7050187.

Liousse, C., E. Assamoi, P. Criqui, C. Granier, and R. Rosset. 2014. "Explosive Growth in African Combustion Emissions from 2005 to 2030." *Environmental Research Letters* 9 (3): 0350003. https://doi.org/10.1088/1748-9326/9/3/035003.

Ministry of Works and Transport. 2009. *National Transport Master Plan Including a Transport Master Plan for the Greater Kampala Metropolitan Area (NTMP GKMA)*. Kampala, Uganda: Ministry of Works and Transport.

Ministry of Works and Transport. 2010. *The Study on Greater Kampala Road Network and Transport Improvement in the Republic of Uganda: Final Report Executive Summary*. Kampala, Uganda: Ministry of Works and Transport.

Nabukalu, Catherine, and Reto Gieré. 2019. "Charcoal as an Energy Resource: Global Trade, Production and Socioeconomic Practices Observed in Uganda." *Resources* 8 (4): 1–27. https://doi.org/10.3390/RESOURCES8040183.

Nsamba, Hussein Kisiki, Robert Ssali, Sarah N. Ssali, Fahad Matovu, John Wasswa, and Hussein Kivumbi Balimunsi. 2021. "Evaluation of the Cooking Cultures and Practices in Rural Uganda." *Journal of Sustainable Bioenergy Systems* 11 (1): 33–44. https://doi.org/10.4236/jsbs.2021.111003.

Official Journal of the European Union. 2005. "Directive 2004/107/EC of the European Parliament and of the Council of 15/12/2004 Relating to Arsenic, Cadmium, Mercury, Nickel and Polycyclic Aromatic Hydrocarbons in Ambient Air." *Official Journal of the European Union* 23 (3): 3–16.

Okure, Deo, Joel Ssematimba, Richard Sserunjogi, Nancy Lozano Gracia, Maria Edisa Soppelsa, and Engineer Bainomugisha. 2022. "Characterization of Ambient Air Quality in Selected Urban Areas in Uganda Using Low-Cost Sensing and Measurement Technologies." *Environmental Science and Technology* 56 (6): 3324–39. https://doi.org/10.1021/acs.est.1c01443.

Petkova, Elisaveta P., Darby W. Jack, Nicole H. Volavka-Close, and Patrick L. Kinney. 2013. "Particulate Matter Pollution in African Cities." *Air Quality, Atmosphere and Health* 6 (3): 603–14. https://doi.org/10.1007/s11869-013-0199-6.

Raffuse, Sean M., Dana C. Sullivan, Michael C. McCarthy, Bryan M. Penfold, Hilary R. Hafner, and Sonoma Technology. 2007. *Ambient Air Monitoring Network Assessment Guidance*. Research Triangle Park, NC: US EPA Air Quality Assessment Division.

Roy, Rana. 2016. "The Cost of Air Pollution in Africa." OECD Development Centre Working Paper No. 333. OECD Publishing, Paris.

Sserunjogi, Richard, Joel Ssematimba, Deo Okure, Daniel Ogenrwot, Priscilla Adong, Lillian Muyama, Noah Nsimbe, and Martin Bbaale. 2022. "Seeing the Air in Detail: Hyperlocal Air Quality Dataset Collected from Spatially Distributed AirQo Network." *Data in Brief* 44:108512. https://doi.org/10.1016/j.dib.2022.108512.

Republic of Uganda. 2019. *The Kampala Capital City (Amendment) Act, 2019*. Kampala: Republic of Uganda. https://www.kcca.go.ug/media/docs/KCCA-Amendement-Act-2019.pdf.

Uganda Bureau of Statistics. 2020. *The Uganda National Household Survey*. Uganda National Survey Report 2019/2020. Kampala: Uganda Bureau of Statistics.

Uganda Communications Commission. 2021. *Market Performance Report*. Kampala: Uganda Communications Commission.

Uganda Gazette. 2019. "The National Environment Act 2019." *Uganda Gazette* 111 (10): 1–178.

Van Brussel, Suzanne, and Huib Huyse. 2019. "Citizen Science on Speed? Realising the Triple Objective of Scientific Rigour, Policy Influence and Deep Citizen Engagement in a Large-Scale Citizen Science Project on Ambient Air Quality in Antwerp." *Journal of Environmental Planning and Management* 62 (3): 534–51. https://doi.org/10.1080/09640568.2018.1428183.

Wehubit. 2022. "Helping Communities Combat Air Pollution through Digital Technologies." Wehubit, July.

WHO (World Health Organization). 2018. "9 out of 10 People Worldwide Breathe Polluted Air, but More Countries Are Taking Action." WHO news release, May 2.

WHO (World Health Organization). 2021. *WHO Global Air Quality Guidelines*. Geneva: WHO.

15

Case Study of Mental Health, Illness, and Resources in Yaoundé, Cameroon

Michael Guy Toguem and Barnard Christian Bela Zomo

1. Introduction

In 2013, mental health was made a priority at the World Health Assembly through the Global Action Plan for Mental Health. This priority was reinforced in 2016 by the introduction of mental health–related goals in the Sustainable Development Agenda (Okasha 2002; Sankoh, Sevalie, and Weston 2018). Since then, the Cameroon government has taken several steps to achieve these goals.

Cameroon is a lower-middle-income country located in Central Africa, with a population of 26.55 million (World Bank Group, n.d.; World Data 2024). The country is divided into ten regions, with Yaoundé as the political capital and Douala as the economic capital (Presidency of the Republic of Cameroon, n.d.).

2. Mental Health Services in Yaoundé

Mental illness is defined in this chapter as "a clinically significant alteration in thinking, emotional regulation, or behavior" (WHO 2022). Symptoms tend to vary for different conditions but might include hallucinations, hopelessness, and impulsive reckless behavior (WHO 2001). The history of conventional mental health service in Cameroon dates back to 1974 with the creation of a psychiatric unit at the Jamot Hospital in Yaoundé and a second one at Hôpital Laquintinie de Douala. Since then, two important milestones have been reached in mental health services in Yaoundé and in Cameroon as a whole. The first milestone was in 2015 when Cameroon's Ministry of Public Health launched the country's first-ever Mental Health Days from December 15 to 17. The Ministry of Public Health acknowledged Cameroonians who experience mental disorders and the need for a national strategy to address the mental health needs of the population. This was followed by the inclusion of some psychiatric illnesses in the minimum package of health coverage, the introduction of psychiatric courses into the training of health professionals, the training of psychologists and psychiatrists at the University of Yaounde 1; and the publication of the first-ever mental health legislation and plan in 2016 (Demassosso 2021; Toguem, Christian, and Fotso 2022).

The second milestone came in 2020, paradoxically with COVID-19, which emphasized the need for psychological support for those isolated due to the pandemic. This prompted the government to recruit and place psychologists, mental health nurses, and psychiatrists at the forefront of managing the psychological issues associated with COVID-19 (Mviena et al. 2020). A hotline was established, with telephone counseling provided to those with psychological distress related to COVID-19 and any other persons in need. In addition, public psychiatric services were expanded in the country. In the western region, a psychiatric nursing school was created, and the psychiatric units were expanded to six of the twenty health districts of the region (Toguem, Christian, and Fotso 2022). Psychiatric services also expanded to include people with mental illnesses living on the streets of Yaoundé. The Yaoundé councils adopted the initiative in 2021 to provide treatment to people with severe mental illness who live on the streets and to reunite them with their families for social reintegration (Heles 2021). So far, fewer people with mental illness are on the streets, but the sources of funding for this intervention and its expected duration of implementation are unclear.

These initiatives and services demonstrate that leaders in Yaoundé are gradually understanding the importance of mental health and disorders. Meanwhile, there is a need to understand the interplay between culture, the urban environment, and perceptions of mental health by residents of Yaoundé to be able to implement effective interventions. In this chapter, we explore the aforementioned concept, as well as the challenges and the policies that can be implemented to improve mental health in Yaoundé.

3. What Does Mental Health Mean to an Everyday Person in Yaoundé?

The people of Yaoundé, like most Africans, have grown up in a culture that is less individualistic and more collectivist compared to countries in the West (Oluwatoyin Folayan et al. 2020). This community-oriented culture emphasizes shared traditional beliefs. It tends to prioritize society over the self and society's expectations over the needs of the self (Tirupati and Ramachandran 2020). While community-oriented culture has many benefits, it also presents some challenges, especially in regard to considering mental well-being, which requires a greater sense of self and in some cases the prioritization of self over community.

Some traditional beliefs also consider abnormal behavior to be a choice to misbehave or a consequence of evil spirits. This is why when a person presents with symptoms of mental illness, the first people usually consulted in Yaoundé are the clerics and the traditional healers. The patients are sometimes blamed for their condition because they are assumed to have joined a cult. Sometimes someone else is blamed for the illness because they are considered a wizard. This practice of blaming can lead to emotional and physical abuse (Tanyuy et al. 2021).

To date, little effort has been made to raise awareness about mental illnesses, substance use, or suicide in Yaoundé. This is due in part to the small number of mental health services and mental health professionals. Yaoundé has the highest number of psychiatrists in the country: ten for 4 million people, followed by the city of Douala, which has three psychiatrists for 4 million people. In the western region of Cameroon, in 2020, there were 1.87 mental health workers per 100,000 population (Toguem, Christian, and Fotso 2022). A lack of awareness and information on mental health and disorders creates an opening for misinformation, which reinforces stigma. Stigma creates more barriers for the few people with mental disorders who want professional help and increases the burden of the illness for those receiving treatment (Dubreucq, Plasse, and Franck 2021).

4. Mental Health Services

To change misconceptions about mental illness, mental health services need to include mental health promotion and awareness. The city of Yaoundé has ten psychiatrists, or one psychiatrist per 400,000 inhabitants, all of whom are civil servants. These psychiatrists provide clinical psychiatry, teaching, research, and administrative functions and are often called on to intervene in other cities since Yaoundé remains by far the city with the highest number of psychiatrists in the country.

Furthermore, the city has only one school that trains psychiatrists: the

Faculty of Health Sciences of the University of Yaoundé 1, with an average of one to two students per year, and some leave the country after graduation. This school is also the only one in the country. Two schools train psychologists: the Faculty of Arts, Letters and Humanities of the University of Yaoundé 1 and the Institute de formation aux professions de la psychologie. And four schools train psychiatric nurses.

General practitioners in Douala, who are representative of general practitioners in the country, are unable to identify and manage depressive disorders (Toguem, Christian, and Fotso 2019) because they do not perform any rotations in a psychiatry unit during training (Ministry of Higher Education 2015).

Although mental health services have expanded in Yaoundé in recent years, two main barriers to care remain: affordability and stigma (World Bank Group 2013). To partially address this issue, on May 5, 2021, the Department of Mental Health at the Ministry of Public Health started implementing community- and hospital-based care for mentally ill and wandering people in the city. The project is funded by the Yaoundé City Council and involves reaching people in the community to educate them about mental illnesses and to treat diagnosed cases. The impact of this intervention on the population's perception of mental illnesses is still to be measured. We are seeing, however, that some people are beginning to change their perceptions and behaviors toward relatives with mental illness. This mainly happens when they observe some signs of recovery from the illness. Family members usually wish they had come to the hospital sooner (Tsiele 2021). There is no shared social security insurance in Yaoundé, however, which creates obstacles to seeking early medical care. The only insurance available is private insurance based on the payment of a premium, which covered 2 percent of the Cameroonian population in 2015 (Sigu 2015). Some private insurance covers mental disorders.

The penal, civic, and family code has made certain provisions to protect the rights of persons who are living with a mental illness or may have an episodic alteration of their mental state. For example, chapter 2, articles 78 and 79, of the penal code states that a person with a mental illness, including a person acting under the influence of a substance, given that the ingestion of the substance was under duress or without the ingesting person being aware that they were taking a substance, may have his or her criminal liability waived or mitigated. In chapter 2, article 489 of the civil code, which deals with the age of majority, it is stated that an adult who is in a habitual state of imbecility, insanity, or fury shall be prohibited from the civilian liabilities of adulthood, even if that person has intervals of lucidity (Toguem, Christian, and Fotso 2022). Meanwhile enforcing these laws is very hard with the few numbers of mental health professionals.

Even though the topic of mental health is relatively new in the city of Yaoundé, there is a universal culture of aspiration for a better life. This applies to anything that can improve quality of life, from community infrastructure to health, education, food security, and so on. Below are some of the factors that can impact the mental health of Yaoundé's citizens (WHO 2014).

5. Housing

In Yaoundé, 60 percent of the population live in slums, and more than 80 percent of the people living in Yaoundé are classified as poor (UN-Habitat, n.d.). Living in slums has been associated with a higher risk of mental health problems, such as depression, anxiety disorders, and substance use, which contributes to keeping these individuals in poverty and adversity (UNODC 2020). In the city of Ouagadougou, Burkina Faso, West Africa, Duthé and colleagues reported that the citizens with the poorest living conditions were those most likely to develop a major depressive episode (Duthé et al. 2016).

6. Education

The school enrollment rate between the ages of 6 and 18 is 84 percent, with a sex ratio of 1.03 in favor of women. For those who do not attend school, high school fees are the reason (National Institute of Statistics, 2018; World Food Programme 2017). This means that those who do not attend school are likely to come from poor backgrounds, which implies that they are likely to experience poverty and all the negative health and mental health consequences of poverty (WHO 2014).

7. Food Security

In 2017, 2.7 percent of the population of Yaoundé was food insecure, and 38.3 percent reduced their food consumption in response to food shortages (World Food Programme 2017). This figure is expected to have increased as a result of the decrease in purchasing power that stemmed from the

COVID-19 pandemic. In addition, the war in Ukraine has increased the cost of producing and importing food and oil. Given that most people in Yaoundé get their food from the market, food insecurity is a major threat to households in the city (National Institute of Statistics 2018). Findings suggests that food insecurity can negatively affect mental health. The mental alteration is higher with a higher level of food insecurity, and the effect can be chronic. It can lead to mental illnesses such as depressive disorders and anxiety disorders (Naicker, Mathee, and Teare 2015; Trudell et al. 2021). To address this, the Cameroon government has decided to limit food exports and fund fish farming. The effect of this measure needs to be assessed, however, as the cost of food has not yet returned to what it was before 2022 (Tjeg 2022).

8. Major Adverse Life Events

During 2017, 81.8 percent of Yaoundé households experienced shocks. This included 2.2 percent who experienced erratic rainfall or drought, 11.2 percent flooding, 11.2 percent crop or livestock diseases or pests, 7 percent damaged houses, 49.4 percent illness or death of a household member, 48.7 percent loss of job or income, 51 percent increased food prices, 2.2 percent increased prices or lower access to credit, 4.9 percent insecurity, and 12.8 percent other (World Food Programme 2017). In South Africa, Williams and colleagues noted that adverse life events increased psychological distress. The effect was cumulative and proportionate to the magnitude of the adverse event (Williams et al. 2007). These shocks can lead to depressive disorders and post-traumatic stress disorders, and they can limit access to health services, as one must pay out of pocket (WHO 2014).

One of the reasons people lose their homes is destruction by the council of Yaoundé. This usually happens because of construction in unauthorized or environmentally risky areas, or as a necessity for infrastructure projects. Poorer neighborhoods are more affected and are often not relocated, which can affect the mental well-being of those residents (Kaze 2020). On the other hand, to address the housing crisis in Yaoundé, the government has built several social housing units. Their entry price on the market is 10 million CFA francs. Some people buy several and resell them on a secondary market at a higher price. The minimum monthly salary is 36,270 CFA francs, and the minimum cost of building a new home is 12 million CFA francs, which can be afforded by only 4.4 percent of the Cameroonian population (CAHF 2019;

Happi 2021; Republic of Cameroon 2014). Clearly these social housing units, as currently structured by the government, cannot reach their target population, which keeps those in need of housing in the same living conditions.

9. Crimes

In 2017, 4.9 percent of Yaoundé residents experienced a security threat (World Food Programme 2017). These included assaults and armed banditry, ritual crimes, and criminal food poisoning, which caused several deaths. The city's poorer neighborhoods tend to have higher incidences of crime, in a context where poverty continues to increase in the country (GOV. UK, n.d.; World Bank Group 2024). Violence usually occurs as a consequence of intoxication and substance use (UNODC 2020). Injected drugs can lead to other health conditions, including blood-borne diseases such as HIV, hepatitis B, and hepatitis C when contaminated material is used. The government has taken steps to address this by collaborating with the United Nations Office on Drugs and Crime (UNODC) in the AIRCOP project, which aims to eliminate drug trafficking in Cameroon (UNODC 2016, n.d.).

Based on a systematic review and meta-analysis on the social determinants of gender-based violence in sub-Saharan Africa, Muluneh and colleagues (2021) noted alcohol and other substance use to be among the factors responsible for gender-based violence. Alcohol consumption is a major problem in Cameroon, with 8.9 liters of pure alcohol consumed per capita in 2016 (WHO 2018). One in three pregnant women consume alcohol during pregnancy (Kingsley et al. 2018). There is no awareness of the risk of this behavior. In Yaoundé, there is a positive culture built around alcohol, which is sometimes considered a treatment for certain diseases, good for health, and a good additive for cooked foods. To address all of this, it is necessary to have an alcohol and drug policy, which is not available in Cameroon (Toguem, Christian, and Fotso 2022). There is also no rehabilitation center for substance use in Yaoundé. The government initiated the building of a rehabilitation unit in the city and in all ten regions of the country, but these are still pending (Lietbouo 2019).

10. Conclusion

Since 2015, the government has made mental health a priority in Cameroon. There are several good initiatives but they suffer insufficiencies, including a lack of coordination of efforts, scientific evidence to support the activities, and culturally sensitive interventions, as well as the attrition of skilled mental health workers in the country (WHO 2001).

To be more effective and efficient, the city needs to conduct scientific studies to assess the burden of mental illnesses in Yaoundé, to understand the prevalence of different conditions, and to define the interventions needed and the indicators that can be used to monitor impact. Similar studies helped to significantly improve the mental health system in Southeast Asia using tools provided by WHO, such as WHO-AIMS (Sharan, Sagar, and Kumar 2017). By defining the indicators and the tools needed, stakeholders can then project the burden in the future, define the resources required, and determine how to address the identified issues. Doing so will include developing a drug and alcohol policy, finding ways to retain and make use of the psychiatrists trained in Yaoundé, and involve all other sectors whose actions affect the mental health of citizens, such as urban planners, educators, law enforcement, the food industry, and religious leaders. Mental wellness should be actively promoted with culturally sensitive messages. The services can be made accessible to the poor by creating a social security fund (WHO 2001).

REFERENCES

CAHF (Centre for Affordable Housing Finance in Africa). 2019. "Understanding Housing Finance Markets in Cameroon: 2019." CAHF, May 1. https://housingfinanceafrica.org/documents/understanding-housing-finance-markets-in-cameroon-2019/.

Demassosso, Didier. 2021. "Reflecting on Four Leaps in Mental Health Development in Cameroon." *Global Mental Health*, July 21. https://globalmentalhealth.ucsf.edu/news/reflecting-four-leaps-mental-health-development-cameroon.

Dubreucq, Julien, Julien Plasse, and Nicolas Franck. 2021. "Self-Stigma in Serious Mental Illness: A Systematic Review of Frequency, Correlates, and Consequences." *Schizophrenia Bulletin* 47 (5): 1261–87. https://doi.org/10.1093/schbul/sbaa181.

Duthé, Géraldine, Clémentine Rossier, Doris Bonnet, Abdramane Bassiahi Soura, and Jamaica Corker. 2016. "Mental Health and Urban Living in Sub-Saharan Africa: Major Depressive Episodes among the Urban Poor in Ouagadougou, Burkina Faso." *Population Health Metrics* 14:18. https://pophealthmetrics.biomedcentral.com/articles/10.1186/s12963-016-0084-2.

GOV.UK. n.d. "Foreign Travel Advice: Cameroon." GOV.UK. Accessed February 20, 2023. https://www.gov.uk/foreign-travel-advice/cameroon/safety-and-security.

Happi, Christian. 2021. "Logements sociaux: le gouvernement travaille à revoir ces prix à la baisse." *Actu Cameroun* (blog), July 1. https://actucameroun.com/2021/07/01/logements-sociaux-le-gouvernement-travaille-a-revoir-ces-prix-a-la-baisse/.

Happi, Christian. 2022. "Lutte contre la vie chère: le gouvernement rend 'obligatoire' le dépôt préalable des barèmes de prix de certains produits." *Actu Cameroun* (blog), April

18. https://actucameroun.com/2022/04/18/lutte-contre-la-vie-chere-le-gouvernement-rend-obligatoire-le-depot-prealable-des-baremes-de-prix-de-certains-produits/.

Heles, Augustine Stéphanie. 2021. "Hôpital Jamot: la Mairie de la ville de Yaoundé prend en charge une centaine de malades mentaux." Communauté Urbaine de Yaoundé, December 30. https://yaounde.cm/wpsite/2021/12/30/hopital-jamot-la-mairie-de-la-ville-de-yaounde-prend-en-charge-une-centaine-de-malades-mentaux/.

Kaze, Béatrice. 2020. "Cameroun: Yaoundé ordonne déguerpissements." Coalition Internationale de l'Habitat, September 9. https://hlrn.org/french/activitydetails.php?id=pnBqZg==.

Kingsley, Tekuh Achu, A. Ndalam, J. Dissongo, M. Ekono, A. Dieudonne, and Y. Jacques. 2018. "Epidemiological Profile of Drugs Use Habits among Pregnant Women in Yaoundé Cameroon: The Case of Alcohol and Tobacco." *International Journal of Public Health and Safety* 3 (3): 1000161.

Lietbouo, Alain Georges. 2019. "Cameroun: le gouvernement en action pour lutter contre la drogue (REPORTAGE)." *French News*, June 26. http://french.xinhuanet.com/2019-06/26/c_138175884.htm.

Ministry of Higher Education. 2015. *Programmes harmonisés de la filière médicale au Cameroun*. Yaoundé, Cameroon: Republic of Cameroon Ministry of Higher Education. http://www.fmsb-uninet.cm/wp-content/uploads/2016/05/Programme-Medical.pdf.

Muluneh, Muluken Dessalegn, Lyn Francis, Kingsley Agho, and Virginia Stulz. 2021. "A Systematic Review and Meta-Analysis of Associated Factors of Gender-Based Violence against Women in Sub-Saharan Africa." *International Journal of Environmental Research and Public Health* 18 (9): 4407. https://doi.org/10.3390/ijerph18094407.

Mviena, Justine Laure Menguene, Mahamat Fanne, Rumbidzai Gondo, Ambele Judith Mwamelo, Linda Esso, Emilienne Epée, Georges Alain Etoundi Mballa, and Yap Boum. 2020. "How Mental Health Care Is Changing in Cameroon because of the COVID-19 Pandemic." *Lancet Psychiatry* 7 (10): e62–63. https://doi.org/10.1016/S2215-0366(20)30390-4.

Naicker, Nisha, Angie Mathee, and June Teare. 2015. "Food Insecurity in Households in Informal Settlements in Urban South Africa." *South African Medical Journal* 105 (4): 268–70. https://doi.org/10.7196/samj.8927.

Nguini, Aline Florence. 2022. "Lutte contre la vie chère: Le gouvernement va booster la filière poisson." Cameroon Radio Television, March 22. https://www.crtv.cm/2022/03/lutte-contre-la-vie-chere-le-gouvernement-va-booster-la-filiere-poisson/.

Okasha, Ahmed. 2002. "Mental Health in Africa: The Role of the WPA." *World Psychiatry* 1 (1): 32–35. https://www.ncbi.nlm.nih.gov/pmc/articles/PMC1489826/.

Oluwatoyin Folayan, Morenike, Brandon Brown, Bridget Haire, Chinedum Peace Babalola, and Nicaise Ndembi. 2020. "Considerations for Stakeholder Engagement and COVID-19 Related Clinical Trials' Conduct in Sub-Saharan Africa." *Developing World Bioethics* 21 (1): 1–54. https://doi.org/10.1111/dewb.12283.

Presidency of the Republic of Cameroon. n.d. "Presentation of Cameroon." Presidency of the Republic of Cameroon.Accessed June 21, 2024. https://www.prc.cm/en/cameroon/presentation.

Republic of Cameroon. 2014. *Décret n° 2014/2217/PM du 24 juillet 2014 portant revalorisation* du Salaire Minimum Interprofessionnel Garanti (SMIG). Republic of Cameroon, Prime Minister's Office, July 24. https://www.spm.gov.cm/site/?q=fr/content/d%C3%A9cret-n%C2%B0-20142217pm-du-24-juillet-2014-portant-revalorisation-du-salaire-minimum.

Sankoh, Osman, Stephen Sevalie, and Mark Weston. 2018. "Mental Health in Africa." *Lancet Global Health* 6 (9): e954–55. https://doi.org/10.1016/S2214-109X(18)30303-6.

Sharan, Pratap, Rajesh Sagar, and Saurabh Kumar. 2017. "Mental Health Policies in South-East Asia and the Public Health Role of Screening Instruments for Depression." *WHO South-East Asia Journal of Public Health* 6 (1): 5. https://doi.org/10.4103/2224-3151.206165.

Sigu, Marjorie. 2015. "Moins de 2% des Camerounais ont une assurance maladie." Assurland.com, June 29 https://www.assurland.com/mutuelle-sante/actualites/moins-de-2-des-camerounais-ont-une-assurance-maladie_124473.html.

Tanyuy, Colins B., Chinyere M. Aguocha, Emeka C. Nwefoh, and Mispar G. Wankam. 2021. "Social Representation of Abuse of Persons with Severe Mental Illness in Jakiri, Cameroon: A Qualitative Study." *International Journal of Social Psychiatry* 67 (7): 946–54. https://doi.org/10.1177/0020764020972432.

Tirupati, Srinivasan, and Padmavati Ramachandran. 2020. "Schizophrenia, Recovery and the Individual-Cultural Considerations." *Australasian Psychiatry* 28 (2): 190–92. https://doi.org/10.1177/1039856219889320.

Tjeg, Paul. 2022. "Lutte contre la vie chère: le Cameroun limite les exportations de certains produits pour satisfaire la demande nationale." *EcoMatin* (blog), April 27. https://ecomatin.net/lutte-contre-la-vie-chere-le-cameroun-limite-les-exportations-de-certains-produits-pour-satisfaire-la-demande-nationale/.

Toguem, Michaël Guy, Eyoum Christian, and Jean-Baptiste Djemo Fotso. 2019. "Comportement des médecins généralistes de la ville de Douala au Cameroun face aux troubles dépressifs." *Pan African Medical Journal* 34:37. https://doi.org/10.11604/pamj.2019.34.37.16715.

Toguem, Michael Guy, Manasi Kumar, David Ndetei, Francois Erero Njiengwe, and Frederick Owiti. 2022. "A Situational Analysis of the Mental Health System of the West Region of Cameroon Using the World Health Organization's Assessment Instrument for Mental Health Systems (WHO-AIMS)." *International Journal of Mental Health Systems* 16 (1): 18. https://doi.org/10.1186/s13033-022-00528-9.

Trudell, John Paul, Maddison L. Burnet, Bianca R. Ziegler, and Isaac Luginaah. 2021. "The Impact of Food Insecurity on Mental Health in Africa: A Systematic Review." *Social Science and Medicine* 278:113953. https://doi.org/10.1016/j.socscimed.2021.113953.

Tsiele, Carine. 2021. "Malades Mentaux Errants: Yaoundé s'organise." *Société*, May 7. https://www.cameroon-tribune.cm/article.html/39831/fr.html/malades-mentaux-errants-yaounde-sorganise.

UN-Habitat. n.d. "Cameroon." UN-Habitat. Accessed June 21, 2024. https://unhabitat.org/cameroon.

UNODC (UN Office on Drugs and Crime). 2015. "Launch of the AIRCOP Project in Cameroon." UNODC, September.https://www.unodc.org/westandcentralafrica/en/aircop---cameroon-launch.html.

UNODC (UN Office on Drugs and Crime). 2016. "L'ONUDC lance deux cellules aéroportuaires anti-trafics à Yaoundé et Douala." UNODC, October 6.https://www.unodc.org/westandcentralafrica/fr/2016_10_14_aircop-cameroon-cells.html.

UNODC (UN Office on Drugs and Crime). 2020. *Socioeconomic Characteristics and Drug Use Disorders*. World Drug Report 2020. New York: UNODC. https://wdr.unodc.org/wdr2020/en/socioeconomic.html.

WHO (World Health Organization). 2001. *"The World Health Report 2001, Mental Health: New Understanding, New Hope."* Geneva: WHO.

WHO (World Health Organization). 2014. *Social Determinants of Mental Health*. Geneva: WHO.

WHO (World Health Organization). 2018. *Global Status Report on Alcohol and Health 2018*. Geneva: WHO. https://www.who.int/publications-detail-redirect/9789241565639.

WHO (World Health Organization). 2022. "Mental Disorders." Fact sheet. WHO, June 8. https://www.who.int/news-room/fact-sheets/detail/mental-disorders.

Williams, Stacey L., David R. Williams, Dan J. Stein, Soraya Seedat, Pamela B. Jackson, and Hashim Moomal. 2007. "Multiple Traumatic Events and Psychological Distress: The South Africa Stress and Health Study." *Journal of Traumatic Stress* 20 (5): 845–55. https://doi.org/10.1002/jts.20252.

World Bank Group. n.d. "Cameroon." World Bank Group: Data. Accessed June 22, 2024. https://data.worldbank.org/country/cameroon.

World Bank Group. 2013. "Better Access to Health Care for All Cameroonians." World Bank Group, September 26. https://www.worldbank.org/en/country/cameroon/publication/better-health-care-access-for-all-cameroonians.

World Bank Group. 2022. "The World Bank in Cameroon: Overview." World Bank Group. Last updated March 12, 2024. https://www.worldbank.org/en/country/cameroon/overview.

World Data. 2024. "Cameroon: Country Data and Statistics." WorldData.info. Last updated July 2024. https://www.worlddata.info/africa/cameroon/index.php.

World Food Programme. 2017. *Cameroon—Comprehensive Food Security and Vulnerability Analysis (CFSVA)*. December. Rome: World Food Programme. https://reliefweb.int/report/cameroon/cameroon-comprehensive-food-security-and-vulnerability-analysis-cfsva-december-2017.

16

Case Study of Improving Education to Address Determinants of Health in Arusha, Tanzania

Neema Mduma and Dina Machuve

1. Education and Health

Significant evidence shows that education is a determinant of good health. Education is also a catalyst for development and a health intervention (Zajacova and Lawrence 2018). A well-educated community will develop skills, values, and attitudes needed to live healthy and fulfilled lives, make informed decisions, and respond to local and global challenges. Education is also associated with higher earnings and other economic opportunities (Raghupathi and Raghupathi 2020). In many societies, people with higher levels of education tend to have fewer financial hardships, achieve higher social and professional ranks, and have more access to services that promote better health, thus increasing life expectancy.

In Arusha, a city in northern Tanzania, education is considered an important determinant of health and well-being. A significant portion of the population, however, has not attained higher levels of education, and school dropout is still a problem. To address this, investment in education at all levels needs to be given special attention. In 2015, the government of Tanzania responded by abolishing school fees in public secondary schools to increase access to higher education. Following this, secondary school enrollment surged from 1.4 million in 2015 to 2.3 million in 2019 (United Republic of Tanzania 2020). The increase in the number of students in public secondary schools can also be attributed to the construction and renovation of education facilities, such as classrooms, latrines, laboratories, playgrounds, and dormitories; higher numbers of qualified teachers, particularly in science and mathematics, reviewing and amending education policies, acts, and curricula to be in line with the current pace of science and technology; as well as an emphasis on being gender and disability inclusive (UNESCO 2015). All these efforts were made with the aim of ensuring that children acquire quality education that will help to promote development and lead to a better and healthier life in the future.

Additionally, the curricula for both primary and secondary school education were reviewed to include topics such as general cleanliness and hygiene, nutrition, sexual and reproductive health, and many other health-related subjects. Despite all the government's efforts to ensure that students attain free quality education, however, there have been a few setbacks, including the problem of school dropouts. In most parts of Tanzania, school dropout is prominent in lower education, that is, primary and ordinary level secondary education, with an estimated rate of 36 percent (UNESCO 2017). Reports from several studies show that girls are most vulnerable to school dropout, and only 66 percent finish their secondary school studies compared to boys, whose completion rate stands at 77 percent. The school dropout problem leaves young people with less knowledge and practical skills needed for a better and healthier life.

This chapter discusses the links between education and health and how dropping out of school can have detrimental effects on the health of communities. We also closely review the factors that contribute to the school dropout problem, current strategies and efforts to reduce dropouts, and how emerging technologies such as machine learning can play a role in addressing the problem, thereby leading to well-educated and healthier communities in Arusha and in other areas of Tanzania and Africa at large.

2. Factors Contributing to School Dropout

The education system in Tanzania is composed of seven years of basic primary education, four years of ordinary secondary, two years of advanced level secondary, and three years of college or university degree. Although the first two stages of education (i.e., primary and ordinary level secondary) are compulsory and currently free, few residents complete these levels of education. Among the factors that hinder students from completing their studies is the problem of school dropout. In most parts of Tanzania, including Arusha, a person who finishes primary and secondary education has a greater chance of being employed and obtaining a job that offers benefits, including health insurance, giving them access to better health care. On the other hand, those who drop out of primary or secondary schools are

Fig. 16.1. Factors that contribute to dropping out of school. Courtesy of Marco Tibasima.

more likely to struggle with finding good jobs and, in most cases, are forced to work in high-risk jobs that offer limited or sometimes no health benefits (Banks 2016).

The causes of school dropout are many and differ between places and communities, but they can generally be grouped into school-level factors (e.g., school distance), cultural factors (e.g., early marriage), household-level factors (e.g., female involvement in household chores), and economic factors (e.g., parental investment) (figure 16.1; Mduma, Kalegele, and Machuve 2019).

School distance was among the top factors reported to significantly contribute to dropping out of most schools in Tanzania (UNICEF and MoEST 2018). Most students that dropped out of school in Arusha were those traveling long distances to school, more than 10 km. The school distance contributes to students losing interest in studying, as they must either walk long distances, hitchhike, or struggle with public transport, which they are often denied because students pay half fare. Most parents reported worrying about the safety of their children when they had to leave very early in the morning to walk to school. Thus, the likelihood of students who live far from school to drop out is much greater compared to those traveling shorter distances.

Cultural factors such as early marriages were also a major cause of school dropout (UNPFA 2019). Many pastoralist communities in Arusha, including the Maasai, Arusha, and Iraqw still believe that educating girls will change their attitudes and make them less appealing to potential spouses. The traditional thinking of not educating girls is not isolated to pastoralist communities; in other parts of Arusha, numerous parents believe that educating girls is a waste of resources since they will leave and get married elsewhere or will become unsuitable for marriage. Thus, parents tend to arrange marriages for their schoolchildren when they reach puberty, resulting in increased school dropout cases.

Household-level factors such as household chores were also observed to contribute to school dropout (Pezzulo et al. 2022). These factors affect both genders, but girls are at higher risk compared to boys due to cultural expectations of most communities in Arusha. In some cases, girls are reported to drop out of school to help their families with income activities or babysitting their younger siblings while parents are out looking for work.

Economic factors such as parental investment in children's education can also contribute to school dropout (Danovska 2018). Despite the free education policy in Tanzania, some parents still feel a huge burden of having to support other basics, such as school uniforms and stationery needed by their children. Some parents also feel more comfortable investing in education for boys while neglecting girls, with a belief that boys will take care of them in the future. Parental-gender bias occurs particularly when parents must choose who to send to school due to limited resources and low income. Thus, the probability of children, particularly girls, dropping out of school increases in families with low income and lower parental investment in education.

3. Efforts to Address School Dropout

The continued school dropout trend in Arusha despite the provision of free education has led to the establishment of several initiatives involving the government, teachers, parents, students, and communities to try to address the problem. Both regional and central governments are working hard to ensure that school-age children attend and finish their studies. Among the issues the government is now keen to address is the shortage of qualified teachers in public schools; for example, in June 2022, around 9,800 teachers for both primary and secondary schools were employed (MoEST 2022). Other efforts to increase the number of teachers, such as adding education programs in higher learning institutions, offering scholarships to students taking education courses, and so forth, are in place to ensure that the teacher-student ratio follows the agreed standard of the Ministry of Education, Science and Technology (Otieno 2022). Furthermore, secondary schools were built in every ward to reduce the distance students have to travel to school and to ensure that every enrolled student gets access to secondary education. These ward schools are constructed following the mandatory requirements for all necessary infrastructures, including latrines, laboratories, and dormitories, particularly in places where settlements are very scattered, such as the Maasai communities in Arusha.

Teachers are organizing regular meetings with parents to discuss students' academic progress and other issues that might help in improving their education. Children with poor school attendance and bad academic performance are discussed during these meetings, and strategies such as close follow-up at home and in school are employed for improving students' attendance and monitoring their academic progress. Extracurricular activities such as sports, games, and role play are organized, and students are encouraged to participate to motivate and inspire them to love school. Several primary and secondary schools in Arusha, such as St. Jude, Nalopa, Nganana, Shalom, Ilboru, Tengeru (boys), Kikwe, and Arusha (girls) have introduced the idea of linking students with higher learning institutions to expose and inspire them to work hard and pursue higher education.

Prior knowledge and academic records of students have also been used to identify early signs of school dropout. For example, students who do not perform well in subjects like mathematics and English, or who miss classes for more than twenty days in a year, are more likely to have less interest in continuing with their studies, hence dropping out of school. Several strategies, such as remedial classes for subjects considered difficult and that drive most students to give up on their studies, have been developed to help improve performance. These subjects could also serve as good indicators for school dropout and be given special attention whenever there is mass failure. Parents have also been highly encouraged to assist and support their children with homework and other school assignments by creating and committing to study time, particularly during the weekends. In addition, parents are reminded that it is their responsibility to ensure that children have enough meals to support their learning process at home and school. This is also aligned with communication mechanisms to assist children in speaking to their parents on other issues, academic or social. These strategies aim to ensure that children stay in school and complete their education despite the challenges they could encounter during their educational journey.

4. Technological Initiative to Reduce School Dropout in Arusha

Traditional approaches to address the problem of school dropout have not completely eradicated the problem, indicating the need for other, innovative solutions. The use of technologies such as machine learning, which can predict outcomes based on input data, could considerably assist in addressing the school dropout problem, since data on students' attendance and academic performance are available. Machine learning is simply the study of computer algorithms that give machines the ability to learn without being explicitly programmed (Badillo et al. 2020). The use of machine learning models to address several problems has gained much attention, particularly in sectors such as finance (Hoang and Wiegratz 2022), health care (Nayyar, Gadhavi, and Zaman 2021), and education (Munir, Vogel, and Jacobsson 2022).

The specific machine learning model highlighted here responds to knowledge gaps and limitations on the capabilities of other approaches to address the issue of school dropout identified by the communities in Arusha and by other research. The developed machine learning model, known as BakiShule (two Swahili words meaning "stay in school"), was deployed in some secondary schools in Arusha to help in early prediction and identification of students who are at risk of dropping out of school and suggest proper measures for interventions. The model was developed on a set of eighteen features, or variables, collected by a nonprofit Twaweza organization with the aim of assessing children's learning levels across Tanzania (Mduma 2020). Features such as the main source of household income, male and female pupil-to-latrine ratios, whether the school has a girls' privacy room, the region, the district, the village name, student gender and age, whether parents check on their child's exercise book once in a week, number of household meals consumed per day, whether a student read any books with their parent in the last week, whether parents discussed their child's progress with the teacher during the last term, enumeration area type (peri-urban, rural, urban), household size, parent-teacher meeting ratio, pupil-classroom ratio, and pupil-teacher ratio were used to assess factors contributing to the problem of school dropout. Student gender and age, whether parents checked on their child's exercise book at least once in a week, number of household meals consumed per day, whether a student read any book with their parent in the last week, and whether a parent discussed their child's progress with a teacher in the last term were identified as factors strongly associated with the problem of school dropout. Other factors, such as village, household size, and so on, were observed to have a lesser contribution to the problem. The BakiShule machine learning model was able to identify factors that were ignored or believed to have no or little contribution to the school dropout problem. This was made possible because machine learning models are able to mine nonlinear information from the features and their association with outcomes.

Development of the BakiShule tool was governed by following the prototyping software development approach. This approach was selected for its ability to receive feedback from users for improving the final product. The goal was to develop a more simplified version of the tool and give users feedback and evaluation. The tool was then improved in response to users' input and the process repeated till the users approved the final product. Education officers, parents, teachers, and machine learning specialists were all included in the tool development process, since the system was created primarily to assist educational stakeholders in identifying students at risk of dropping out of school. Functional requirements, including student dropout prediction, features with high contributions to the dropout prediction, the best model and visualization of school dropout, were gathered. Nonfunctional requirements covering scalability, usability, performance, accessibility, and consistency were also considered during the development of the tool. Flask framework was selected to facilitate the development of the tool since it supports the development of simple but expandable core functionality.

BakiShule allows users to input student information generated from six features that showed strong contribution to the dropout problem. Based on the input information, the deployed model, an ensemble of logistic regression and multilayer perceptron, helps to predict and identify students who are at risk of dropping out of school. BakiShule has been able to correctly identify and predict students at risk of dropping out of school with an accuracy of 85 percent.

After the tool development, the team of machine learning specialists was

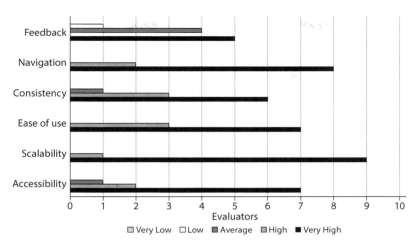

Fig. 16.2. End-user evaluation results for machine learning specialists.

invited to undertake technical tests specifically to evaluate the proposed non-functional requirements provided by end-users. Evaluators were required to rate each of the presented aspects using the following scale—Very High, High, Average, Low, or Very Low—by ticking one of the boxes and giving reasons for ratings below Average (figure 16.2).

Additionally, education stakeholders in Arusha were invited to evaluate the proposed functional requirements as end-users. Most of the evaluators (90 percent) were satisfied with the tool's ability to predict student dropout and rated it very high. Despite its accurate performance and high ratings, however, the tool had measured only a few schools in Arusha. For early intervention, there is a need to expand its application to reach more schools within Arusha and other regions where dropout rates are high.

5. Conclusion

This chapter's case study focuses on the use of machine learning to address the education problem of school dropout in the city of Arusha, Tanzania. The machine learning tool is one of several initiatives used to address the problem of school dropout in Arusha. The tool predicts and identifies early students who are likely to drop out of school and proposes effective measures for intervention.

While significant progress has been made to ensure access to free education in Tanzania, several setbacks, including school dropout, have significantly hindered the implementation of a free education for all policy. Providing free and quality education that will in turn improve the health behaviors of the community requires continuous investment based on informed and credible scientific and social findings. The traditional and technological initiatives used to address school dropout and new areas of focus can have significant value for teachers, parents, education stakeholders, policymakers, and development partners invested in improving the well-being of communities by ensuring students, especially girls, graduate from primary and secondary school. The success of this developed machine learning tool in addressing the school dropout problem has the potential to help Arusha and other cities in Africa to achieve the global agendas of promoting Sustainable Development Goal (SDG) 4, which stresses the importance of quality education, a social determinant of good health and well-being (SDG 3) among communities.

REFERENCES

Badillo, Solveig, Balazs Banfai, Fabian Birzele, Iakov I. Davydov, Lucy Hutchinson, Tony Kam-Thong, Juliane Siebourg-Polster, Bernhard Steiert, and Jitao David Zhang. 2020. "An Introduction to Machine Learning." *Clinical Pharmacology and Therapeutics* 871–85.

Banks, Nicola. 2016. "Youth Poverty, Employment and Livelihoods: Social and Economic Implications of Living with Insecurity in Arusha, Tanzania." *Environment and Urbanization* 28 (2): 437–54

Danovska, Ketija. 2018. "Reasons behind Children Drop out of Primary Schools with Unequal Socio-Economic Preconditions." Bachelor's thesis, Södertörn University, Fleminsberg, Sweden.

Hoang, Daniel, and Kevin Wiegratz. 2022. "Machine Learning Methods in Finance: Recent Applications and Prospects." *European Financial Management* 29 (5): 1657–1701.

Mduma, Neema. 2020. "Data Driven Approach for Predicting Student Dropout in Secondary Schools." PhD diss., Nelson Mandela African Institution of Science and Technology https://dspace.nm-aist.ac.tz/handle/20.500.12479/898.

Mduma, Neema, Khamisi Kalegele, and Dina Machuve. 2019. "Machine Learning Approach for Reducing Students Dropout Rates." *International Journal of Advanced Computer Research* 9 (42): 156–69.

MoEST (Ministry of Education, Science and Technology). 2022. *The National Science, Technology and Innovation Policy*. United Republic of Tanzania, MoEST.

Munir, Hussan, Bahtijar Vogel, and Andreas Jacobsson. 2022. "Artificial Intelligence and Machine Learning Approaches in Digital Education: A Systematic Revision." *Information* 13 (4): 203.

Nayyar, Anand, Lata Gadhavi, and Noor Zaman. 2021. "Machine Learning in Health care: Review, Opportunities and Challenges." In *Machine Learning and the Internet of*

Medical Things in Health care, edited by Krishna Kant Singh, Mohamed Elhoseny, Ahmed A. Elngar, and Akansha Singh, 23–45. San Diego: Elsevier Science and Technology.

Otieno, Kennedy Omondi. 2022. "Teacher Training and Provision of Quality Education in Public Secondary Schools in Arusha City." *Journal of Research Innovation and Implications in Education* 6 (2): 177–87.

Pezzulo, Carla, Victor A. Alegana, Andrew Christensen, Omar Bakari, and Andrew J. Tatem. 2022. "Understanding Factors Associated with Attending Secondary School in Tanzania Using Household Survey Data." *PLoS ONE* 17 (2): 1–18. https://doi.org/10.1371/journal.pone.0263734

Raghupathi, Viju, and Wullianallur Raghupathi. 2020. "The Influence of Education on Health: An Empirical Assessment of OECD Countries for the Period 1995–2015." *Archives of Public Health* 78 (1): 1–18. https://doi.org/10.1186/s13690-020-00402-5

UNESCO. 2015. *Better Life, Better Future*. Paris: UNESCO.

UNESCO. 2017. *Estimation of the Numbers and Rates of Out-of-School Children and Adolescents Using Administrative and Household Survey Data*. Paris: UNESCO.

UNICEF and MoEST (Ministry of Education Science and Technology). 2018. *Tanzania Verification of the Out-Of-School Children Study*. Global Initiative on Out-of-School Children. New York: UNICEF.

United Republic of Tanzania. 2020. "Pre-Primary, Primary and Secondary Education Statistics in Brief." President's Office—Regional Administration and Local Government, United Republic of Tanzania.

UNPFA (United Nations Population Fund Africa). 2019. "Fact Sheet: Child Marriage." UNFPA Tanzania. https://tanzania.unfpa.org/sites/default/files/pub-pdf/Factsheet_CM_UNFPA_14Oct.pdf.

Zajacova, Anna, and Elizabeth M. Lawrence. 2018. "The Relationship between Education and Health: Reducing Disparities through a Contextual Approach." *Annual Review of Public Health* 39: 273–89. https://doi.org/10.1146/annurev-publhealth-031816-044628.

17

Case Study of Integrated Planning as Pathway for Healthy Informal Settlements in Nairobi, Kenya

Jane Weru and Patrick Njoroge

1. Introduction

Nairobi, a city of about 4.6 million people, is a sprawling metropolis with two faces: the well-planned formal city, where its middle and upper classes live, and the informal unplanned city, where its poor reside. These two cities are like night and day. Nairobi's formal city is a city of skyscrapers, well-planned residential neighborhoods, and shopping malls, while its poor settlements are dense bustling localities, with narrow streets and next to no services. Yet these two faces of the city are symbiotic and live off each other. The residents of the city's poor neighborhoods, who constitute about half of Nairobi's inhabitants, are the cleaners, the drivers in its offices, and the workers on its factory floors. They are also the caregivers, gardeners, and cooks in many middle-class homes. The close relationship between the residents of these two faces of Nairobi implies that the plight of one is eventually visited on the other.

This chapter explores the condition of water and sanitation and the impacts of poor and insufficient sanitation services on the urban poor in three of the largest informal settlements in Nairobi: Mukuru Kwa Njenga, Kwa Reuben, and Viwandani. The chapter illustrates the effects of paltry services on the mental and physical health of residents of the three settlements, with special emphasis on the plight of women.

2. Informal Settlements

Based on a door-to-door enumeration carried out in 2016, the three informal settlements of Mukuru Kwa Njenga, Kwa Reuben, and Viwandani sit on about 689 acres of prime city property and are home to over 100,000 households (Corburn et al. 2017; University of Nairobi 2010). These 689 acres were initially government land zoned for industrial use and allocated to various individuals for the development of small industries. The people allocated the land, however, failed to develop it as required, and it lay vacant for many years. Slowly and over a period of about thirty years, the land was encroached and built on by individuals who constructed temporary one-room houses out of sheets of corrugated iron, which they rented out to the city's poor.

As in many informal settlements in Nairobi, insecure land tenure and the constant threat of eviction is a perennial source of anxiety for the residents of Mukuru. Tenure insecurity and the informal occupation of land has many negative impacts. Among these are the lack of planning and the failure of the state to recognize the area as a human settlement and therefore allocate resources for the provision of essential services (Weru 2013). With a state that has been largely absent for many years, it is not surprising that this area has paltry services and deplorable living conditions. The informal settlements of Mukuru are extremely dense, with an average of about 212 households living on one acre of land. Due to these high densities and the lack of planning, vehicular and pedestrian access is limited to narrow roads and winding footpaths with open drains running along their edges.

Of grave concern to the residents is the state of water and sanitation services in their settlements. The main source of water in Mukuru is the city's water utility company, Nairobi Water and Sewerage Company. Fresh water is piped to Nairobi by the water company from several dams situated outside the city's boundaries. This water is then piped to the edges of the three settlements. With recurrent droughts and an ever-increasing population, water scarcity is a common occurrence in Nairobi. Luckily, Mukuru has a high water table with plenty of underground water. To augment the scarce water resources within the city, the government during the COVID-19 crisis drilled eleven bore holes in various parts of the three settlements. The water pumped from these boreholes is accessed by the residents through public water taps at no cost. This water is salty, however, and can be used only for laundry, cleaning, or bathing.

The fresh water piped to the edges of Mukuru by the water utility company is often illegally reticulated by water vendors to different parts of the three settlements. Water vendors ordinarily use flimsy low-quality pipes laid overground and usually passed through drains running along the area's footpaths and roads. These exposed poor quality pipes are prone to breakage and habitually let in dirty, contaminated water. Many water vendors do not pay for the water they supply, and water pillage and spillage are common occurrences in this area.

Water, in Mukuru, is sold by water vendors to residents at a cost of about KES (Kenyan shillings) 5 for a 20 liter jerrycan. This water is accessed through taps situated within water kiosks located at different points in the three settlements. Water shortages are a common occurrence, however, with taps running completely dry for up to one month. These shortages are especially common during the dry months. Scarcity during these periods leads to increased costs as water is ferried by handcarts in jerry cans from one part of the city to the other. One 20 liter jerrycan of fresh water costs up to KES 20 during times of scarcity.

Mukuru has only 1,472 fresh water access points. It is therefore not surprising that residents complain of the inordinately long time it takes to fetch water. Long disorderly queues at water points are a common sight and a constant source of stress and conflict. This situation is exacerbated by the fact that water vendors close their businesses between 7 and 8 p.m., and a common grievance is that they are not open during the evening, as most people are not available to fetch water during the day.

The lack of running water within plots often means that handwashing facilities are generally not available. During the COVID-19 crisis, however, handwashing was practiced more diligently than usual. Most of the residents living in plots during the outbreak each contributed about KES 50 to buy liquid soap and water containers. With time, though, the practice of providing soap and water for handwashing was dropped when residents no longer perceived COVID as a threat.

3. Sanitation

One of the most challenging problems faced by the residents of Mukuru is the lack of toilets. Nearly all, 94 percent, of the residents of Mukuru are tenants who pay an average monthly rent of about KES 2,000 to structure owners who do not own the land they have built on. Most structure owners in Mukuru occupy long narrow plots of land. The shape of these plots inevitably influences the layout of housing in Mukuru. Housing units in a single plot are often constructed around a long, narrow enclosed courtyard with a gate at one end. Ordinarily ten to sixteen single-room houses share a courtyard, which is used for hanging clothes and as a communal space. One pit latrine and one bathroom built at the end of the courtyard serve all the residents. Not all plots have toilets, however, and a survey conducted in 2016 revealed that the three settlements had only 3,863 pit latrines (Corburn et al. 2017; University of Nairobi 2010).

The majority of toilets in Mukuru are pit latrines with a few dry toilets, called Fresh Life, provided by Sanergy, a social enterprise firm. Toilets in many plots are heavily used and fill up quickly. Once full, these pit latrines are manually exhausted by young men using ropes and buckets. The raw waste from latrines is emptied into drums and ferried away by handcarts, known as ambulances, to be emptied into nearby rivers or drains. During the rainy season, pit latrines often flood and spew out their raw waste in the open.

Due to the high water table, most plots in the Reuben area of Mukuru do not have toilets, and residents must use public toilets or other means to relieve themselves. Public toilets in Mukuru are not free and are run by individuals or groups as small businesses. Apart from toilets, these facilities sometimes provide bathrooms and almost always have water and soap for handwashing. The private use of public toilets is not cheap, and households must pay between KES 5 and 10 depending on whether it is a short or long call. Residents indicate that they spend between KES 900 and 1,200 per month for toilet use, a cost that is too high for many households.

For those without toilets, use of containers, such as buckets, within their plots is a common coping strategy. After use, waste is disposed of in public toilets for a fee, or in the open drains outside homes, along which water pipes run. The disposal of waste in public drains is prohibited and is often done furtively. If caught, one is evicted from their home or made to clean the drains by the area chief.

Open defecation is another coping strategy that is often practiced in Mukuru during the early morning hours. The use of carrier bags for toilet uses and as receptacles of human waste is quite ubiquitous. These used bags are normally thrown on rooftops or dumped indiscriminately along footpaths and into nearby drains. It is therefore not surprising that cholera outbreaks and other ailments are a common occurrence in this area, especially during the rainy season (Corburn et al. 2017; University of Nairobi 2010).

The lack of strong government presence in Mukuru has created a gap that has been filled by informal governance structures. These governance struc-

THE CHALLENGE OF FUTURE DEVELOPMENT

ELECTRICITY

Mukuru households must pay

45%–142%

more for their monthly electricity bills than residents enjoying formal Kenya Power provision.

WATER

Mukuru residents pay

172%

more per cubic meter of water than rates paid by residents living in formal areas.

In a bid to meet the rapid population growth in Mukuru, illegal, poorly constructed medium-rise structures are now a common occurrence.

HOUSING

Not only is Mukuru's water and shelter of extreme low quality, but households also must bear the inequitable burden of higher per-unit costs than their wealthier neighbors.

Loose soil and dumps   **Low-quality construction**   **Unplanned development**

POVERTY TAX

The research revealed the quality of water, electricity, and sanitation services enjoyed by the people of Mukuru are extremely inferior and pose a safety and public health risk not only to the residents but to the rest of the city. Not only are Mukuru's essential services of extremely low quality, but households also must bear the inequitable burden of higher per-unit costs than the rest of the city. This poverty penalty, where the poor pay more for lower-quality services, is clearly illustrated above.

Fig. 17.1. A depiction of the poverty penalty (a.k.a. poverty tax). Source: Akiba Mashinani Trust.

tures work closely with the area chief, a government official, to control development and often extract rents from those who want to construct housing, build kiosks for informal trade, or provide services such as water. These additional costs are inevitably passed on to the consumer. The lack of state involvement or regulation in service provision means that the people pay more for being poor, which is known as a poverty penalty (figure 17.1).

4. Menstrual Hygiene

For the women of Mukuru, managing one's menstrual cycle without access to a toilet is a harrowing experience. Women not only struggle to find ways of accessing affordable menstrual hygiene products but also must work out how to find the privacy needed to use these products. Additionally, the disposal of used sanitary towels is a common challenge for many.

In response to the high sense of deprivation that the women of Mukuru experience, in 2013, they launched a sanitation campaign dubbed "Too Pressed To Wait" (Anderson 2014). A critical objective of the campaign was to expose the terrible sanitation conditions suffered by residents and to further highlight the negative impacts of this situation, not only on the lives of the people of Mukuru but also on the rest of the city. The women hoped that the campaign would help build a sense of urgency within the government to plan the area, build the necessary infrastructure, and provide the required services.

Numerous meetings were held by women as part of this campaign. In these meetings the women observed that the deplorable sanitation conditions in Mukuru were humiliating to them and had therefore remained largely concealed and unspoken of. One main aim of this campaign was therefore to empower women to speak openly and without shame about intimate sanitation and reproductive health matters, which were often seen as taboo. In discussions held between the women, it was agreed that the prevailing conditions were the fault of not only the people of Mukuru but also the state in failing to provide the necessary infrastructure and services. It was therefore agreed that to improve living conditions and the unique sanitation problems of women, everyone had to be present in discussions: men, women, professionals, and political leaders. As the months went by, more and more women began to see the need to speak up on the issue of sanitation. They talked about the challenges of being a woman living in a one-room house and needing to use the toilet at night in a plot that does not have a toilet. They shared their fears of stepping out of their homes into the dark unlit pathways of their settlements and the constant threat of rape that accompanies such a journey.

The women opened up about the challenges of menstrual hygiene, especially the humiliation faced when they are forced to change their sanitary towels in front of their families. Many complained that they suffered infections because they were unable to frequently change their towels. Women who had given birth and were required to sit in warm saltwater baths to aid healing complained that they often did not have the privacy to do so in their single-room homes and consequently suffered numerous infections.

An essay-writing competition for primary school girls ages 12–15 was carried out in May 2013 to highlight the issue of inadequate sanitation and its implications on young girls. Twenty-one informal schools in Mukuru Kwa Njenga and Kwa Reuben participated in the competition. In total four

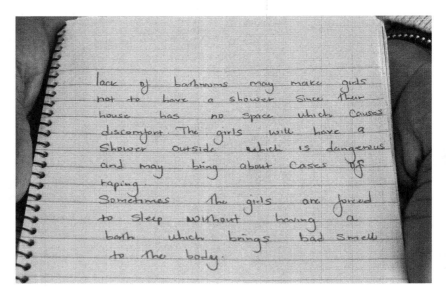

Fig. 17.2. Excerpt from a young girl's essay on living with inadequate bathroom facilities. Courtesy of Agnes Owang.

hundred girls wrote essays that lucidly reflected their day-to-day experiences without toilet and bathroom facilities (figure 17.2). The women also explained that the lack of bathrooms undermined their dignity and brought a sense of shame and humiliation.

Of great concern to the children and women of Mukuru is a lack of proper solid waste management, which leads to ridicule of menstrual hygiene, lack of bathrooms, rape, degraded environmental conditions, disease due to poor sanitation, and lack of sanitary towels and other hygiene products.

5. The Mukuru Special Planning Area

The Constitution of Kenya provides that "the state may regulate the use of land and any interest in or right over any land in the interest of defense, public safety, public order, public morality, public health, or land use planning" (Kenya Law Reform Commission 2010b, article 66). Article 42 guarantees the right to a clean and healthy environment, to clean and safe water in adequate quantities, while article 43 guarantees citizens "the right to the highest attainable standard of health, which includes the right to health care services, including reproductive health care," and the right to "accessible and adequate housing, to reasonable standards of sanitation, to be free from hunger, and to have adequate food of acceptable quality" (Kenya Law Reform Commission 2010a).

According to the Physical and Land Use Planning Act (2019), a county government may declare an area a Special Planning Area if that "area has unique development, natural resource, environmental potential or challenges; that area has been identified as suitable for intensive and specialized development activity; the development of that area has significant effect beyond that area's immediate locality, the development of that area raises significant urban design and environmental challenges; or the declaration is meant to guide the implementation of strategic national projects; or guide the management of internationally shared resources" (Republic of Kenya 2019).

As a response to the many development challenges facing the people of Mukuru, the county government of Nairobi in August 2017 declared the three settlements of Mukuru Kwa Njenga, Kwa Reuben, and Viwandani as a Special Planning Area. The declaration was made under the provisions of section 23 of the Physical Planning Act. This act gives county governments the authority to declare an area with unique development problems and opportunities as a Special Planning Area. Upon declaration, a county government is required to co-develop integrated development plans in an inclusive manner with the people affected.

The city county government has, with the help of forty-two organizations and through a rigorous community engagement process, developed a Mukuru Integrated Development Plan that now awaits the approval of the county assembly. Mukuru Special Planning Area takes a holistic approach to dealing with the challenges facing the residents of Mukuru. The plan addresses the root causes of these problems and seeks to implement the corrective measures agreed on. Some of the proposed measures are the provision of adequate sanitation, clean and affordable water, proper roads, drainage, and proper waste disposal systems. These measures ensure that the causes of diseases are addressed. In addition, the plan proposes the construction of three hospitals, which are already operational. Further measures aimed at uplifting the residents out of poverty have also been crafted. The health benefits of the water and sanitation plan are depicted in figure 17.3.

The national government during the COVID-19 pandemic began implementing the Mukuru Integrated Development Plan. It opened up and tar-

Fig. 17.3. Benefits of a water and sanitation plan in the Mukuru Special Planning Area. Source: Akiba Mashinani Trust.

macked roads, laid water and sewage infrastructure, built three hospitals, provided affordable and clean water through prepaid water dispensers, and began to connect plot-level toilets to the sewer. Further implementation of the plan will reduce flooding; the spread of disease-causing bacteria and toxic chemicals; food contamination; and disease vectors such as mosquitoes. Reduced flooding will also minimize displacement, hence reducing post-traumatic stress disorder, depression, and anxiety after flooding. This will also lower the prevalence of major outcomes of flooding like cholera, soil transmitted helminth infections, chronic diarrhea, typhoid, and vector-borne illnesses such as malaria.

6. Conclusion

Poor sanitation has negative effects on the health and well-being of the Mukuru populace. Lack of adequate sanitation services not only affects the residents' physical health but also undermines their confidence, erodes their overall sense of dignity, and impinges on their mental health. One of the direst consequences is the impact of poor sanitation on children. According to the African Population Health Research Center (APHRC), an estimated 41 percent of children experience intestinal parasites related to contaminated water, waste, and food, which can contribute to stunted growth (Faye et al. 2019). Stunted growth in childhood can contribute to lifelong disease susceptibility and premature death. In making the declaration of Mukuru as a Special Planning Area, the opportunity to positively influence the lives of a large marginalized population was not lost on the city government. The government hopes that the Special Planning Area will also play a critical role in the economy and general well-being of the whole city.

REFERENCES

Anderson, Mark. 2014. "Nairobi's Female Slum Dwellers March for Sanitation and Land Rights." *Guardian*, October 29.

Corburn, Jason, Vincent Agoe, Marisa Ruiz Asari, Julieth Ortiz, Regan Patterson, Peter Ngau, Munyua Mwaura, Dainah Kinya, Barale Bosibori, and Isaacnezer Kang'ethe. 2017. *Situational Analysis of Mukuru Kwa Njenga, Kwa Reuben and Viwandani*. Technical Paper. Nairobi, Kenya: University of Nairobi Department of Urban and Regional Planning.

Faye, Cheikh Mbacké, Sharon Fonn, Jonathan Levin, and Elizabeth Kimani-Murage. 2019. "Analysing Child Linear Growth Trajectories among Under-5 Children in Two Nairobi Informal Settlements." *Public Health Nutrition* 22 (11): 2001–11.

Kenya Law Reform Commission. 2010a. "43. Economic and Social Rights." Constitution of Kenya. https://www.klrc.go.ke/index.php/constitution-of-kenya/112-chapter-four -the-bill-of-rights/part-2-rights-and-fundamental-freedoms/209-43-economic-and -social-rights.

Kenya Law Reform Commission. 2010b. "66. Regulation of Land Use and Property." Constitution of Kenya. https://www.klrc.go.ke/index.php/constitution-of-kenya/117 -chapter-five-land-and-environment/part-1-land/233-66-regulation-of-land-use-and -property.

Republic of Kenya. 2019. "Physical and Land Use Planning Act, 2019." *Kenya Gazette Supplement*, July 22.http://kenyalaw.org/kl/fileadmin/pdfdownloads/Acts/2019/Physical andLandUsePlanningAct_No13of2019.pdf.

University of Nairobi. 2010. *Mathare Valley, Nairobi, Kenya: 2009 Collaborative Slum Planning and Upgrading*. Nairobi, Kenya: University of Nairobi Department of Urban and Regional Planning, UC Berkeley City and Regional Planning, and Pamoja Trust.

Weru, Jane. 2013. "Security of Tenure for the Urban Poor: A Critical Tool for Sustainable Social and Community Resilience." *Huffington Post* (blog), January 27, 2013. https:// www.huffpost.com/entry/security-of-tenure-for-th_b_2559995.

18

Case Study of Prospects of Digital Health for Africa in Nairobi, Kenya

Pauline Bakibinga, Dennis J. Matanda,
and Elizabeth Bakibinga

1. Introduction

In an increasingly digital world, the use of technology is a critical investment in the achievement of sustainable development (UN 2016). For all the Sustainable Development Goals, the use of digital technologies is highlighted as a tool to ensure that no one is left behind (UN 2016). In the health care sector, the use of digital technologies to reduce access gaps and improve quality of care has grown exponentially in the past decade, but especially since 2020, when COVID-19 was declared a pandemic (Whitelaw et al. 2020).

In sum, digital technologies are electronic resources, systems, tools, and devices used to generate, process, and store information. Digital health, a growing field, has been defined as "a discrete functionality of digital technology that is applied to achieve health objectives" by the World Health Organization (WHO). On the other hand, e-health is broadly defined as the use of information and communication technology (ICT) to deliver health information and services (Eysenbach 2001). The benefits of digital health innovations have been experienced in various health sectors, including disease surveillance, data collection and analysis, clinical management of patients, record keeping and support for health care workers, among others. The benefits of digital health technologies are most appreciated in many low resource countries, including countries in sub-Saharan Africa, given their immense potential to improve health access by overcoming distance and cost barriers (Olu et al. 2019). Digital health technologies ensure continuity of health care service delivery and health education during disruptions, enable early detection of epidemics and surges in numbers, and have the added advantage of ensuring access to remote health consulting services, thus protecting patients and health workers (Bakibinga-Gaswaga et al. 2020; Olu et al. 2019; WHO 2019).

Globally, countries that have benefited from digital health technologies are those with health systems responsive to the needs of the population, especially the marginalized or hard to reach, and for whom health enterprise architecture (HEA) is ingrained in the different components of the health system (Jonnagaddala et al. 2020). HEA is defined as a tool that enables alignment of the needs of the health sector to ICT implementation (Jonkers et al. 2006). With the combined goals of controlling investments and related risks, improving program performance and ultimately health outcomes, HEA demonstrates an organization's desired future status as well as the current structures, the state of its information systems, data, and hardware.

The WHO African Region has thus far benefited the least from the use of digital health for several reasons. Africa's inability to harness the immense potential of the digital health revolution is fueled by poor infrastructure, the digital divide and illiteracy, erratic electricity supply, and the high cost of installing ICT infrastructure amid prevailing poor policy environments (Bakibinga-Gaswaga et al. 2020). Variations in countries' implementation of HEA across the subregion make comparisons across interventions difficult given the heterogeneity in quality, objectivity, and completeness of strategies employed (Olu et al. 2019). For instance, the implementation of HEA in sub-Saharan Africa has not supported a comprehensive analysis and more sustainable development outcomes, and thus inequalities, discriminatory practices, and unjust power relations still persist in the health sector. Consequently, there is an opportunity presented by a human rights-based approach to health programming (London 2008) in general and for digital health programs in particular to address health access gaps. The human rights-based approach envisages development efforts anchored in a system of rights whereby states implement and are accountable to obligations established by international law. Under this arrangement, civil, cultural, economic, political, and social rights provide a guiding framework for development plans, policies, and processes.

Drawing on our experiences and the existing literature, using Nairobi, Kenya, as an example of an African city with a fast-growing urban population, which has harnessed digital health technologies, this chapter serves three overarching roles. First, it provides an overview of the current policy environment governing the use of ICT in health in Kenya. Second, it describes the governance of health services as well as access to, utilization of, and challenges of health services in Nairobi, with emphasis on the city's growing urban poor population. Last, the chapter demonstrates how the use of digital health technologies has been implemented across different health system components, existing challenges, and how a human rights-based approach to e-health policy and programming would reduce inequalities and improve health outcomes, especially for the urban poor.

2. Context

Kenya is recognized as a leader in sub-Saharan Africa in the use of technologies across all sectors of the economy. The 2022 Agility Emerging Markets Logistics Index, a ranking of the world's fifty leading emerging markets, ranked Kenya second to South Africa in Africa and number 28 globally (Agility 2022). The ranking assesses the overall competitiveness of countries based on their logistics strengths, business climates, and digital readiness. Kenya's position as a regional leader is driven by its growing mobile penetration rate, currently over 119 percent (CCK 2020), as telecommunication service providers innovate and add value-based solutions to their products. This figure is driven by the number of users with multiple sim cards. On the other hand, internet usage is 27 percent, with the majority using mobile internet. Although there is growing appreciation of the value of digital technologies in the achievement of sustainable development, the Kenyan health sector has not fully harnessed the immense potential of such technologies in improving service delivery. A plethora of digital innovations have been developed and are currently in use. The innovations span the health systems' building blocks as defined by the WHO: service delivery, health workforce, health information systems, access to essential medicines, financing, and leadership/governance (WHO 2007). The innovations in these core components of the health system in Kenya vary by component and county and continue to grow supported by the existing policy environment.

2.1. Policy Environment for E-health

The place of ICT in Kenya's health sector is informed by different policies and strategies. Kenya's health policy (2014–2030), in part, aims at planning, designing, and installing ICT infrastructure and software for the management and delivery of essential health care. Yet the national e-health policy (2016–2030) seeks to "create an enabling environment for the sustainable adoption, implementation and efficient use of e-Health products and services at all levels of health care delivery in the country." Kenya's Ministry of Health has an e-Health Unit whose roles include policy guidance, setting of standards, and supporting related national systems (Ministry of Medical Services and Ministry of Public Health and Sanitation 2010; Kang'a et al. 2017). Among the systems are the District Health Information Software (DHIS2; Manya et al. 2012), patient identifier, Digital Health Atlas, and the Master Facilities list. Such systems are implemented in conjunction with development partners. Since 2008, Kenya has implemented an HEA that has undergone iterations in 2015–16 with updates ongoing in 2022. In a bid to provide further guidance on the use of ICT in health, policies and strategies specific to particular components have been developed.

To drive the implementation of ICT in the health sector, the government of Kenya has regulations and guidelines for its human resources for health. The national e-health policy calls for the integration of ICT capacity building into existing training, including continuous professional development through e-learning. The National Continuing Professional Development (CPD) Regulatory Framework stipulates ICT as a CPD course that should account for 10 percent of the necessary CPD points, thus enabling in-service health workers to obtain the requisite ICT knowledge and skills. For different health professionals, including nurses, clinical officers, and community health assistants, a certificate in computer applications from a recognized training institution is a minimum requirement for employment.

Health products and technologies (HPT) is one of the eight investment areas of the Kenya Health Policy. Informed by the 2012 Kenya National Pharmaceutical Policy (MoH 2012), the HPT investment area's mandate is to enable the availability and rational use of effective, safe, and affordable health products and technologies. A commendable step in the nation's innovations to ensuring reliable supply chains is the 2020–25 HPT Supply Chain Strategy (MoH 2020a), launched at the time the COVID-19 pandemic took root and disrupted the already fragile health systems and their supply chains. Among its six focus areas is to harness the use of ICT in the establishment and maintenance of HPT supply chains.

3. Nairobi City County: Population, Health Care Provision, and Challenges

3.1. Population

Nairobi, Kenya's capital, is home to over four million people. Nairobi typifies the rapid urban growth rate seen across sub-Saharan Africa, at 4.1 percent annually (KNBS 2019). This rapid growth in population, however, has not been matched with growth in infrastructure and services. This has paved the way for unchecked growth in informal settlements. Nairobi's informal settlements, despite making up only 5 percent of the total residential land area of the city, are home to up to 60 percent of the city's residents. The settlements are characterized by inequality, poverty, overcrowding, insecurity, and lack of basic amenities and infrastructure, like safe drinking water and decent housing (Bakibinga et al. 2022). As a result, the residents experience poor health outcomes as demonstrated in population-level indicators, such as higher infant, child, and maternal morbidity and mortality, than those seen in other urban and rural areas (APHRC 2002, 2014). Many government initiatives to reduce health inequalities do not effectively benefit the urban poor in Nairobi, despite their physical proximity to both public and private services (APHRC 2002, 2014; Bakibinga et al. 2022; KNBS 2019).

3.2. Management

The 2010 Kenyan constitution transitioned the country into a devolved system of governance at two levels—the national government and forty-seven semiautonomous county governments (GoK 2010). Under this system of governance, the health service delivery function is devolved to county governments, while the national government is responsible for policy and regulatory functions. The Nairobi City County government is therefore responsible for delivery of health services in the city. Nonetheless, in March 2020, the Nairobi City County government signed an agreement with the national government that led to the transfer of four core functions (including delivery of health services) from the county government to the national government. Thereafter, Nairobi Metropolitan Services was formed under the Executive Office of the President as per Executive Order No. 1 of 2020 and mandated to deliver health services in the city until it officially handed back all previously transferred functions to the new Nairobi county government on September 30, 2022.

3.2.1. HEALTH CARE PROVISION

The Kenya Health Policy 2012–2030 provides a framework detailing the institutional and management structure under the devolved system (MoH 2014). Under this framework, health care is organized in a four-tiered system: (1) community health services—comprising all community-based demand creation activities, including the identification of cases that need to be managed at higher levels of care; (2) primary care services—all dispensaries, health centers, and maternity homes for public and private providers; (3) county referral services—all public and private hospitals operating in, and managed by, a given county; and (4) national referral services—facilities that provide highly specialized services and all tertiary referral facilities. The counties are responsible for three levels of care: community health services, primary care services, and county referral services (MoH 2014). The delivery of health services in Nairobi city is spearheaded by Nairobi city county government. Key functions include recruiting health workers and ensuring universal health care, including access to health services at all health centers and hospitals in Nairobi. This entails offering preventive, curative, protective, and reproductive health services through a network of over eighty health centers and three hospitals spread across the city.

In Nairobi's informal settlements, formal health care provision is largely provided by the private sector (Ekirapa, Mgomella, and Kyobutungi 2012; IFC 2016) because public health facilities are either few or nonexistent in these settlements. Where they are present, residents are often unable to access them because of unconducive opening hours of the facilities, insecurity at night, and perceived poor attitudes of health care workers (Bakibinga et al. 2016; Emina et al. 2011; Essendi, Mills, and Fotso 2011; Fotso and Mukiira 2012). Most slum dwellers are informal workers and leave home before the facilities open and return when they are closed. This pattern renders them a hard-to-reach subpopulation, as unfavorable working hours may mean that services are closed by the time they seek them; they are rarely at home even when home-based services are available to other members of the community. Informal workers can also be constantly on the move looking for employment opportunities, making follow-up and referral for long-term care impossible and resulting in higher opportunity cost due to lost wages if they must seek care (Rockefeller Foundation 2015). The near absence of the public sector has paved the way for a vibrant private sector, which is fairly unregulated, resulting in poor quality health services (Bakibinga et al. 2014). The private sector includes both clinics and pharmacists (Bakibinga et al. 2021). Support to private health care providers in the settlements is critical to any efforts targeted at improving the health and well-being of the residents (Bakibinga et al. 2014).

3.2.2. CHALLENGES

The health challenges facing Nairobi city are not unique; the same general challenges bedevil the devolved health sector in Kenya (Kimathi 2017). The issues are many, ranging from capacity inadequacies, human resources, infrastructure, enabling legal framework, financial resources, and the relationships between county and national government (GoK 2007; Kibui et al. 2015; MoH 2014; C. Mwangi 2014). For example, the transition of health service delivery functions from national to county governments has been characterized by various inconsistencies, including poor understanding of the system, management issues, and lack of coordination between the two levels. Challenges in resource distribution have also been reported, with the national government inconsistently allocating funds to counties and thus stalling health service delivery functions at the county level. Delays in funds disbursement have led to frequent strikes by health care workers over salaries, lack of medications, and other basic necessities at health facilities (Kimathi 2017). Regarding management of county health facilities, many health personnel lack adequate strategic management skills. For instance, the procurement of goods and services at the county level has faced myriad challenges, including entrenched corruption, which has affected the quality of procured products and service delivery (Mutai 2015; Mwamuye and Nyamu 2014).

4. Examples of Current Digital Health Interventions in Nairobi

Informed by the prevailing policy and legal environment as well as growing mobile penetration, service providers in Kenya continue to develop innovations that seek to address service delivery gaps in order to promote universal health coverage. Current interventions include innovations in the different health system building blocks.

4.1. Service Delivery

4.1.1. CLINICAL MANAGEMENT OF PATIENTS

Over the years, different health care providers have developed solutions to improve access and quality of services. Some innovations have focused on providing remote care for patients with chronic conditions such as diabetes and hypertension, while others provide general health care. Innovations like Afya Pap provide vital health information to patients with diabetes, track blood sugar and pressure, and enable direct communication with health care workers (Baobab Circle 2018). More recently, in the initial stages of the pandemic, a number of service providers adopted digital technologies to reduce health service delivery gaps. Several hospitals in Nairobi partnered with health insurance schemes to promote continuity of health care to their clients. Many of these, however, were not sustained after the restrictions were eased. Even then, the services catered to groups that were already advantaged through access to medical insurance schemes or money to pay for the services.

4.1.2. DISEASE SURVEILLANCE AND HOUSEHOLD MAPPING

One of the benefits of digital technologies in the health sector is the ability to ensure real-time sharing of health events. The Government of Kenya (GoK), with relative success, uses its self-service portal (Chanjo) to collect information about people vaccinated against COVID-19 (MoH 2020b). This system is still actively used. In the Kibera, Korogocho, and Viwandani slums of Nairobi, GIS methods to map households and structures has enabled researchers to know pockets of communities with specific health problems (Yeboah et al. 2021).

4.1.3. HEALTH PROMOTION AND EDUCATION AND COMMUNITY HEALTH CARE

In Kenya, and in Nairobi in particular, the use of digital health technologies in delivering door-to-door services as well as vital health information has been successful. This relies on the country's community health strategy, which uses community health volunteers (CHVs) to conduct home visits and share information and education materials with residents. The biggest beneficiaries of this service are residents of urban informal settlements.

The services include registering women and infants to allow for follow-up and completion of vaccination doses (APHRC 2018) as well as screening for pregnant and postpartum women and neonates with danger signs (Bakibinga et al. 2017), among others.

4.2. Health Information Systems

The DHIS-2, a national level system for collating statistics on health indicators, has been in operation in Kenya for over a decade (Manya et al. 2012). It is used to report health events at community unit, facility, sub-county, county, and national levels. Electronic medical records (EMR) systems are in operation in the public and private sectors (Kang'a et al. 2017; Muinga et al. 2020). Some are program specific, such as those for HIV/AIDS, while others are used in different health service delivery departments, such as outpatient, billing, radiology, laboratory, and inpatient (Muinga et al. 2020). Many of these rely on open source software and could be integrated with the DHIS-2 if frameworks to support this were in place and standardized. Interoperability and integration rely on standardization; however, this has not yet been fully achieved, as several differing standards are still in operation. Without alignment and effective implementation, the landscape of digital health information systems is fragmented, which results in duplication of efforts and makes health information difficult to share and secure (Bakibinga et al. 2020; Muinga et al. 2020). With the completion of the updates and successful implementation of the HEA, whose goal is to have a system that is "shared, interoperable and secure," it is anticipated that the country's health sector will be more organized and will benefit from the digital revolution.

4.3. Access to Essential Medicines

The last mile delivery (LMD) of medicines is an essential component of health service delivery without which compliance and disease control are not possible. LMD of essential medicines has grown exponentially in the past decade, with many online pharmaceutical companies setting up shop in Kenya's urban areas, including Nairobi. Online pharmacies are increasingly common, providing services to customers who can either pay or have health insurance (D. Mwangi 2022). By design, these services tend to benefit people in middle- or high-income neighborhoods in Kenya's cities. Some of the innovations to reduce frequent stock-outs and promote LMD of essential medicines include using riders to deliver (McCoy 2013), reporting stock-outs with phone-based (SMS) services (Githinji et al. 2013), decentralizing supplies (Tran et al. 2021), introducing digital solutions to order and track stocks, and establishing online pharmacies that use both web and digital applications to obtain orders and deliver medicines to users.

In a major move to address frequent stock-outs, the Kenya Medical Supplies Authority (KEMSA) recently rolled out the application Electronic Proof of Deliveries (e-POD) (UNFPA 2020). The KEMSA e-POD app is GPS enabled to facilitate correct deliveries and ensure confirmation of receipts and acknowledgment of commodities, while monitoring orders to reduce delays. The service is currently in its pilot phase and anticipated to reach all counties in the near future. Because of KEMSA's mandate to deliver to specific facilities (MoH 2019), this new service is not available to many private health care businesses, which are responsible for the majority of health care delivery in Kenya. KEMSA's e-POD application is in addition to Qualipharm, a mobile-based digital reporting tool by the United Nations Population Fund (UNFPA) and HealthStrat (UNFPA 2021). Designed for the public sector, Qualipharm serves the dual purpose of monitoring the consumption of family planning commodities at the facility, subcounty, and county levels and improving the quality of data reported. Despite these initiatives, however, persistent challenges include inadequacies in governance, regulation, and quality assurance; transparency and accountability in the supply chain; human resource management; and coordination of stakeholders across the public and private sector (MoH 2020a). Additionally, the above initiatives on improving supply chain management are currently designed to benefit only the public sector.

4.4. Financing

Kenya's health financing is through the National Health Insurance Fund (NHIF). The NHIF and other forms of health insurance, however, are only accessible to approximately 30 percent of the population, favoring the better-to-do individuals (Kazungu and Barasa 2017; Otieno et al. 2019). This leaves the majority of the population exposed to catastrophic health expenditure, as they have to pay out of pocket or rely on social networks to meet their medical bills. This health care funding gap has opened opportunities for innovators to create digital financing solutions. One such endeavor is the M-TIBA, a medical insurance scheme developed as a partnership between

PharmAccess Foundation, Carepay, and Safaricom (M-TIBA 2015). M-TIBA allows the user of the platform to save and use the funds toward a specific health care need. Over the years, M-TIBA has grown to bring insurance providers on board.

4.5. Human Resources for Health

Digital health technologies provide opportunities to support health workers by advancing their skills. The Ministry of Health has an online portal for continuing professional education for health workers (MoH 2022). The e-learning portal is a training platform for health workers on Kenya's Health Information System applications, such as the Master Health Facility List and the DHIS-2, as well as key topics in the screening and managing of common illnesses.

5. Leaving Many Behind: Challenges of Implementing Digital Health in Nairobi

While some challenges are specific to individual areas of the health system, there are broad systemic barriers to harnessing the value of technology in different sectors of the economy. As elsewhere in sub-Saharan Africa, Kenya's failure to benefit from the immense potential of the digital health revolution is dependent on several critical issues. As the government of Kenya, through its Ministry of Health, work toward improving the HEA, these challenges are critical considerations.

5.1. Poor Policy Environment

Inasmuch as the country has defined different policy instruments, existing guidelines are either weak or not fully implemented. For instance, while the HEA seeks to promote shared, interoperable, and secure systems, innovators continue to operate in silos, with many failing to go to scale. Kenya's legal and policy environment regarding e-health is fluid and has enabled innovators to implement digital health innovations with multiple systems that often do not speak to each other (Muinga et al. 2020). This makes integration and interoperability difficult. While some developers rely on frameworks developed for high-income countries, those frameworks cannot be fully implemented in low- and middle-income countries given the management and technical expertise, capital investment, and infrastructure needed to deploy and sustain them. For example, a recent study on the digital systems landscape in public health facilities demonstrated that individual facilities primarily invest in digital systems to cater for administrative functions (Muinga et al. 2020). Auxiliary services, such as laboratory and radiology, existed as stand-alone systems. While users highlighted challenges related to system and infrastructure support, system usability, and limited knowledge and skills, the developers and vendors reported that full rollout of the systems was impaired by the lack of appropriate data sharing policies and inadequate funding, among other challenges.

5.2. Digital Divide and Illiteracy

A combination of digital illiteracy and digital divide are major challenges to fully realizing the benefits of digital technologies in the health sector in Kenya (Bakibinga et al. 2020). Digital health innovations implemented in the past have not been fully appreciated or have failed to be sustained because end users do not have the requisite skills to run the interventions. For example, a project implemented in Nairobi's informal settlements to improve CHVs' ability to screen and refer mothers and neonates with danger signs (signs that sick neonates show, such as inability to feed, convulsions, and high temperatures) reported implementation challenges related to the failure of CHVs and clinicians to use the system due to their limited digital knowledge and skills (Bakibinga et al. 2020). Furthermore, although household ownership of cell phones is almost universal in Nairobi, women are least likely to own phones. As such, they have to rely on their partners' phones to access vital information and services.

In addition to the above challenges, poor ICT infrastructure, the high cost of installing ICT infrastructure, and poor energy supply are prevailing concerns for effective implementation of digital health innovations in Nairobi and in Kenya generally.

6. Additional Opportunities for the Urban Poor: Leaving No One Behind

Although many value-based digital health innovations continue to grow in Nairobi, by design these leave over two-thirds of Nairobi city's population out because they are targeted at people who can either pay or have health insurance (D. Mwangi 2022). In Nairobi's informal settlements, health insurance coverage ranges between 27 to 43 percent, with recent studies showing that this number remarkably decreased following the COVID-19 pandemic and associated responses (Bakibinga et al. 2022; Kazungu and Barasa 2017; Kibe, Kisia, and Bakibinga 2020; Otieno et al. 2019). Many residents of Nairobi's informal settlements lost income and thus were unable to either enroll or keep up with their monthly premiums. In addition, erratic power supply in these settlements and limited availability of gadgets are major deterrents for the effective use of digital health innovations for this section of the city's population (Bakibinga et al. 2020). As such, deliberate policy decisions and innovations are needed to reduce health access gaps. There are opportunities created by existing systems.

6.1. A Human Rights-Based Approach to Programming Digital Health

Digital health innovations are preferred tools to strengthen health systems because of their ability to overcome physical/spatial and economic barriers, thus enabling disadvantaged population groups to access care. The current digital health landscape in sub-Saharan Africa and in Kenya in particular, however, is increasing health inequities and inequalities (Saboga-Nunes, Bittlingmayer, and Bakibinga 2022). This is because many of the digital health innovations in Nairobi continue to benefit those with means to pay. There is an opportunity presented by a rights-based approach to health programming (London 2008) in general and for digital health programs in particular to address health access gaps. The place of a human rights-based approach in promoting the achievement of universal health access is appreciated globally, and particularly in Kenya, given its ability to reduce health inequities and inequalities (London 2008). With a human rights-based approach, every person's right to the enjoyment of the highest attainable standard of health is respected and protected by law. A human rights-based approach is premised on the following principles—legality, non-discrimination and equality, participation, accountability, and empowerment—that in sum serve to guide health policy and service delivery, ensuring that services are available, accessible, acceptable, and of quality (WHO 2017). The current Sustainable Development Agenda includes Goal 16 on the rule of law, emphasizing the role of legal, policy, and regulatory frameworks in enabling the measurement and attainment of targets set (UN 2015).

In Kenya, the current health policy draws from the provisions made in the constitution guaranteeing the right to health for all. Nevertheless, the policy fails to define ways to address the specific needs of population groups that are more vulnerable and need more or accelerated attention in the realization of their health and well-being. This is despite its emphasis on people-centered, participatory, and multisectoral approaches to realizing universal health access. The policy provides a foundation to respond to the health care needs of marginalized and vulnerable population groups, such as the urban poor (Maalim, McVeigh, and Mannan 2014). A human rights-based approach would ensure that marginalized groups, such as the urban poor, internally displaced persons, and women who are least likely to have cell phones, are included in the designing of products, and that value-based products are affordable and accessible to them (Bakibinga and Bakibinga-Gaswaga 2019). Such innovations could include those that target low-technology users (feature phones) and enable savings with minimum premiums for low-income earners. Two existing strategies could harness digital health and a human rights-based approach to reduce existing health inequalities for urban poor residents of Nairobi.

6.2. The Community Health Strategy

As a response to prevailing health worker shortages, the government of Kenya established the community health strategy, in which CHVs were identified as the first line of primary health care (GoK 2005; Bovbjerg et al. 2014). Using CHVs to deliver health information and basic health care is a proven strategy. In urban poor communities such as those in Nairobi, CHVs play a critical role that needs to be harnessed by empowering this cadre of health workers with digital skills and tools to bridge existing health care gaps (Bakibinga et al. 2020; Osindo et al. 2016). In the urban poor communities of Nairobi, CHVs usually go beyond their stipulated roles of health education, health assessments, and referrals to support community members during different health crises. As such, empowering them with essential digital skills, involving them in the development of digital health innovations, and supporting them through implementation processes with adequate resources, including mental health services and financial and social support, would have a positive ripple effect on the health and well-being of residents in Nairobi's informal settlements.

6.3. Public-Private Partnerships for Health

Given the role that private health care providers play in delivering essential care to residents of informal settlements, supporting the sector in

316   Case Studies

harnessing digital health innovations has the potential to reduce current health inequalities.

7. Recommendations

7.1. Digital Health Innovation Research to Identify Ideal Models for Different Population Groups

In the inaugural guidelines for digital health interventions, the WHO stressed the absence of a strong evidence base to inform the use of digital health technologies in the different components of the health system. Indeed, many innovations across the world have not been studied systematically because they lack a clear conceptual framework or are not reported at all. As such, innovators continue to develop technologies that have been completed elsewhere without the benefit of learning from previous and related solutions. For better planning and identification of appropriate health service delivery models, disaggregated data are necessary. Therefore, there is need for more structured evidence generation embedded in the conceptualization of innovations. This requires strategic partnerships between users, policy actors, innovators, and researchers. Evidence generation techniques would need to combine different social and technological research methods, such as participatory action research, cocreation of solutions with community members, and the use of digital technologies to enable real-time relaying of information and GIS methods to map localities.

7.2. Policy Formulation Supported by Robust Research

Policies that are informed by both human rights and gender equality considerations are needed to reduce existing inequities and inequalities, with emphasis on vulnerable and marginalized groups, such as the urban poor and women. More opportunities to include direct beneficiaries in the policy formulation processes are needed.

As the government considers improving the policy and regulatory environment for e-health in Kenya based on robust scientific evidence, additional efforts are needed to improve ICT infrastructure investment as well as ensure sustainable power supply. These initiatives demand a multisector approach, including both the government and development partners. Given that a significant proportion of the urban population is poor, it is critical to consider their input in the design of digital health technologies, as they are often marginalized and face enormous challenges in accessing e-health services. Case in point is whether the poor who are neither employed nor have health insurance are able to pay for digitization from infrastructure level to access. Such reflections need to be considered to ensure that the system is responsive to the unique needs of the poor through consultation. Critical inputs from ICT, energy, infrastructure, education, labor, and social protection ministries might go a long way in ensuring that existing challenges are addressed.

8. Conclusion

As the global community seeks to achieve sustainable development in general, and universal health coverage in particular, the use of digital technologies presents opportunities to bridge prevailing inequity and inequality gaps. Current innovations, however, exist in poor policy and legal environments, weak health systems, and prevailing digital illiteracy and limited digital skills, as well as poor ICT infrastructure, inadequate power supply, and a high cost of installing ICT infrastructure. These are in addition to economically related access hindrances, especially for marginalized and vulnerable subpopulations, who are generally poor, unemployed, and lack health insurance. A human rights-based approach to the implementation of digital health in Nairobi, embedded in existing strategies such as the community health strategy and public-private partnerships for health, is necessary to ensure that no one is left behind. People-centered, participatory, and multisectoral approaches are needed to address existing gaps to ensure that Kenya adequately benefits from the digital health revolution.

REFERENCES

Agility. 2022. *Agility Emerging Markets Logistics Index 2022: Agility Ventures*. Sulaibiya, Kuwait: Agility. https://www.agility.com/en/emerging-markets-logistics-index/.

APHRC (African Population and Health Research Center). 2002. *Population and Health Dynamics in Nairobi's Informal Settlements*. Nairobi, Kenya: APHRC.

APHRC (African Population and Health Research Center). 2014. *Population and Health Dymanics in Nairobi's Informal Settlements*. Nairobi, Kenya: APHRC.

APHRC (African Population and Health Research Center). 2018. "Improving the Timeliness of Administering Birth Dose Vaccines Using a Digital Platform in Nairobi Slums: A Stepped Wedge Design." APHRC, "What We Do" page. https://aphrc.org/project/improving-the-timeliness-of-administering-birth-dose-vaccines-using-a-digital-platform-in-nairobi-slums-a-stepped-wedge-design/.

Bakibinga, Pauline, and Elizabeth Bakibinga-Gaswaga. 2019. "Access to Healthcare for the

Urban Poor in Nairobi, Kenya: Harnessing the Role of the Private Sector in Informal Settlements and a Human Rights-Based Approach to Health Policy." In *Handbook of Global Urban Health*, edited by Igor Vojnovic, Amber L. Pearson, Gershim Asiki, Geoffrey DeVerteuil, and Adriana Allen, chapter 9. New York: Routledge.

Bakibinga, Pauline, Remare Ettarh, Abdhalah K. Ziraba, Catherine Kyobutungi, Eva Kamande, Nicholas Ngomi, and Jane Osindo. 2014. "The Effect of Enhanced Public–Private Partnerships on Maternal, Newborn and Child Health Services and Outcomes in Nairobi–Kenya: The PAMANECH Quasi-Experimental Research Protocol." *BMJ Open* 4 (10): e006608. https://doi.org/10.1136/bmjopen-2014-006608.

Bakibinga, Pauline, Caroline Kabaria, Ziraba Kasiira, Peter Kibe, Catherine Kyobutungi, Nelson Mbaya, Blessing Mberu, et al. 2021. "Pharmacies in Informal Settlements: A Retrospective, Cross-Sectional Household and Health Facility Survey in Four Countries." *BMC Health Services Research* 21 (1): 945. https://doi.org/10.1186/s12913-021 -06937-9.

Bakibinga, Pauline, Eva Kamande, Lyagamula Kisia, Milka Omuya, Dennis J. Matanda, and Catherine Kyobutungi. 2020. "Challenges and Prospects for Implementation of Community Health Volunteers' Digital Health Solutions in Kenya: A Qualitative Study." *BMC Health Services Research* 20 (1): 888. https://doi.org/10.1186/s12913-020 -05711-7.

Bakibinga, Pauline, Eva Kamande, Milka Omuya, Abdhalah K. Ziraba, and Catherine Kyobutungi. 2017. "The Role of a Decision-Support Smartphone Application in Enhancing Community Health Volunteers' Effectiveness to Improve Maternal and Newborn Outcomes in Nairobi, Kenya: Quasi-Experimental Research Protocol." *BMJ Open* 7 (7): e014896. https://doi.org/10.1136/bmjopen-2016-014896.

Bakibinga, Pauline, Lyagamula Kisia, Martin Atela, Peter M. Kibe, Caroline Kabaria, Isaac Kisiangani, and Catherine Kyobutungi. 2022. "Demand and Supply-Side Barriers and Opportunities to Enhance Access to Healthcare for Urban Poor Populations in Kenya: A Qualitative Study." *BMJ Open* 12 (5): e057484. https://doi.org/10.1136/bmjopen -2021-057484.

Bakibinga, Pauline, Abdhalah K. Ziraba, Remare Ettarh, Eva Kamande, Thaddaeus Egondi, and Catherine Kyobutungi. 2016. "Use of Private and Public Health Facilities for Essential Maternal and Child Health Services in Nairobi City Informal Settlements: Perspectives of Women and Community Health Volunteers." *African Population Studies* 30 (3): 3113–23. https://doi.org/10.11564/30-3-926.

Bakibinga-Gaswaga, Elizabeth, Stella Bakibinga, David Baxter Mutekanga Bakibinga, and Pauline Bakibinga. 2020. "Digital Technologies in the COVID-19 Responses in Sub-Saharan Africa: Policies, Problems and Promises." *Pan African Medical Journal* 35 (2): 38. https://doi.org/10.11604/pamj.supp.2020.35.2.23456.

Baobab Circle. 2018. "Afya Pap: Empowering You to Do the Best for Your Health." Afya Pap. https://www.afyapap.com/.

Bovbjerg, Randall R., Lauren Eyster, Barbara A. Ormond, Theresa Anderson, and Elizabeth Richardson. 2014. *Integrating Community Health Workers into a Reformed Health Care System*. Research Report. The Urban Institute, March.

CCK (Communications Commission of Kenya). 2020. *Fourth Quarter Sector Statistics Report for the Financial Year 2019/20*. Nairobi, Kenya: CCK.

Ekirapa, Akaco, George S. Mgomella, and Catherine Kyobutungi. 2012. "Civil Society Organizations: Capacity to Address the Needs of the Urban Poor in Nairobi." *Journal of Public Health Policy* 33 (4): 404–22. https://doi.org/10.1057/jphp.2012.33.

Emina, Jacques, Donatien Beguy, Eliya M. Zulu, Alex C. Ezeh, Kanyiva Muindi, Patricia Elung'ata, John K. Otsola, and Yazoumé Yé. 2011. "Monitoring of Health and Demographic Outcomes in Poor Urban Settlements: Evidence from the Nairobi Urban Health and Demographic Surveillance System." *Journal of Urban Health* 88 (2): 200–218. https://doi.org/10.1007/s11524-011-9594-1.

Essendi, Hildah, Samuel Mills, and Jean-Christophe Fotso. 2011. "Barriers to Formal Emergency Obstetric Care Services' Utilization." *Journal of Urban Health* 88 (2): 356–69. https://doi.org/10.1007/s11524-010-9481-1.

Eysenbach, Gunther. 2001. "What Is E-Health?" *Journal of Medical Internet Research* 3 (2): e833. https://doi.org/10.2196/jmir.3.2.e20.

Fotso, Jean-Christophe, and Carol Mukiira. 2012. "Perceived Quality of and Access to Care among Poor Urban Women in Kenya and Their Utilization of Delivery Care: Harnessing the Potential of Private Clinics?" *Health Policy and Planning* 27 (6): 505–15. https://doi.org/10.1093/heapol/czr074.

Githinji, Sophie, Samwel Kigen, Dorothy Memusi, Andrew Nyandigisi, Agneta M. Mbithi, Andrew Wamari, Alex N. Muturi, et al. 2013. "Reducing Stock-Outs of Life Saving Malaria Commodities Using Mobile Phone Text-Messaging: *SMS for Life* Study in Kenya." *PLoS One* 8 (1): e54066. https://doi.org/10.1371/journal.pone.0054066.

GoK (Government of Kenya). 2005. *Reversing the Trends: The Second National Health Sector Strategic Plan of Kenya*. Nairobi: Government of Kenya.

GoK (Government of Kenya). 2007. *Kenya Vision 2030*. Nairobi: Government of Kenya.

GoK (Government of Kenya). 2010. "The Constitution of Kenya." Kenya Law. https://www.kenyalaw.org.

IFC (International Finance Corporation). 2016. *The Business of Health in Africa: Partnering with the Private Sector to Improve People's Lives*. Washington, DC: International Finance Corporation, World Bank Group.

Jonkers, Henk, Marc M. Lankhorst, Hugo W. L. ter Doest, Farhad Arbab, Hans Bosma, and Roel J. Wieringa. 2006. "Enterprise Architecture: Management Tool and Blueprint for the Organisation." *Information Systems Frontiers* 8 (2): 63.

Jonnagaddala, Jitendra, Guan N. Guo, Sean Batongbacal, Alvin Marcelo, and Siaw-Teng Liaw. 2020. "Adoption of Enterprise Architecture for Healthcare in AeHIN Member Countries." *BMJ Health and Care Informatics* 27 (1): e100136. https://doi.org/10.1136/bmjhci-2020-100136.

Kang'a, Samuel, Nancy Puttkammer, Steven Wanyee, Davies Kimanga, Jason Madrano, Veronica Muthee, Patrick Odawo, et al. 2017. "A National Standards-Based Assessment on Functionality of Electronic Medical Records Systems Used in Kenyan Public-Sector Health Facilities." *International Journal of Medical Informatics* 97: 68–75. https://doi.org/10.1016/j.ijmedinf.2016.09.013.

Kazungu, Jacob S., and Edwine W. Barasa. 2017. "Examining Levels, Distribution and Correlates of Health Insurance Coverage in Kenya." *Tropical Medicine and International Health* 22 (9): 1175–85. https://doi.org/10.1111/tmi.12912.

Kibe, Peter Mwangi, Lyagamula Kisia, and Pauline Bakibinga. 2020. "COVID-19 and Community Healthcare: Perspectives from Nairobi's Informal Settlements." *Pan African Medical Journal* 35 (suppl. 2): 106. https://www.ncbi.nlm.nih.gov/pmc/articles/PMC 7687469/.

Kibui, Agnes W., Ruth K. Mugo, Grace Nyaga, L. M. Ngesu, I. N. Mwaniki, and Bernard Mwaniki. 2015. "Health Policies in Kenya and the New Constitution for Vision 2030." University of Nairobi. http://erepository.uonbi.ac.ke/handle/11295/97062.

Kimathi, Leah. 2017. "Challenges of the Devolved Health Sector in Kenya: Teething Problems or Systemic Contradictions?" *Africa Development* 42 (1): 55–77.

KNBS (Kenya National Bureau of Statistics). 2019. "2019 Kenya Population and Housing Census Results." KNBS, November 4. https://www.knbs.or.ke/?p=5621.

London, Leslie. 2008. "What Is a Human-Rights Based Approach to Health and Does It Matter?" *Health and Human Rights* 10 (1): 65–80. https://doi.org/10.2307/20460088.

Maalim, Mohamed Isaack, Joanne McVeigh, and Hasheem Mannan. 2014. "Kenya's Vision for an Equitable, Rights-Based Health System Fails to Address Specific Health Needs and Barriers to Accessing Health Care of Vulnerable Populations." *Africa Policy Journal*, May 21.

Manya, Ayub, Jørn Braa, Lars Helge Øverland, Ola Hodne Titlestad, Jeremiah Mumo, and Charles Nzioka. 2012. "National Roll Out of District Health Information Software (DHIS 2) in Kenya, 2011—Central Server and Cloud Based Infrastructure." In *IST-Africa 2012 Conference Proceedings*, vol. 5, n.p. Dublin: IIMC.

McCoy, Jessica H. 2013. "Overcoming the Challenges of the Last Mile: A Model of Riders for Health." In *Handbook of Healthcare Operations Management: Methods and Applications*, edited by Brian T. Denton, 483–509. International Series in Operations Research and Management Science. New York: Springer. https://doi.org/10.1007/978-1-4614 -5885-2_19.

Ministry of Medical Services and Ministry of Public Health and Sanitation. 2010. *Standards and Guidelines for Electronic Medical Records Systems in Kenya*. Nairobi, Kenya: Ministry of Medical Services and Ministry of Public Health and Sanitation. http:// guidelines.health.go.ke:8000/media/Standards_and_Guidelines_for_EMR_Systems .pdf.

MoH (Ministry of Health). 2012. *Sessional Paper 4 of 2012 on the Kenya National Pharmaceutical Policy*. Nairobi, Kenya: Ministry of Health.

MoH (Ministry of Health). 2014. *Kenya Health Policy 2014–2030*. Nairobi, Kenya: Ministry of Health.

MoH (Ministry of Health). 2019. *Kenya Medical Supplies Authority Strategic Plan 2019–2024*. Nairobi, Kenya: Ministry of Health.

MoH (Ministry of Health). 2020a. *Health Products and Technologies Supply Chain Strategy 2020–2025*. Nairobi, Kenya: Ministry of Health.

MoH (Ministry of Health). 2020b. *The Kenya COVID-19 Self Service Portal: The Chanjo Portal (MOH NVIP)*. Nairobi, Kenya: Ministry of Health.

MoH (Ministry of Health). 2022. "MoH Virtual Academy." Ministry of Health, Kenya. https://elearning.health.go.ke/.

M-TIBA. 2015. "M-TIBA: Changing Lives." *M-TIBA* (blog). 2015. https://mtiba.com/about-m-tiba/.

Muinga, Naomi, Steve Magare, Jonathan Monda, Mike English, Hamish Fraser, John Powell, and Chris Paton. 2020. "Digital Health Systems in Kenyan Public Hospitals: A Mixed-Methods Survey." *BMC Medical Informatics and Decision Making* 20 (1): 1–14.

Mutai, Abraham Kiplangat. 2015. "Devolution on Trial in Kenya: Case Study on Isiolo County." *Somalia Newsroom*, January 12, 2015. https://somalianewsroom.com/devolution-on-trial-in-kenya-case-study-on-isiolo-county/.

Mwamuye, Mwatsuma Kitti, and Henry Muchiri Nyamu. 2014. "Devolution of Health Care System in Kenya: A Strategic Approach and Its Implementation in Mombasa County, Kenya." *International Journal of Advanced Research* 2 (4): 263–68.

Mwangi, Caroline. 2014. "Accessibility to the Kenyan Health Care System: Barriers to Accessing Proper Health Care." Bachelor's thesis, Arcada, Nylands svenska yrkeshögskola. http://www.theseus.fi/handle/10024/70364.

Mwangi, Denis. 2022. "List of Most Popular Online Pharmacies in Nairobi." *Pulselive Kenya*, February 18. https://www.pulselive.co.ke/news/list-of-most-popular-online-pharmacies-in-nairobi/wyz8fgv.

Olu, Olushayo, Derrick Muneene, Juliet Evelyn Bataringaya, Marie-Rosette Nahimana, Housseynou Ba, Yves Turgeon, Humphrey Cyprian Karamagi, and Delanyo Dovlo. 2019. "How Can Digital Health Technologies Contribute to Sustainable Attainment of Universal Health Coverage in Africa? A Perspective." *Frontiers in Public Health* 7:341. https://www.frontiersin.org/articles/10.3389/fpubh.2019.00341.

Osindo, Jane, Pauline Bakibinga, Nicholas N. Ngomi, Eva Kamande, Peter Muriuki, and Catherine Kyobutungi. 2016. "Challenges and Opportunities for Promoting Maternal, New Born, and Child Health in Urban Informal Settlements: Perspectives of Community Health Volunteers in Nairobi, Kenya." *African Population Studies* 30 (3): 3124–32. https://repository.mut.ac.ke/xmlui/handle/123456789/4554.

Otieno, Peter O., Elvis Omondi Achach Wambiya, Shukri F. Mohamed, Hermann Pythagore Pierre Donfouet, and Martin K. Mutua. 2019. "Prevalence and Factors Associated with Health Insurance Coverage in Resource-Poor Urban Settings in Nairobi, Kenya: A Cross-Sectional Study." *BMJ Open* 9 (12): e031543. https://doi.org/10.1136/bmjopen-2019-031543.

Rockefeller Foundation. 2015. *Insights into Urban Informal Workers and Their Health*. New York: Rockefeller Foundation. https://www.rockefellerfoundation.org/wp-content/uploads/Insights-Into-Informal-Workers-and-their-Health.pdf.

Saboga-Nunes, Luis, Uwe H. Bittlingmayer, and Pauline Bakibinga. 2022. "The Digital Lifeworld and Salutogenesis." In *The Handbook of Salutogenesis*, edited by Maurice B. Mittelmark, Georg F. Bauer, Lenneke Vaandrager, Jürgen M. Pelikan, Shifra Sagy, Monica Eriksson, et al., 625–34. Cham: Springer.

Tran, Dan N., Phelix M. Were, Kibet Kangogo, James A. Amisi, Imran Manji, Sonak D. Pastakia, and Rajesh Vedanthan. 2021. "Supply-Chain Strategies for Essential Medicines in Rural Western Kenya during COVID-19." *Bulletin of the World Health Organization* 99 (5): 388–92. https://doi.org/10.2471/BLT.20.271593.

UNFPA (United Nations Population Fund Africa). 2020. "Taking Reproductive Health Commodities to the Last Mile." UNFPA Kenya, March 13. https://kenya.unfpa.org/en/news/taking-reproductive-health-commodities-last-mile.

UNFPA (United Nations Population Fund Africa). 2021. "E-POD App for Last-Mile Delivery of Family Planning Commodities Wins Global Health Supply Chain Award." UNFPA Kenya, December 27. https://kenya.unfpa.org/en/news/e-pod-app-last-mile-delivery-family-planning-commodities-wins-global-health-supply-chain-award.

United Nations. 2015. "Transforming Our World: The 2030 Agenda for Sustainable Development." United Nations Department of Economic and Social Affairs. https://sdgs.un.org/2030agenda.

United Nations. 2016. "Harnessing Science, Technology and Innovation for the Sustainable Development Goals." United Nations Department of Economic and Social Affairs. https://www.un.org/en/desa/harnessing-science-technology-and-innovation-sustainable-development-goals.

Whitelaw, Sera, Mamas A. Mamas, Eric Topol, and Harriette G. C. Van Spall. 2020. "Applications of Digital Technology in COVID-19 Pandemic Planning and Response." *Lancet Digital Health* 2 (8): e435–40. https://doi.org/10.1016/S2589-7500(20)30142-4.

WHO (World Health Organization). 2007. *Everybody's Business—Strengthening Health Systems to Improve Health Outcomes: WHO's Framework for Action*. Geneva: World Health Organization. https://apps.who.int/iris/bitstream/handle/10665/43918/9789241596077_eng.pdf.

WHO (World Health Organization). 2017. *Human Rights and Health*. Geneva: World Health Organization.

WHO (World Health Organization). 2019. *WHO Guideline: Recommendations on Digital Interventions for Health System Strengthening*. Geneva: World Health Organization. https://www.who.int/reproductivehealth/publications/digital-interventions-health-system-strengthening/en/.

Yeboah, Godwin, João Porto de Albuquerque, Rafael Troilo, Grant Tregonning, Shanaka Perera, Syed A. K. Shifat Ahmed, Motunrayo Ajisola, et al. 2021. "Analysis of Open-StreetMap Data Quality at Different Stages of a Participatory Mapping Process: Evidence from Slums in Africa and Asia." *ISPRS International Journal of Geo-Information* 10 (4): 265. https://doi.org/10.3390/ijgi10040265.

V LOOKING TO THE FUTURE

The last two chapters focus on what we must do to address the challenges and take advantage of current and future opportunities to create healthier cities in Africa. Individuals from multiple professions, including public health professionals, urban planners of housing and transport services, physicians, nurses, community health workers, policy advocates, urban water and waste managers, and many others, are needed. Educational and training programs that focus on the study of urban health problems, interventions, and policy are needed. Local, national, and regional governance is also needed to ensure that African cities achieve the goals stated in national, regional, and global health agendas.

19

Educating the Next Generation of Urban Health Scholars

Damilola Odekunle, Feyisayo A. Wayas, Lambed Tatah, Meelan Thondoo, and Elaine O. Nsoesie

1. Introduction

The field of urban health in Africa needs professionals with the necessary knowledge, skills, and context expertise to address current and emerging health challenges and to create healthy, equitable, and sustainable cities. The urban health workforce is multisectoral and interdisciplinary, including all professionals whose work aims to improve health in urban populations and cities (Freudenberg and Klitzman 2005). This includes a broad list of professions: public health professionals, urban planners of housing and transport services, physicians, nurses, community health workers, policy advocates, urban water and waste managers, and many others. Accomplishing the goal of creating a robust urban health workforce in Africa requires an understanding of what trainees and early career researchers perceive as opportunities and obstacles in urban health programs.

To this end, this chapter includes the perspectives of four early career urban health professionals from Africa. We highlight what we perceive as the education, training, and opportunities needed to develop a robust urban health workforce in Africa. Our perspectives focus specifically on the needs of the early career urban health professionals in programs that aim to train professionals to lead urban health research and implementation. The chapter is divided into three major sections that cover selected topics in addition to specific recommendations for policymakers and academic institutions in Africa and beyond. The first section focuses on the opportunities and training needed to conduct relevant research aimed at addressing current and future urban health challenges in Africa. The second section focuses on current gaps in training. The third section is a case study—an assessment of early career researchers' training needs.

2. Opportunities for Urban Health Education

The approach by which institutions train the cadre of urban health professionals faces challenges in Africa. Until recently, urban health has been poorly defined compared to rural health, which has long been incorporated into many training programs in Africa. In the 1970s and 1980s, the World Health Organization and other international organizations launched initiatives to improve primary health care in rural areas, which included training programs for rural health personnel. These programs were aimed to train community health workers, nurses, and other health care professionals to provide basic health care services in rural areas. Since then, there has been a gradual expansion of training programs for rural health personnel in Africa, often supported by international aid and partnerships (Declaration of Alma-Ata 1978; WHO Regional Office for Africa 2008). As Africa is still largely rural, its systems have not adjusted to respond to the health challenges posed by urbanization. African educational institutions at all levels rarely have programs, capacity, and resources dedicated to urban health education. Besides, urban health professionals may require core training in other disciplines, such as data sciences, implementation research, and systems thinking, which are also underdeveloped in many institutions in Africa.

A focus on training a cadre of urban health researchers and practitioners is strategic for moving forward the urban health agenda regionally and globally (Vearey et al. 2019). The research needs are evident from the endless list of urban health issues that need proper characterization. Oni and colleagues (2016) discuss six priority areas where new researchers will immediately contribute to African urban health research: obesity and food insecurity nexus, urban context as a tool for health promotion, urban health governance and policy, community strengthening for healthy inclusive cities, health systems in an urbanizing context, and migration, urbanization, and health. The myriad urban health challenges in Africa indicate that the current training programs on the continent might just need minor reorientation to incorporate urban health–relevant topics. To sustainably address these health research needs, however, urban health professionals must increase intersectoral urban health literacy, apply healthy urban governance

Educating the Next Generation of Urban Health Scholars   327

and systems approaches, and develop participatory and collaborative urban health planning processes.

Ultimately, there is a need to develop improved institutional training programs at all educational levels to produce a new generation of African urban health scholars and practitioners who are literate across sectors and disciplines. The new generation should have specialized skills in systems thinking to conduct implementation and transdisciplinary research. They also need to act as interlocutors and catalysts between diverse urban governance actors, meaningfully leading engagement with different stakeholders on why urban health matters and why often challenging cross-sectoral collaboration should be a priority.

African institutions can take advantage of new opportunities to foster urban health education. The increased global momentum on urban health provides platforms for raising awareness of the training needs of urban health professionals. That means a potential increase in training resources from governments and international organizations, including training offered at the World Health Organization, which can benefit urban health practitioners and others interested in learning and contributing to the health of urban residents. Online learning and training platforms and ongoing collaborations among cities in the south are two rapidly growing initiatives that can facilitate theoretical and practical knowledge transfer on urban health in Africa.

3. Gaps in Urban Health Training

Cities are now more than ever in agreement with the Sustainable Development Goals (SDGs). There is also increased attention about the critical role that health educators and professionals play in improving urban health. This is reflected in the growing consideration given to urban health education in recent decades (Hahn and Truman 2015; McNeill, Stephens, and Walker 2022; Nekhorosheva et al. 2021; Vearey et al. 2019; Zodpey and Tiwari 2016). There are still gaps in urban health training, however, that limit the formation of professionals able to holistically address ongoing and future city health concerns.

In 2019, Corburn and colleagues published a commentary on global challenges and opportunities in urban health education. Their commentary offers a call to action for a new approach to urban health training to target various systemic problems, such as the lack of undergraduate or graduate-level training programs at universities that focus on urban health (Corburn et al. 2019). The handful of students with an interest in the subject are typically found in departments of geography, public health, urban planning, or environmental studies. More and more institutions are offering at least one class or course in urban health; however, these usually concentrate on either a particular group of urban diseases (such as noncommunicable diseases or communicable diseases, but rarely both) or the physical, constructed, social, or health care contexts. Few university-level programs in urban health offer training in mixed methodologies, participatory action research, or policy analysis; instead, they tend to concentrate on a small number of methodological specialties, such as spatial epidemiology or neighborhood ethnography. Urban governance—or the institutions, social movements, economic policies, laws, and regulations that work together to influence who is included in decisions and the transparency of decision making—is not included in urban health education in schools of public health. Only a few university programs provide possibilities for supervised fieldwork or practicum in urban health. The client-focused studio models used in architecture and urban planning are exceptions. Few university-based urban health training programs are concentrated on urbanizing regions in sub-Saharan Africa, Asia, or Latin America, where rapid urbanization is occurring. Most urban health education programs frame the issue generally rather than delving deeply into one or more cities or comparing across cities.

While many of the aforementioned challenges apply to sub-Saharan Africa, this section does not aim to capture all possible gaps that exist in urban health training for scholars in Africa. It highlights specific topics identified by early career researchers.

3.1. Influencing Policy

Training researchers in how policies are developed, implemented, and evaluated in African cities is important because policies affect how governments invest in health in many countries. Therefore, understanding how policies are developed and how young urban professionals can participate is essential for creating change. Otherwise, the translation of research to policy might take much longer than required for timely impact. Currently, urban health researchers who are interested in creating new policies or policy correctives lack opportunities to learn about the basic process, including the different actors involved in crafting policies and how to engage with them.

3.2. Methods

There are gaps in methods taught in urban health training programs. Methods such as implementation science, geospatial techniques, and impact assessment in addition to epidemiology, biostatistics, demography, and governance can be useful in creating effective solutions. Additionally, advances in technologies such as artificial intelligence (AI), machine learning, remote sensing (satellite imagery, drones), genome sequencing, robotics and automation, among others, offer new opportunities for advancing urban health in Africa. These technologies can be used for collecting and processing data for policy decisions and evaluation. There are many examples demonstrating the applications and challenges of using these technologies for disease prevention, surveillance, and management during the COVID-19 pandemic (Bakibinga-Gaswaga et al. 2020; Maharana et al. 2021; Mbunge et al. 2022).

AI technologies, for example, can be applied toward improving disease diagnosis and detection, as well as assisting in clinical decision making, especially in cities with a shortage of health care workers. Many startups and academic researchers are developing technologies in cities across Africa. For example, researchers at the Artificial Intelligence Lab at Makerere University in Uganda are developing AI mobile-based tools for diagnosis of malaria (Makerere Artificial Intelligence Lab, n.d.; Nakasi et al. 2020; Quinn et al. 2016). True-Spec, a startup in Yaoundé, Cameroon, has developed AI-based tools for identifying fake medications. Poor quality antimalarial medications have been associated with about 122,000 deaths each year for children younger than 5 years in sub-Saharan Africa (Renschler et al. 2015).

Other examples include the use of machine learning, AI, and statistical methods to extract information from large datasets from satellite images, social media, and cell phones (which are widely used across the continent) to study social and economic determinants of health. Remote-sensing imagery from satellites and drones has many applications in the mapping of buildings and settlements, water scarcity, population estimation, and response guidance during natural disasters and conflicts (Quinn et al. 2018). Researchers have used aerial images to create datasets that aim to capture the impact of apartheid in shaping neighborhoods in cities in South Africa (Sefala et al. 2021). When combined with data analytics, 3D printing could be used for policy and advocacy by rendering a realistic representation of the physical environment. For example, in Sierra Leone, 3D printing has been used to understand disparities in school performance across chiefdoms and to represent distances from communities to schools in Freetown, which has assisted decisions on the allocation of school buses to various communities. Data from social media sites (including Instagram) and search engines (such as Google) have been used to study health information seeking and sharing of data on social determinants of health (Abebe et al. 2019; Jalal et al. 2019; Kekere, Marivate, and Hattingh 2022; Nsoesie et al. 2021).

While the aforementioned applications are not focused specifically on urban health, there are opportunities for adapting these technologies and their applications to address problems that might be more prevalent or unique to urban Africa. In this book, specific examples in the Case Studies section focus on the use of technology in digital health, air pollution surveillance, and improving primary school retention rates for girls.

To take full advantage of these technologies, governments and institutions in Africa need to invest in human capital development, specifically toward skills-based learning, such as digital literacy, computer coding, entrepreneurship, and critical thinking. Grassroots organizations such as Data Science Africa (2017), Deep Learning Indaba (n.d.), and Data Scientists Network (n.d.) offer unique opportunities for training subject matter experts in the use of data science methods, including AI and geospatial analysis, to address local problems.

While it might not be possible to easily integrate these methods into urban health programs, it is important for trainees to know that these methods exists and that there are opportunities for developing these skillsets.

3.3. Mentorship

Structured mentorship opportunities in teaching, research, academia, and grant writing are beneficial to trainees. Upon graduation, many trainees, depending on their jobs, are expected to acquire funding, perform rigorous research, write and publish impactful papers, and teach effective courses without the necessary mentorship needed to do so. In many institutions, lecturers are expected to teach three or more courses a semester, which is demanding, making it difficult to create the time needed to mentor graduate

Educating the Next Generation of Urban Health Scholars   331

students. Further, opportunities for networking, attending conferences, developing new skills, and sharing knowledge across fields and institutions are lacking.

3.4. Gender Inequity and Inequality

Commentaries on gaps in urban health training (e.g., Corburn et al. 2019; Frenk et al. 2010) have paid scant attention to gender inequality and inequity in urban health education. The 2030 Agenda for Sustainable Development, however, features a stand-alone goal (SDG 5: Gender Equality) that aspires to achieve gender equality and empower all women and girls (United Nations 2015), including a target to stop all forms of discrimination against women and girls. Similarly, there are eleven references to gender-responsive interventions in the New Urban Agenda (NUA; United Nations 2017). This implies that gender equality and equity have high prominence in development strategy and policy.

Gender equality and equity should be core in urban health training, embedded in curricula, enrollment, career track designation, students, and faculty, and enacted by institutional policies and regulations, particularly because for female urban health educators and professionals, gender inequity and inequality are major obstacles to access, reentry ,and retention in employment systems (Newman 2014).

That said, a quick review of the websites of some of the best universities in Africa (Times Higher Education 2022) reveals that at the undergraduate and postgraduate levels, the institutions running urban health–related programs inadequately focus on gender-related curricula and gender-related theories within their program structures. The training structure primarily deals with urban health issues associated with the growth of urban populations in developing countries and emerging middle-class populations. The institutions particularly focus on environmental health, urban health problems of developing countries, and health of slum areas, affluent areas, migrants/ refugees, children, the elderly, and populations at high risk (e.g., commercial sex workers, males who have sex with males, injection drug users).

Considering the increasing prevalence of gender-based health issues and the widening gender disparities, inequalities, and exclusions in African cities today (Tolhurst et al. 2022), key gender topics, such as protecting women from violence and abuse, defending their property rights, ensuring equality in access to health, education, employment, and political participation, and other issues of gender equality, must be identified and incorporated into the curricula of these African institutions.

Extant literature opines that the integration of gender into curricula and health training is challenging because of the following: lack of time and space to include gender in the curriculum, difficulties with conceptual clarity, doubts about gender inclusion in the curriculum, professors' lack of interest in or time for gender studies, gender inequality in the medical community and in knowledge, neglecting the presence of other genders and treating women's difficulties as gender issues, gender classification in obstetrics or birthing themes, and strengthening of the connection between women's health and reproduction (Frye, Putnam, and O'Campo 2008; Siller et al. 2018; Verdonk et al. 2009). Continually excluding solid gender-related syllabi and gender-related theories or partially addressing gender-related topics will make gender education, equality, and equity difficult in urban health education and training.

In several African countries, institutional gender-blind policies (i.e., laws and procedures that do not account for gender factors) are preventing students, especially females, from partaking in practicums, classes, and other curricular offerings because the tertiary institutions fail to consider potential conflicts between educational requirements and students' caregiving responsibilities (Griffin 2007; Newman et al. 2011). As a result of such gender blindness, students often receive inadequate support, which makes it difficult for them to enroll in school or to continue their studies. This is the case in Tanzania, Kenya, and Uganda, where there are high attrition rates in programs related to urban health. Gender-blind policies and practices can drastically alter the educational environment and prospects for students, as well as influence their decision to forgo a particular professional path.

For faculty, a glance at the websites of the top one hundred African universities also reveals that more men are teaching urban health and its related programs. For instance, in a department with ten staff members, only an average of four are female educators. This is the case at the Department of Public Health, University of Ibadan. There is a need for a gender-diverse faculty in African tertiary institutions who have the expertise and adequate knowledge of the disparities and inequity between men and women; who consider gender as an individual scientific concept and are aware of the topics and aspects to cover in gender education; who understand that the extent of gender education in urban health training is beyond discussing the physical and behavioral distinctions between men and women in cities; and who have the time to engage in gender studies in urban health.

3.4.1. WHY IS GENDER EQUITY AND EQUALITY IMPORTANT IN AFRICA'S URBAN HEALTH EDUCATION AND TRAINING?

First, at least a basic understanding of how gender affects the production of urban health is crucial since it has large-scale effects on every member of the urban population. Second, a gendered approach shows that, despite substantial changes in gender roles over the past fifty years, men and women frequently occupy different physical and social spaces in metropolitan regions, which may serve to maintain long-standing gender roles in society and the gendered division of labor (Hubbard 2004). The effects of this spatial stratification on gender inequalities and inequities in urban health outcomes are significant. Third, several urban health educators focus on social justice components of urban life, concentrating on how the unequal distribution of resources within the urban environment negatively affects the health of its least powerful citizens and residents.

3.4.2. HOW DO WE REDUCE GENDER INEQUITY AND INEQUALITY IN URBAN HEALTH TRAINING IN AFRICA?

First, urban health trainers must incorporate theories about how and why urban, gendered social, and physical environmental factors interact to promote health in both women and men in cities. Second, urban health educators should teach on the effects of the urban environment on health from a gender perspective. Third, urban health trainers should integrate a gender approach into their methodology and pedagogy to foster the understanding of urban health problems and urban populations to build the capacity of urban health students to appreciate integrated concepts and theoretical perspectives of urban health. Finally, the institutions must redesign the curriculum to change the structure of gender-related knowledge to identify the gender-related concepts and enhance educators' professional knowledge of gender.

Reducing gender gaps and inequalities in urban health education at the undergraduate and postgraduate levels at African tertiary institutions will allow us to better understand how the urban environment influences and creates disparities in men's and women's health and well-being.

4. Case Study: The Global Diet and Activity Research Network Early Career Researchers Forum

Undoubtedly, the early career researchers in urban health are the next generation of urban scholars who need to be strengthened to combat urban health challenges in Africa. It is imperative to recognize that the road to achieving urban health goals in Africa is a long one with unique curves and bumps. Hence, it requires seasoned mentors to equip upcoming scholars with the essential skills, tools, and resources to sustainably and effectively navigate and tackle the increasing urban health challenges in Africa. Furthermore, it is important to provide a platform for early career researchers to identify their skills, knowledge, and training gaps, safe places for capacity building and opportunities to utilize the capacities developed.

To buttress these points, we draw lessons from the case study of an international research network, the Global Diet and Activity Research (GDAR) Network, focused on urban health (https://gdarnet.org/), which comprises members from Brazil, UK, Jamaica, Kenya, Cameroon, South Africa, and Nigeria at varying career levels, ranging from undergraduates to professors. Although the network, like most international research networks, has members from both high-income countries (HICs) and low- and middle-income countries (LMICs), more than half of its members are from African countries, and more than three-quarters from LMICs. More importantly, this network also has an early career researchers forum, focused on providing equitable strengthening of capacities for the next generations of urban health scholars as one of its key objectives. Other objectives include sharing experiences and promoting leadership and expertise to build the next generation of research leaders.

Within the GDAR early career researchers forum, an early career researcher is identified as a researcher who is not yet able to write and apply independently for a research grant as a principal investigator or work independently in their field and who would like to develop expertise (academic or nonacademic) to a senior level. The vision of the early career researchers forum is to develop a cadre of independent researchers from the GDAR Network within each specific field of research.

The objectives of the GDAR early career researcher forum are:

- To provide a platform for sharing ideas and expertise on research taking place in the network
- To work together to produce innovative research outputs that can affect different spheres of influence
- To help each other develop research expertise and capacities
- To provide social opportunities for early career researchers from the GDAR Network for networking

While the GDAR Network unfolds for the next year (2021–25), so far, several activities have been conducted to kick-start the early career researchers forum and aim for achieving the vision and set objectives. First, an online training needs assessment of GDAR early career researchers was conducted to make equitable plans to bridge training need gaps. Three major categories of needs were identified, most of which were primarily unique to the GDAR early career researchers cohort. These major needs were split into two large categories:

1. Improving on general research skills such as presentation, management skills, or similar areas, and on specialized research skills, such as methodological, data analysis, grant writing, and comparative analysis, skills necessary for scientific research across different sites
2. Building professional networks and exposure to higher-level research-related activities

The training needs assessment was useful to clarify early career researcher members' expectations of the forum. They were given the opportunity to further refine their needs in terms of training, networking, and mentorship. More specifically, they underlined their needs for training on data analysis, research methods, individual skills exchange, grant writing, paper writing, project management, and structured mentorship. They also highlighted that they wanted to grasp opportunities for exchange visits with early career researchers from other cities to replicate ideas and skills.

Second, the GDAR early career researchers forum plans and runs a regular monthly feedback meeting, during which they discuss current issues, opportunities, and challenges. If needed, the notes from these meetings are submitted for input by senior research members. These meetings are also used to validate structured plans to prepare early career researchers for chairing and planning agendas outside the forum.

Third, the GDAR early career researchers forum uses a wide range of resources to stay updated on urban health resources and opportunities across the network, including:

- A live document for capacity building, in which the training gaps, field of expertise, and training needs of each early career researcher are frequently updated and reviewed
- Training opportunities related to urban health, which are regularly circulated within the training forum
- Updates on easy communication virtual platforms such as WhatsApp and Slack
- Online surveys on the benefits and importance of the ECR forum as well as expectations

So far, several benefits have emerged from the establishment and running of the GDAR early career researchers forum:

- Sharing training opportunities and discussions around career development and capacity building
- Maintaining a safe place for early career researchers to ask questions and experiment with leadership roles
- Providing a learning platform and an excellent networking forum, where people at the early career researcher level are open to sharing their experiences, including challenges in their areas of work
- Promoting diversity in terms of sites (localities), academic backgrounds, courses, and levels of education.

Further plans are currently being made to address the gaps and needs highlighted from GDAR early career researcher members. These plans include writing opportunities on manuscripts that are first or second authored by early career researchers and shared co-working processes to apply for relevant grants, individually and collaboratively. While logistics and financial barriers are being considered to bridge the gaps involved in face-to-face mentoring and exchange visits, virtual platforms are being used for such conversations. The process of undergoing frequent surveys and keeping communication channels open has been and is still crucial for monitoring and evaluating the forum and for reaching out to senior GDAR and non-GDAR colleagues for capacity building.

Notably, the early career researchers forum has made great strides within

Educating the Next Generation of Urban Health Scholars 337

a year, which might not have been achieved without the forum's building a safe place for capacity strengthening and opportunities, starting a quarterly blog on various topics relevant for early career researchers, organizing NIHR representatives to present on "Opportunities and Fellowships for Early and Mid-career Researchers" and "Applying for a Successful NIHR Grant," and inviting senior colleagues to share their career journeys and tips for development.

It is incontestable that those starting their career journey are more likely to be successful with help from seasoned senior colleagues, as well as from other early career researchers, strengthening each other based on diverse areas of expertise and training and being willing to indicate their inadequacies in the skills and expertise required.

Highlighted findings:

- To educate the next generation of urban scholars, training opportunities and platforms with well-defined goals and objectives are essential.
- An early career researchers forum is an essential safety and strengthening platform for career development.
- Leave no one behind.
- Equity of early career researchers in Africa is important in any international network.
- Regular monitoring and evaluation is essential to identify gaps and expectations and to develop realistic plans to bridge the gaps.

5. Conclusion

There is a need to inclusively train a generation of scholars studying urban health in Africa, who will influence policies that will lead to the design of cities that encourage health and well-being. This chapter includes the perspectives of four early career researchers on the challenges we have experienced and observed in urban health training. Through a case study and examples of current gaps in training, it highlights a need for bridging regional divides across Africa and between Africa and other regions to enable the sharing of information and practices that can benefit local practitioners. It also highlights the need for more structured programs and funding mechanisms that support urban health research training. Furthermore, investment in research institutes and centers focused on advancing public health research and supporting evidence-based policy interventions in Africa will go a long way in strengthening urban health research capacity.

REFERENCES

Abebe, Rediet, Shawndra Hill, Jennifer Wortman Vaughan, Peter M. Small, and H. Andrew Schwartz. 2019. "Using Search Queries to Understand Health Information Needs in Africa." *Proceedings of the International AAAI Conference on Web and Social Media* 13:3–14.

Bakibinga-Gaswaga, Elizabeth, Stella Bakibinga, David Baxter Mutekanga Bakibinga, and Pauline Bakibinga. 2020. "Digital Technologies in the COVID-19 Responses in Sub-Saharan Africa: Policies, Problems and Promises." *Pan African Medical Journal* 35 (2): 38.

Corburn, Jason, Blaise Nguendo-Yongsi, Waleska Teixeira Caiaffa, Tolu Oni, and Gerard Salem. 2019. "Urban Health Education: Global Challenges and Opportunities." *Journal of Urban Health* 96:510–13.

Data Science Africa. 2017. "Data Science Africa 2017." Data Science Africa. http://www.datascienceafrica.org/dsa2017/.

Data Scientists Network. n.d. Data Scientists Network. Accessed June 30, 2024. https://www.datasciencenigeria.org/.

Declaration of Alma-Ata. 1978. "International Conference on Primary Health Care." *WHO Chronicle* 32 (11): 428–30.

Deep Learning Indaba. 2020. "Strengthening African Machine Learning." Deep Learning Indaba. https://deeplearningindaba.com/2020/.

Frenk, Julio, Lincoln Chen, Zulfiqar A. Bhutta, Jordan Cohen, Nigel Crisp, Timothy Evans, Harvey Fineberg, Patricia Garcia, Yang Ke, and Patrick Kelley. 2010. "Health Professionals for a New Century: Transforming Education to Strengthen Health Systems in an Interdependent World." *Lancet* 376 (9756): 1923–58.

Freudenberg, Nicholas, and Susan Klitzman. 2005. "Teaching Urban Health." *Handbook of Urban Health: Populations, Methods, and Practice*, edited by Sandro Galea and David Vlahov, 521–38. New York: Springer.

Frye, Victoria, Sara Putnam, and Patricia O'Campo. 2008. "Whither Gender in Urban Health?" *Health and Place* 14 (3): 616–22.

Griffin, Anne-Marea. 2007. *Educational Pathways in East Africa: Scaling a Difficult Terrain.* Kampala, Uganda: Association for the Advancement of Higher Education and Development.

Hahn, Robert A., and Benedict I. Truman. 2015. "Education Improves Public Health and Promotes Health Equity." *International Journal of Health Services* 45 (4): 657–78.

Hubbard, Phil. 2004. "Revenge and Injustice in the Neoliberal City: Uncovering Masculinist Agendas." *Antipode* 36:665–86.

Jalal, Mona, Kaihong Wang, Sankara Jefferson, Yi Zheng, Elaine O. Nsoesie, and Margrit Betke. 2019. "Scraping Social Media Photos Posted in Kenya and Elsewhere to Detect and Analyze Food Types." In *Proceedings of the 5th International Workshop on Multimedia Assisted Dietary Management*, 50–59. New York: ACM.

Kekere, Temitope, Vukosi Marivate, and Marié Hattingh. 2022. "Exploring COVID-19 Public Perceptions in South Africa through Sentiment Analysis and Topic Modelling of Twitter Posts." *African Journal of Information and Communication*, no. 31, 1–27.

Maharana, Adyasha, Morine Amutorine, Moinina David Sengeh, and Elaine O. Nsoesie. 2021. "COVID-19 and Beyond: Use of Digital Technology for Pandemic Response in Africa." *Scientific African* 14:e01041.

Makerere Artificial Intelligence Lab. n.d. "About Us." Makerere AI Lab. Accessed June 30, 2024. https://air.ug/.

Mbunge, Elliot, John Batani, Goabaone Gaobotse, and Benhildah Muchemwa. 2022. "Virtual Healthcare Services and Digital Health Technologies Deployed during Coronavirus Disease 2019 (COVID-19) Pandemic in South Africa: A Systematic Review." *Global Health Journal* 6 (2): 102–13.

McNeill, Cynthera, Umeika Stephens, and Tara Walker. 2022. *Urban Health: A Practical Application for Clinical Based Learning.* Detroit, MI: Wayne State University Library System.

Nakasi, Rose, Ernest Mwebaze, Aminah Zawedde, Jeremy Tusubira, Benjamin Akera, and Gilbert Maiga. 2020. "A New Approach for Microscopic Diagnosis of Malaria Parasites in Thick Blood Smears Using Pre-Trained Deep Learning Models." *SN Applied Sciences* 2:1–7.

Nekhorosheva, Elena, Leonid Denisov, Elena Alekseycheva, and Daria Kasatkina. 2021. "Health Literacy in the Urban Health Infrastructure: Who Maintains Healthcare and How." *SHS Web of Conferences* 98:02007.

Newman, Constance. 2014. "Time to Address Gender Discrimination and Inequality in the Health Workforce." *Human Resources for Health* 12:1–11.

Newman, Constance, Anastasiah Kimeu, Leigh Shamblin, Christopher Penders, Pamela A. McQuide, and Judith Bwonya. 2011. "Making Non-Discrimination and Equal Opportunity a Reality in Kenya's Health Provider Education System: Results of a Gender Analysis." *World Health and Population* 13 (2): 23–33.

Nsoesie, Elaine Okanyene, Wuraola Fisayo Oyewusi, Opeyemi Osakuade, and Olubayo Adekanmbi. 2021. "A Comparative Analysis of Semi-Supervised and Self-Supervised Classification for Labeling Tweets about Police Brutality." Paper presented at the 35th Conference on Neural Information Processing Systems, Sydney, Australia, December 6–14 (online).

Oni, Tolu, Warren Smit, Richard Matzopoulos, Jo Hunter Adams, Michelle Pentecost, Hanna-Andrea Rother, Zulfah Albertyn, Farzaneh Behroozi, Olufunke Alaba, and Mamadou Kaba. 2016. "Urban Health Research in Africa: Themes and Priority Research Questions." *Journal of Urban Health* 93:722–30.

Quinn, John A., Rose Nakasi, Pius K. B. Mugagga, Patrick Byanyima, William Lubega, and Alfred Andama. 2016. "Deep Convolutional Neural Networks for Microscopy-Based Point of Care Diagnostics." In *Proceedings of Machine Learning for Healthcare*, 271–81. San Diego, CA: PMLR.

Quinn, John A., Marguerite M. Nyhan, Celia Navarro, Davide Coluccia, Lars Bromley, and Miguel Luengo-Oroz. 2018. "Humanitarian Applications of Machine Learning with Remote-Sensing Data: Review and Case Study in Refugee Settlement Mapping." *Philosophical Transactions of the Royal Society A: Mathematical, Physical and Engineering Sciences* 376 (2128): 20170363.

Renschler, John P., Kelsey M. Walters, Paul N. Newton, and Ramanan Laxminarayan.

2015. "Estimated Under-Five Deaths Associated with Poor-Quality Antimalarials in Sub-Saharan Africa." *American Journal of Tropical Medicine and Hygiene* 92 (6): 119.

Sefala, Raesetje, Timnit Gebru, Luzango P. Mfupe, Nyalleng Moorosi, and Richard Klein. 2021. "Constructing a Visual Dataset to Study the Effects of Spatial Apartheid in South Africa." Presented at NeurIPS 2021, December 6.

Siller, Heidi, Nikola Komlenac, Heike Fink, Susanne Perkhofer, and Margarethe Hochleitner. 2018. "Promoting Gender in Medical and Allied Health Professions Education: Influence on Students' Gender Awareness." *Health Care for Women International* 39 (9): 1056–72.

Times Higher Education. 2022. "Best Universities in Africa 2023." Times Higher Education, November 9. https://www.timeshighereducation.com/student/best-universities/best-universities-africa.

Tolhurst, Rachel, Sally Theobald, Beth Chitekwe-Biti, Jane Wairutu, Jackie Waithaka, Stanley Mburu, Lilian Otiso, and Haja Wurie. 2022. "Interrogating Gender Inequalities in African Cities." African Cities Research Consortium (ACRC), March 8. https://www.african-cities.org/interrogating-gender-inequalities-in-african-cities/.

United Nations. 2015. *Transforming Our World: The 2030 Agenda for Sustainable Development*. New York: United Nations.

United Nations. 2017. *Resolution Adopted by the General Assembly on 23 December 2016: 71/256, "New Urban Agenda."* New York: United Nations.

Vearey, Jo, Isaac Luginaah, Ng'weina Francis Magitta, Dativa J. Shilla, and Tolu Oni. 2019. "Urban Health in Africa: A Critical Global Public Health Priority." *BMC Public Health* 19 (1): 1–4.

Verdonk, Petra, Yvonne Benschop, Hanneke de Haes, Linda Mans, and Toine Lagro-Janssen. 2009. "'Should You Turn This into a Complete Gender Matter?' Gender Mainstreaming in Medical Education." *Gender and Education* 21 (6): 703–19.

WHO (World Health Organization) Regional Office for Africa. 2008. *Report on the Review of Primary Health Care in the African Region*. Brazzaville, Republic of Congo: WHO Regional Office for Africa.

Zodpey, Sanjay, and Ritika Tiwari. 2016. "Landscaping Teaching and Training of Urban Health as a Part of Health Professional Education in India." *Journal of Health Management* 18 (3): 351–60.

20

Urban Health

2030 and Beyond

Blessing Mberu and Elaine O. Nsoesie

1. Regional and Global Health Agendas

Two-thirds of the world population are projected to live in urban areas by 2050. Together with global demographic and climate change, natural disasters, and pandemics, cities face a growing challenge to provide healthy, equitable, and sustainable living and working conditions for their residents (WHO 2022). Consequently, urban health has gained increased global attention in recent years, with global organizations and agendas focusing attention on the need for research, policies, and actions to help cities protect and promote the health of their residents. Beyond linkages to other goals, the United Nations Sustainable Goal 11 specifically aims to make cities and human settlements inclusive, safe, resilient, and sustainable (United Nations 2015). Further, the World Health Organization (WHO) has developed the Urban Health Research Agenda (UHRA), which is a set of global urban health research priorities for 2022–2032, covering environmental health, climate change, tobacco, housing, healthy diets, physical activity, road safety, and emergency preparedness and response, with the overarching goal of supporting states, actors, and communities in achieving health, equity, and sustainability targets (WHO 2022).

For urban Africa, the aforementioned issues are typical of the health challenges across the region. Urban health is increasingly being recognized as an important emerging field that has long been neglected in the region. In some countries, urban health is such a new reality that while several programs are already addressing urban health issues and undertaking research in the same, they are not identified as urban health even at the university level because they are subsumed into the general focus on health. Nonetheless, the field has recently begun to gain traction, with more and more researchers and funders recognizing the specific importance of addressing urban health challenges through multisectoral approaches. With about 62 percent of the urban population in sub-Saharan Africa living in slums or slum-like conditions and having much worse health than those in nonslum urban areas and the rural poor (Ezeh et al. 2017), the often assumed urban advantage is being challenged in many cities in relation to health and socioeconomic indicators, raising intricate social policy challenges around resilience and viability of life in cities in many countries (Mberu et al. 2014, 2016). As noted in several chapters, there have been concerted calls to address the health of the urban poor in Africa, as their health indicators will determine whether Africa will achieve global agendas of inclusive and sustainable urbanization. African and Africanist scholars have called for the recognition of slums as spatial entities that highlight neighborhood effects, particularly how the shared physical and social environment of slums concentrates risks and contributes to the loss of health of its residents. The distinction of slum health from urban health will enable the mainstreaming of the same and the implementation of the Sustainable Development Goals and the New Urban Agenda (Ezeh et al. 2017).

Being a relatively young and emerging area in the African context and beyond the health of slum dwellers, scholars and experts in the region have identified many domains of urban health that are important but remain nearly untouched. While issues of maternal and child health, malnutrition among children, infectious diseases like malaria and HIV, and some noncommunicable diseases like diabetes and hypertension are more researched, huge gaps in knowledge have been identified. These include how principles of equity can be applied to research to improve the outcomes of city dwellers, as well as on the risk factors of noncommunicable diseases, including nontraditional epidemiological risk factors and commercial determinants of health (WHO 2022). Other areas with huge gaps in knowledge, policy, and actions, but in which there is expert consensus, include transport systems; urban food systems; mental health and well-being and associated urban stressors; intersectoral and multisectoral collaboration and integrated approaches to urban health; multifaceted waste management systems; effective research methods for collecting data in city settings, as well as effective intervention research methods; pollution and air quality monitoring; climate change and resilience; political aspects of urban health, including health governance and accountability in city health systems; and the use of citizen science for advocacy in urban health.

Against the backdrop of the foregoing, emerging visions for urban health opportunities in the African context lie in the fact that Africa is a rapidly urbanizing continent, and research interest is building in the field in various areas. The Sustainable Development Goals are identified as offering a framework for African countries to move toward sustainable cities, and hence is a guiding framework for research, policy, and action. There is an opportunity to integrate health into economic development agendas, leveraging regional bodies to prioritize health in cities across Africa. There is an increasing emergence of experts and urban health research institutions, especially within Africa, as well as the respective need for more, which will contribute to evidence generation for improving health and shaping thinking on urban health in the region.

The COVID-19 pandemic has been seen as offering an opportunity for cities to build more resilience for future epidemics and pandemics, but this will require governments to commit to human capacity development. Windows of opportunity for urban health are expressed in some local development agendas, such as Kenya's Big 4 Agenda and Rwanda's interest in technological innovations. There are opportunities for integrating urban health into the rebuilding agendas of countries emerging from civil war, such as Somalia and South Sudan; deploying citizen science, especially using young people for evidence generation, advocacy, and community interventions; and engaging in the greater regional politics of urban health, building on the visions of the Africa Union Agenda 2063 and the New Africa Free Trade Agreement (African Union 2019). These platforms, further discussed below, will enable researchers and practitioners to push urban health–related agendas that are beyond an individual country's control.

2. The Africa We Want (Agenda 2063) and the African Continental Free Trade Area

The linkages between regional agendas and urban health in Africa is typified by Agenda 2063, which aims to transform Africa into the global powerhouse of the future, bringing wide-ranging and sustainable growth, self-determination, freedom, progress, and shared prosperity (African Union 2019). One of the main goals of the agenda is to ensure that Africans are healthy and well-nourished, with sufficient levels of investments to expand access to quality health care (African Union 2019). The African Continental Free Trade Area (AfCFTA), which aims to establish a single market for a wide range of goods and services across the fifty-five African countries, is one of the most important projects of the African Union in pursuit of the fulfillment of Agenda 2063.

Beyond the economic and prosperity aspirations of these laudable regional initiatives are increasing questions around their critical direct and indirect implications for health. Outside the potentials of unlocking possible growth, contribution to improved socioeconomic security, and enabling of production and trade in health-fostering commodities, AfCFTA may directly or indirectly affect critical social determinants of health, including food security, housing, essential and health care services, the environment, and early childhood development (Machemedze 2023; SEATINI 2023). Further, liberalized trade could adversely affect other factors related to health and well-being, including the environment for health and health services, increased consumption of unhealthy products, and cross-border spread of disease (Machemedze 2023; SEATINI 2023). These challenges have raised important research questions relating to how these risks can be effectively addressed, creating unique research opportunities to provide evidence to governance actors to inform policy and implementation initiatives across the region.

3. Urban Governance, Politics, and the Future of Cities in Africa

Urban governance is primarily "the processes through which government is organized and delivered in towns and cities and the relationships between state agencies and civil society, which include citizens, communities, private sector actors, and voluntary organizations" (Raco 2020). For urban health, governance is about how local, national, regional, and global governance processes, institutions, and policies work together for human health and well-being in urban areas. It includes formal institutions empowered to enforce compliance and informal mechanisms through which people and institutions either have agreed to or perceive to be in their interest (Commission on Global Governance 1995). Muggah (2012) suggests that "global, national, and local governance challenges are most immediate and visible on the city frontlines." Accordingly, urban health and well-being is shaped by many "formal and informal policies, budgetary and regulatory decisions made at global, national, city and local scales as well as negotiations over access to power and services that may enhance or detract from urban health and wellbeing" (International Council for Science 2011).

There is growing international consensus that the failure or crisis of governance in developing countries is at the heart of the worsening urban crisis (Lewis et al. 2019; Nwaka 2005), with African cities continuing to present multiple health risks, especially when they are poorly governed or fail to sufficiently prioritize health in all policies (Laros and Jones 2014). Consequently, urban governance has become an important factor of urbanization in most countries, with a corpus of experts and practitioners pointing to how the rules, norms, and practices of formal and informal governance institutions (states, international organizations, and nonstate actors) tackle health challenges. While cities have little ability to alter the broader legal framework of governance or increase their boundaries beyond their current legal authority, they have legal levers that give them many tools to improve how government and governance work for the benefit of city residents (Burris and Lin 2021). These tools can be deployed for health promotion, including the familiar uses of law to regulate behavior like smoking and drinking.

The identified gaps that exist include how governance processes outside the health sector can be harnessed toward the protection and promotion of human health, together with how strengthened urban governance frameworks, policies, processes, and tools can protect and promote health in sustainable ways. Muggah (2012) calls for "reinforcing the capabilities and participation of nonstate civic actors" as a "key tenet of urban governance" in "promoting the 'interaction' of local residents and associations with public institutions, including mayors and line services." This is not only as "a matter of rights and citizenship," but is "practically connected to ensuring the survival of interventions and local buy-in to action plans." These governance challenges warrant in-depth inquiry and analysis by policy experts and practitioners from the public and private sectors, as well as civil society, to discuss, share, and document good governance practices for urban health across urban Africa.

Further, some key challenges from expert reflections for urban health and research in the African context vis-à-vis urban governance include the lack of skills among implementers, the siloed work among government sectors, and the failure of African governments to own research funding. There is also the lack of bottom-up participatory approaches in the governance structures in the region, together with the problems of government and management. Notwithstanding, there are opportunities to integrate health into political and economic development agendas by leveraging regional bodies and regional agendas, such as Agenda 2063 and AfCFTA, to prioritize health in cities across Africa. This calls for an integrated urbanization research approach that addresses governance, development, and complex health problems in rapidly growing cities. Building on global agendas around universal health access and leaving no one behind, platforms should be provided for urban health to address vulnerable and marginalized urban informal settlements and subpopulations, including women, children, people with disabilities, and urban refugees, who remain huge parts of urban Africa. A focus on how government sectors can work together through intersectoral and multisectoral approaches to improve urban health will remain paramount moving forward, to include health departments, land and urban planning, national treasuries and ministries of finance and education, among others. According to the 3D Commission (2021), the 2030 SDG agenda, beyond breaking down traditional silos, is the integration of "economic, social, and environmental dimensions of sustainable development and the interlinkages existing within and across the goals" (3D Commission 2021). It builds "on more cross-sectoral decision-making and multistakeholder partnership approaches, identifying various nexuses, clusters, or links among sectors." Elements of intersectoral perspective have found increasing embrace among researchers through interdisciplinary and transdisciplinary partnerships and collaborations in problem identification and evidence generation in urban health research in Africa. At the levels of national and subnational governments, elements of intersectoral collaboration are increasingly being demonstrated in terms of multisectoral decision making for health, as well as "collaboration and multidisciplinary and multisectoral identification of challenges and co-creation of solutions" (3D Commission 2021).

In sum, central to the importance of urban governance for urban health in Africa is the perspective that those who control political power control the destiny of nations and territories by monopolizing the allocation of resources through their control of budgets and the legal instruments of decision making via policies and program prioritization and implementation. They also have a monopoly on instruments of coercive action through the control of legal institutions and law enforcement apparatchik of state. Consequently, favorable disposition and prioritization of urban health policies

Urban Health: 2030 and Beyond   347

and actions by urban governance actors together with a critical mass of expertise related to the same will remain paramount for urban health programming, urban health equity, and sustainability in the region.

3. Conclusion

There is a need for policy and governance at local, national, and global levels that align with global, regional, national, and community goals. Additionally, to produce research to address these challenges, health needs should be prioritized in urban policymaking; investments and programs should be created to address gaps in training, capacity, and expertise; different sectors such as urban planning and education should be included in urban health agendas; different sectors and institutions, including secondary schools, government, ministries of health, universities, and policymakers should be engaged; and slum communities and other vulnerable urban subpopulations should be engaged and elevated in urban health priorities.

REFERENCES

3D Commission. 2021. *Data, Social Determinants, and Better Decision-Making for Health: The Report of the 3-D Commission*. Boston: 3D Commission.

African Union. 2019. "Agreement Establishing the African Continental Free Trade Area." African Union, May 30. https://au.int/en/treaties/agreement-establishing-african -continental-free-trade-area.

Burris, Scott, and Vivian Lin. 2021. "Law and Urban Governance for Health in Times of Rapid Change." *Health Promotion International* 36 (1): i4–i12.

Commission on Global Governance. 1995. *Our Global Neighborhood: Report of the Commission on Global Governance*. Kobe, Japan: Global Development Research Center. https:// www.gdrc.org/u-gov/global-neighbourhood/.

Ezeh, Alex, Oyinlola Oyebode, David Satterthwaite, Yen-Fu Chen, Robert Ndugwa, Jo Sartori, Blessing Mberu, Gerardo J. Melendez-Torres, Tilahun Haregu, and Samuel I. Watson. 2017. "The History, Geography, and Sociology of Slums and the Health Problems of People Who Live in Slums." *Lancet* 389 (10068): 547–58.

International Council for Science. 2011. *Report of the ICSU Planning Group on Health and Wellbeing in the Changing Urban Environment: A Systems Analysis Approach*. Paris: International Council for Science.

Laros, Marlene, and Freda Jones, eds. 2014. *The State of African Cities 2014: Re-Imagining Sustainable Urban Transitions*. Nairobi, Kenya: UN-Habitat.

Lewis, Dan, Gulelat Kebede, Alison Brown, and Peter Mackie. 2019. *Urban Crises and the Informal Economy: Surviving, Managing, Thriving in Post-Conflict Cities*. Nairobi, Kenya: UN-Habitat.

Machemedze, Rangarirai. 2023. "Addressing Health Implications of the African Continental Free Trade Agreement in East and Southern Africa." EQUINET Discussion Paper

131. Harare: Regional Network for Equity in Health in East and Southern Africa (EQUINET). https://equinetafrica.org/sites/default/files/uploads/documents/Diss%20131%20AfCTA%20and%20health%20Sep2023.pdf.

Muggah, Robert. 2012. Researching the Urban Dilemma: Urbanization, Poverty and Violence. Ottawa: International Development Research Centre (IDRC).

Mberu, Blessing, Caroline W. Kabiru, Donatien Beguy, and Alex C. Ezeh. 2016. "Consolidating Research on Population Dynamics and Health of the Urban Poor in Sub-Saharan Africa: An Overview." *African Population Studies* 30 (3): 3016–21.

Mberu, Blessing, Joyce Mumah, Caroline Kabiru, and Jessica Brinton. 2014. "Bringing Sexual and Reproductive Health in the Urban Contexts to the Forefront of the Development Agenda: The Case for Prioritizing the Urban Poor." *Maternal and Child Health Journal* 18:1572–77.

Nwaka, Geoffrey I. 2005. "The Urban Informal Sector in Nigeria: Towards Economic Development, Environmental Health, and Social Harmony." *Global Urban Development Magazine* 1 (1): 1–11.

Raco, Mike. 2020. "Governance, Urban." In *International Encyclopedia of Human Geography*, 2nd ed., edited by Audrey Lynn Kobayashi. Amsterdam: Elsevier. https://www.sciencedirect.com/topics/social-sciences/urban-governance.

SEATINI (Southern and Eastern African Trade Information and Negotiations Institute). 2023. "Brief 49: Addressing Health Implications of the African Continental Free Trade Agreement in East and Southern Africa." SEATINI, in the EQUINET, September. https://equinetafrica.org/sites/default/files/uploads/documents/EQ%20Polbrief49%20AfCFTA%20and%20health%202023.pdf.

United Nations. 2015. *Transforming Our World: The 2030 Agenda for Sustainable Development*. New York: United Nations.

WHO (World Health Organization). 2022. *Setting Global Research Priorities for Urban Health*. Geneva: World Health Organization. https://apps.who.int/iris/bitstream/handle/10665/363443/9789240041820-eng.pdf?sequence=1.

Index

2020–25 HPT Supply Chain Strategy, 305
2030 Agenda for Sustainable Development, 214, 331

abortion, 216
Abuja, Nigeria, 172
accessibility, 119–20; housing and, 97; WASH and, 131; water and, 114–17
Accra, Ghana, 146
adaptation, 80–81, 86, 88
Addis Ababa, Ethiopia, 165
Adelaide Statement on Health in All Policies, 98
adolescence, 215
affordability pathway, 115; housing and, 97–98; mental health resources and, 274
Africa, partitioning of, 22–24
Africa Clean Cooking Energy Solutions (ACCES), 148
African Commission on Human and Peoples' Rights, 96
African Continental Free Trade Area (AfCFTA), 343–44
African Development Bank Group, 166
African exceptionalism, 36–38
African Population Health Research Center (APHRC), 300
African Union Agenda 2063, 130
African Urban Food Security Network (AFSUN), 66, 71; Household Hunger Scale and, 87; rural-urban linkages and, 85
Africapolis, 33
Africa Renewable Energy and Access program, 148
Africa Union Agenda 2063, 343
Africa Union Commission, 214
Afya Pap, 309
agency, 67
Agenda 2063—The Africa We Want, 214, 343–44, 346
Agility Emerging Markets Logistics Index (2022), 304
agro-pastoral economies, 38

AIRCOP project, 277
air pollution, 255–59; air quality management and, 259–62, 267–68; ambient air quality and, 142–46, 149–53; digital data access and, 262–63; education and, 264; greenhouse gases and, 172–73; household cooking and, 146–49; transport and, 265–66; transportation and, 159, 171–72
AirQo, 256, 260, 262–63, 267–68
air quality management, 142–46, 149–53, 255–56, 264–68; air pollution, 142–46; Kampala and, 256–60; monitoring and, 261–63
air quality monitoring (AQM) networks, 150–51, 153
al-Askar (the city of sections), 16
alcoholism, 56, 277; homelessness and, 100
Alexandria, Egypt, 16–17
al-Fustat (the city of tents), 16
al-Qatta'i (the Quarters), 16
al-Shabaab, 201
alternative livelihoods, 24
amputation, 203
animals, 126
Arab Spring (2010), 200
Archer et al., 86
architecture, 24–25, 26
ARISE program (ariseconsortium.org), 224
Armed Forces of Liberia (AFL), 197
artificial intelligence (AI), 261, 329
Arusha, Tanzania, 282–86; education and, 287–90
asbestos exposure, 103
Asia, 145–47, 167, 278
assets, utility of, 86
"A Systems Approach to Air Pollution in East Africa" study (ASAP East Africa), 145

BakiShule machine learning model, 287–88
Bamako, Mali, 16
Battersby, Jane, 68
Battersby and Watson, 68
Beall et al., 196

350   Index

behavioral change, 217
behavioral risk factors, 232, 234–35, 242, 244
Beijer et al., 100
Belgian Congo, 26
Benin City, Nigeria, 4, 20–22
Benin Empire, 16, 20–22
Biomass Energy Initiative for Africa (BEIA), 148
biomass fuels, 143, 146–48, 150–51, 153
birth registration, 50–51, 59
Blantyre (Malawi), 118
Boko Haram, 197, 200, 204
Botswana, 17, 33
Britain, 21–22, 25–27
built environment, 234–36, 243–44; colonization and, 25–26; urban environmental conditions and, 241
Burnett et al., 68
Bus Rapid Transit (BRT), 160, 163–64, 167, 173–75, 176

Cairo, Egypt, 16; rural areas absorbed into, 36
Cameroon, 276–78; Boko Haram and, 201; mental health services in, 271–75
Cameroon Ministry of Public Health, 271
Cape Town, South Africa: 17; Open Street program in, 243; shared sanitation in, 128
capillary approach, 20
capitalism as extractive economy, 24
Carrigan et al., 176
cash transfers, 88
Centre for Research on the Epidemiology of Disasters, 233
cervical cancer, 217
Chad, 201
Chanjo (self-service portal), 309
childbirth, 185, 187–89, 192, 215–16, 220, 222–24
child marriage, 216, 223
children, 51, 74, 113, 127; child-headed households (CHHs) and, 224; diarrheal disease in, 125; food price increases and, 85; housing and, 8; physical activity and, 236; South African support grants for, 88. See also maternal health care
Child's Rights Act (Nigeria), 224–25
Chirgwin et al., 129
chronic poverty, 202
circular migration, 38, 70. See also rural-urban migration

cities, urban areas contrasted with, 33
citizen science, 260, 263, 267
city-specific partnerships, 267
civic conflict, 196, 198–99, 205–6
civil conflict, 196–97, 202–3, 205
civil registration and vital statistics systems (CRVS), 50, 59
Clean Air Cities Declaration, 172
Clean Cooking Alliance (CCA), 148–49
climate change, 60, 341–42; clean cooking and, 147; food security and, 66, 73; slum conditions and, 55, 58; transportation and, 170, 172–73; urban environmental conditions and, 232–35, 239–40, 241, 242–44
co-design, 132, 316
Coker et al., 257
colonization, 22–24; urban planning and, 25–28
community ablution blocks (CABs), 121–22, 128
community health volunteers (CHVs), 309, 313, 315
community participation, 10, 224, 243–44; air quality management and, 255–56, 260–61, 264–68; community health services and, 307, 309–10; community health strategy and, 315–17; digital platforms and, 262–63; food security and, 85; professional training and, 326
commuter buses, 163–64
comparative geography, 86, 87–88
conflict, 195–96, 205–7; definitions of types of, 196–200; health impacts of, 201–5; social impacts of, 201; terrorism as, 200–201
contraception, 215–17, 220
cooking pollution, 143, 146–49, 152–53
coping strategies: food security and, 81; index of, 86–87
Corburn at al.: professional training and, 327
corruption, 195
COVID-19 pandemic, 126, 294, 302, 305, 309; food security and, 56, 73, 276; mental health resources and, 272
credit, 81
crime: 51–52; conflict and, 199; mental health and, 277; motorcycles used for, 162; transportation and, 171
crisis narratives, 34–35
crowding, 54
cultural identity, 96–97
curfews, 26

Dahomey, Kingdom of, 17

data collection, 10; air quality management and, 256, 260, 262–63, 266–67; from air quality monitoring, 145–46, 150; disaggregation of, 105, 316; evidence-based policies and, 225; gaps in, 151; housing sector and, 105–6; policy programming and, 40–41; in real-time for transportation, 176; slums and, 6, 221; WASH and, 130

Data Science Africa, 330

Data Scientists Network, 330

Daudey, Loïc, 120

debt, 81, 85

Deep Learning Indaba, 330

delegated management model, 116

Democratic Republic of the Congo, 169

Demographic and Health Surveys (DHS), 191; perinatal care and, 185

demographics, 214, 216

demonstrations, 199–200

diabetes, 309

diarrheal diseases, 102, 104, 127, 129; handwashing and, 123

diet, 234–35, 237, 238–39, 242, 244; diversity of, 56, 71, 88. See also food security; nutrition

Digital Health Atlas, 305

digital technology, 10, 302–4, 313–17; air quality management and, 262–63, 267; COVID-19 and, 309; illiteracy in, 313; mapping with, 176; Nairobi and, 308–11; payment platforms and, 167; professional training and, 329–30

disability adjusted life years measure (DALYs), 142

disease, 113, 127–29; air pollution and, 142–43; animals and, 126; environmental pollution and, 57–58; housing and, 102; hygiene and, 123–27; slum conditions and, 55; triple burden of, 73

displacement, 197, 201–3, 205–6. See also internally displaced persons (IDPs)

District Health Information Software (DHIS-2), 305, 310, 312

Djenné, Mali, 17

Doe, Samuel, 197

Domestic Violence Act (Sierra Leone), 223

Douala, Cameroon, 271, 273–74; community participation in, 243; transience and, 39

dropouts, 282–85, 290; efforts to address, 285–89

drought, 55; food security and, 74; mental health and, 276

Durban, South Africa, 128

Duthé et al., 275

East Africa, 17, 66, 69–70, 71–73, 88

economic development. See socioeconomic development

economic growth, 36–39

Edo Kingdom, 20

education, 282–83, 285–89; conflict and, 206; food security and, 85; lack of sanitation impact on, 127; mental health and, 275; policies for, 289–90; road access and, 189; sexual and reproductive health and, 216; WASH and, 113–14. See also professional development; training

Egypt, 4; precolonial era and, 15

e-health, 302, 304–5, 312, 316–17

elderly, 51–52

electoral violence, 200, 202

electricity, 146–49; air pollution and, 152–53; housing lack of, 103

electronic medical records (EMR) systems, 310

Electronic Proof of Deliveries app (e-POD), 311

employment, 52, 206; food security and, 73–74; road access and, 186, 189–91; sexual and reproductive health and, 216

Ending Child Marriage (ECM) (Malawi), 223

EndSARS movement, 200, 203

energy, 146–49, 150–51, 152–53, 313, 317; poverty and, 149

environment, 75, 238; built environment and, 235–36, 244; urban food access and, 237–38; urbanization and, 231–35, 239–43. See also air pollution; pollution

e-ridesharing, 162–63

Eritrea, 196

Eswatini, 33

Ethiopia, 17, 22, 33; Eritrean war and, 196; food security and, 71; tuberculosis study in, 100

ethnic heterogeneity, 220

Europeans, 22–26; Benin City and, 21; segregation from, 27–28

European Union Air Quality Directives, 264

eviction, 54, 96–97, 99–100, 102, 106; civic conflict and, 198

extractive capitalism, 24

extreme heat, 55
Ezeh and Mberu, 41

fecal sludge management, 118–19. *See also* sanitation; solid waste management
Federal Road Safety Corps (FRSC), 169
fertility, 38, 213, 215, 222, 224
fire, 104
floods, 55, 74, 276
food environment, 234–35, 237–38, 239
food hygiene, 123, 125
food security, 68–71, 85–88; adaptation and, 80–81; conflict and, 202–3; definition of dimensions of, 67; measurement of, 86–87; mental health and, 275–76; price increases and, 74–75; professional training and, 326; slum conditions and, 55–57; sustainability and, 66–69. *See also* diet; nutrition
formal housing, 99, 101, 106
For the City Yet to Come (Simone), 2
fractal design, 21
France, 27
fuel efficiency, 176

gender, 215, 332; bias and, 285; equity and, 331–33; food security and, 73–74; road access unequal outcomes for, 189–92; violence and, 80
gender-based violence, 204, 207, 219–20, 223, 225; mental health and, 277
Gender Equality and Women's Empowerment Act (Sierra Leone), 223
Geographic Information Systems (GIS), 309
geospatial context, 87–88
Ghana, 101–2, 104, 169
Ghana Empire, 16
girls, 283, 285, 290; menstrual hygiene and, 297–98; privacy rooms for, 287. *See also* menstrual hygiene; women
Glazener et al., 169
Global Burden of Disease Study (2019), 232; road injuries and, 161
Global Diet and Activity Research (GDAR) Network, 334–36
global health policy, 60; air quality studies and, 145; development agendas and, 214; food security and, 68, 87–88; governance and, 344–47; policy and, 341–45
Global North, 238
Global South, 70
Gordon, Deborah, 172

governance, 195–99, 201, 205–6; community health strategy and, 315; COVID-19 and, 343; digital technologies and, 309, 311–12, 316; global health agenda and, 344–47; health care provision and, 305–8; informal systems and, 295; professional training and, 326, 328; transportation and, 175; underdevelopment and, 221; WASH and, 130–31
grassroots organizations, 330
Great Zimbabwe, 15, 17, 19–20, 28
greenhouse gases, 170, 172–74, 176
Guttmacher-Lancet Commission on Sexual and Reproductive Health and Rights (2016), 215

Hadza people, 24
handwashing, 123–27, 294
health care use index, 188–89, 191
health enterprise architecture (HEA), 303, 305, 312
Health in All Policies (HiAP) approach, 107
health insurance, 218, 309–11, 313; digital technologies and, 317; mental health and, 274
health products and technologies (HPT) investment strategy, 305
HealthStrat, 311
HIV/AIDS, 41, 216–17; conflict and, 204; digital technologies and, 310; migration and, 218; risky sexual behaviors and, 220
homelessness, 99–100; varying definitions of, 105
Household Hunger Scale (HHS), 87
households, 73–75, 80–81, 85–88; air pollution and, 142–45, 150–53; cell phone ownership in, 313; digital mapping of, 309; education and, 285; food security and, 66–68; handwashing facilities in, 123; housing costs and, 97–98; hunger measurement in, 87–88; lack of sanitation facilities and, 122; shared sanitation and, 129
housing, 9, 96–100, 104–7; affordability pathway and, 100–102; colonial employer-provided control of, 26; mental health and, 275, 276–77; safety and, 102–4; slum conditions and, 53–55; urban environmental conditions and, 241
Housing Health and Safety Rating System (HHSRS), 106
human development, 70

Index 353

Human Development Index, 38
human rights–based approach, 303–4, 314–15;
digital technologies and, 317; gender equality and, 316; mental health resources and,
274; right-based policy options and, 222
hunger, 24; household measure of, 87–88.
See also food security
hygiene, 123–27. *See also* menstrual hygiene;
sanitation; water; water sanitation and
hygiene (WASH)

Ibekwe et al., 172
Ile-Ife, Nigeria, 16–17
immigration, 199, 204
immunization, 184
India, 28
Indian Ocean Rim circulation system, 20
Indigenous food practices, 73
Indigenous people, 23, 25, 28
inequality, 50, 68, 241; gender equity and,
331–33; road access and, 189–92
inflation, 74–75, 85
informal settlements, 1–4; affordability and,
101; community health care and, 309; conflict and, 195, 202; demolition of, 198–99;
digital technologies and, 313–15; health
care provision and, 306–7; housing and,
97–100, 102–6; planning and, 292–94;
sanitation and, 119; sexual and reproductive health and, 224; urban environmental
conditions and, 241; water service providers and, 116–17. *See also* slums
informal systems, 295; conflict and, 199; food
and, 68, 73, 80, 238; informality's creative
spirit and, 37; schools and, 297; transportation and, 166, 175
information and communication technology
(ICT), 302–5; infrastructure for, 313, 316–17
infrastructure, 8–10; nonmotorized transportation and, 165; roads and, 166; slum
conditions and, 58. *See also* road access;
transportation
insecurity, 196, 204. *See also* food security
interdisciplinary study, 3
internally displaced persons (IDPs), 202–7;
postdisplacement settlement of, 206
International Conference on Population and
Development (ICPD) (1994), 214
International Covenant on Economic Social
and Cultural Rights (1966), 96
international networks, 334, 337

International Organization for Migration,
218
Internet of Things (IoT), 151, 267
intersectoral collaboration, 243–44
intimate partner violence, 217, 223
Islam, 200–201

Jinja Industrial Park, 265, 267
Johannesburg, South Africa, 24; intersectoral
action in, 243; sanitation costs in, 121; transportation and, 164, 175
Joint Monitoring Programme (JMP), 114, 120;
excreta flow diagrams and, 118
Juillard et al., 169
Juma et al., 51

Kampala, Uganda, 256–59; air quality management and, 259–62, 265–67
Kampala Capital City Authority (KCCA),
259–60
Kenya, 312–13; Constitution of, 298; digital
technologies and, 304–5, 308–12, 314–17;
food security and, 71; healthcare provision
and, 306–8; motorcycle accidents in, 161;
national reproductive health policy in, 223;
service delivery models in, 41; sexual and
reproductive health and, 219–20; transportation and, 169; vehicular emissions in,
144; youth-related programs in, 224
Kenya Health Policy, 305, 307
Kenya Integrated Household Budget Survey
(KIHBS), 105
Kenya Medical Supplies Authority (KEMSA),
311
Kenya Ministry of Education, 51
Kenya Ministry of Health, 305, 312
Kenya National Pharmaceutical Policy (2012),
305
Kerma, Sudan, 17
Keygnaert et al., 217
Kisumu, Kenya, 116
KOKO Networks, 148–49
Korogocho slum, 53
Koutonin, Mawuna, 20
Kuba, Kingdom of, 15

Lagos, Nigeria, 164–65, 174, 176; EndSARS
demonstrations, 200; housing fuel sources
in, 103; motorcycle taxis in, 161; ridesharing services in, 163; traffic accidents
in, 168–69

354 Index

Lagos Metropolitan Transport Management Authority, 175
Lancet Commission on Adolescent Health and Well-Being (2013), 215
land evictions, 198. *See also* eviction
land use policies, 173–74; segregation and, 27; transportation and, 177
last mile delivery (LMD) of medicines, 310
Latin America, 146
lead exposure, 103, 166
Lenoir, Rene
Liberia, 197
life expectancy, 142–43
Lighting Africa, 149
light rail systems, 165
local governance, 40–41, 345; global health agenda and, 343
Lord's Resistance Army (LRA), 197
low- and middle-income countries (LMICs), 41, 334; climate change and, 232–33; urban advantage assumptions and, 37
Luba, Kingdom of, 15
Lusaka, Zambia, 128–29

Maasai people, 285–86
machine learning, 262, 267, 329; addressing dropouts with, 287–90; education and, 283
Mackett and Thoreau, 170
Madagascar, 27
Makerere University, 260, 329
Makindye Division (Kampala), 266
Malawi, 33, 101, 223
malnutrition, 72–73, 233; urban environmental conditions and, 234, 237. *See also* diet; food security; nutrition
Manga et al., 121
Mapungubwe, 19
marginalization, 37, 50–51, 59
marriage, 215–17, 223–24, 285
mass transit, 151, 166, 176
Master Health Facility List, 305, 312
maternal health care, 184–88; conflict and, 204; mortality and, 216; road access and, 188–92
Mberu et al., 53
McConville et al., 121
megacities, 32
menstrual hygiene, 114, 123, 126–28; Mukuru and, 296–98; privacy and, 7. *See also* hy-

giene; sanitation; water; water sanitation and hygiene (WASH)
mental health, 8, 276–78; built environment and, 236; conflict and, 204–5; equitable access to, 206–7; homelessness and, 100; housing and, 98–100, 104; migration and, 218–19; sexual and reproductive health and, 220–21; slum conditions and, 56; Yaoundé and, 271–75
mentorship, 330–31
methodology, 329–30
migration, 38, 69–70, 326; rural-urban form of, 38–39, 99. *See also* displacement; internally displaced persons (IDPs)
Milan Urban Food Policy Pact (MUFPP), 70, 88
Misagu, Jean Pierre, 203
Mogadishu, Somalia, 201
mold, 102
Mombasa, Kenya: solid waste management in, 199
Monrovia, Liberia, 197
morbidity and mortality, 216; air pollution and, 142–43; conflict and, 203–4; homelessness and, 100; housing and, 102; perinatal care and, 184, 188; slum conditions and, 51
Moser et al., 86
motorcycles, 160–62
motorization, 144, 149–50; air quality management and, 265–66; sedentary lifestyles and, 235, 239. *See also* transportation
movement, restrictions on, 23, 25–26
Mowafi and Khawaja, 52
M-TIBA, 311
Muggah, Robert, 344–45
Mukuru Integrated Development Plan, 299
Mukuru Kwa Njenga (Nairobi slum), 7, 292–96; menstrual hygiene campaign and, 296–98; Mukuru Special Planning Area in, 298–301
Mukuru Special Planning Area, 298–301
multisectoral approaches, 346
Muluneh et al., 277
Muslim conquest, 16

Nairobi, Kenya, 7, 81, 98, 102; al-Shabaab terrorist attacks in, 201; Dandora dumpsite pollution in, 57–58; digital technologies and, 303–4, 308–9, 313–15, 317; food security and, 57, 68, 74–75, 80–81, 85; health care provision and, 306–7; last mile delivery (LMD) of medicines and, 310;

Mukuru Special Planning Area in, 298–99; planning and, 292–93; school birth registration requirements in, 51; sexual and reproductive health and, 220, 224; solid waste management in, 199; transportation deaths in, 53; Urban Health and Demographic Surveillance System (NUHDSS), 88

Nairobi City County government, 306

Nairobi Metropolitan Services, 306

Nairobi River, 58

Nairobi Urban Health and Demographic Surveillance System (NUHDSS), 102

Nairobi Water and Sewerage Company, 293

National Continuing Professional Development (CPD) Regulatory Framework, 305

National Environmental Management Authority (NEMA) (Uganda), 260

National Health Insurance Fund (NHIF), 311

National Institute for Health and Care Research (NIHR), 337

National Male Involvement Strategy for the Prevention of Sexual and Gender-Based Violence (Sierra Leone), 223

National Patriotic Front of Liberia (NPFL), 197

National Union of Road Transport Workers (NURTW), 164

natural disasters, 55

neighborhood pathway, 98, 104

neighborhoods, 96, 98, 103–4, 106

New Africa Free Trade Agreement, 343

New Urban Agenda, 214, 331, 342

Nigeria, 105, 168–69, 204, 224–25; Benin Empire colonial incorporation into, 22; conflict and, 197–201, 204; demolition of Otodo Gbame slum in, 198–99; housing costs and, 98; State Anti-Robbery Squad (SARS), 200; town planning acts as model in, 25

Niger Republic, 203

noise pollution, 172

noncommunicable diseases (NCDs), 203–4, 231–35, 237, 239–44; built environment and, 244; four primary types of, 232; urbanization and, 238–39

nonmotorized transportation (NMT), 53, 164–65

nonslum urban areas, 59–60

Nubia, 15

nutrition, 72–73; food security and, 67–68;

housing and, 100; urban environmental conditions and, 238. *See also* diet; food security; malnutrition

Nyasaland (present-day Malawi), 25

obesity, 73, 169, 236–37, 326

Okure et al., 257, 261

Olasunkanmi, O., 170

Oni et al., 326

Open Streets Exchange, 243

Organization for Economic Cooperation and Development (OECD), 33

Ouagadougou, Burkina Faso, 275

Oyo Empire, 16

Pakistan, 167

paratransit, 163

participatory approaches, 316, 345; air quality management and, 256, 261–62, 264, 266, 268; professional training and, 327–28

pastoralism, 24, 285

Patton et al., 216

PayGo, 152

perinatal care, 184–88; road access and, 188–92. *See also* maternal health care

pharmacies, 310–11

physical activity, 169–70, 231–32, 234–36, 242–44; social environment and, 238–40

Physical and Land Use Planning Act (2019) (Kenya), 299

Pinto, Lourenço, 4

piped water supply, 114–17

pit latrines, 118–19, 121, 295

policy, 50, 130; air pollution and, 150–53; digital technologies and, 303–5, 308, 312–13, 314–17; food security and, 87–88; gender equity and, 331–32; global health agendas and, 341–44; governance and, 344–47; health care provision and, 306–7; professional training and, 326, 328–30, 337; sexual and reproductive health and, 222–25; substance abuse and, 277–78; transportation and, 167, 173–75; urban environmental conditions and, 239–41, 243–44; urban health research and, 40–41

political economy, 20

pollution, 56, 57–58, 102–3, 104–5. *See also* air pollution

Pongou and Serrano, 220

population, precolonial era, 17

356 Index

population growth, 34–36; sexual and reproductive health and, 222, 224. *See also* rapid urbanization; urbanization rates
post-traumatic stress disorder (PTSD), 205, 219, 276
poverty, 59, 88, 104, 152; conflict and, 196, 199, 202, 206; definition of chronic forms of, 52; food security and, 66, 69–70; mental health and, 277–78; poverty penalty and, 115, 296; sexual and reproductive health and, 216, 221; urbanization and, 37–38. *See also* informal settlements; slums
precolonial era, 15–17, 19–22; largest cities in Africa in 1800, 17
pregnancy, 216–18, 220, 222, 224; air pollution and, 143
prenatal care. *See* maternal health care; perinatal care
primary care services, 307
privacy, 104
private service providers: criminal groups as, 199; health care, 306–8, 310–11, 315, 317; public services provided by, 51; water supply and, 115–17
professional development: 325–28; gender equity and, 331, 332–33; networks for, 335. *See also* education; training
programming urban health research, 40–41
Project Gaia, 148, 149
pro-poor approaches, 115–16
prototyping software development approach, 288
psychiatric services, 271–72, 273–74
public-private partnerships, 152, 315, 317
public space, 125–26, 235
public transport, 9
public transportation, 53; informal transport (dominant mode of), 163
Pygmy people, 24

Qualipharm, 311
quality pathway, 98, 102–4

railway system, 26
Ramesh et al., 129
Ramlal et al., 128
rapid urbanization, 1–2, 4; air pollution and, 143–44; air quality management and, 257; complex health factors and, 39–41; conflict and, 195, 197, 201, 203; food security and, 69; global health agenda and, 343; housing

and, 97; lack of planning and, 49; population trends and, 213–14; professional training and, 328; transportation and, 166; water and, 114. *See also* urbanization; urbanization rates
referral services, 307, 315
refugee camps, 205–6
regional initiatives, 343–44, 346–47
Registration of Customary Marriage and Divorce Act (Sierra Leone), 223
regulation, 166–67, 175
rental housing, 101
reproductive health, 214–17, 218–19, 221–25; lifelong need for services and, 206–7; menstrual hygiene campaigns and, 297; migration and, 217–19; slums and, 219–21
research, 129–30; early career researchers and, 334–37; programming for urban health, 40–41
resilience, 7, 58, 86
respiratory conditions, 102–3
Revolutionary United Front (RUF), 197
risky sexual behaviors, 7–8, 220
Rite and Hine, 167
road access, 9, 183, 185–89; inequality and, 189–92; lack of, 53; low investment in, 166; waste management and, 57. *See also* transportation
road hierarchy arrangement and management strategy, 175
road traffic accidents (RTAs), 168–69; Global Burden of Disease Study and, 161
Ross, Ronald, 27
rural areas, 4; access to clean cooking technologies in, 147; electrification of, 148; food security and, 66; health training and, 326; urban advantage and, 214; urbanization and, 35–36, 38–39
rural-urban linkages: food security and, 56–57, 70, 85–86; food security measurement and, 86
rural-urban migration, 38–39, 99

safety net, 86
Sahara Desert, 146
sanitation, 117–21; absenteeism due to lack of, 127; menstrual hygiene and, 296–98; Mukuru and, 294–96; shared facilities and, 120–23; slum campaign benefits and, 7; slum conditions and, 54–55; Special Planning Areas and, 299–300. *See also* hygiene;

menstrual hygiene; water; water sanitation and hygiene (WASH)

San people, 24

Savi, Benin, 17

segregation, 27–28; colonial state formation and, 23; slums and, 50

sensitization, 59, 129, 131

sensor technologies, 151, 153, 262

service delivery, 41, 58, 308–10, 314, 316

sewer systems, 118, 121–22

sexual health, 214–17, 217–19, 221–25, 222; lifelong need for services and, 206–7; menstrual hygiene campaigns and, 297; migration and, 217–19; slums and, 219–21

sexually transmitted infections, 204, 216

sexual violence, 204, 217–20

Shona people, 19–20

Sierra Leone, 8; 3D printing and, 330; civil war in, 197, 202–3, 222; racial segregation and, 27; sexual violence as national emergency in, 222–23

Simone, AbdouMaliq, 2

skills-based learning, 330

slave trade, 22–23

slums, 6–7, 40–41, 58–60; air pollution and, 144, 150; apartheid townships as, 23; conditions in, 53–57; data disaggregation and, 106; demolition of, 198; displacement and, 197; electrification of, 148; food security and, 66, 68–71, 80–81, 85–88; food security shocks specific to, 74–75; global health agenda and, 342, 347; marginalization within, 50; mental health resources and, 275; non-slum urban areas and, 59; nutrition security and, 72–74; rapid urbanization and, 49; sexual and reproductive health and, 219–21, 224; socioeconomic changes and, 52; transportation and, 53; urban advantage and, 221; vulnerable groups and, 51. See also informal settlements

social disruption, 201–2

social environment, 233–34, 238–39

social exclusion, 170–71; migration and, 218

social protection, 88

social security insurance, 274, 278

socioeconomic development: air pollution and, 144; conflict and, 195–96, 198–99, 202, 204–6; dropouts and, 285; housing and, 98; sexual and reproductive health and, 218–20, 222–24; status and, 191; WASH and, 113; water and, 115

solid waste management (SWM), 150–51, 199, 298. See also fecal sludge management; sanitation

Somalia, 204; Islamic State in, 201; US conflict in, 196

South Africa, 71, 103, 217; apartheid in, 23; child support grant in, 88; informal food environment in, 238; pass laws in, 25; xenophobic violence and, 199, 203

Southeast Asia, 167, 278

southern Africa, food security in, 66, 69, 71–73, 75, 80, 88

Southern Rhodesia (Zimbabwe), 25

sovereign conflict, 196, 205

spatial diversity, 262

spatial policies, 27. See also rapid urbanization; urbanization; urban planning

Special Planning Areas, 298–301

stability pathway, 98–100

states, colonial establishment of, 23–24

St. George's Castle (Elmina, Ghana), 26

stigma, 273–74

structural inequalities, 68

substance abuse, 56, 205, 219

Sudan, 17

supermarkets, 68, 71, 73

supply chain management, 311

surveillance, 25

sustainability, 107, 213; conflict and, 205; food security and, 66–69, 87–88; global health agenda and, 341–43, 345–47; transportation and, 166–67, 175, 177; water infrastructure and, 126

Sustainable Development Agenda (UN), 68–69

Sustainable Development Goals (SDGs), 56; air pollution and, 150, 152; digital technologies and, 302, 314; education and, 290; energy access and, 147; global health agenda and, 341–42, 346; housing and, 98; professional training and, 327; rapid urbanization and, 213; sexual and reproductive health and, 225; WASH and, 113–14, 130–31

Swahili, 17

syndemics, 233

Tanganyika (present-day Tanzania), 26

Tanzania, 282–85, 287, 289

Tanzania Ministry of Education Science and Technology, 286

taxis, 162–63

Taylor, Charles, 197
teachers, 282, 285–86, 287–88
technology, 10
tenure security, 24, 97, 101, 106, 115, 119–20;
   informal settlements and, 99, 293
terrorism, 200–201
tetanus vaccine, 184–85, 188–89, 192
3D Commission (2021), 346
3D printing, 329–30
Timbuktu, 16
"Too Pressed To Wait" sanitation campaign,
   297
Town Planning Act (1948), 25
trade, precolonial centers of, 16–17, 19–22
traditional beliefs, 273
traffic management systems, 176
training, 325–28, 334–37; gender equity and,
   331–33; on methods, 329–30. *See also* education; professional development
transportation, 8–9, 159, 166–68, 173–77;
   air pollution and, 144, 153; air quality
   management and, 265–66; greenhouse
   gases and, 172–73; health risks of public,
   168–71; maternal health care and, 192;
   motorized vehicles for, 159–64; nonmotorized forms of, 164–65; urban environmental conditions and, 243. *See also* road access
tricycles, 162
Tswana agro-towns, 17
tuberculosis, 100
Twaweza organization, 287

Uganda, 197, 256–60, 261, 263–64, 267; National Development Plan (NDP III), 257
Uganda Ministry of Public Health, 274
Uganda Ministry of Works and Transport,
   266
underdevelopment, 221
UN-Habitat, 104; housing and, 107
United Nations (UN), 56, 68–69, 213; food
   environment and, 238; Global Strategy for
   Women's, Children's, and Adolescent's
   Health, 215; housing and, 96–97; right to
   water and sanitation and, 113; sexual and
   reproductive health and, 215; sustainable
   cities and, 341; urbanization rate projections and, 32
United Nations Children's Fund (UNICEF),
   114
United Nations Office on Drugs and Crime
   (UNODC), 277

United Nations Population Fund (UNFPA), 311
United States Centers for Disease Control
   and Prevention (CDC), 96
United States Environmental Protection
   Agency, 170
United States-Somalia conflict, 196
Universal Declaration of Human Rights
   (1948), 96
universities, 328, 331–32
University of Ibadan, 332
unresolved conflict, 196
urban advantage, 37, 49–50, 60, 214, 221
urban agriculture, 71
urban areas, definitions of, 32–33
Urban Health Research Agenda (UHRA), 341
urbanism, Western ideas of, 34–35
urbanization, 24, 35–36, 38, 326; built environment and, 244; conflict and, 196, 205;
   early history of, 4–5; and economic growth,
   36–39; hygiene and, 123; noncommunicable
   diseases and, 231–35, 238–39, 241–44; population trends and, 213; sexual and reproductive health and, 221; slums and, 49. *See
   also* rapid urbanization
urbanization rates, 1, 32, 34–36, 222, 257. *See
   also* rapid urbanization
urban planning: air pollution and, 144, 151;
   emergence as disciple of, 25–28; Great
   Zimbabwe and, 20; housing and, 107; lack
   of, 293; precolonial Benin City and, 20–22;
   precolonial variety of, 15; special planning
   areas and, 298–301; underdevelopment
   and, 221
urban primacy, 69

vacuum service providers, 118–19
Van Kempen et al., 172
violence. *See* conflict; gender-based violence;
   sexual violence
Violence Against Persons (Prohibition) Act
   (2015), 225
Viwandani slum (Nairobi), 53
vulnerable groups, 51, 58–59

Walata, Mauritania, 16
Wanyama AutoSafety, 266
waste management, 57–58, 150–51, 199, 298;
   housing conditions and, 104. *See also* fecal
   sludge management; sanitation
water, 114–17; animal contamination of, 126;
   girls' responsibility to collect, 113; hand-

washing and, 123–25; lead exposure in, 103; Mukuru and, 293–96, 299–300; pollution and, 58; slum conditions and, 54–55; slum costs of, 51. *See also* hygiene; menstrual hygiene; sanitation; water sanitation and hygiene (WASH)

water sanitation and hygiene (WASH), 9–10, 113–17, 129–32; conflict and, 199; housing and, 102; hygiene and, 123–27; sanitation and, 117–21, 128–29; shared sanitation facilities and, 120–23

White et al., 38

WHO/UNICEF Joint Monitoring Programme (JMP), 54

Williams et al., 276

women, 113–14, 128, 236; conflict and, 204–5; gender equity and, 331–33; menstrual hygiene and, 126–27

World Bank, 148–49, 159, 173, 175

World Health Organization (WHO), 107, 125, 142, 232; air pollution and, 145–46; air quality and, 255; climate change and, 170;

digital technologies and, 302–3, 316; global research priorities set by, 341; healthy housing concept of, 96; Joint Monitoring Programme (JMP) of, 114; lead exposure limits and, 103; mental health prevalence and, 218; prenatal care and, 184; professional training and, 327; road traffic accidents and, 169

xenophobic violence, 199, 202–3

Yaoundé Cameroon, 276–78; mental health services in, 271–75

Yoruba people, 16

youth, 7–8, 242; high proportion of, 213; migration and, 217; sexual and reproductive health and, 219–21, 221, 223, 224–25; sexual risk-taking behavior among, 220

Zimbabwe, 105. *See also* Great Zimbabwe

zoning, 27

Zulus, 15

Explore other books from **HOPKINS PRESS**

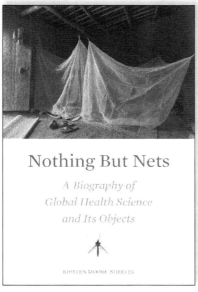

JOHNS HOPKINS UNIVERSITY PRESS | PRESS.JHU.EDU